Thailand
The Politics of
Despotic Paternalism

Cornell University

Thak Chaloemtiarana

Thailand
The Politics of
Despotic Paternalism

SOUTHEAST ASIA PROGRAM PUBLICATIONS
Southeast Asia Program
Cornell University
Ithaca, New York
2007

Cornell Southeast Asia Program Publications
640 Stewart Avenue, Ithaca, NY 14850-3857

Studies on Southeast Asia No. 42

Printed in the United States of America

ISBN-13: 978-0-8772-7772-9 hc / ISBN-10: 0-8772-7772-9 hc
ISBN-13: 978-0-8772-7742-2 pb / ISBN-10: 0-8772-7742-7 pb

Cover Design: Julie Manners

TABLE OF CONTENTS

FOREWORD TO SECOND PRINTING

It is very humbling yet satisfying to know that there continues to be interest in this book almost thirty years after its publication. I am also honored that it has been chosen as one of the books to be republished as part of the commemoration of the 72nd anniversary of the Coup of 1932. When the book was finished, my ideological leanings made me hope that it would stir readers into action that would inhibit praetorian officers from intervening in and dominating Thai politics. Although the book was about military dictatorship posing as the champion of atavistic and nativist concepts of democracy, it was in fact a veiled attempt to get students and scholars to closely examine the roots of that dictatorship—why it was successful and in which direction it would lead future political development.

Similar to the youth of those days, I was very impatient for change, and like many, I even romanticized radical upheavals. My own timidity probably saved me from joining a cause that may have proven costly to the lives of the innocent. Moving from the context of time and space of the 1970s and with the blessing of hindsight, and now advancing age, I can say that the impatience for political change expressed in my youth was just that: impatience, with little understanding of how society works. As a lived experience, political change seemed to creep forward at a snail's pace; however, looking now from the more detached perspective of the middle-aged (or even the aged) observer, I can say that a lot has happened since the People's Party staged their rally in front of the Royal Equestrian monument seventy-two years ago, toppling absolute monarchy in Siam.

Even the youthful promoters' idealist goal of achieving democratic rule within a defined timetable proved unviable. To complicate matters, what constitutes democratic rule, political participation, legitimacy, party politics, the rule of law, and other major principles of governance were contested ideas from the start. Some embraced Western definitions while others argued for localized and indigenous ones. No one had a clear idea of what would be most suitable for Thailand. Liberal democracy was attractive as a modern blueprint for governance, but the question lay in its translation. I would suppose that no particular group or leader can write a script or formula for what is ideal, what will work, and what will not. Democratic political development is still a messy process with gains and losses, dead ends, sidetracks, and the occasional fleeting victory. There is nothing pure and universal about democracy as a global ideology. Forms of democracy change over time and are particular to both time and space. Experience and context proved more powerful than ideology in defining democracy for Thailand. This book studies one context where regime agency defined democracy in a particular Thai context.

Although to the naked eye political change appears to be the product of a mechanistic process (be it an election, protests, upheaval, or military coups d'état), it is, in fact, also organic in nature. Over time, political tastes and opinions affect a broad spectrum of social and political values that ultimately support and tolerate new forms of political life. I am not advocating a purely deterministic theory of politics, but I want to be able to make room for innovative programs (both good and bad) that may eventually introduce a new behavior and norms for political action. For example, one should not go overboard in lamenting the rise to power of the provincial *"chao pho,"* or godfathers. Their political power was the result of a phase of Thai democracy where popular elections relied on influential rural canvassers who used local knowledge to intimidate voters and politicians and to engage in an economy of vote buying. If we were to ignore the criticism of public intellectuals and royalist conservative critics (politics makes for strange bedfellows), this particular period could be seen as one path of political development in Thailand, since during this time the national political system was forced to open its doors to include the provincial political elite and the rural electorate (even if some were selling their votes).

In my mind, this turn of events can be taken as a positive one, a move towards more participation. This is not to say that I favor vote buying, intimidation, corruption, and so forth, but in my opinion, even a condition marred by such practices will eventually lead to a new form and a future modification of national politics. The recent push for political reform as written into the 1997 constitution is an illustration of this point. The dynamics of politics can be viewed in dialectic terms: the urban and the rural; the military and the civilian; the parties of the angels and those of the demons; the royalist/conservatives and the liberal/radicals, and so on. Observers of these dynamics hope that the resolution of tensions will lead to something better. I want to believe, and indeed do believe, that in the long view, this "march of history" will lead to a better life for all.

To fully appreciate politics, one has to remove oneself from its details, the leaves and tree, to look at the larger political landscape—the forest itself. In some sense, to the layperson politics means reading the daily papers (especially the gossip on page four) and relishing the details of intrigue, the rumor mill, and the minutiae of politics. But it is up to the scholar to ingest this entire morass of information and pick the important features in order to construct a logical whole. There is both success and failure in this enterprise, and even the successes are—at best—partial ones. What the scholar can hope for is to produce a work that will intrigue others, that will lead to more and better questions, and that others will build upon, even though the work itself may have to be torn down and eventually rejected and discarded. Such is the price of scholarship and of the scientific revolution.

This book was, in fact, an accident of history. It is the stepchild of a research project that I started in 1970. My initial dissertation proposal, which was funded by the London-Cornell Fund, was to examine the intersection of political and social differentiation and its effect on the Thai military. The hypothesis was that as society developed (on the path to economic industrialization), demands for political development in terms of expanding participation may or may not have affected the professionalization of the Thai military. The likelihood of military intervention in society will remain high if, in spite of socioeconomic changes, the professionalization of the officers' corps remains low. Back in the late 1960s and early 1970, studies such as the one I proposed were very much in vogue. Political scientists were trying to reconcile the fact that seemingly free (that is, pro-Western) and aspiring democratic polities were under military rule in Southeast Asia and in Latin America. Thailand, Burma, Laos, Vietnam, and Indonesia were all controlled by military regimes.

But two months after my arrival in Bangkok to conduct field research, Field Marshal Thanom staged a coup against himself in November 1971. The constitution that provided for elections was discarded in favor of a Sarit-style interim constitution in an attempt to stifle the growing rumblings in parliament and academic circles calling for immediate elections and more open politics. The coup resulted in the usual "closing of ranks" in the military, and it was not a good time for some nosey political scientist to be interviewing military officers about "professionalism" when, in fact, the military itself had just intervened in the political process. This setback was serendipitous because it forced me to look for another viable project, as I was already committed to spend the year doing field research. I ultimately settled on studying the Sarit regime as a system of politics that monopolized power through the manipulation of atavistic political concepts and the promotion of "Nation, Religion, and King," where the nation was protected by the military, religious dissent was to be controlled by the state, and where the role and place of the king would be rationalized as a modern political institution.

In my judgment, Thanom's coup was an attempt to rejuvenate and to maintain the political system that Sarit devised. I was also concerned that this turning back of the clock and holding back of progress was dangerous because the policies that Sarit implemented—such as *phatthana* (improvement of infrastructure), counter-insurgency, privatization of government enterprises, and encouragement of foreign investment—accelerated social and economic changes that were to become more and more out of step with a rigid political system that choked off participation. I pointed out that such an incongruity between the three spheres would eventually lead to conflict and rupture. In current language, the rise of civil society and its political demands for participation will lead to tensions in a strict and restrictive political system.

Although the use of force and the staging of military coups to determine political succession had become institutionalized in Thailand since 1932, Thanom's coup lacked the force—and rationale—of many of the earlier coups. Thanom's coup was seen as a last resort of the military leaders to remain in power. It was a coup against the rising demands of civil society, and not against a clear political rival, such as previous preemptive strikes against the People's Party or rival military factions. In fact, three members of parliament took the coup leaders to court, accusing them of unconstitutional acts. These three representatives of civil society were summarily jailed for their audacity, as the constitution was revoked and the new constitution gave dictatorial power back to the coup leaders. It is interesting to note that the lawsuit filed was in the criminal court, where the three accused Thanom and seventeen others of using force to "inflict injury and to intimidate to people in order to topple the constitution." The three were arrested and imprisoned by order of the accused, that is, by Thanom acting as Leader of the Revolutionary Council.

The use of military force to overthrow and replace governments in fact became a "legitimate" part of the Thai political process beginning with the June 1932 coup. Therefore, one can say that Thai democratic aspiration is flawed from the start. Nevertheless, if one were to look at historical precedents, one would see that the use of force by the elite to seize power followed historical practice from the times of the kings of the many early kingdoms that dotted the landscape. To help legitimize their claim to power, the 1932 promoters posed as the logical successors to the "modernizing" Chakkri kings; in this instance, the royals were forcefully displaced and replaced by the new elite of educated military and civilian bureaucrats. But group leadership soon gave way to traditional practices in which the political unit was to be defined by a leader, a person of the sort Oliver Wolters called "a man of prowess." And, as we know, in time the fallout between the civilian and military factions within the People's Party ended, with the latter dominating political leadership.

Out of that struggle, Field Marshal Phibunsongkhram rose to the top. In past times, Phibun would have founded a new dynasty (and some would claim that he would have liked to do so). The Phibun regime lasted (with some interruptions) from 1935 until his ouster by Sarit Thanarat in 1957. Quite a lot of ink has been spilt over the Phibun regime, but unfortunately, not much has been written about Sarit. I would argue that the Sarit regime lasted from 1957 until 1973; this includes the period that Thanom was prime minister. This book mainly deals with the period when Sarit was still alive and jumps briefly towards the end to talk about the trauma of 1973. It unfortunately glosses over the entire Thanom period, which is important to understand, as it laid the groundwork for the political "unrest" of the second half of the 1970s. (Benedict Anderson's article, "Withdrawal Symptoms," covers the sociological changes of the 1960s and early 1970s and provides some detail of the genesis of those changes.[a])

Although I am most gratified and humbled that some scholars and students still refer to this book, I am disappointed that not more have taken it to task. The criticisms I have seen about this book have been fair and helpful. But most of the discussions have focused on some details that were left out and some questions of interpretation. I am particularly impressed with the review of Ukrit Pattamanant in the *Journal of Political Economy* (*Warasan Setthasat Kan Muang*), vol. 3, no. 4, June 1984.

Several friends and critics have chastised me for loosely appropriating the concept of *"phokhun"*[b] to describe the Sarit leadership. I admit that the concept was applied ahistorically. But I would continue to contend that it is appropriate as a descriptive concept to help highlight the kind of leadership that Sarit himself (with a lot of prompting from Luang Wichit) espoused. It is true that the sources used came from self-affirming speeches and official government documents, and I would agree that I presented little evidence that such a concept was ever in the consciousness of the public. My only response is that the book presents a theorizing exercise that provides a plausible roadmap for researchers to make some sense of the Sarit political system. It was clear to me, from my understanding based on textual analyses and my own lived experience, that the public both feared and admired Sarit. Few would dare to call him a dictator, as they would later call his successors. This study was one of the first to label his leadership as somewhat of a contradiction: that is, he was a "paternalistic despot," for which the Thai term that I coined is *"phokhun uppatham baeb phadetkan."*

Whether he believed in the idea of the *phokhun* is not the issue here. My point is that Sarit was able to appropriate that concept for his own use to justify his paternalistic rule. The "despotic" part of that rule had little to do with the idea of the *phokhun*. Here, Sarit was using his own training in the army as commander in chief. The word of the superior officer is law. In the military, this rule is enforced and enforceable. He was also tapping into one stereotype of Thai masculinity, that of the *nakleng*. In this instance, the model of the virile man is perhaps closely related to the Hanuman character in the Thai Ramayana. Desirable masculine traits would include, among other things, physical strength; mental fortitude and decisiveness;

---

[a] Benedict R. O'G. Anderson, "Withdrawal Symptoms: Social and Cultural Aspects of the October 6 Coup," *Bulletin of Concerned Asian Scholars* 9,3 (July–September 1977).

[b] *Phokhun*: the Thai term referring to the first kings of Sukhothai in the thirteenth century.

combativeness; loyalty to friends; heavy alcohol consumption (without getting drunk); and awkwardness with the ladies (he gets them in the end nevertheless).

Paternalistically, while acting as father of the people, Sarit would urge his bureaucrats to be his eyes and ears; he would visit his "children" in the provinces; he would supervise the putting out of fires; he would keep the streets clean; and he would promise a good life for his children. Sarit also wanted to be a decisive and strong leader. He was able to do this by citing authority that he gave himself based on "legal" constitutional powers. The dreaded *Matra*, or Article, 17 of the Interim Constitution of 1959 (it had only 20 articles, compared to the 336 articles in the current 1997 constitution) provided him the legal and constitutional basis for dictatorial rule. As dictator and despot, he would use his absolute power to intimidate and jail social misfits and teddy boys and hooligans, as well as writers, journalists, monks and intellectuals, and he would order the execution of arsonists, *phi bun* (millenarian religious leaders), and political rivals. In short, Father was a very nasty man.

Looking back now, I can see that I could have spent more time writing in some detail about the historicity of the concept of *phokhun* and the public understanding of the concept. I could have, and perhaps should have, spent more pages on the intimidation of the Sangha, especially the controversial case of Phra Phimonlatham. And surely there is much more work to be done with the section on the actual programs that undergirded Sarit's *phatthana* policies. In addition, a whole chapter could have been written about his persecution of the progressive and radical thinkers whose works were repressed and banned under his regime. Most of these works were rehabilitated just prior to the events of October 6 and October 14, to fuel the fire of youthful souls and minds. With the cachet of being "banned and dangerous," certain books, such as Jit Phumisak's *Chomna Sakdina Thai* and Kulab Saipradit's *Lae Pai Khangna*, had an inordinate appeal and impact on the generation of political activists of the 1970s. Of course, others have written about those topics: for example, Somboon Suksamran and Peter Jackson on Phra Phimonlatham; Robert J. Muscat, Pasuk Pongpaichit, and Chris Baker on economic development; and Yuangrat Widel, Kasian Tejapira, and Craig Reynolds on radical thinkers. Some built on what this book started, and others disagreed with some of my assertions. I am grateful that they took notice.

Granted, there are gaps in the book which many of my esteemed critics have kindly pointed out over the years. I want, nevertheless, to reiterate here the purposes of the study when it was undertaken. Parenthetically, although it would be wonderful to rewrite the book, it is also good to reprint the volume as it stands to remind us of the limitations placed upon it by the context of time and space. It might be interesting to the reader to get a glimpse of the book's original intentions and what I believe to be its contributions to the field of Thai studies.

Prior to the birth of the nation state, Oliver Wolters[c] (*History, Culture, and Region in Southeast Asian Perspectives*, revised edition) theorized that political communities in Southeast Asia could be defined as "Mandala States." These states had control of territory, but there were no real defined borders. Thongchai Winichakul's later

---

[c] O. W. Wolters, *History, Culture, and Region in Southeast Asian Perspectives*, revised edition (Ithaca, NY: Cornell Southeast Asia Program, 1999).

study, *Siam Mapped*, supported Wolters's theory.[d] The strength and longevity of the Mandala State were contingent upon the leader's forceful personality; he is the "man of prowess" whose will and leadership guarantees the state's future and prosperity. This leadership is not transferable to heirs, and thus the state waxes and wanes according to the strength of its leader. Of course the exception to Wolters's theory could be the Angkorean kingdom under Jayavarman II, who instituted the idea of the *chakravatin* (universal ruler), which later evolved into the *devaraja* cult. Under this new statecraft also based on the Hindu science of government, the kings could inherit power/dharma. This emphasis on the strong leader has been carried over into modern times. Max Weber may call it charismatic leadership, but in Thai political understanding the concept is embedded in many aspects of leadership. Kingship and the divine nature of the king is one such manifestation. What then, will be the basis for legitimacy for a civilian leader? Can it be based solely on legal-rational institutions?

I wanted to investigate the effectiveness of civilian political leadership after the overthrow of absolute monarchy, focusing especially on the type of leader who could command the attention and compliance of the Thai public. Following the 1932 coup, Thai politicians experimented with the idea of a "group" leadership, but even in group leadership, there is always the need to find someone who is the *primus inter pares*. And as we have seen, Phibun eventually emerged as the leader of the 1932 Promoters. It did not take long for him to declare himself "*phunam*," or the supreme leader, taking a page out of Hitler and Mussolini's play book. No matter whether one is a fan or not, Phibun's leadership during the mid to late 1930s left lasting effects on Thai political culture, affecting the way we dress, the way we pay respect to national symbols, the way we treat women, children and the elderly, and the way the Thai public is conditioned to follow the dictates of the state. But just as important, that leadership style became a possible model and even perhaps the prototype for Sarit, who succeeded Phibun in 1957. In fact, even during his early career, Sarit was already competing with Phibun (and to a certain extent Phao) as the emerging charismatic political personality.

Following a short period under Phibun during which more open democratic practices (party politics, open debates, Hyde Park speeches, overtures to socialist countries, and so forth) were experimented with and tolerated, Thailand once again experienced a regime that, for all intents and purposes, could be defined by its leader. I remember that, growing up as a child during and after the Sarit coup of 1957, there was some excitement in the air, a sense that something was happening or was about to happen. People became fascinated once again with a strong and decisive leader, one who exuded (and cultivated) charisma, one who valued modern scholarship (the advice of technocrats and the World Bank), and a military man who was prone to use harsh and decisive measures against those deemed as enemies of the state and public decency. For a Buddhist country used to the idea of a righteous ruler, Sarit was a bit of an aberration. He was someone who was willing to personally and publicly order executions and to declare that he alone would shoulder the responsibility for the action. Compared to his successor, Thanom, who would also order executions, Sarit did not immediately *tham bun,* or make merit, to add to his bank of merit, as did Thanom. That perhaps added to his aura of power: as

---

[d] Thongchai Winichakul, *Siam Mapped: A History of the Geo-body of a Nation* (Honolulu, HI: University of Hawai'i Press, 1994).

someone with amply stored merit, he was the most meritorious, and most powerful, in the land. Such a person used to be the king. As Lucien Hanks pointed out in his seminal article,[e] merit and power in Thai culture are closely linked. Needless to say, I was fascinated with this new leadership and wanted to find out why this sort of leader was both feared and revered. The study of Sarit was a natural and logical extension of my initial dissertation topic on the modern Thai military. Professionalization of the Thai military was based on mainstream social science modernization theory. But from ground-level research and experience, I felt that somehow "culture" still played a role.

The study of politics can be both a science and an art. As a science, it is based on empirical data leading to the detection of patterns of behavior, outcomes, and predictability. As art, politics involves the grand art of deception, where the perception of power is almost as effective as its possession. I found in my study that Sarit was the master of both. His brutish rule, especially when directed against those he saw as enemies (personal and national), demonstrated to everyone that he was the supreme authority in the land. He held the power of life and death based on his command of the police, armed forces, and secret service. Furthermore, his absolute power was backed by Article 17 of the Constitution. However, what is artful, in my mind, was his invocation of the indigenous roots of such leadership. My late friend Toru Yano of Kyoto University was first to alert me to the possibly atavistic nature of Sarit's ideas about governance. His study made me think about how indigenous and even historical interpretations of Western political concepts were used by this leader. Working from this premise, I began to view "Thai democracy" on its own terms, and not as something to be dismissed as a political ploy of conservative forces, or as a messy, inferior hybrid for which one must apologize to outside observers.

My study showed that Sarit's speeches were sprinkled with the imagery of the leader acting as father of the people. His idea of Thai democracy and representation theory were also based on Thai understanding. Good (that is, moral) local administrators can "represent" the needs of the public. They can then "represent" those ideas to the father of the people. The idea of access and accountability is modified to mean that the leader/father visits his children to listen and to observe their needs directly. Sarit gained direct access to the people by traveling in army vehicles and convoys to the countryside; he would camp in tents near villages during his many visits. Accountability has to do with the beneficent intentions of the father, which can be equated with karmic merit and valorization of the father in Thai beliefs about the family. And in responding to this leader, the Thai people should believe in the cliché that "father knows best what is good for the family." Even his harshest actions were justified in this mode—as father, he must punish his children and others who go astray. Not only is the punishment good for the family but it is also necessary for their well-being. I admit that I may have been overly enthusiastic in reaching for an indigenous concept to describe this modern and yet anachronistic leadership style.

I remember my friend Charnvit Kasetsiri chiding me for picking the *phokhun* concept to describe Sarit's leadership. Charnvit accused me of pandering to sensationalism and of inventing a marketable label. He believed that Sarit was *phadetkan*, nothing but a dictator. I, on the other hand, liked the tension created by a

---

[e] Lucien M. Hanks, "Merit and Power in the Thai Social Order," *American Anthropology* 64 (1962), pp. 1247–61.

contradicting imagery of father as despot. Regardless of my friend's sentiments, I wanted to illustrate that politics is "local." No matter how hard one tries to adapt foreign political forms and concepts (in this case, Western democratic practices), they will work better if they resonate with local beliefs, past and present. Although it is true that as time goes by even foreign forms become institutionalized as indigenous ones, I would contend that even the Thai title of Prime Minister, or *Nayok Ratthamontri,* is but a syncretic concept that combines many layers of local indigenous ideas.

To reiterate, my original study of the Sarit regime was an attempt to tease out the Thai part of the concept of democracy, that is: What is "Thai Democracy"? And as I had discovered, Thai ideas concerning the representation and prerogatives of the leader are quite different from Western understanding. I would suggest here that concepts embedded in the Sarit regime's construction of democracy remain, lurking in the background of the "demi-democracy" or *prachathippatai khrung bai* of the Prem regime[f] and even in the current "corporatist state" of the Thaksin regime. I do not subscribe to the idea of a singular democracy. Thai democracy is a distinct entity—no better or worse than others. It arises in a certain time and place, and we need not make excuses for it looking different from Western models (of which there are also many). However, this does not mean that we should accept what is. There is always room for improvement; political development (hopefully changes for the better) involves the exercising of options that are presented to the political system. As an aside, I believe that both the Prem and Thaksin regimes warrant serious study, as they mark important pivotal points in the development of Thai politics. In my mind they are just as significant as the Phibun and Sarit regimes. These two forceful leaders bring with them a certain style, or genre, of Thai leadership.

The other really important feature of the Sarit regime was its acquiescence to the economic development model put forward by the World Bank: more privatization, industrialization, and commercialization of the agricultural sector. Although I did not focus on the details of this aspect of the regime, it is not because I judged it to be unimportant, but because I was more focused on how the regime artfully inserted this policy into the daily lives of the public through a publicity campaign that appealed to the common man's sense of need and well-being. Under the catchy slogan of *"nam lai, fai sawang, thang di, mi ngan tham, bandarn suk"* (Water flows, the lights are bright, the roads are good, there is work for the people. Such is happiness), Sarit was able to promote a new economic concept to the Thai people. This idea was *"phatthana"* or "development."

Under the rubric of *phatthana,* many economic projects were carried out without much scrutiny by or objection from the public. The idea that Thailand should do its best to leave the ranks of the "underdeveloped" world reminds me of the call to make Siam *"than samai"* and *"siwilai"*—modern and civilized—at the turn of the twentieth century. Although the terms *than samai* and *siwilai* have fallen out of grace, the idea of *phatthana* is still quite current. In fact, the Sarit regime's justification for economic practices and policies modeled to fit the dominant capitalist international economic system has been well documented (see, for instance, Robert J. Muscat, *The*

---

[f] In describing Thai democracy as represented by the Prem regime, some have compared it to a national boat sailing along with half of its sails—an incomplete democratic "vessel." In this phrase, again, one finds a tendency to apologize for Thailand's form of democracy.

Fifth Tiger, 1994[8]). And one can say that the Sarit regime laid the foundation for Thailand's *phatthana* (path forward) industrialization and economic prosperity. Of course, this policy did not help the poor or the rural sector, as they became the fuel and fodder used to fire the engines of rapid economic development which benefited the urban sector and the capitalist/entrepreneurial class. Ironically, it was only the peripheral effects of the Vietnam conflict and the building of a modern transportation infrastructure for military purposes that allowed provincial entrepreneurs to capitalize on construction and transportation and transform themselves into a powerful political force in later years. These rural entrepreneurs became powerful *"chao pho"* or "godfathers" of the 1980s. And it is under the auspices of "democracy" and the implementation of elections that these provincial leaders were able not just to be players in national politics, but to eventually control it through their control of parliament. The tension created by the resentment of the remnants of the bureaucratic polity and liberal forces against the rural (and perhaps less educated) politicos has animated politics in Thailand from the 1990s to the present. The coup of 1991, the dastardly events of May 1992, and the reform movement of the late 1990s were reactions to Thai democracy of the 1970s and 1980s.

Another intention was to make it apparent that Sarit's power, no different from Phibun's and those who would follow them, was based on the control of a few garrisons in Bangkok. In spite of its saber rattling, the Thai military is mostly an internal force used to support a particular political regime. This praetorian nature of Thai politics continued unabated as those who claimed to be professional soldiers, democratic soldiers, and the unrepentant political soldiers continued their regular and sometimes deadly game of coups and counter coups. Ironically, the military coup of 1991 (led by General Sunthorn Kongsomphon) justified its action by accusing parliament of being under the control of rural MPs and thereby creating a "parliamentary dictatorship" that turned a blind eye to corruption. The coup itself exposed in very graphic and textual terms the bankruptcy of new ideas for statecraft in Thailand. The leaders returned to the gamebook of the last successful military coup d'état, which was the Sarit master plan. Amazingly, the coup leaders took the Sarit Coup Proclamations out of mothballs and foisted them on the Thai public once again. The verbatim republication of the coup declarations was to me like a bad nightmare, *déjà vu* in its worst form.

The unsavory intentions of the 1991 coup leaders who tried to turn the clock back to a bygone period were somewhat laughable. Thai society was no longer the same as the one Sarit faced in 1957. Through the policy of *phatthana* and industrialization, it had become more and more differentiated, richer, better educated, and politically savvier. The attempt by General Suchina to anoint himself the new leader failed. His subsequent tug-of-war with Major General Chamlong (a reformed professional soldier) led to a public and an international scolding for both by King Bhumibol. For all intents and purposes, I was among the many who believed that future political interventions by the Thai military were most unlikely. But as we shall see, I was proven wrong. It is my opinion that Thai society, and especially the economy, have become too complex and too complicated for the praetorian military officer to control. Politics today has become more sensitive to the Dow Jones and the indices of the Security Exchange of Thailand than to the internal

---

[8] Robert J. Muscat, *The Fifth Tiger: A Study of Thai Development Policy* (New York, NY: M. E. Sharpe, 1994).

power struggles of the armed forces. Rent-seeking businesses that had relied on their connections with military leaders turned their attention to new political allies. In fact, the old rent seekers eventually became the landlords who controlled national politics. The king's public spanking of Suchinda and Chamlong illustrated the extent of the king's political influence and stature. The rationalization of the role of the monarchy in post-absolutist rule began in earnest during the Sarit period. While Phibun tried to circumscribe the king's influence, Sarit put it into use as part and parcel of the new political system.

It is most interesting to me that while most Thai scholars focus their debate on the suitability of the *phokhun* concept to describe Sarit, non-Thai scholars are less bothered by that assertion because it allows for an acknowledgment that the Sarit regime normalized the relationship between the king and the modern state. In fact, I argued that Sarit made a place for the king in his political system. While Sarit can be the father of the people, the king is the father of the Thai nation. "Nation" encompasses all Thais—past, present and future. In the Sarit regime, the then youthful king was allowed to play an open public role and to be able to gain the love and respect of the "nation." Up to that time, it was unclear what role the monarchy would be able to play after the 1932 Revolution. Phibun as prime minister did not want the king to compete with this authority and leadership. Sarit, on the other hand, was able to incorporate the king into national politics by "elevating" his position as a legitimating authority of his regime and a symbol of the nation. Under Sarit, the state ideology of "King/ Nation, Religion" was placed upfront and forward. King and Nation were closely identified as equivalents, diverging from the Phibun idea of "king, Military/ Nation, Religion," where "king" was in the lower case, the military protected the nation, and religion was somewhat ignored. In addition, to diminish the prestige of the king, Phibun coined a new slogan—*"Chua phunam, chat phonphai"* (Trust the Leader and the nation will escape danger)—for good measure.

In my understanding, the relationship of the monarchy and Sarit should be seen as a symbiotic one. After Sarit's death in 1963, the popularity and influence of the king and of the royal family were firmly established, and royal prestige grew rapidly under the subsequent regimes of less powerful leaders who had no way to curb royal prestige and influence. By the mid-1970s, the palace, and in particular the king, became a formidable force in Thai politics. Although scholars now agree that the king plays a very important role in contemporary Thai politics as the voice of reason, there are indeed concerns about the future role of the monarchy.

Institutionally, the throne is posed as the embodiment of the Thai nation by the armed forces. Soldiers need something symbolic that they can focus on that is the equivalent of an "absolute value," that is, something worthy to die for. In many cases, people are willing to die for a religious cause, an ideological cause, or for the nation. Because the concept of nationhood is so elusive and hard to concretize, the Thai armed forces have always seen the nation in terms of the preservation of the throne. During a time when the Thai military was politically powerful, the combination of the armed forces and the authority of the king proved an unbeatable combination. However, as the political system has expanded to include new socio-economic groups, the centrality of the military, and perhaps eventually that of the monarchy, must become diluted and be transformed. Already, we have seen the new contours of another form of Thai democracy and the possible rise of a new political star, one who embodies some of the characteristics of successful strong leaders of the past. But the emerging paradigmatic leadership combines a brashness verging on bullying tendencies that are coupled with the entrepreneurial talents appropriate for the current global economy. Already, one can feel the tension that this new regime is causing. Tension is not in itself a bad thing, because without tension there would be no action and no movement.

The Thaksin Shinawat government was formed after his Thai Rak Thai party gained overwhelming mandates in the 2001 and 2005 elections. However, Thaksin quickly squandered his chance to help promote a stable democracy of the sort envisioned by the framers of the 1997 Constitution. His government, faced with a very weak opposition in parliament, proceeded to bully the press, to intimidate human rights workers, to use unsavory police tactics to deal with drug dealers and the growing unrest in the three southern Thai Muslim provinces, and to undermine the integrity of independent watchdog agencies, such as the Constitutional Court, the Audit Bureau, the Anti-crime and Corruption Commission, and the Elections Commission. Five years into his administration, opposition groups began to coalesce. State enterprise workers, academics, students, city dwellers, members of the media, and some of his former rich cronies joined together to stage large public protests and demonstrations against Thaksin. Thaksin countered by bussing in his supporters from the rural areas. It is ironic that Thaksin's Thai Rak Thai party, the party of the ultra-rich, had to rely on the provincial and rural poor for support.

Rumors began to spread that the palace was unhappy with Thaksin's style of leadership. Many Thais believed that the prime minister was competing with the king for popularity. The divisiveness in Thai society, the deteriorating situation in the southern provinces, the perceived nepotism of Thaksin in promoting his relatives and friends to key military and police positions, and the perceived displeasure of the palace precipitated a surprise military coup d'état led by the heads of the armed forces, including the police chief. The coup of September 19, 2006 took place while Thaksin was in New York attending a meeting at the United Nations.

The coup group called itself "The Democratic Reform Council with the King as Head of State." Like many coup leaders before them, they were granted an audience with the king that was used to legitimize their actions. The coup group immediately banned political gatherings, closed down community radio stations, blocked access to foreign news reporting, warned the press not to print divisive opinions, and abrogated the 1997 constitution. This coup group is the first to use "Democracy with the King as Head of State" as part of its name. Previous reform councils left unstated what was, in fact, to be "reformed"; this group makes it clear that one of their chief concerns is to insure that Thailand remains a democratic country with a constitutional monarchy. Senior military officers and some members of the king's Privy Council may have been worried about rumors that Thaksin was contemplating the establishment of a republic with the help of former student activists from the 1970s. Some of these activists, now prominent members of Thaksin's Thai Rak Thai party, had ties with the now defunct Communist Party of Thailand following the October 6, 1976 massacre of students at Thammasat University. The name chosen for the coup group clearly links it to General Prem, the head of the king's Privy Council. General Prem was instrumental in promoting the use of this political system during his premiership (1980-1988).

Immediately following the coup d'état, the Democratic Reform Council promised to return democracy to Thailand by October 2007. It promised to appoint an interim government and national assembly, to draft a new interim constitution within two weeks, and to convene a constitutional drafting assembly. To calm anxieties, it instructed the newly formed Elections Commission to plan for nationwide elections for city and provincial council representatives. Although it is too early to confirm or reject the coup group's claim that it is not interested in power, one can make several observations. First, the coup d'état did not elicit a clear rejection by the public. In fact, initial polls conducted by the Suan Dusit Poll optimistically showed that 83.9 percent of their sample approved of the takeover. Secondly, several respected scholars and public intellectuals, such as Professor Sanel Chamarik, accepted the coup as a way to put an end to Thaksin's political leadership, which had undermined the 1997 Constitution. Such assertions by respected scholars helped soften the impact of this use of coercion. Thirdly, even though the US, the UN Secretary General, and other world leaders condemned the coup, their condemnation seemed weak, insincere, and ineffective. Therefore, one can surmise that the seizure of power by the military is a *fait accompli* that will not jeopardize Thailand's acceptance by the international community. In addition, public opposition from groups and individuals in Thailand has been muted by many who support the coup.

Even though I do not endorse Thaksin's behavior or his leadership, I still cannot condone his dismissal by military intervention. Thai democracy has made great progress since 1932, and in the last fifteen years, competition for political leadership has followed rules set by the constitution. Certainly, there are flaws in the constitution, flaws that become obvious when it is subjected to the clever manipulation of the law by politicians. But these flaws should be corrected and amended, not used to justify the overthrow of a legally elected government. During the past decade and a half, the Thai public have become politicized, socialized, and accustomed to open debate, discussion, and peaceful resolution of political differences. The coup of 2006 is without a doubt a setback to Thailand's democratization process.

This coup d'état by the Thai military is, by twenty-first century standards, peculiar, quaint, and anachronistic. One television host in the United States, noticing that Thais were handing out flowers and meals to the soldiers, remarked that if there were to be a coup, this is how it should be conducted. Perhaps he was referring implicitly to the 1960s, when hippies were putting flowers in the gun barrels of the national guardsmen in San Francisco. But to the Thai public that has witnessed nineteen or more military coups and counter coups, the appearance of soldiers and their antiquated tanks in the streets is not that unfamiliar. In fact, for some, it was comforting to know that there is extra-legal recourse to rid the country of "crooked politicians." The fact that political intervention can still be carried out by the military, with tacit support from the king, makes future democratically-elected leaders vulnerable and imperfectly protected by the rule of law.

Unfortunately, this coup reinforces the false dichotomy in Thai politics that elections are always *dirty* because they can be manipulated by *crooked politicians*, while, on the other hand, the intentions of the *professional and disciplined military officers* are more *noble* and more *pure*. Furthermore, as long as the king is highly revered by the Thai public, there will be continued competition for his support and blessing. In the Thai setting, the military always has an edge. Military officers (excluding the police) receive their swords and commissions from the king. Military officers also pledge annually their allegiance to the throne in elaborate public ceremonies. Politicians, on the other hand, have less connection and less access to the king. Realizing that his public image as a loyal servant of the crown was eroding, Thaksin and his cabinet began wearing yellow shirts to honor the king's sixtieth year on the throne. This practice soon spread to other civilian officials. But in the end, wearing yellow did not protect the civilian politicians from those in military uniform.

The question that begs to be answered is whether there can be such a thing as a good coup d'état. If one were to believe the Suan Dusit poll showing that an overwhelming number of Thais favor the military action, the answer is possibly yes. And if this coup group does not advocate Sarit-like atavistic political ideas that would derail decades of democratic gains, then one could perhaps make a case that the coup can be compared to a surgical removal of a cancer. This analogy has been used, of course, numerous times by other military coup leaders. Nonetheless, a different analogy seems to me to be more appropriate. The Thai body politic no doubt suffers the aches and pains of the maturing process. It is still young and finding its way, but by no means is this young body politic suffering from terminal cancer. More likely, behavioral adjustment and mild medication are only needed to help nurture this young Thai body politic. Unnecessary major surgery could stunt its growth and development ... that is, if it does not kill the patient first.

Ithaca, New York

October 2006

Army Captain Sarit with his mother Chanthip, a native of Mukdahan,
Nakhon Phanom Province, circa 1935-1939.

Graduation day, March 26, 1928. Sarit is third from the left of the second row from the top. He
graduated tenth out of forty-two cadets and was assigned to the Army First Battalion.

"Everyone cheated" Sarit told the demonstrators protesting the April, 1957 dirty elections. The demonstrators did not want to listen to Phibun (standing glumly left of Sarit), who was prime minister but demanded that Sarit talk to them. Government House, March 2, 1957. Six months later Sarit stages a coup d'état

Another turning point in Thai-US relations: Sarit meets with President Eisenhower after his coup against Phibun and turns pro-American. January, 1958. Sarit had come to the United States to undergo surgery on his liver and pancreas at Walter Reed hospital. A heavy drinker, he would die of cirrhosis of the liver five years later.

Sarit and Thanom after the October 20, 1958 coup. Parliament was dissolved and the two ruled as Head and Deputy Head of the Revolutionary Council. Sarit also became Prime Minister, Supreme Military Commander, Army Chief, and Acting National Police Chief. Thanom became deputy premier and Minister of Defense.

Sarit's last cabinet meeting, November 19, 1963, at the Government Guest House in Bangsaen, Chonburi Province. Sarit (back to camera) is flanked by Thanom, Prince Wanwaithayakorn, and Thanat Khoman.

Sarit shares a lighter moment with King Bhumibol at one of their regular meetings to discuss matters of state. (No date; reprinted in Sarit's cremation volume sponsored by the Thai Army, no pagination)

ACKNOWLEDGMENTS

The idea of republishing this book, albeit its Thai version, was first proposed by Acharn Charnvit Kasetsiri to the Thai Textbook Project Foundation to commemorate the seventy-second anniversary of the Revolution of 1932. Three books were selected. The other two are the translation of Benjamin Batson's *The End of Absolute Monarchy in Siam*, and Charnvit Kasetsiri and Thamrongsak Petchlertanan's 1932 *Revolution in Siam*. These three books continue to be standard texts in many Thai universities, and their earlier editions are no longer available. The recent Thai edition of *Thailand: The Politics of Despotic Paternalism* was ably re-edited by Acharn Thamrongsak. He added new pictures to help illuminate the text and also translated the new introduction and postscript. At the book launch in May 2005, Acharn Chalong Soontravanich kindly organized a symposium at Chulalongkorn University where current scholars discussed the contributions of this book to Thai studies. The symposium also marked the end of the fifth cycle of my life, a time when most Thai colleagues retire.

The republication of this English version is the brainchild of my Cornell colleague, Tamara Loos, who convinced the Cornell Southeast Asia Program Publications editorial board that this book might still be useful to students of Thai politics. When the first edition was published in 1979, only one thousand copies were printed. It quickly sold out within the year, partly because there were few books in English on Thai politics at that time. This republication is also a joint effort with Silkworm Press, which will market the book in Thailand and in Asia. I want to express my thanks to Tamara Loos for her confidence that there is still value in this book, to Deborah Homsher and Fred Conner of the SEAP publications office who painstakingly made sure that my workmanlike prose was correct and readable, and to Thamora Fishel for checking the transliteration of Thai words. The more perceptive of you will notice that the cover of this book differs significantly from the black and white cover of the original. Hardly any reader has made the connection of that somber cover to that of a cremation volume; the subliminal message of "cremating military dictatorship" was unrealized. And in spite of the military intervention of September 19, 2006 that overthrew the elected Thaksin Shinawat government, I hope that this more colorful and cheerful red cover will convey to you that indeed Thai politics faces a brighter future, having survived despotic paternalism.

INTRODUCTION

Previous authoritative works on modern Thai politics have failed to give adequate stress to the importance of historical and cultural constraints on the nature of its development.[1] They tend to concentrate upon functional aspects of the modern political system and misjudge conceptually the central idea of modernization and development in the Thai context which should be subsumed under the traditional concern for the consolidation of power and leadership status.[2] Thai politics should be considered and understood from the historical perspective involving a study of traditional political values that faced stresses and strains from the impact of modernism. On the paradigmatic level, the main characteristics of modern Thai politics could be briefly listed as follows—authority is patrimonial and absolute; political behavior is affected by the interplay of royal, military, and bureaucratic power relations; the traditional political structure is hierarchical and segmented; the rigidity of the political structure persists in the face of rapid social change, which causes tension and eventual political instability.[3]

Historically, the development of the concept of power, authority, and legitimacy took two forms. Firstly, the "traditionally" Thai reification of the patriarchal system was argued and substantiated by the now famous stone inscription attributed to King Ramkhamhaeng of Sukhothai through which the ruler was idealized as the father-figure *(phokhun)* who rules over his domain in a paternalistic, yet autocratic, manner.[4] This basis for power and authority was to be replaced during the Ayutthaya period by the *devaraja* cult influenced by court Brahmans of the Khmer civilization.[5] Through the process of Khmerization or Hinduization, the king

---

[1] Examples are David A. Wilson, *Politics in Thailand* (Ithaca, NY: Cornell University Press, 1962); Frank C. Darling, *Thailand and the United States* (Washington, DC: Public Affairs Press, 1965); Fred W. Riggs, *Thailand: The Modernization of a Bureaucratic Polity* (Honolulu, HI: East-West Center Press, 1966), and William J. Siffin, *The Thai Bureaucracy: Institutional Change and Development* (Honolulu, HI: East-West Center Press, 1966).

[2] For an exception, note the iconoclastic Norman Jacobs, *Modernization without Development: Thailand as an Asian Case Study* (New York: Praeger, 1971).

[3] The future of this paradigm is at present in doubt. The politics of the post-1960s is marked by the emergence of new socio-economic groups and conflicting ideologies. These forces have created a great impact upon the prevailing structure of Thai politics, threatening to replace it with a socio-economic and political structure defined in terms of class and cross-cutting interests transcending traditional boundaries of political segmentation. For an interesting study reflecting this change, see Benedict Anderson, "Withdrawal Symptoms: Social and Cultural Aspects of the October 6 Coup," *Bulletin of Concerned Asian Scholars,* IX (July–September, 1977), pp. 13-30.

[4] See Damrong Rachanuphab, *"Laksana kanpokkhrong prathet sayam tae boran"* [Ancient Siamese Administration], (speech delivered before the Samaikhayachan Samakhom, Bangkok, October 8, 1927).

[5] James N. Mosel "Thai Administrative Behavior," in *Toward a Comparative Study of Public Administration,* ed. Willam J. Siffin (Bloomington, IN: The Department of Government, Indiana University Press, 1957), p. 284.

established claims to be a personification of cosmic values and hence derived power and legitimacy from the religio-cosmological interpretation. This framework of royal authority was transferred to the early Ratanakosin period, where changes were made during the Chakkri Reformation of Rama IV, and particularly later in Rama V's reign.[6] As *devaraja*, the king had become increasingly isolated from the public and deviated from the *phokhun* ideal type. However, during the reign of Rama IV, several measures were instigated to bring the position of the king closer to his subjects. Taboos against looking at or touching the king were removed, and his subjects were allowed to petition the king directly, reminiscent of the practices described in the Ramkhamhaeng inscription.[7] Rama V went one step further by releasing his subjects from the obligation of prostrating themselves before the king. Nevertheless, the monarch still retained the aura of the absolutist god king.

The revolution of 1932, while effectively depriving the royalty of its centrality in the process of politics, did not in effect bring about a revolution in the modern political sense. What is significant seems to be the stress exerted upon the concept of power and legitimacy heretofore invested in the personage of the monarch. The new leaders had to present an alternative legitimizing source. The foreign idea of constitutionalism was apparently weak in Thailand because it was foreign and not thoroughly appreciated by the general public. There were attempts to disregard the historical and traditional position of the throne as a legitimizing institution, even to the point of suggesting a republican form of government. In the end, as their predecessors of 1911 had done before them,[8] the leadership within the People's Party backed down and retained the monarchy, asked for its forgiveness, and allowed it to exercise the sanctioning prerogative of legitimization. The constitution became not a product of the people's work and toil but a royal gift from a benevolent king. As the generous provider of this gift, the throne maintained a moral superiority over the leaders of the People's Party.

This aspect of the genesis of modern Thai politics must be understood clearly. As the gracious donor, the monarchy retained a foothold in the Thai constitutional adventure. The image of the patriarchal king was preserved by this action, establishing a political order under which both king and subject continued to maintain interlocking moral obligations to guide and determine the future of

---

[6] The traditional roots of this change came during the period of King Trailok of Ayutthaya in the 1450s, whose administrative reforms created functionally specialized ministries. Under Trailok, rationalization of the *sakdina* graded hierarchization of the social structure was also carried out.

[7] King Mongkut or one of his sons would appear at the palace wall four times a month to give alms to the poor and receive petitions from the people. See Royal Proclamations of 1856 and 1858 in *Prachum Prakat Ratchakan thi si Po Su, 2394–2400* [Collected Royal Proclamations of the 4th reign, 1851-1857] (Phranakhon[?]: Ongkan Kha khong Khurusapha, 2503 [1960]), pp. 263, 264.

[8] The Revolt of 1911, or Kabot R.S. 130, was an attempt made by young army officers to overthrow the absolute monarchy and find new political means to modernize Thailand. They were distressed with the situation in Siam as it compared to other countries, especially Japan in Asia. The plot never got off the ground as the secret was leaked. Arrests were made. Correspondences smuggled out of prison indicated how the plotters were later grateful to the king for dealing with them fairly. In response, several of the conspirators confirmed their allegiance to the throne. See Lieutenants Rian Sichan and Net Phunwiwat, *Kabot R.S. 130* [The Revolt of R.S. 130] (Bangkok: National Student Center of Thailand, 1974).

constitutionalism in Thailand.[9] Thus the Thai monarchy, unlike those in other constitutional systems, retained a special position in the new political system whereby the throne was not merely the object of politics, but in fact the "subject" of politics. Thus any true political understanding of modern Thai politics must take into account that the special position of the monarchy is a requisite of the political system.[10]

The tension between the monarchy and the leadership of the People's Party continued throughout the period from 1932 to 1957. In particular, Marshal Phibunsongkhram, who took over real control of national leadership from the mid-1930s, tried first to ignore and undermine the throne's precarious position as the traditional legitimizer of political power by imposing upon the Thai society modern concepts of the state and leadership. This tension between king and minister was not satisfactorily removed until the coming of age of Marshal Sarit Thanarat, who staged a coup against Phibun in 1957 and subsequently took power in 1958.

The dualism between the authority of the king and his chief minister, and the traditional dualism inherent in the rival concepts of king as *devaraja* and *phokhun*, became the central concerns of the new leadership under Sarit.[11] The traditional concepts of power and leadership were conceptually and pragmatically secularized to accommodate the two spheres of leadership, so that the king retained his cosmological and historical links with legitimating symbolism while the *de facto* non-royal leadership derived its legitimacy from both the constitutional symbolism described above, as well as the more mundane aspect of a secular patriarchy. Thus, in this modern sense, the Sarit period was significant because during this time the position of the prime minister became the most powerful in the national leadership, having tapped cosmological sanctions through the close association with, and receiving active/tacit support from, the throne, while also deriving legitimacy and support from the public through Sarit's own systematic promotion (by demonstration) of the atavistic concept of the national leader as *phokhun*.[12] This development could be viewed as the normalization of conflicting concepts of leadership based on historical, cosmological, and patriarchal ideals and the ahistorical and socially alien concept of modern constitutionalism. Lip service was given to constitutionalism and democratic processes, while the actual practice of politics became, in reality, one of despotic paternalism fashioned from converging historical heritages of patrimonialism and the leadership's militaristic background.

---

[9] For an account of the promoter's dealings with Rama VII after the 1932 coup, see Lt. Gen. Prayoon Phamonmontri, "The Political Change of 1932," in *Thai Politics, 1932-1957*, ed. Thak Chaloemtiarana (Bangkok: Social Science Association of Thailand, 1978), pp. 36-50. Also note Rama VII's detailed criticisms of Pridi's Economic Development Plan in Ibid., pp. 193-236. The king labeled the plan as communist-inspired, which led to the temporary exile of Pridi.

[10] See Benedict Anderson's argument in his "Studies of the Thai State" (paper submitted to the Conference on the State of Thai Studies, Chicago, March 30, 1978), pp. 20-27.

[11] For a detailed account, see Thak Chaloemtiarana, *"Khwamkhit thang kanmuang khong chomphon Sarit Thanarat lae rabob kanmuang baeb phokhun uppatham"* [The Political Thinking of Field Marshal Sarit Thanarat and the Politics of Paternalism], in *Rak muangthai* [Love Thailand], ed. Sombat Chantornwong and Rangsan Thanapbonphan (Bangkok: I Thai Textbook Project, 1976), pp. 35-82.

[12] The argument that Thai politics was marked by a kind of political atavism was first used by Toru Yano, "Sarit and Thailand's Pro-American Policy," *The Developing Economies*, VI (September 1963): 284-299.

The Chakkri Reformation, or modernization, has yet to be fully understood. However, several implications of the reformation can be isolated. Firstly, while it is facile to view the reformation from the standpoint of a traditional society adjusting to the encroachment of Western colonialism and the need to clearly demarcate Siam as a territorially and administratively distinct nation-state, one must not lose sight of the position of the monarchy during the early part of Rama V's reign, during which the king needed the machinery, as well as the structure, to consolidate his weakened hold on actual political power, which had been under the control of several powerful aristocratic families.[13] Modernization in this sense could be viewed as attempts of the monarchy to establish means to consolidate its own weak position.

Secondly, it is perhaps misleading to view the modernization of the Chakkri Reformation as "national" modernization, although there are certain grounds for this line of theorizing. More meaningful, perhaps, would be an analysis focused on the fact that consolidation led to the creation of two institutional power structures that would ultimately compete with the throne for national leadership.[14] I refer to the establishment of the modern bureaucracy and the modern army.

Nothing illuminates better the nature of such modernization than an examination of the historical development of the Thai military. By the middle of the nineteenth century, Siam's traditional enemies had been pacified and colonized. The creation of a modern and professional army seemed a moot issue in view of the military potential of the Western powers in the area. Siam was in no position to resist Western designs militarily if the case ever arose. I will not go into the controversial subject as to how Siam escaped direct colonization. Suffice it to say, the modern army was created not so much for external warfare or the defense of national integrity, but for the purposes of supporting and extending royal authority over a traditionally loosely-held realm.

Traditionally, the armies serving the Chakkri kings in the late eighteenth and early nineteenth centuries were composed of foreign personnel.[15] And by this time the external security of the kingdom was guaranteed by the Western imperial powers. Siam's traditional rivals had been neutralized by the colonial powers, and as a result of this fact, the modern Thai army took on the character of an internal army to be deployed internally for consolidation purposes, a function that has endured to the present time. One of the earliest moves of king Chulalongkorn concerning military matters was to create a special royal bodyguard unit that was well-equipped and professionally trained, which could be seen as an important base of support for the king's faction in trying to wrest power from the aristocratic families.[16] Noel Battye states that Chulalongkorn was aware of the importance of the army in political terms as an organization that could provide adequate force to "put down unlawful persons within the country."[17] From this perspective, the decree instituting military conscription of 1905 could be best understood as the actions of a state that

---

[13] For further discussion, see Thak Chaloemtiarana, "The Evolution of the Monarchy and Government: Institutional Conflicts and Change," in *Asia,* ed. Lauristan Sharp (New York, NY: Asia Society, 1976), pp. 41-56.

[14] Ibid.

[15] Noel Battye, "The Military, Government, and Society in Siam, 1868-1910" (PhD dissertation, Cornell University, 1974), pp. 20, 21.

[16] Ibid., p. 133.

[17] Ibid., p. 132.

required enforcement firepower to maintain internal stability, which had been threatened by the Holy Man and Shan rebellions in 1902; Battye notes that the rebellions prompted and supported the argument "for a national conscript army as an essential instrument of internal governance."[18] Thus under these inauspicious conditions of birth, the modern Thai army emerged as a political instrument of the state, and precisely because it did not have external functions, it followed logical steps of development that led it eventually to dominate the domestic political process.[19] The coup of 1932 marked the turning point.

Under the normal circumstances of an open democratic political system with roots deeply embedded in corresponding social values, the professionalism of the military corps could have evolved. However, such was not the case. Democracy was an alien principle in Thailand; authoritarianism was traditional, thus indigenous. The leaders of the People's Party vacillated between responding to the urge to nurture the seeds of a democratic system and the inclination to revert to old authoritarian values. In this struggle, the military faction was superior, and so it proceeded to pursue its basic function of an internal army, only now it became the political instrument of its own officers, who were bent upon seeking and maintaining their own power and status.[20] Ultimately, the growth of parliamentary democracy was stunted by the antiquarian concerns of military leaders who inherited the old concepts of the hierarchical and segmented Thai political system. Taking the segmentation of the Thai political structure as *a priori* suited the authoritarian nature of military leaders. Politics seen through this framework clearly fit the leaders' military socialization and the army's traditional role in national administration.

The third consequence of the Chakkri Reformation was the effect it had upon the structure of the political system. Toru Yano forcefully argued that the reformation of Chulalongkorn caused the "segmentation" of the Thai political structure. The gist of his argument was that "a segmented society emerged within the formal framework of a unified nation-state—a segmented society that was clearly a product of the

---

[18] Ibid., p. 430. Battye posits that "There is no reason to disbelieve the report of the British Counsel that the army, a novelty to the Siamese scene, was created for 'internal' rather than external military purposes." Ibid., p. 226. Regarding the army's domestic role, Ben Anderson cited Battye and Benjamin Batson, "The End of the Absolute Monarchy in Siam" (PhD dissertation, Cornell University, 1977), who argued that in the mid-1880s young reformers who had been educated in Europe strongly supported the modernization of the military in order to push through domestic reforms against conservative opposition and the provinces. At the same time, they realized the futility of organizing a modern army to defend the country against the West. See Battye, "The Military, Government, and Society in Siam," pp. 263ff. He noted that Baston ("The End of the Absolute Monarchy in Siam." p. 202) brings to attention an issue raised by Prince Boworadet before Rama VII that subversive propaganda could turn military officers against the monarchy. This potential threat was discussed in 1928, perhaps reflecting on the events of 1911. See Anderson, "Studies of the Thai State," footnote 23.

[19] For studies on the Thai military, consult David Wilson, "The Military in Thai Politics," in *The Role of the Military in Underdeveloped Countries*, ed. John J. Johnson (Princeton, NJ: Princeton University Press, 1962), pp. 253-276; Claude E. Welch Jr. and Arthur K. Smith, *Military Role and Rule* (North Scituate: Duxbury Press, 1974); Moshe Lissak, *Military Role in Modernization: Civil-Military Relations in Thailand and Burma* (Beverly Hills, CA: Sage Publications, 1976); and Fred von der Mehden, "The Military and Development in Thailand," *Journal of Comparative Administration* II (November 1970): 323-340.

[20] The best example of this is the 1947 coup d'état. For an account see Suchin Tantikun, *Ratthaprahan Ph. S 2490* [The 1947 Coup] (Bangkok: Social Science Association of Thailand, 1972).

conscious efforts made to establish a rigid hierarchical order under absolute monarchy."[21] The functions of the royal house became more important in policy-making as Chulalongkorn encouraged princes to study abroad and gain knowledge and competency to help the king administer the country. In this way, the previous monopoly of power enjoyed by the highly influential aristocratic families was negated. In addition, the bureaucrats were reduced to strictly neutral functions. Their roles and behavior were closely regulated by law and ordinance. As members of a modern functional administrative structure, they became privileged servants of the throne, constituting a political stratum next in prestige to the royal house but quite removed in status from the general public. The third segment was the peasantry, who were given the status of free citizenship but whose quality of life did not receive much official notice or redress.[22]

Pursuing this line of argument, we find that highly authoritarian rule was thus necessary to maintain national integration and political stability. This system could be controlled as long as the vast peasantry was not subjected to extreme social and economic stresses. Demands on the administration were to be minimized (although they had never posed any real threat in the past). Tight authoritarian rule was also needed to control both the civilian and military bureaucracies, as the nature of the modern functional bureaucracy was meritocratic, valuing accomplishment and talent, and therefore opposed to the ascriptive norms prescribed by the royal house and inherent in the absolute monarchial system.

This conflict of values became critical within the confines of the bureaucracy as it began to mature by the first half of the twentieth century. The Revolution of 1932 could be seen as a manifestation of the conflict between the standards of "merit" and "blood".[23] The Chakkri Reformation, while considered as a modernizing influence, could be understood clearly from the viewpoint earlier stated that it was for power consolidation of the royal house. While it did create non-royal bureaucrats on a grand scale, the top echelon was to remain within the grasp of the royal family members. As long as the bureaucracy was in its nascent state and that the royal princes were clearly capable administrators, the system continued to persist. However, this condition became exacerbated with the passing of time, as civilian and military officials reached bureaucratic maturity and the royal house was not able to generate enough capable members following the death of Rama V.[24]

While it is widely considered that the situation described above became endemic during Rama VII's reign, the malady was the result of the policies of King Chulalongkorn—policies that were strikingly at odds with professional and meritocratic standards. Again, policies regarding the military best illustrate this observation. After the law on conscription was passed, civil servants who were conscripted were assigned military ranks equivalent to the ones they had held in the

---

[21] Toru Yano, "Political Structure of a 'Rice-Growing State'," in *Thailand: A Rice Growing Society*, Monographs of the Center for Southeast Asian Studies, ed. Yoneo Ishii (Kyoto: Kyoto University, English-language Series, No. 12, 1978), p. 122 ff.

[22] Yano points out that the benefit of education was not fully extended to the public. On a different level, he argues that "in modernizing, Thailand did not seek to encourage division in its political system. In actuality however, the Chakkri Reformation produced a system in which each stratum maintained its own broad cultural pattern, which embraced political culture as well as lifestyle." Ibid., p. 123.

[23] Chaloemtiarana, "The Evolution."

[24] The monogamous Rama VI and Rama VII did not leave any male heirs.

civilian bureaucracy. In 1906, for purposes of restricting the expansion of the national army, rules of admission to the Military Academy were adjusted so that candidates must be children of reputable parents and be sponsored and guaranteed by commissioned government officials. Furthermore, by 1909 entrance to the three preparatory grades of the military academy were limited exclusively to the sons of the royal house and military officers. Also, a special class was set up for sons of royalty, with the rank of Serene Highness and above, and for male children of military officers with commissioned or warrant rank. Examinations were waived for this special class.[25]

However, royal nepotism ran deeper and was more pervasive in the General Staff of the War Ministry. In 1910, only members of the royalty held the ranks of General and Lieutenant General; and six out of thirteen Major Generals were of royal birth. More than half of the Divisional Commanders were from royal families. Many of these generals were extremely young.[26]

The 1932 Revolution, while allegedly an attempt to "revolutionize" the political system, in fact accepted it as more or less on its own grounds and proceeded to modify it. However, it should be conceded here that attempts were made by the civilian sector within the People's Party under the leadership of Pridi to consider the aspects and benefits of representative democracy seriously; nevertheless, in the final analysis, they had to give in to the political preconditions of the system that grew out of the reformation years. Yano expresses the opinion that

> An important point to keep in mind here is that internal impetus toward modernization was lacking in the Thai social structure. This meant that political modernization had to be artificially devised and imposed from above, and also that the establishment of an authoritarian dictatorship accompanied by expansion of the bureaucracy (*kharatchakan*), and the practice of a formalistic constitutionalism, became inevitable.[27]

Political reality and constitutional idealism clashed in the end, and the People's Party had to make adjustments that ultimately forced it to rely more and more upon the experience and insight of its leaders—itself a form of paternalism—and eventually paved the way for a return to authoritarianism.

Political segmentation after 1932 took on new characteristics. The centrality of the royal house in the decision-making arena was replaced by the new bureaucratic leaders who constituted the government, which in turn was responsible for the destiny of the state (*rat*). On the second tier of the hierarchy, the bureaucracy rapidly expanded as an instrument of the state, generating new bureaucratic leaders from within its own ranks. This particular feature led to the formulation of the Riggsian concept defining Thailand as a bureaucratic polity.[28] Peasants were thus transformed into citizens of the state with rights and privileges—not merely duties, as before—under the new constitution. This new aspect of citizenry was also expressed in the proposals of Pridi in his Economic Plan of 1933.

---

[25] Battye, "The Military, Government, and Society in Siam," pp. 494, 495.

[26] Ibid., 519.

[27] Yano, "Political Structure," p. 127.

[28] Riggs, *Thailand*.

Before the decade ended, the nature of political segmentation took another turn, which inclined the government to reinstate pre-1932 authoritarianism—an ironic twist in the evolution of the state. In 1939, under the dictates of Phibun, the relationship between the state and the citizenry was again readjusted. Under the *ratthaniyom,* or State Convention/Preference Movement, the state and its representative, the government, was elevated to a paramount position above all other social and political elements.[29] The concept of "the state" changed, so that the term was no longer merely legalistic, but now encompassed a wider meaning with ideological implications. It came to resemble similar concepts that had gained currency in Europe, concepts underlying the philosophical foundations of modern totalitarianism. The position of the citizenry was relegated to secondary importance, as the people were now chiefly obligated to perform duties for the glory and survival of the state. With this movement emerged the strongman-savior concept of *phunam,* who became the guardian of the national will and whose decisions were to be unquestionably followed and obeyed by a grateful public. Phibun was well-suited for that role, having tapped the support of the army, which performed its traditional political role as the base for power and instrument for controlling internal unrest.

With the *phunam's* authority grounded in the traditional absolutism of the Thai monarchs legitimized by historical and cosmological sources, the *phunam* era brought forth the specter of a non-royal and secular authoritarian style of leadership which in its fundamental essence approximated, but yet was alien to, traditional Thai political values. The position of the monarch in this system was considered spurious and inconsequential. As a promoter who was responsible for the demise of royal authority, Phibun did not want nor did he permit any rivalry to his recently acquired status. This aspect of Phibun's relationship with the monarchy would continue throughout his career. And as the throne remained the "subject" of politics and the ultimate source of traditional legitimization, Phibun deprived himself of its support. This weakness in Phibun's political armor was to be exploited by his successor, Sarit.[30]

The *ratthaniyom* campaign and the *phunam* cult faded out of the scene of Thai politics following the defeat of Japan in World War II.[31] The interregnum of civilian rule between 1944-1947 was marked by attempts to institute democratic government. It proved to be short-lived, however, as the army staged a coup d' état in 1947 and brought back Phibun as prime minister. For the next ten years, Phibun danced to a different tune, as his power base within the army was severed, having fallen under the control of younger and more aggressive officers. From dictator, Phibun turned democrat. He was able to maintain his position with the support of the army, whose younger generation of leaders were not ready to assume political leadership. In addition, a facade of formalistic constitutionalism was maintained—party politics were allowed, accompanied by parliamentary elections, "Hyde Park" speeches, and regular "press conferences" orchestrated by the prime minister. In reality, however, Phibun used the police to harass his political enemies and to rig ballot boxes. At first,

---

[29] For documents of this period in the English language, see Chaloemtiarana, *Thai Politics,* pp. 244-316.

[30] See Chaloemtiarana, *"Khwamkhit thang kanmuang."*

[31] For the most recent study of this important period, consult Thamsook Numnonda, *Thailand and the Japanese Presence, 1941-1945,* ISEAS, Research Notes and Discussions, No. 6 (Singapore: ISEAS, October 1977).

the army was a tacit partner in this political repression and democratic farce, but as institutional rivalry with the police intensified, and when the new army strongman, Sarit, saw his chance of breaking away from Phibun "gracefully" and seizing power himself, the army withdrew its support from the government. Exploiting public protests against police corruption and brutality and against Phibun's tampering with election results in 1957, the army staged a coup and appointed a civilian caretaker government. In the following year, Sarit staged a *coup de main* and proclaimed Thailand's second "Revolution." This marked the beginning of Thailand's neo-classical authoritarian period, a time for despotic paternalism.

The leaders of the 1957 coup differed fundamentally from those of the 1932 group by the fact that most were army officers who had never attended educational institutions in other countries. Their political outlooks had been shaped almost exclusively by what had happened in Thailand. They were naturally much less impressed than their predecessors with the idea that Western democracy was the final goal of political modernization. It was the members of the Sarit 1957 coup group who were responsible for shaping the new format of Thai politics that endured until October 1973. Under Sarit's leadership, a formal rationalization of the concept "democracy in the Thai context" took place, a development that presents students of Thai politics with a most challenging analytical problem.

With the exception of the Japanese scholar Toru Yano, no foreign academics have shown interest in a systematic study of the important political implications of the period between 1957 to 1963: the Sarit years. Although Sarit's system was carried on after his death by Marshal Thanom Kittikhachon, I feel that the above period laid the essential basis for the system, and its study should thus lead to a clear understanding of the form and character of modern Thai politics.

Although Sarit's ideas were never systematically formulated, it is nevertheless possible to reconstruct the basic ideological tenets of his regime. In their most elementary form, they revolved around Sarit's notion of *pattiwat* — loosely translated as "revolution"— and *phatthana* (development/modernization). Sarit always argued that his coup in 1958 was historically unique in that it installed a revolutionary government to carry out *pattiwat* and *phatthana*. Yet Sarit's *pattiwat* (and *phatthana*) had their own peculiar meanings for him, very different from Western concepts of revolution and development that involve major social, political, and economic changes. Sarit's *pattiwat* was actually "reactionary" in the sense that it encouraged political atavism. For Sarit's idea of a truly Thai political order was based on the three-tiered segmented socio-political system defined in terms of *rat/rattaban* (state/government), *kharatchakan* (bureaucracy), and *prachachon* (people). With this view of the political system established as a guide, Sarit's policies and programs were aimed at maintaining the boundaries between hierarchical sectors while the process of *phatthana* was applied; *phatthana* was meant to reinforce *pattiwat*. Development and modernization were to be extensions of regime paternalism, and great care was to be taken to see that change did not undermine the integrity of traditional boundaries that ordered the political system.

The difficulty inherent in Sarit's ideology lay, of course, in the fact that his conception of the political system was essentially static, and thus vulnerable to rapid social change. While Sarit's *phatthana* was initially devised as a paternalistic program of controlled change, the real consequences were hard to contain and predict. Sarit's ideology, which assumed that socio-economic and political systems are naturally compatible and can be easily juxtaposed in one entity, basically denied the potential for dynamic interaction between the two. The incongruity of economic development and political traditionalism built up growing tensions in Thai society, especially after Sarit's death. For either the political system would have to adjust itself to socio-economic change or the regime would have to employ coercive measures to suppress such change. The dramatic events of the 1970s in Thailand are indicative of the tensions between the two systems.

Sarit's impact on Thai political development is not one that could be readily applauded. His rule was harsh, repressive, despotic, and inflexible. Yet we must make clear assessments of the role he played in the development process of modern Thai politics. It is necessary that scholars answer the questions regarding Sarit's popularity, which was much greater than one would predict, given his distasteful tight-fisted rule; we must also note the system's limitations and built-in flaws, which eventually led to its own disintegration. By answering these questions, we will be able to understand the nature of modern Thai politics and glimpse certain aspects within the system that were inherited from the past and passed on to the present.

Criticisms have been raised regarding the study of the so-called Sarit system. Most critics have been concerned with the normative portrait of Sarit as a despicable individual whose regime was an intolerable experience; they contend that a scholar should discharge his debts to society by exposing Sarit for what he was—a greedy and selfish dictator—in order to help prevent this pattern and style of leadership from recurring. While I share many of their concerns, I would argue that a scholar should not seek to indict or eulogize the subject under study. One should instead attempt to try to study what policies Sarit implemented politically, policies that made him effective as a leader who was respected, hated, obeyed, and above all, feared. It is easy for us to attribute public compliance to fear of dictatorial powers alone. Yet there appears to have been an "elusive quality" in the Sarit leadership, enough to raise the issue of whether Sarit was an anachronism, for it is still common even today to hear people remark that political uncertainty in Thailand could be stabilized by a leader like Sarit. He remains a controversial prototype, and other Thai political leaders are measured through comparisons with him. This enigma needs and dictates academic exploration.

One the theoretical level, one should not merely search for the uniquely Thai aspect of the Sarit leadership. I believe that an understanding of the politics of this period in Thailand would contribute to a wider knowledge of modern patrimonial systems—societies that have been affected or infected by modernism while their political values and traditions, inherited from the recent past, have been paternalistic, militaristic, and authoritarian.

* * *

This book is divided into two distinct yet complementary parts. The first is a narration of the extremely volatile period following the Second World War in which coups and counter-coups became the common tactics of those engaged in political maneuvering. This era was distinctly marked by the lip service given to democratic forms of government, while in reality authoritarian tactics were functioning not too far from the surface of parliamentary rule. This part is important to the study insofar as it provides the backdrop to our understanding of Sarit's political education. I have indulged in a rather lengthy analysis of this period for two reasons, one of which is stated above. The other justification for this decision lies in the fact that no previous study of Thai politics during this important period, which paved the way for the return to a system of traditional authoritarian governance, has been made available to students. Part two analyzes in detail the Sarit regime and the nature of Thai despotic paternalism and the concept of democracy seen within this context.

My original study of the Sarit regime was undertaken in 1971, made possible by generous grants from the Rockefeller Foundation and the London-Cornell Project. The subsequent write-up was supported by the Rockefeller Foundation and the Cornell Southeast Asia Program. The major part of this manuscript was presented to the Cornell University Graduate School to fulfill dissertation requirements. While the central thesis has not been altered, I have made several revisions and updated the manuscript at many points; in particular, the introduction spells out more clearly my aims and certain theoretical concerns. The last phase of preparation was conducted at the Center for Southeast Asian Studies of Kyoto University. To these benefactors I am most grateful. In this regard, I would like to express personal thanks to Larry Stiffel, David Wyatt, and Shinichi Ichimura for their interest in my work.

My intellectual debts to friends and former mentors are enormous. First and foremost, the writing of this book would not have been the satisfying experience that it was without the help, patience, and understanding of Benedict R. O' G. Anderson. Throughout my years in Ithaca and even following my teaching career, he has shaped my intellectual outlook and appreciation of our common discipline. Others in Ithaca have contributed to my academic maturity. Of these I would like to single out George McT. Kahin, Lauristan Sharp, and my numerous colleagues at 102 West Avenue. I am also sure that those of us at 102 would be remiss if we neglected to mention Peggy Lush and her efficiency and love, which she so generously heaped upon her charges.

With regard to my field research, I would like to acknowledge the help received from Jitlada Sirirat, Khun Manop Sirithu, Noranit Sethabut, Phongsak Ditsathat, and my two assistants, Jirawat Lueng-suphabun, and Kamon Phothiyop.

My students and colleagues at Thammasat University also contributed their share in shaping my ideas regarding the Sarit regime. They criticized many of my ideas and provided me with additional food for thought. Several colleagues have read parts of the manuscript and provided valuable criticisms. For this, I would like to thank Sombat Chantornwong, Likhit Dhiravegin, Saneh Chamarik, and Montri Chenvidayakarn.

At Kyoto, I greatly benefited from discussions with the noted Japanese scholar of Thai politics, Toru Yano, who not only gave me his valuable time, but kindly made my stay at the Center most pleasurable and rewarding. I would like to thank Professor Yoneo Ishii for sharing with me recollections of his close association with Marshal Sarit. To my friends, particularly Kenji Tsuchiya, I would like to express my thanks and appreciation for all the big and small favors they had done for me and my family.

Above all, I am grateful to Siu-ling, Thwen, and Khwan for bearing with me and for gamely resettling in strange environments as my academic ports of call continually shift. Needless to say, I bear the sole responsibility for the weaknesses and mistakes in interpretation, unless of course annotated and clearly attributed to others.

T.C.
Kyoto
October 1978

CHAPTER ONE

THE RETURN OF THE MILITARY TO LEADERSHIP AFTER WORLD WAR II

From 1938 to 1943, while Phibun was Thailand's prime minister, Thailand's domestic politics were marked by the promotion of nationalism in the manner of Germany, Italy, and Japan. The targets of this nationalism were the local Chinese and the French in Indochina.[1] It appears that, at the time this nationalistic policy got under way, the People's Party leadership was intact. Phibun and Pridi still cooperated with each other. However, after the landing of the Japanese in Thailand in 1941, Phibun felt he had little choice but to accept the Japanese presence and consequently gradual splits developed among the Thai elite. What happened in Thai politics from 1941 to 1945 is still not clear. While on the one hand, Phibun and Pridi seem generally to have cooperated in attempting to "save" the country from disaster, at times signs of growing conflict also surfaced. Rapid changes in the fortunes of war had considerable effect on their relationship. Phibun was naturally identified with the Japanese cause. Though he seems to have given some indications that he wanted to cooperate with the European–American Allies, these moves came late in the war and his credibility with the Allies was not high. The events of the war and their impact on Thai society also increased Phibun's unpopularity at home. Pridi's stature, on the other hand, grew thanks to his pro-Allied activities and his removal from immediate political responsibility on assuming the position of Regent. Personal rivalry now took the form of institutional rivalry among the "civilians," led by Pridi; the so-called Seri Thai, allied with conservative royalists, headed by Khuang Aphaiwong; and Phibun and the army.[2]

Toward the end of World War II the struggle for political leadership between the mainly civilian groups led by Pridi and the army headed by Phibun came to a head. Pridi had used his elevation to the prestigious but powerless post of Regent after the Japanese landing in December 1941 to stay in the background of the domestic

[1] See G. William Skinner, *Chinese Society in Thailand: An Analytical History* (Ithaca, NY: Cornell University Press, 1957), pp. 261-72, and Luang Wichit Wathakan, *Thailand's Case* (Bangkok: Thammasat University Press, 1941).

[2] The Seri Thai was an underground movement formed by Pridi to cooperate with the Allies against the Japanese. It was a loose organization whose membership came primarily from senior officers in the navy, Isan MPs, students studying in England and the United States, and others who were closely associated with Pridi. Khuang Aphaiwong had been a student in Europe when Phibun and Pridi were planning the 1932 coup. He was not officially a member of the People's Party until after the coup, when he became associated with it as a junior member. For personal accounts of this period consult translations in Thak Chaloemtiarana, ed., *Thai Politics, 1932–1957* (Bangkok: Social Science Association of Thailand, 1978), pp. 322–440.

political struggle to disassociate himself somewhat from the wartime regime.[3] He bided his time, nourishing the illegal Seri Thai movement on which he hoped to build a future power base to contest the army's control of political leadership and its monopoly of the means of violence.[4]

The Seri Thai has been described in various accounts, but there is no good objective account of all its diverse groups and activities.[5] Roughly speaking, there were three main components. The first was the local organization led by Pridi (code name: "Ruth"), Luang Adul ("Pulau"), and Admiral Luang Sinat Yotharak ("Champa"). The American group was led by Ambassador Seni Pramote and had a membership of close to ninety individuals.[6] They worked closely with the Overseas Strategic Service, but only a few were actually sent to Thailand, entry being made from China. The English section had no particular leader and was composed of students studying in England. According to Puey's account in Direk's book, they numbered around fifty-four members, thirty-seven of whom were later attached to the British army.[7] A few of them were trained paratroopers who were parachuted into the country. The work of the Seri Thai members from the United States and England was mainly to set up radio transmission centers to send intelligence reports to the Allies in China and India. Contact between the Seri Thai abroad and those within the country was established by March 1944, when Seri Thai members from England and the United States entered the country. Most of them were captured by the police and sent to Bangkok, where Luang Adul, the police chief and second in command to Pridi, took charge of them. Puey's narrative indicates that the other Seri Thai members received considerable cooperation from the government—officials, police, navy, and army officers. They had to rely heavily on police and local administrative officers' help in their task of establishing transmitting stations in various provinces. The bulk of the Seri Thai, however, were those working in the country prior to contact with the United States and British sections. (Little is known of their activities, although Chiep has written briefly of his personal experiences in the southern provinces. He gives the impression that many Isan MPs were also involved.)

Net's account gives a rather curious picture of certain anti-Japanese efforts made by Phibun. Before the coming of the Seri Thai members from abroad, Phibun allegedly started his own "Seri Thai" plans. At the end of 1942. he sent Lt. General Jira Wichitsongkhram and Col. Net Khemayothin up to the Shan States to try to

---

[3] Pridi had been the minister of finance. An account of the career of Phibun up to 1952 can be found in Charun Kuwanon, *Chiwit Kantosu khong Chomphon P. Phibunsongkhram* [The Life and Struggles of Field Marshal P. Phibunsongkhram] (Bangkok: Akson Charoenthat Press, 1953).

[4] General Luang Adul Detcharat was both the chief of the national police and head of the Seri Thai armed units. When Pridi became prime minister after the war, Luang Adul took over Phibun's position as army chief. For accounts of Seri Thai activities, see Nai Chanthana (pseud.), *XO Group* (Bangkok: Akson Samphan Press, 1964); Chiep Amphunan, *Mahawitthayalai khong khaphachao* [My University] (Bangkok: Ruamsan Press, 1957); and Nicol Smith and Blake Clark, *Into Siam* (New York, NY: Bobbs-Merrill Co., 1945).

[5] See Chiep Amphunan, *Mahawitthayalai*; Nai Chanthana, *XO Group*; Smith, *Into Siam*; Direk Chaiyanam, *Thai kap Songkhram Lok khrang thi Song* [Thailand and the Second World War] (Bangkok: Phrae Phitthaya Press, 1967); and Net Khemayothin, *Ngan Taidin khong Phan-ek Yothi* [Underground Activities of Colonel Yothi] (Bangkok: Fuang Akson Press, 1967).

[6] Direk, *Thai kap Songkhram,* pp. 472-474.

[7] Ibid., pp. 380-434.

establish contacts with the Kuomintang's 93rd Division.[8] Phibun's negotiators wanted to assure the Chinese that Thailand did not consider them as enemies and that the Japanese had forced the Thai army to send troops to occupy the Shan states to clear the way for a Japanese offensive into Burma. Net claims that Phibun also intended to move the national capital and the army to Petchabun as part of a contingency plan to fight the Japanese.[9] In 1943, Phibun had already transferred a part of the command headquarters of the army's field forces to Petchabun in anticipation of a future struggle with the occupation forces. But when parliament failed to pass a bill for moving the capital, Phibun's plans could not be realized and he was forced to resign. His attempts to establish contacts with the Chinese could not be followed up.

If this version were correct, Phibun would have had reason to feel bitter at the failure of his bill. He could well have felt that the Seri Thai had double-crossed him since his plans were known to Luang Adul, who surely would have informed Pridi.[10]

Meanwhile, the Seri Thai movement became more clearly defined. The top leaders were Pridi, Police General Luang Adul, and Lt. General Luang Sinat (who took charge of the military after Phibun's fall). Luang Sangwon and Thahan Khamhiran led officers from the navy who joined the Seri Thai. Furthermore, according to Net's account, about fifty young men were secretly sent by Pridi (Thammasat students), Luang Adul (police officers), and Luang Sinat (army officers) to train at Colombo. However, most of them did not see action for the war ended first.

Estimates given by Nai Chanthana suggest that in Bangkok–Thonburi, the Seri Thai forces numbered close to ten thousand men composed mainly of soldiers from the First Army Division, whose commander belonged to the movement. Naval forces under Luang Sangwon and the police under Luang Adul were also included in that estimate. It is interesting to note that mention is made of Chinese residing in the capital who agreed to help. They were members of various Chinese associations.[11]

Although there appears to be an overestimation of the membership figures, one thing is quite clear—the Seri Thai toward the end of the war was quite active and had a considerable following. Second, the civilians under Pridi's leadership came to

---

[8] An account offered by Lt. Colonel Sawaeng Thapphasut in *Sri Krung* (May–June, 1947) indicates that contact with the 93rd Division was made only in February 1944, when the outcome of the war was obvious.

[9] Net, *Ngan Taidin*, p. 321, suggests that Luang Adul fully cooperated with Phibun on this plan. For a recent study of Thai–Japanese relations of this period, see Thamsook Numnonda, *Thailand and the Japanese Presence, 1941-1945* (Singapore: ISEAS, Research Notes and Discussion Papers, No. 6, October 1977).

[10] It is interesting that Thawee Bunyaket, a follower of Pridi, wrote in the preface of Net's book that Phibun's plan to move the capital to Petchabun was a commendable thought but that it was not feasible. However, Thawee Bunyaket evidently did not see that, from Phibun's military perspective, Petchabun was strategically located and could be defended by a small number of troops.

[11] Nai Chanthana, *XO Group*, pp. 363, 364, 380. The author continues to list other forces: 4,300 from Petchburi, 1,000 from Hua Hin, 800 from Nakhon Phanom, 1,200 from Udon, 200 from Nongkhai, 4,000 from Mahasarakham, 132 from Chacherngsao, 2,000 from Chonburi, and 3,000 from Ubon. He also mentions that the Seri Thai had built fourteen secret airfields, most of which were located in the Isan area. These figures appear exaggerated and probably included soldiers, marines, and policemen whose commanding officers were Seri Thai.

see the Seri Thai as a force that could become politically important if it could be sustained as an ongoing organization.

As mentioned earlier, the climax of the Phibun–Pridi rivalry came when, on July 24, 1944, parliament refused to pass a government bill moving the capital to Petchabun.[12] Two alternatives were formally open to Phibun—resign or dissolve parliament. Phibun inclined to the former course for two reasons. First, he thought that simply by threatening to resign he might be able to convince parliament to reverse itself on the grounds that there was no other person suitable for the job. Second, he knew his resignation had to be accepted by the regents before it became valid. At that time, there were two regents, Pridi and Lt. General Prince Athit.[13] Phibun was on friendly terms with the Prince and was sure that his resignation would not be accepted, on the grounds that the country was in a delicate wartime situation and that the dissolution of the government would endanger the country's security.

However, before Phibun could make a definite decision, parties unknown made his resignation threat public.[14] Most Thai leaders by now realized that, with Japan losing the war, Phibun's leadership would not facilitate rapprochement with the Allies and that, if Thailand was to avoid or survive a punitive post-war settlement, a new leadership was imperative. In fact, it is probable that parliament's refusal to pass the bill proposed by Phibun was in itself an indication of the way the wind was blowing. This may also explain why Phibun did not put up any great fight and resigned on July 26, 1944. His retirement to Lopburi, the army's stronghold, and his continuing refusal to relinquish the post of Supreme Commander of the Armed Forces, can be seen as attempts both to save face and to cling to some of his power.

It was speculated that Pridi had engineered Phibun's downfall. A majority of the MPs certainly regarded Pridi as an able and sincere leader who believed in democracy and who would be acceptable to the Allies. His position was immediately strengthened when his co-regent, Prince Athit, resigned, and parliament appointed Pridi as the sole regent of Thailand. Yet he continued to move cautiously.

Khuang Aphaiwong, the deputy speaker of parliament, was given the chance to form a cabinet, which was overwhelmingly approved by the assembly with 101 votes out of a total of 122. The choice of Khuang was an adroit one, for Khuang was not only a respected leader, but was acceptable both to Pridi and to Phibun and his followers.[15] With Khuang as prime minister, it was hoped that the domestic tension created by the sudden expulsion of Phibun and his sullen retreat to Lopburi would be eased. A good indication of Khuang's role (and Pridi's blessing) was that the new government proclaimed again the original People's Party's platform—the Six

---

[12] *Phraratchabanyat Anumat Phraratchakamnot Rabieb Borihan Nakhonban Petchabun lae Phraratchakamnot Chatsang Phutthamonthon* [Decree to ratify the administrative code of the Petchabun municipality and to approve the creation of a Buddhist Circle]. See Pla Thong (pseud.), *Phakkanmuang Thai* [Thai Political Parties] (Bangkok: Kaona Press, 1965), p. 64.

[13] Phrachaoworawongthoe Phraongchao Athit Thipapha.

[14] See Pla Thong, *Phakkanmuang*, pp. 66, 67. Shortly after Phibun's resignation, Prince Athit left the regency and followed Phibun to Lopburi.

[15] In an earlier struggle between Phibun and parliament, Phibun rejected parliament's choice for speaker. Parliament had elected Thawee Bunyaket (a Pridi man) as speaker, but Phibun refused to approve the appointment. Parliament gave in and elected Rear Admiral Krasae Prawahanawin; Khuang was the choice for deputy in both instances. Phibun voiced no opposition to Khuang's selection. Ibid., pp. 60–63.

Principles, namely, independence, peace, economic independence, equality, liberty, and education.[16] Phibun's role in Thai politics was subsequently further curtailed. He was appointed political adviser and was deprived of his position of supreme military commander when Khuang announced the abolition of that post.[17]

When the war ended, the main problem facing Thai leaders was less domestic politics than Thailand's difficult international position. So, having done the job of establishing a civilian government, Khuang resigned in August 1945 to make way for a better qualified person to negotiate with the Allies.

The most obvious choice was Seni Pramote, who was ambassador to the United States and an organizer of the Seri Thai movement. When the war began and Phibun came out in favor of the Axis Powers, Seni refused to deliver the government's declaration of war to the American government. Instead, he openly supported the Allies and helped found the Seri Thai, which trained people for missions in Thailand against the Japanese. Given his excellent US connections, Seni was a good choice for the position of prime minister to negotiate with the Allies. In view of the hostile attitude of the British and French, it was widely felt that every attempt should be made to gain strong United States diplomatic support.

In his capacity as regent, Pridi accordingly invited Seni back to become prime minister.[18] In the meantime, Thawee Bunyaket, a Pridi supporter, became interim premier for seventeen days.

Once Seni took over the helm of government, the process begun in 1944 reached its climax. The Allies' list of war criminals had included some Thai leaders, among whom Phibun was most outstanding. Partly to prevent trials by Allied tribunals, the Seni government rushed to pass the War Criminal Act of 1945, empowering Thai courts to review the wartime acts of Thai leaders.[19] Phibun and fourteen others were then arrested and legal proceedings instituted under the new law. However, the so-called war criminals were quickly released once the courts ruled that the law could not be applied *ex post facto*.[20]

KING ANANDA

On reaching the age of twenty-one, King Ananda returned to Bangkok from Switzerland in December 1945. The regency was now dissolved, but Pridi was given the title of elder statesman by parliament, with the official duty of advising the king and parliament on national matters.[21] In the meantime, Seni's negotiations with the Allied Powers resulted in an agreement with Great Britain, signed on January 1, 1946. Having achieved this agreement, Seni resigned and asked for the dissolution of

---

[16] W. Ch. Prasangsit, *Phaendin Somdet Phrapokklao* [Rama VII's Reign] (Bangkok: Aksonsan Press, 1962), pp. 226, 227. Pridi was the acknowledged author of the platform.

[17] Khuang traveled to Lopburi to ask Phibun to resign from his military post. See Khuang's private account, reproduced in Kiat (pseud.), *Ruang Khong Nai Khuang* [Khuang's Story] (Bangkok: Phinit Pracha Press, 1970), pp. 88, 89.

[18] Seni Pramote, *Chumnum Wannakhadi thang Kanmuang* [Collection of Political Writings] (Bangkok: Thai Watthanaphanit Press, 1968), p. 208.

[19] *Ratchakitchanubeksa* [Royal Thai Government Gazette], Vol. 62, October 11, 1945, p. 591. Subsequently referred to as *Ratchakitcha*.

[20] San Dika (Dika Court), *Khamphiphaksa San Dika Khadi Adchayakon Songkhram* [Ruling of the Dika Court on War Criminals], Case no. 1/2488, March 23, 1946.

[21] *Ratchakitcha*, vol. 62, December 11, 1945, p. 62.

parliament to pave the way for elections.[22] Although Seni was well-known abroad, he was relatively new on the domestic scene and was not considered a "politician." Unlike Pridi, Khuang, and Phibun, Seni did not have a personal base of support. His assumption of the post of prime minister had been due to special circumstances, and when he had carried out his responsibilities, Seni graciously resigned.

At this juncture, Pridi seems to have had second thoughts about his relation with Khuang, who as prime minister had proved to be no man's pawn and was developing into a political leader in his own right. Thus, after the elections of 1946, Pridi backed Direk Chaiyanam for the premiership. But Khuang was able to garner enough support from MPs, both elected and appointed, to give him the go-ahead to form a government. This was the first time in Thai history that an elected member of parliament was given the chance to form a government. Previous prime ministers had either been members of a coup or been appointed members of the assembly.

Khuang's cabinet was composed mainly of elected MPs, but it was little more than a loose coalition of political factions. There were no organized political parties as yet, and Khuang's control over parliament was weak.[23] Khuang's government lasted only a few weeks. A group of MPs led by Thongin introduced a bill calling for price controls on basic commodities. The bill was given the pet name "bill to control the price of sticky rice."[24] The government opposed the bill on the grounds that it would not help the people much and that it was nearly impossible to enforce. Parliament nevertheless passed the bill by a vote of 65 to 63.[25] Khuang's defeat and subsequent resignation came about because many of his supporters who were given cabinet portfolios were out visiting members of their constituencies to celebrate their

---

[22] Many MPs had opposed the War Criminal Act on grounds that it was unfair to declare a national leader a criminal just because he was on the losing side. Seni was afraid that this would upset the Allies. As a solution he proposed new elections, which were long overdue. The previous election had been held in 1938.

[23] Since 1932, no formal political party existed. The People's Party was misnamed, for it was closer to a political association or group. Political parties did not come into being in Thailand until 1946, when Pridi's government promulgated the Constitution of 1946, which explicitly allowed the free organization of political parties. Under this constitution, six parties were organized; the Progressive Party, led by Kukrit Pramote, which supported Khuang; the Unionist Party, which supported Pridi; the Democratic Front Party, which also supported Pridi; the Democrat Party, which incorporated the Progressive Party and was headed by Khuang; the Prachachon Party, headed by Liang Chaiyakan; and the Labor Party. For a concise study of this, see Aphinya Charunphon, "Khwam mai mankhong khong Phakkanmuang Thai [The Instability of Thai Political Parties]," in *Sat Kanmuang* [Political Animal], ed. Chai-anan Samutwanit, Setthaphon Khusiphithak, and Sawaeng Rattanamongkhonmat (Bangkok: Thai Watthanaphanit Press, 1971), pp. 179-209.

The split in the strong Isan faction of parliament had helped Khuang. MPs from Isan were nominally Pridi supporters. However, the jockeying for ministerial positions between Thongin Phuriphat (Ubon) and Liang Chaiyakan (Ubon) resulted in Liang going over to Khuang's side as a cabinet member. Thongin then formed the Sahachip (Unionist) Party to back Pridi and oppose the Khuang government. Rear Admiral Luang Thamrong Nawasawat, another Pridi supporter, organized the Naew Ratthathammanun (Democratic Front) Party to incorporate Pridi MPs, who refused to join Thongin because of his "provincial" background.

[24] *Phraratchabanyat Pakpai Khaoneiw* [Decree to display the price of sticky rice]. Sticky rice is consumed by Northeasterners, and the term is used in a derogatory way by non-Northeasterners.

[25] *Raingan Prachum Saphaphuthaen Ratsadon* [Report of Parliamentary Meetings], Report no. 14/2489, March 18, 1946.

ministerial appointments and were not expecting this countermove by the Pridi people. It is still puzzling to many why Khuang resigned so readily, since the bill was not a major government policy bill and he could have asked for a second reading while regrouping his forces.[26]

Khuang's resignation caught Pridi off-balance. No one had expected Khuang to surrender so easily. The question of who might be a credible successor to Khuang loomed large, and the only other person of obvious stature was Pridi himself. It might have seemed less than appropriate for Pridi, holding the prestigious title of Elder Statesman, to stoop down and accept the premiership. But after a campaign by Pridi's parliamentary supporters, which made it appear that Pridi was forced to take the office because of popular demand, he became prime minister on March 24, 1946[27] amid rising organized opposition.[28]

A new constitution was promulgated after Pridi took office, replacing the Constitution of 1932, which was now fourteen years old.[29] The Constitution of 1946 called for a bicameral system—a house of representatives and a senate.[30] Article 14 allowed for the establishment of political parties, the first time that parties were to be recognized as such. The Sahachip and the Naew Ratthathammanun parties backed Pridi's government, while opposition was provided by the Prachathipat (Democrat Party). As battle lines were being drawn, but before anything serious erupted, the young King Ananda was found shot in bed on June 9, 1946. Pridi's credibility as protector of the throne came into question and his government was later forced to use repressive measures to quell rumors of his involvement.[31] Despite investigations ordered by Pridi, his popularity declined. In an attempt to preserve his political influence, Pridi resigned from the premiership complaining of poor health. Rear Admiral Luang Thamrong took over and became Pridi's front man.

Pridi's faction continued to run parliament,[32] and the approval of Luang Thamrong as the new Prime Minister was easily secured.[33] The Democrat Party, acting as opposition, attacked the government for its inability to control economic conditions as well as for its inability to solve the mystery of the death of Rama VIII.

---

[26] Kiat, *Ruang khong Nai Khuang,* pp. 179, 180. According to Khuang's memoirs, the law was a later version of something the Assembly had discussed previously and agreed was not plausible. Thongin was also convinced that it was a bad policy at that earlier date. When the bill came up again and was pushed through by Pridi supporters, Khuang said he resigned in protest as a political move that would force his government to carry out a policy that parliament knew was impossible. Because of this incident, writers have labeled Khuang the "sensitive" premier.

[27] *Ratchakitcha,* vol. 63, March 25, 1946, p. 118.

[28] The Democrat Party was formed during this period with Khuang as its head. Among the more prominent founders were Kukrit Pramote (Seni's brother and head of the Kao Na Party), Liang Chaiyakan, and Yai Sawitachat. Kiat, *Ruang khong Nai Khuang,* p. 180.

[29] Pridi headed the drafting committee during Khuang's government.

[30] Articles 24, 29. The members of the senate were selected members of the lower house for a term of six years.

[31] *Bang Ruang kieokap Phrabaromasanuwong nai rawang Songkram Lok krang thi Song* [Stories concerning members of the royalty during the Second World War], distributed on the occasion of Pridi's 72nd birthday. It tries to show that Pridi was not anti-royalty.

[32] The elections of August 5, 1946, assured a majority for the Pridi faction. Pridi and Luang Thamrong were elected from Ayutthaya. Khuang and Kukrit won in Bangkok.

[33] *Ratchakitcha,* vol. 63, August 26, 1946, p. 1.

In May 1947, the Democrat Party called for a session to question the government; the session lasted seven days. The debates were broadcast over the radio and received a wide audience. Although the government was able to win the vote of confidence, Luang Thamrong resigned to form a new cabinet. Five months after the approval of this new government, it was ousted by an army coup d'état.

THE ARMY COUP OF NOVEMBER 8, 1947

The Revolution of 1932, which overthrew the absolute monarchy, ushered in an era of military domination of politics and national leadership. From the time that General Phraya Phahon took office in 1933 until the fall of Phibun in 1944, the army had enjoyed its first golden age of political rule. The army was able to remain the most powerful force in Thai politics until challenged by Pridi. International circumstances, the upsurge of Pridi's popularity, and the support of the Seri Thai posed a challenge to the army's control. Phibun's "miscalculation"[34] had forced him to make way for Pridi and other civilians to conduct negotiations with the Allies. The years 1944 to 1947 marked the apex of civilian power.[35] Indeed, under civilian leadership, Thailand's international relations were normalized and international respectability was achieved. Negotiations with the United Kingdom regarding the Shan states and parts of Malaya taken by Phibun during the war were settled and a general agreement was signed on January 1, 1946.[36] Thailand was accepted into the United Nations on December 15, 1946, after the Luang Thamrong government agreed to pass a bill nullifying the Anti-Communist Act[37] to please the Soviet Union and returned to France territory seized during the war.[38] Establishing diplomatic relations with the Soviet Union was another part of the price for United Nations recognition. Thailand's return to international respectability would actually make it easier for army officers to stage a coup d'état in 1947, for international recognition of a new regime could now be readily obtained. Some weaknesses in the government also worked to the advantage of the coup leaders, for in spite of the successes noted here, the civilian government had faced a number of acute difficulties, many of them economic in nature. The most important appear to have been the rice shortage and the declining value of the baht.

Production of rice during the war years had not fluctuated very greatly except in 1942, when floods reduced the tonnage by over one million. In 1945, however,

---

[34] Phibun wanted to be on the winning side, and Japan at that time was supreme, having routed the British and Americans. Moreover, earlier appeals to Western powers had resulted in hollow promises that indicated no assurances of military aid. Some authors have argued that Phibun hated the Japanese but had no other alternative. See Siri Premchit, *Prawatsat Thai nai Rabob Prachathipatai 30 Pi* [30 Years of Democracy in Thai History] (Bangkok: Kasem Bannakit Press, 1962), pp. 231 ff.

[35] Luang Thamrong, although a naval officer, was only a stand-in for Pridi.

[36] *Ratchakitcha*, vol. 63, January 11, 1946, p. 63. "Formal Agreement for the Termination of the State of War between Siam and Great Britain and India," in Direk, *Thai kap Songkhram*, pp. 812–845. Article 2 states "The Siamese Government declare [*sic*] as null and void all purported acquisitions of British territory made by Siam later than December 7th, 1941 ..." Thailand agreed to relinquish all claims to territory occupied by Thailand with the help of the Japanese during the war.

[37] *Ratchakitcha*, vol. 63, November 11, 1946, p. 561.

[38] Returned to France on November 17, 1946. Direk, *Thai kap Songkhram*, p. 676.

figures released by the Ministry of Agriculture indicated a serious drop back to the level of 1942. Meanwhile, the population had increased dramatically. In addition, the Japanese occupation authorities had made heavy demands on the country's rice supply. Last, by the terms of the agreement signed between Thailand and the United Kingdom, Thailand was obligated to deliver 1,500,000 tons of rice free of charge to the British by September 1, 1947.[39]

The shortages, however, were not merely the result of these factors. Much of the blame lay with the government's own policies. In 1946, two bills were passed by parliament allowing the government to inspect rice holdings, prevent hoarding, control the internal flow of rice, and acquire rice at will. Luang Thamrong summed up the government's intentions on the occasion of his answering the questions of the Democrat MPs. Luang Thamrong said,

> Our greatest advantage is the advantage to the state in acquiring money. We have gone to certain measures, even to force rice from farmers without compensation. Frankly, whatever the people have blamed me for doing ... I concede that they are true, but I did it to save the country from destruction ... I guarantee with my neck that no one will die of hunger, but that we will also receive money.[40]

Even though the state collected money on the rice sales, its control policies created loopholes for illegal trafficking in grain. Thus, while domestic prices were controlled and the export price for the British was very low, rice commanded the fair sum of two hundred to five hundred pounds sterling per ton in neighboring Malaya.[41] Because of this wide discrepancy, smuggling and government corruption were inevitable. Newspapers began an exposé of government corruption and rising illegal sales of rice, which were noted in relation to the severe shortages in the major cities. *Phim Thai* reported on October 9, 1947, that though 2,700 sacks of rice were allotted to five provinces, only one province had received its quota, while the rest of the rice had presumably been misappropriated by government officials for redistribution on the black market. The government's weak excuse for its ineptness in controlling widespread corruption was that it lacked sufficient machinery and

---

[39] Ibid., pp. 579, 580, 734. Later on, Pridi was able to renegotiate this part of the agreement. Under the revised plan, Thailand was to sell 1,200,000 tons of rice to Britain at the rate of 12 pounds 14 shillings per ton. This was to be honored within twelve months or the remainder would have to be delivered without charge. Another modification was negotiated by the Luang Thamrong government, whereby the amount to be delivered was reduced to 600,000 tons and was to be sold at a flat rate of 20 pounds per ton. The Thai government found it hard to fulfill even this obligation, and in September 1947 still another readjustment was made, increasing the price to 33 pounds 6 shillings 6 pence per ton, together with the stipulation that domestic prices should come under control and exports must also be restricted until the end of 1948.

[40] *Raingan Prachum Sapha,* Report no. 7/2490, May 23, 1947. The reasoning was unclear because the agreements with the British prevented the government from selling rice on the world market.

[41] W. D. Reeve, *Public Administration in Siam* (New York, NY: Royal Institute of Pacific Relations, 1953), p. 36. Also see James C. Ingram, *Economic Change in Thailand since 1858* (Palo Alto, CA: Stanford University Press, 1970), pp. 87-92.

manpower.[42] The problem of the rice shortages and the government's monopoly over the rice trade was to be one of the main reasons given by the military for staging its 1947 coup. Field Marshal Phin Chunnahawan, a leader of the coup, remarked that although Thailand was one of the world's richest rice countries, the people had to line up to buy low-grade rice.[43]

Another economic problem faced by the post-war nation was inflation. Although this was not directly the fault of the government, and a period of two years was perhaps not long enough to bring about definite solutions, the army nevertheless later justified its intervention by citing the inability of the government to alleviate this crisis. Inflation was one result of the wartime economy; the government had been compelled to print and circulate a lot of money in response to forced loans imposed by Japan to finance its forces in the country. It was reported that between 1941 and 1945, the amount loaned to Japan was 1,230,701,083 baht.[44] Also, government spending during the war years and immediately after far exceeded revenues, which contributed to the inflationary trend.[45] To a certain extent, the post-war general agreement with Great Britain limiting Thai exports[46] meant that the country was denied major foreign-exchange earnings during the critical period immediately following the Japanese occupation.[47]

Attempts were made by the post-war governments to ease this problem. Khuang recalled all one thousand baht notes and for a period of four months allowed public gambling, which was taxed, to try to collect more revenue. Pridi fared a little better by being able to secure loans from the United States and India.[48] Luang Thamrong's government resorted to the sale of gold bullion to act as a run-off for the over-circulation of banknotes and to induce foreign exchange.[49] The *Annual Report* of the Bank of Thailand in 1947 revealed that 339,489.62 grams of gold were sold domestically for 14,785,960.57 baht and 7,998,030.162 grams were sold in the United States for $8,999,985.72.[50]

Other sources of governmental corruption and inefficiency were among the grievances cited by the 1947 coup leaders. The government established cooperative stores that reputedly sold goods at cheap prices. Although this project started with good faith, these stores quickly became the source of further corruption and black marketeering. It was estimated that the government lost fifty million baht during the

---

[42] Sawang Lanlua, 37 *Pi haeng Kanpattiwat* [37 Years of the Revolution] (Thonburi: Pho Sam Ton Press, 1969), p. 250.

[43] Phin Chunnahawan, *Chiwit kap Haedkan khong Chomphon Phin Chunnahawan* [The Life of Field Marshal Phin Chunnahawan] (Bangkok: Prasertsiri Press, 1970), p. 84.

[44] *Anuson nai Ngan Phraratchathan Pleungsop Phrachaoworawongthoe Phraongchao Wiwatthanachai Chaiyan* [Cremation Volume of Prince Wiwatthanachai], 2504, p. 204. Prince Wiwatthanachai was the Governor of the National Bank during that period.

[45] Bank of Thailand, *Raingan Prachampi 2491* [Annual Report 1948].

[46] See Article 13 of the Agreement. The commodities in question were rice, tin, rubber, and teak.

[47] Direk, *Thai kap Songkhram*, p. 726.

[48] Cremation Volume of Prince Wiwatthanachai, p. 114. $10 million from the United States and 50 million rupees from India.

[49] Pla Thong, *Phakkanmuang*, pp. 117–121. Prince Wiwatthanachai resigned in protest over the gold-selling policy. The Democrat MPs also opposed the move.

[50] Bank of Thailand, *Raingan Prachampi 2492* [Annual Report, 1947].

short period of their operation.[51] The government's grant of hoes and cloth to its parliamentary supporters for distribution in their respective constituencies was also a source of complaint. These were war-surplus goods that the government had given to the MPs as rewards for their support. However, instead of giving these commodities to the people, many MPs sold their share to merchants for a profit. The army was thus able to claim later that the government was unable to control its own administrative bureaucracy, as well as allowing rampant civil disorder in the cities and countryside.[52]

Robberies and petty crimes were committed daily in the cities and countryside in defiance of government authority. This was the heyday of the *Sua*.[53] Piracy was also a growing concern in the south along the Malay Peninsula. These social phenomena could be attributed to general post-war conditions of economic depression, social uprootedness, easy acquisition of arms through the black market, and the sudden demobilization of troops. The last factor proved to be especially important, as we will see below. For while the Ministry of Defense deplored the lawless acts of its troops, a majority of officers felt concern for the well-being of their men and resented the actions of the civilian government, which they saw as responsible for the degeneration of the army.[54] (Field Marshal Phin expressed his feelings when he described how he was forced to flee to Bangkok after being warned that bandits were planning to raid his house and no one could give him protection. He was also upset over the fact that a car belonging to the king had mysteriously disappeared, indicating that even royal property was no longer safe.[55])

Neither were economic troubles the civilians' only problems. Prachuab Thongurai asserted in his book, *Phak Kanmuang Thai*, that Pridi misjudged the people's feelings regarding the monarchy and the death of King Ananda.[56] The government's handling of the investigation left room for doubt and criticism. Indeed, the government's actions fed speculation that Pridi himself was behind the tragedy. Preliminary investigations suggested that the death could have been an accident, for the shot was fired in the king's chambers and the pistol was still in the king's hand. Assassination and suicide were ruled out on vague and circumstantial evidence.[57]

---

[51] Pla Thong, *Phakkanmuang*, p. 118. These stores operated for six months, from December 1946 to May 1947.

[52] This theme was common in justifying army coups after 1947. The Sarit coups of 1957 and 1958 were followed by a mass program of social rehabilitation for public enemies such as the *anthaphan* (hooligans), thieves, and drug addicts. The Thanom coup of 1971 was justified by the rise of crime and the need for severe government measures not possible under a democratic system of government. It is interesting to note that in the highly successful movie "Z," which depicts the coup d'état by the military in Greece, the opening scene shows a conference in which an army officer berates his colleagues for tolerating the presence of the "social cancer" and stressing the necessity to take strong measures against it.

[53] *Sua* (tiger) denotes personal attributes of ferocity, cunning, daring, and cruelty. *Sua* is a prefix used before the names of successful bandits whose exploits sometimes become legend.

[54] *Phim Thai*, April 1, 1947. Lt. General Jira Wichit-songkhram said that "banditry is like a contagious disease that spreads from the outside into military ranks."

[55] Phin, *Chiwit*, pp. 83, 84.

[56] Pla Thong, *Phakkanmuang*, p. 108.

[57] Ministry of Interior, *Prakat khong Krom Tamruad* (Announcement of the Police Department), June 10, 1946. The king was observed to have been happy earlier and had scheduled audiences for various people later on during the day. Assassination was deemed "inconceivable."

However, this did not deter hostile discussion by the press and members of the Democrat Party. The government's response was poorly judged. Initially, police warnings were issued to quell spreading rumors of foul play. On June 18, 1946, the government appointed a committee to investigate the affair further. The committee was composed of senior court justices, the speaker of the house, the president of the senate, three high-ranking princes, three representatives of the armed forces, and two others. While this was going on, rumors continued to spread. On July 2, Pridi declared a state of emergency and proceeded to censor the press and arrest those who openly discussed the possibility of his involvement. A few newspaper editors were arrested and two MPs were jailed on charges of libel.[58]

The work of the investigating committee was not concluded until October 1946, after Pridi had already resigned. The wording of its published summation complicated matters further. While hinting at possible foul play, its conclusions sounded suppressed. Roughly translated, the statement made public was as follows:

> The Committee has considered all evidence presented by the police as well as evidence revealed to the people. And after having reviewed testimonies, evidence, and other circumstantial facts in all aspects, the Committee feels that the cause behind the death of King Ananda is as follows: accident—the Committee could not see how it was possible; as for the other two—assassination or suicide—the former lacks conclusive evidence but again could not be ruled out completely because of the position of the corpse; in the case of the latter, suicide was possible but there appeared to be neither reason nor evidence to lead one to that conclusion. Therefore, the Committee cannot rule conclusively that it was either one of the two.[59]

Because of this inconclusiveness, discussions and rumors continued to flourish. One famous incident occurred just a month before the military takeover. This involved the testimony of a woman who said that she had overheard a conversation in which one of the king's pages implicated Pridi in the death of the king. She reported that the page revealed that Pridi had sent someone to assassinate the king. The woman and two other persons were promptly arrested for smearing the character of Pridi, who was still elder statesman.[60]

Pridi and Luang Thamrong were aware of their weak position. Shortly before the army coup in 1947, Pridi called a meeting of his followers to discuss further tactics. However, instead of considering concrete proposals, mutual recriminations occurred, which brought about misunderstandings between Luang Thamrong and Luang Adul Aduldejcharat, the army chief.[61] The final consensus was that the cabinet

---

[58] The two MPs arrested were both Democrats. Liang Chaiyakan (Ubon) was arrested for shouting while inside a movie theater that Pridi was behind the assassination of the king. The other MP was Chote Khumphan (Bangkok).

[59] *Railaiat lae Khwamhen khong Khanakammakan Sobsuan Prutikan nai kan thi Phrabatsomdet Phraporamenmaha Ananthamahidon Sadet Sawannakhot* [Details and Opinions of the Committee to Investigate the Death of King Ananda] (Bangkok: Thammasat University Press, 1946), p. 51. The possibility that this was an accident was not considered seriously, for the committee noted how very careful the king was in handling firearms.

[60] See *Sayam Nikon,* early October 1947 issues.

[61] *Anuson nai Ngan Phraratchathan Pleungsop Phon-ek Luang Adul Aduldejcharat* [Cremation Volume of General Luang Adul], 1970. See particularly article by Police Lt. Colonel Thien

should be reshuffled. Amidst this cabinet crisis, several MPs and certain newspapers urged General Luang Adul to take drastic measures to control corruption. However, Luang Adul was a former Seri Thai and a Pridi supporter. He knew that his grip on the army was tenuous, for many had resented his appointment to the position of army chief, and he did not feel ready to test the limits of his powers.[62]

Luang Thamrong's new government came under increasingly heavy criticism from the Democrats, who called for a general questioning session in parliament. In May 1947, six months before the coup, the Democrats invoked Article 34 of the 1946 Constitution to call for such a session. There were eight issues that the opposition party put forward: peace and order, the currency crisis, bad economic policies, weak foreign policy, corruption, neglect of the livelihood of civil servants, failure to promote national education, and the death of King Ananda.[63]

Luang Thamrong's government was able to weather the weeklong, grueling attack from the Democrats.[64] Nevertheless, the publicity given to the affair was tremendous, for citizens could turn on their radios to keep up with the debate.[65] Speculation and widespread discussion by the public did not help to stabilize the political situation. Rumors of coups and counter-coups became pervasive, leading to still more confusion.

A last key reason for the 1947 coup was the discontent in the army. It was enraged at being blamed for "losing the war." It felt that it had fought well, if briefly, during the war, and that its achievements were not recognized but rather were tarnished by the propaganda issued by the Seri Thai. The army's greatest hero and wartime leader, Phibun, had been put on trial and army troop strength had been cut down by the civilian leadership. In addition, the country's wartime territorial gains had been abandoned, and its internal state was very bad.

Immediately after the Japanese invasion in December 1941, Phibun's government had ordered that troops be mobilized, and a field army was sent to the Shan States in Burma. This army, given the name Kongthap Phayap (North Army), was dispatched to take the city of Kengtung. This expeditionary force met little opposition. However,

---

Sukoson. Thien described how Luang Thamrong challenged Luang Adul to take over his job, but Adul declined. He was the police chief during the war and second in command of the Seri Thai. After Pridi became prime minister, Luang Adul was appointed the army's commander-in-chief. As police chief, Adul had lost touch with the army.

[62] His fears were later confirmed when he proved unable to order the troops back to their barracks during the army coup of 1947. Charun states that Luang Adul had warned Pridi of the pending coup (*Chiwit Kantosu*, pp. 357, 358). It appears that in police and army circles, the coup was an open secret. (See Chiep, *Mahawitthayalai*, pp. 1-110.) According to Charun, Pridi said that there was no need to arrest the plotters, for Luang Adul was instructed to inform them that the government was about to resign. But as later events showed, Pridi's gesture was not enough to placate army demands. This episode appears to indicate that Pridi realized his own weakness, and that without international constraints and military backing, civilian governments could not stand for long.

[63] *Raingan Prachum Sapha*, Report no. 1/2490, 1947, p. 29.

[64] Voting resulted in an affirmation of confidence by 86 to 55. *Raingan Prachum Sapha*, Report no. 11/2490, May 27, 1947.

[65] The Thamrong government felt sure that it still held a majority in parliament and believed that its openness would appease public and military uneasiness. For a detailed account of Thamrong's life history, see Siri Premchit, *Chiwit lae Ngan khong Phonrua-tri Thawan Thamrongnawasawat* [Life and Work of Rear Admiral Thawan Thamrongnawasawat] (Bangkok: Samnakphim Saengtham, 1977).

the troops had to fight the elements to get from one place to the other. Because of the lack of motorized transportation, that campaign was carried out on foot and on horseback. It appears that casualties ran high because of sickness and hard marching rather than because of combat activity. Nevertheless, the army was proud of its 1941 northern campaign, which won and held parts of the Shan States, which were renamed Saharat Thai Dem (Former United Thai States).[66]

At the war's termination in 1946, the Thai government (under Khuang) agreed to return the Former United Thai States to the British, and troops in that area were ordered back home.[67] The withdrawal was not conducted in an orderly manner, and the soldiers encountered many hardships. Resentment against the government quickly built up. According to testimony given by General Jira Wichitsongkhram, then minister of defense and former commander of the north army, the withdrawal was complicated by the demands of the Allies. In his remarks before parliament, General Jira said that because the Allies insisted on immediate removal of Japanese troops by railway, considerable suffering was inflicted on the Thai troops, who had already pulled up stakes, packed, and were ready to return to bases by the same train.[68] Lacking adequate transportation and government funds, the soldiers were left to fend for themselves. Many decided to walk home and broke ranks to do so. Army officers were helpless in this situation and could only watch while the command structure deteriorated. Colonel Chuai Chawaengsaksongkhram, the minister of the interior, criticized the handling of the troop withdrawal, saying that it was not done according to the proper military procedure of returning to base and holding debriefing sessions before the troops were sent home. The confused and inept handling of the affair added fuel to the growing resentment of the army. Many officers blamed the problem on the Pridi–Khuang leadership, which complied with Allied demands at the cost of sacrificing army discipline and morale. Far from being received with open arms as heroes, the army was deprived of any triumphant return.

The feeling of disgust prevailing in the officer corps can be glimpsed in the words of Lt. General Kat Katsongkhram, a leader of the 1947 coup. He wrote:

> After we had withdrawn [from the Shan States], we were subjected to more inhuman torture. There was an order to relieve officers of their duties. Some were relieved of their commands while marching from Lampang to Chiengrai. Some were attacked and killed on buses, others were wounded and died in Bangkok ... [69] The whole army [North Army] withdrew in sad disorder. People looked at Thai soldiers as if they were Japanese prisoners of war ... Many attacked the army both directly and indirectly. The common soldiers wore tattered uniforms, which could not be replaced since there were none to replace them. Military codes of conduct were loosened because army units remained in

---

[66] Japan had promised Thailand parts of the Shan States as a reward for joining the war on its side.

[67] Japan had also helped Phibun regain Siemreap and Battambang from the French in March 1941. See John F. Cady, *Southeast Asia* (New York, NY: McGraw-Hill Inc., 1964), pp. 564, 565. These territories, too, had to be restored to the French.

[68] *Raingan Prachum Sapha,* Report no. 3/2490, May 19, 1947.

[69] Many of the soldiers and officers were attacked and robbed by bandits along the way. A large number of soldiers also had to turn to looting to feed themselves.

name only; the troops were worn out and tired in body and soul. People believed that there was no use in having an army anymore.[70]

The forced retirement of army officers after the war was also a major cause for resentment. As we shall see, of the four chief planners of the 1947 coup, only one was still on active duty. Phibun was also in retirement. The British authorities had a part in trying to eliminate the power of the army, for it was Great Britain that urged Seni to disband the field forces and cut down on troop strength. In fact, the British were quite insistent about this point.[71]

The army was acutely aware of the lean times it faced. It was a bitter comedown after the era of nationalism of the wartime Phibun regime. The new Constitution of 1946 barred military officers from active political roles, for under Article 24, section 2, it was stipulated that members of the senate could not be a *kharatchakan* (government official). This was also the case for members of the lower house and of the cabinet. Thus it was legally impossible to be commander-in-chief of the army and prime minister at the same time, a potent combination of offices which Phibun and later Sarit and Thanom found most useful. The change also meant that the army could not "load" parliament with active-duty officers to ensure that the assembly would be partial to its aspirations.

Still another major area of army complaint was the great influence of Seri Thai people. The army viewed the intrusion of Seri Thai military officers into its command structure as the civilian leadership's subversive attempt to control the army. Pridi's supporters did indeed assume positions of leadership in the army after Phibun was "fired" by Khuang in 1944. At first, Luang Sinat took over the task of directing the army; later, Luang Adul replaced him in the Thamrong government. Both Sinat and Adul were prominent Seri Thai leaders close to Pridi. Another cause for army concern was the appointment after 1945 of Rear Admiral Luang Sangwon Suwannachip as adjutant general of the armed forces and police chief. Luang Sangwon had been Seri Thai's liaison with the navy. General Kat, who had himself been a Seri Thai collaborator, noted that while it was all right to heap praise on the Seri Thai movement, it was not fair that the press and some politicians should belittle the army. He was referring to some individual's assertions that in the fifty years or so of the army's existence it could not accomplish what the Seri Thai did in two years, that is, steer the country safely toward an alliance with the winning side.[72] He noted that many army officers were deeply hurt by these statements; indeed, several were extremely angry.

General Net Khemayothin wrote in his book *Ngan Taidin khong Phan-ek Yothi* (Underground Work of Colonel Yothi) that the army suffered the injustice of being looked down upon by some Seri Thai ministers who insisted that the army would probably fall into the hands of another dictator and therefore should best be disbanded, since a small country such as Thailand did not need such a large force.[73]

---

[70] Kat Katsongkhram, *Ruang Kamlang lae Amnat khong Prathetchat* [The Country's Force and Power] (Bangkok: Rat Phakdi Press, 1949), pp. 26, 27. Luang Kat himself did not participate in the Northern Campaign. He had chosen to go to China and worked for the Seri Thai. He was also a 1932 Promoter. Also see *Anuson Ngansop Phon-tho Luang Kat Katsongkhram* [Cremation volume of Lt. Gen. Luang Kat], April 20, 1967.

[71] Seni, *Chummun Wannakhadi*, p. 22.

[72] Kat, *Ruang Kamlang*, pp. 28, 29.

[73] Net, *Ngan Taidin*, p. 735.

As for the soldiers, during the war they worked hard and made sacrifices. But once the war ended, they did not receive adequate attention and care. Even worse, they were humiliated by the Seri Thai people. The sense of hurt turned to frustrated anger. With little prodding and invitation, they reacted.[74]

It would be naïve to assume that Pridi and Luang Thamrong were not aware of the army's restlessness or the imminent threat of a coup d'état. However, they seem to have underestimated the ability of the "retired" officers to get support from other officers who still commanded troops. Instead, they seem to have relied excessively on the influence of Luang Adul, the army chief, and the police and the navy chiefs.

According to Police Captain Chiep Amphunan, a Pridi supporter and a former Seri Thai, he warned Luang Thamrong of the coup, but the prime minister's reply appeared to come from a weary man who did not know what to do next. Luang Thamrong said that he had played the game according to the rules set up by the Constitution and was ready to resign.[75] He later revealed that he had confronted Luang Adul with the coup rumors and was given Luang Adul's assurance that the army was still under his control.[76] When the American Ambassador, Edwin Stanton, visited Luang Thamrong in order to query him about a possible army coup, he was given the reply that the government had control of the army and the police, and that the navy was essentially in the prime minister's back pocket.[77]

Signs of things to come began to emerge with the announcement of Phibun's return to active political life. After his trial, during which he was acquitted on the technical point that the war crimes bill could not be retroactive, Phibun had vowed that he had had enough of politics and would lead the quiet life of a common citizen. However, in 1947, he announced that he would organize a Conservative Party to vindicate himself from the accusations leveled against him and his previous administrations. He said that he could no longer remain still and felt compelled to break his own earlier resolution. He anticipated resistance from the Seri Thai but appeared ready to face them. Field Marshal Phin, then a retired officer, came out to defend the honor and integrity of Phibun as a national leader.[78]

There were four chief planners of the army coup of November 8, 1947. Phin Chunnahawan, a retired lieutenant general, was its most prominent leader. Phin was a soldier in the classic sense, having fought in the Indochina war as deputy commander of the Isan Army. During the Northern Campaign, he was commander of the third division of the Northern Army and was in charge of the capture of

---

[74] Ibid., p. 751. The sacrifices he referred to were not sustained in combat, but rather from facing the harsh elements and from the lack of adequate medical supplies. See page 105.

[75] Chiep, *Mahawitthayalai*, pp. 565, 566.

[76] Thepwithun Nutkasem, "Khrang nung mua phom mai mi Phasutha chaasai [Once upon a time when I had no land on which to live]," *Prachachat* (October 31, November 5, 1970), p. 45. Luang Thamrong later revealed to the press that he had made up his mind to resign and had told Phibun of this decision. *Sayam Nikon,* January 21, 1948. On November 8, the day of the coup, the cabinet met with Pridi and a decision was made to let Luang Adul form a new government.

[77] Edwin F. Stanton, *Brief Authority* (London: Robert Hale Ltd., 1957), p. 207.

[78] *Sri Krung,* March 22, 1947. For a good account of what follows and particularly the 1947 coup, see Suchin Tantikun, *Ratthaprahan 2490* [The 1947 Coup d'état], Senior Thesis, Thammasat University, 1970.

Kengtung. Phin had, as his right-hand man, Colonel Phao Siyanon, who was also relieved of duty after the war. Phao was a former aide to Phibun and acted as liaison between the coup planners and Phibun. The next most important character in the drama was Luang Kat Katsongkhram, who held the rank of group captain of the air force at the time of the coup. Kat had been a participant in the 1932 Revolution and had distinguished himself during the suppression of the Boworadej Rebellion. He had been Phibun's deputy minister of finance from March 1942 to October of the following year. He had resigned because of his dissatisfaction with the way the government had complied with the demands of the Japanese. He had left for exile in China and was in Kunming from 1944 to 1945, acting as a Seri Thai working closely with the Allies.[79] After the war and upon his return from China he was appointed a member of the senate.

The other two members were not as distinguished. Lt. Colonel Kan Chamnongphumiwet had been a 1932 Promoter. Together with many others he was relieved of duty at the end of the war. The last member of the planning group was the only officer still on active duty at the time of the coup. He was Colonel Sawat Sawatikiat, director of the army commissary department.

None of these men had command of the troops necessary for a military takeover, nor did they have national stature or reputations. However, they were sure that Phibun would provide the necessary symbolic leadership for the *Khana Ratthaprahan* (Coup Group).[80] They felt they could count on some friends still on active duty to raise the necessary troops. They also gambled on the assumption that most army officers were so tired of being put down by the Seri Thai and civilian leaders that they would not offer any resistance to a coup, and would indeed give tacit approval.

The Coup Group subsequently put forward six reasons that prompted their action:

1. The coup d'état was carried out for the nation as a whole and not for the sake of any individual group.
2. The coup that overthrew the government of Luang Thamrong will form a new government that will respect the principles of Nation, Religion, and King, as well as act according to the spirit of the constitution.
3. The coup was conducted to uphold the honor of the army, which has been unjustly treated.
4. The coup will restore efficient administration and improve the people's livelihood.
5. The coup will make it possible to clear up the assassination plot against the king and to arrest those responsible.
6. The coup will rid the country once and for all of vestiges of communism and insure that the nation will cherish the Buddhist religion forever.[81]

One could extract from this statement a basic philosophy of the new leadership. Roughly, it involved the trilogy of Nation, Religion (Buddhism), and King. The leaders saw the army's "clientele" as being these three, which were conceived in

---

[79] Cremation Volume of Luang Kat, no pagination.

[80] Members of the Coup Group sometimes use the Thai initials r.p. (*rattha prahan*) after their names as signs of distinction.

[81] W. Ch. Prasangsit, *Phaendin Somdet*, pp. 170, 171.

absolute terms. They believed the actions of civilians threatened these values. The concessions made by the Pridi/Thamrong group to the Allies, with their dire effects upon the economy and the well-being of the people, threatened the nation. The recognition of the Soviet Union and the repeal of the Anti-Communist Act, as well as the increased agitation of the local Chinese community, threatened nation, monarchy, and religion.[82] The death of King Ananda was also perceived as Pridi's attempt to subvert the institution of the monarchy. Point five clearly indicated that the army considered the King's death (assassination) as a major issue. In general, the statement can be seen as an indictment of Pridi, whom the army now portrayed as anti-royalist and even communistic in his ideology. On the other hand, point three revealed the stark fact that the coup was an army affair and that it was done in its own interest and to regain its self-respect. If the civilian leadership were allowed to continue its demoralizing campaign, the solidarity and *esprit de corps* of the army would deteriorate to the point that it would fall victim to political manipulation of internal army affairs.

In any case, the turning point for the coup planners came when they were able to solicit the support of Colonel Sarit Thanarat, the young military commander of the First Regiment of the army's powerful First Division. Colonel Sarit had participated in the Shan States campaign and seems to have wanted to resign after the war for fear of being forced to do so.[83] But after consulting with a monk and various soothsayers who predicted future military fame, Sarit changed his mind. Apparently Sarit had had no previous political role, for he was not forced out of active duty like other officers; better still, he was given the command of the sensitive First Regiment, stationed in Bangkok. He was noted for his forceful character, and for being a first-rate army officer.

At first Sarit was apprehensive about participating in politics. He had even sternly reprimanded Lieutenant Channarong Wichanbut, a junior officer under his command, who tried to approach Sarit about the coup.[84] However, he knew that many of his officers wanted to take part in an army coup, and he was probably aware that he could not hold out too long if he wanted to remain popular with his junior officers. So shortly before the coup, Sarit called a meeting of his battalion commanders and other senior regimental officers to discuss the possibilities of a coup and to decide the regiment's future course. By the end of the meeting he was convinced that the First Regiment should not stand idly by, but should join the foray and act on behalf of the army. Indeed, of all the elements within the army that took an active part in the coup, the First Regiment was the largest single component. With the First Regiment the coup plot had the firepower it needed.

---

[82] G. William Skinner, *Leadership and Power in the Chinese Community of Thailand* (Ithaca, NY: Cornell University Press, 1967), p. 16. Skinner reports that many in the postwar Chinese leadership held left-wing sentiments nurtured by the communist Chinese underground and communist newspapers.

[83] The basis for most retirements was the post-war general demobilization. However, British pressure to whittle down the Thai army, and the desire of Pridi to weaken the army, no doubt had certain additional effects.

[84] *Prawat lae Phonngan khong Chomphon Sarit Thanarat, Khanaratthamontri Phim nai Ngan Phraratchathan Pluengsop* [Biography and Work of Field Marshal Sarit Thanarat, published by the Cabinet for his cremation ceremony], April 17, 1964, p. 43, hereafter referred to as Cremation Volume of Sarit Thanarat (Cabinet edition).

The coup plans called for the arrest of Pridi, Luang Thamrong, and Luang Sangwon by the First Regiment. Pridi's capture was to be carried out by troops from the Second Battalion. Forces from the Third Battalion were to arrest Luang Thamrong. Soldiers from the First Battalion were to arrest Luang Sangwon.[85] As it turned out, all the intended victims escaped arrest in time. Sarit himself went to arrest the prime minister, who was reported to have been at a celebration at Suan Amphon, but this venture was also unsuccessful.[86] Meanwhile, General Luang Adul, the army chief, went about frantically ordering troops back to their barracks, but Sarit had convinced them earlier that victory was for the taking and that they should not give up under any circumstances.[87] The plan to use the First Regiment's headquarters as the coup command post was abandoned in favor of the defense ministry. Sarit was able to gain easy access there, for the security troops posted around the ministry were men from his own command. Later he was joined by the military academy's Lt. Colonel Thanom Kittikachon, who brought with him carloads of fully armed military cadets.

In preparation for the coup, Luang Kat had drafted a new replacement constitution. It was hidden under a red water jar to foil discovery. (This was the reason why the Coup Group's constitution was later known as the "under the waterjar constitution.") Now Luang Kat, Thanom, and a score of military cadets went to see Regent Krommakhun Chainatnarenthon, to get him to endorse the document. Luang Kat brought along Prince Chakraphanphensiri, his son-in-law, to facilitate the audience with the regent. Since the most salient feature of this document was the theoretical increase of the king's powers, the coup group must have hoped to win some conservative royalist backing.[88]

Meanwhile, at the coup headquarters, a highly emotional Phin conducted an interview with the press. With sad and tear-filled eyes, he said that the army had had to act for the sake of the people.[89] It could not stand by and watch while the country deteriorated. The civilian governments, while criticizing Phibun, had proved no better, for they were corrupt and inefficient. The mysterious death of the king, the plight of the farmers who fell victim to corrupt MPs, and the shortage of rice were more than he or the army could take.

The Coup Group then justified its actions with an official announcement the next day:

Proclamation No. 1
    Beloved Brothers and Sisters:
        The military, civilian officials, police, and the Thai people have unanimously agreed that the present situation in Thailand could not be solved by the government, [a failure that has] resulted in misery for our brothers and sisters. The present government is also aware that it could not solve these problems—the worsening conditions of living and the rice shortage. In addition, it has

---

[85] W. Ch. Prasangsit, *Phaendin Somdet*, pp. 198–200.

[86] Cremation Volume of Sarit Thanarat (Cabinet edition), p. 45.

[87] Ibid. Sarit had urged his troops to fight for victory and not to return to the barracks once the action began. He said that there was no use for them as soldiers to return to "die" at their own camp. He pointed out that failure would be equivalent to life in prison.

[88] Cremation Volume of Luang Kat, no pagination.

[89] Krom Khotsanakan, *Khao Khotsanakan*, X (November, 1947), pp. 1052–1062.

allowed widespread corruption, even though the government has the power to stop it ... Furthermore, some politicians have used politics as a cover for graft and corruption in the midst of the people's hardships and have without shame accumulated riches in self-interest. At a time when people are starving, the government and other opportunists live in wealth and extravagance and ignore the cries of the people. The corruption and inefficiency within official circles have grieved all.

Because of our concern for the people and hatred for corruption, we were forced to take over power to force the resignation of the government and create a new one according to the constitution to help reduce graft and corruption and to rid the people of their woes.

Therefore, for peace and quiet, we urge the public, both Thai and foreigners, to remain peaceful and not do anything to obstruct our work. Civil servants should carry on with their duties as usual and wait for future directives. On November 9, 1947, government officials should work as usual.

Khana Thahan (Military Group)
November 9, 1947

The Pridi Constitution of 1946 was now replaced by Luang Kat's version, which was more royalist in nature. Under this the new constitution, the king could theoretically exercise more power through a provision by which he could delay the passing of a bill by refusing to sign it into law.[90] In emergencies the king could pass laws in the absence of a parliamentary session, and such laws would later be presented for review by the assembly.[91] Under articles 78 and 79, the king could also dismiss any member of the cabinet or the whole cabinet by royal decree. He could also appoint members of the senate. Although on paper the king appeared to have gained wide new prerogatives, in practice he was limited by a new institution, the *Aphirathamontri* (Privy Council), an appointed body controlled by the army.

Phibun's role in the coup appears to have been essentially symbolic. Although he was in retirement, he was still a well-known leader, as well as a respected army officer. Through use of his name, the Coup Group could solicit acquiescence from the people and gain wide support in the army. But it was too soon to bring Phibun into the government. (It was enough for the moment to restore him to the position of commander-in-chief of the army.) The powers would not have forgotten his role during the war. For this and other reasons, the Coup Group invited Khuang to form a government. By allowing Khuang to head a new cabinet for the time being, the army was able to claim publicly that it was not out for its own political power.

THE KHUANG INTERIM GOVERNMENT

Phibun had personally assured Khuang that the army would support his government, and urged on him the necessity of forming a new government to avert further strife within the armed forces.[92] Khuang agreed on the condition that the army and the Coup Group would not interfere with government affairs but would only be responsible for the maintenance of peace and order.

---

[90] Article 30.

[91] Article 80.

[92] Kiat, *Ruang khong Nai Khuang,* p. 295.

With great tact and ability, Khuang was able to persuade prominent and respected men to join his cabinet.[93] Certain members of the appointed cabinet had questioned the legality of such a government and the legal authority of the Coup Group to instruct Khuang to form one.[94] Khuang's cabinet list was approved by Phibun, and the Coup Group and was endorsed by parliament shortly thereafter.[95] On November 13, Phibun wrote a letter to Khuang officially turning over the powers of government from the Coup Group to the new cabinet.[96]

Khuang's government was able to solve the rice-shortage problem immediately by allowing the free movement of rice from one province to another. In the face of an initial unwillingness on the part of Great Britain to recognize his government, Khuang insisted that his government was both democratic and peace loving. Within a short time, recognition was indeed granted by the world's major powers. Meanwhile, rumors of a counter coup by the Pridi clique continued to thicken, and this made Khuang very uneasy. However, he was lucky to be able to gather around him enough prominent civilians to deter any immediate action from Pridi's followers.[97]

In the meantime, a struggle for power within the Coup Group shook the fragile stability of the Khuang government. The press hotly criticized the promotion of Luang Kat from the rank of colonel to lieutenant general in one huge step.[98] Luang Kat had demanded promotion to the rank so that he would be on par with Phin, whom he saw as his major rival to succeed Phibun. However, the Coup Group could not yet deal effectively with Luang Kat, for they feared that any sign of an internal rift might prompt an attack from the ousted Pridi clique. Phin became army chief after Phibun, and Kat assumed the position of deputy chief. But the jockeying for power continued. Kat hoped to get the defense department portfolio, but it was awarded to Lt. General Luang Chatnakrop, a Coup Group member close to Phibun. On one occasion, to test his influence, Kat even ordered the withdrawal of security troops from the defense ministry and the ministry of finance, two strategic places that symbolized the Coup Group's control of government.

While Kat was challenging Luang Chart and Khuang, another area of friction between the Coup Group and the government appeared. Phibun and Phin wanted to make sure that the police would be on their side in the event of any action taken by

---

[93] Democrat Party members resented the fact that members of the cabinet were "outsiders."

[94] Doubts concerning the legality of the coup and the formation of a new government were "resolved" when the Coup Group announced its Proclamation No. 18, declaring that *de facto* power was theirs through the coup d'état and that the Coup Group could legally turn over political leadership to any designated government of its choice.

[95] See letter in Suchin, "Ratthaprahan 2490," p. 69. Khuang's cabinet was approved by the newly appointed senate acting as parliament until new elections could be held. Kiat, *Ruang khong Nai Khuang*, p. 312.

[96] By this time, MPs who had supported Pridi were in hiding or were afraid to show opposition to the Coup Group.

[97] Kiat, *Ruang khong Nai Khuang*, pp. 323–328. Kiat said that he had examined the private memoirs of Dr. Thongplaew Cholaphum, who recorded the Satthahip meeting of Pridi and his followers. According to the document, after seeing the list of Khuang's choice of ministers, Pridi and his allies all agreed that these men were the superior candidates; based on that assessment, they decided it would be inadvisable to seek power.

[98] Kat held the rank of colonel and group captain at the time of the coup. As a reward for himself, he asked for the promotion. Smarting from public criticism, he challenged his tormentors to stage a coup, something, which he said, was hard to accomplish.

Pridi. They suggested that Colonel Phao Siyanon, Phin's son-in-law, become deputy police chief. Lt. General Luang Sinat,[99] the minister of the interior, resented the Coup Group's interference with his work. He reacted by remarking in public that a person of Phao's qualifications could not become even a patrolman let alone deputy police chief.[100]

After the election for members of the lower house in January 1948, the Democrats were able to capture a majority in parliament, and Khuang was again given the mandate to form a government. However, signs of the Coup Group's displeasure became increasingly apparent. Leaflets were distributed in the capital urging the public to demand that Phibun become prime minister and criticizing Khuang's government for not being able to run the country properly. Phibun, Phin, and Kat publicly denied any connections with the efforts, and Khuang was able to proceed with the installation of his cabinet. There was little change in Khuang's new cabinet compared with the previous one. The most noticeable absence was that of Luang Sinat, the interior minister. Khuang did not want to risk further friction with the Coup Group and took over the interior portfolio himself for lack of a better replacement. Khuang wanted to keep Luang Sinat in his cabinet as a guarantee to the Seri Thai, but Sinat would accept no offers short of the ministry of defense or of the interior, and defense was out of the question (for Luang Chart was the Coup Group designee). Khuang also wanted Phin to join his cabinet, for he reasoned that this would help control interference from the Coup Group, especially from Luang Kat. However, Phin had different ideas. He could not divide his time between the cabinet and the Coup Group, for he did not trust Luang Kat. Phin and Luang Kat were like two tigers in the same cave, each waiting to pounce on the other.

Khuang's new government did not last long. On April 6, 1948, four leading members of the Coup Group visited him.[101] This incident is the infamous *chi nai Khuang,* or Khuang's "hold up/mugging." The officers who called on Khuang at his house presented him with an ultimatum that his government should "reconsider" itself, that is, resign. The officers stated that the Coup Group was dissatisfied with the government's inability to solve pressing needs. They gave Khuang twenty-four hours to think it over.

Khuang attempted to verify this drastic threat by writing a note to Phibun, demanding clarification. He instructed his brother, who was an army officer, to deliver it personally. Soon after, Phin and Luang Kat came to his house to confirm the Coup Group's demands. Having no other recourse, Khuang resigned. In his resignation letter to the king, Khuang made it clear that he was forced by the army to step down and gave full details of his "hold up" in the letter.[102] Although Khuang's two governments lasted but four months, he was able to solve the rice shortage problem, secure recognition for the government, and give the army time to consolidate its power to await countermoves by the Pridi/Seri Thai forces.

---

[99] Although a former Seri Thai leader in charge of army affairs, Luang Sinat was independent minded and respected both by his former Seri Thai colleagues and by army officers.

[100] Kiat, *Ruang khong Nai Khuang,* p. 335.

[101] Ibid., pp. 363–382. The officers involved were Major General Sawat Sawatikiat, Lt. Colonel Kan Chamnongphumiwet, Colonel Silapa Silapasonchai Ratanawaraha, and Lt. Colonel Lamai Uttayananon. (The first two played important roles in the 1947 coups.) It appears that Phibun did not play a direct part in this affair, but had to accept it as a *fait accompli.*

[102] See Thak Chaloemtiarana, ed., *Thai Politics, 1932–1951* (Bangkok: Social Science Association of Thailand, 1978), pp. 592, 593.

...TRUGGLE FOR SUPREMACY

struggle for political supremacy and internal solidarity lasted from
...n it was finally able to eliminate all other contending factions—
...enges, the Pridi/Seri Thai clique, and the navy. This period
... rebellions and two abortive coup attempts.

...ing of the army was carried out through the prosecution of
...eneral staff coup attempt and later the elimination of Luang
...'état, known as the October 1st Rebellion, was mainly the
...army's general staff.[103] There were nineteen persons
...ment case, charging the defendants with rebellion.[104]
...'s general staff, five were "retired" officers, and one
...ers who did not command any significant forces.
...ior General Net Khemayothin, another general
...e Seri Thai.[105] The government charged the
...the government by force through persuading
...se and to build up secret arms caches. The
...vernment officials, as well as leading army
...ne night of October 1, 1948, coinciding with a
...al Sarit. The planners reasoned that the affair would
...portant army officers and the cabinet.[106] The festivities
...the partygoers so that reaction to the coup would be slow

...ent's case seems to have been well documented. It appears, at least
...hat a coup was in fact planned. However, from looking at the
...ances involved, one cannot help but feel that there was more behind the
...and that the Coup Group exploited the situation as an excuse to stamp out
internal dissent.

In testimony given on behalf of the defense, it was argued that, after the coup of
November 8, 1947, there were many army officers who were satisfied with the initial
act but were appalled by the army's return to political leadership by ousting the legal
Khuang government by force. Most of these officers were general staff officers who
wanted to have more reforms and development within the army. They were of the
opinion that the military should not be involved in politics, for it would divide the
army and turn professional soldiers into the instruments of politicians.[107] The defense

---

[103] For an account see Udom Utthaphalin, comp., *Kabot 1 Tula* [October 1st Rebellion]
(Thonburi: Prayurawong Press, 1950). The book records the court trials of those arrested.

[104] San Aya [Criminal Court], Case no. 2768/2491, November, 10, 1948.

[105] San Aya, Case no. 908/2492, May 17, 1949.

[106] Testimonies from San Aya, Case nos. 2768, 2818/2491 and 788, 908/2492; April 19, 1950. A
petition for closed-door hearings was denied. Also see W. Ch. Prasangsit, *Phaendin Somdet*, p.
274. Prasangsit wrote that the plan was to assassinate Coup Group leaders at Sarit's wedding.
Sarit at this time had assumed command of the army's powerful First Division and was a
rising personality. Almost everybody tried to gain his friendship. The navy denied having any
part in this planned coup and said that it was not harboring Pridi at any of its bases. The
situation during this period was tense, for the army was always on the lookout for potential
trouble from Pridi, the Seri Thai, and the navy.

[107] Ibid.

went on to state that because of the defendants' beliefs they were continually scrutinized and, indeed, persecuted as potential troublemakers. The defense argued that

> Officers who were really concerned with their own duties [as soldiers] therefore were in a very difficult situation. The defendants were officers who did not command troops or weapons of any kind and did not have the authority to give orders to troops. It was therefore easy to accuse and prosecute these men.[108]

The defendants felt that the case was already prejudiced against them, for absolute powers of prosecution and review were given to deputy police chief Phao, a powerful member of the Coup Group. Through him, their case was being manipulated as an excuse to get rid of opposition within the army. Police strong-arms tactics were also used, such as the detention of the defendants' spouses, a tactic employed as leverage to secure admissions of guilt; mysterious deaths of political prisoners while in police custody were also reported. While not denying that they harbored different ideas concerning the work of the army and the Coup Group, the accused men refused to admit that they had planned to overthrow the government by force, mainly because they did not control any troops.

On the other side, the government built up a strong case against the defendants by bringing out testimony that the defendants actually had considered and laid plans for a coup. It was common knowledge within the army that the defendants were not pleased with the army's rate of development, and had asked for the opinions of many officers regarding the best method to rectify this. The government claimed that there was a joint plan among the defendants, the navy, civilian politicians, and the Seri Thai.

The case concluded with court sentences of three years' imprisonment for each of nine defendants, while thirteen others were released. The nine were composed of four officers from the general staff, one junior officer, and four officers who were in retirement.[109] It is interesting to note that the sentences were light, for the defendants received the minimum sentence under the law.[110] Probably the Coup Group merely wanted to set an example to others in the army to emphasize that it would not tolerate any rifts that could weaken its preparation for a counter offensive from Pridi and former Seri Thai members. The light sentences seem to indicate that the main aim was publicity, or an unwillingness to alienate people in the army by excessive harshness.

In another housecleaning action, the new government leaders accused Luang Kat, one of their former allies, of having planned his own coup. The "Luang Kat Rebellion" ended even before it was started on January 27, 1950, when he was arrested and forced to go into exile in Hong Kong.[111] One of the four leading

---

[108] Ibid.

[109] San Aya, *Khamphiphaksa* [Court Ruling], May 20, 1950.

[110] Article 102 of the Criminal Code. Recommended sentence was three to fifteen years.

[111] Cremation Volume of Luang Kat, no pagination. It was known that Phibun feared Luang Kat and encouraged Phao to strengthen his police to counter Kat's attempt to control the army. At first Sarit appeared to have backed Kat, but later he abandoned him for his own ambitious reasons. In effect, the fear of Kat led Phibun to ally himself with Phao more than Sarit, whom he did not trust fully.

members of the 1947 coup, and surely its most colorful, Luang Kat was a victim of his own "hold up" or "mugging" tactics. He had been a thorn in the side of Phibun and the Phin/Phao faction of the Coup Group since his refusal to cooperate with the Khuang government and Luang Chatnakrop, the Coup Group's choice for Defense Minister.

Foiled in his ambition to become defense minister, Kat devoted his time to building up his own *barami* (power and influence) in the army. He frequently toured the provinces and summarily called for meetings of the local officials to listen to his speeches regarding the difficulties involved in staging coups and running the country. Luang Kat's activities annoyed the press and especially Phibun's cabinet ministers, who felt that Luang Kat was interfering in national matters and taking things into his own hands just because he was a member of the Coup Group.

The three ministers in charge of defense threatened to resign unless the Coup Group promised to police its own members. The first sign of Luang Kat's fall from favor was a rigged meeting of all senior army officers called by Luang Chat. Luang Kat was forced to attend. Feeling himself a senior officer, deputy commander of the army, and a leading member of the Coup Group, Luang Kat showed open contempt and disrespect for Luang Chat in the meeting, behavior that earned him a lecture from Luang Chat on the need for tightening up the military code of conduct—a personal affront to Luang Kat.

Luang Kat, however, was not to be easily controlled. A few months later, the cabinet received news that a large sum of Indian rupees had been withdrawn from the treasury without authorization from the minister of finance. Luang Kat had seen fit to take the money and give it to army troops for entertainment. The minister of finance resigned in protest, which gave the press a grand time reporting another Luang Kat "mugging" victim.

Luang Kat's career was cut short in January 1950. The Coup Group decided that it had to eliminate him as a force in politics, for he was a constant source of embarrassment for the army leaders. Phao was given the assignment of arresting Luang Kat. A plan was drawn up whereby Luang Kat was lured to the prime minister's office. Once there, Phao arrested him at gunpoint and informed him he was to be charged with treason and rebellion.[112] Demands to meet Phibun were denied, and Luang Kat was quickly hustled off to Hong Kong after receiving a small amount of money for his exile. He was later formally charged in court with rebellion. It is interesting to note that he was the case's only defendant. Luang Kat remained in Hong Kong for about a year and then decided that he would come back to face charges. The courts quickly dropped his case, but the experience was enough to convince Luang Kat that it was time for him to retire. The elimination of Luang Kat left the leadership of the Coup Group in the hands of the Phin/Phao faction, with Phibun acting as the titular head. But Sarit, whose career quickly blossomed after he was instrumental in suppressing the Palace Rebellion and the Manhattan Rebellion, as described below, would later challenge their leadership.

THE PRIDI/SERI THAI AND NAVY COUNTERMEASURES

After the 1947 coup, Pridi and his Seri Thai followers fled to their former strongholds. Pridi had first escaped to the Sattahip naval base and subsequently left

---

[112] Ibid.

the country for Singapore. His Seri Thai followers returned to their provinces and allegedly tried to organize groups to await a counter coup in Bangkok. Two serious episodes occurred shortly after the army takeover. The first was the arrest of Thim Phuriphat, who was accused of attempting to organize an independent state in Isan. He was arrested in February 1948 and released in 1950. Other Seri Thai leaders from Isan and former MPs were also accused of organizing autonomous states in Isan, to be known as *Sahaphan Rat Laemthong* (Federated States of the Golden Peninsula). The leaders were Thongin Phuriphat, Fong Sitthitham, Thawin Udon, and Tiang Sirikhan. They were all arrested and later released.[113] The Seri Thai movement at this point appeared to be weak and uncoordinated. However, on February 26, 1949, Pridi—together with the Seri Thai and the navy—staged their counter coup, now known as the Palace Rebellion.

Accounts of this coup are very confusing. It is not at all clear who was on whose side.[114] As far as can be ascertained, it was a joint affair of Pridi/Seri Thai elements and factions of the navy, especially the marines under the command of Rear Admiral Thahan Khamhiran and Vice Admiral Luang Sangwon, from Sattahip and Chonburi.

At the same time, the Coup Group was making its own preparations. On the pretext that six tanks had been involved in an attempted coup on February 23, they arranged to have a national emergency declared.[115] They also staged various military exercises involving army and navy forces, the main operation being known as the *Chang Dam Chang Nam* Operation (Black Elephant and Hippopotamus Operation). Military demarcation lines were drawn and each branch of the armed forces was warned to maintain strict security and not intrude into each other's territory.

While the army and navy were conducting their military maneuvers using live ammunition, Pridi and his supporters, armed with modern weapons, "captured" Thammasat University and used it as their headquarters.[116] Another detail broke into the Radio of Thailand and announced over the air that Phibun had been relieved of all duties and that Direk Chaiyanam was now prime minister. Phin, Phao, and Kat were also relieved of their duties. Admiral Luang Sinthu Songkhramchai, the navy chief, was to become the supreme military commander. Rear Admiral Thahan was to assume the position of minister of defense. All troop movements were to be suspended pending further orders from Luang Sinthu. In the meantime, forces led by Captain Wacharachai, a Pridi lieutenant, captured the palace and prepared for battle with the army.

As far as can be ascertained, the original plans of the Seri Thai called for simultaneous uprisings in the provinces that would converge upon the capital together with marine forces from Sattahip and Chonburi. This plan was foiled when

---

[113] Samut Surakhaka, *26 Kanpattiwat Thai lae Ratthaprahan 2089–2507* [26 Thai Revolutions and Coups d'états, 1546-1964] (Bangkok: Sue Kanphim Press), p. 435. The government accused these Isan MPs of trying to stage diversionary events in the Northeast in preparation for a coup by Pridi in Bangkok.

[114] Ibid., pp. 445–469.

[115] The 1949 Constitution prohibited troop mobilization except during a national emergency. The Aphiratthamontri (Privy Council) had denied Phibun's insistence on the need to be at a "ready" state. The "six tanks episode" may have been an army gimmick to force the council's hand.

[116] These modern weapons were obtained from the United States toward the end of the war. They were given to the Seri Thai for their own protection and for possible harassment of the Japanese.

the army arrested most of the Seri Thai leaders in Isan. The marine reinforcements also never appeared, for they were stranded in Bang Pakong because of low tide.[117]

Lt. General Sarit, the commander of the army's first division, was given the job of suppressing the rebels.[118] He was appointed director of the affair and acted with great speed and precision. He ordered his tanks to storm the palace gates and troops from the First Regiment poured in to rout the rebels. However, sporadic fighting occurred elsewhere in the city where misunderstandings arose between navy and army troops. The navy quickly sent an officer to see Sarit to clear things up.

The suppression of the Palace Rebellion was quite harsh. The Coup Group saw its chance to eliminate finally the Seri Thai as a potential contender for power. Numerous arrests were carried out, and a political purge was set in motion. On March 3, 1949, four former ministers were murdered. These men, Thawin Udon (a Seri Thai leader from Roi Et), Thongplaew Cholaphum (Pridi's secretary), Chamlong Dowruang (a Seri Thai leader from Mahasarakham), and Thongin Phuriphat (a Seri Thai leader from Ubon), were killed while being transferred from one prison to another under police escort. The affair was covered up by Phao's police force as being the work of Seri Thai fighters trying to liberate the prisoners.[119]

Having eliminated one major institutional challenge to their power, the army leaders still faced a formidable foe in the navy. The navy was on a par with the army in troop forces and armaments, for it had an efficient and well-trained marine corps, tanks, airplanes, and modern weapons.[120] Furthermore, its headquarters were in Bangkok and its ships were moored in the Chaophraya River, with cannons ready to bombard army strongholds if needed.

The marines' role in the Palace Rebellion was not totally overlooked by the army. After the defeat of the rebels, the Coup Group organized a large celebration to signify solidarity between the armed forces. Rear Admiral Thahan, however, was notably absent, for after the Palace affair he was transferred to Bangkok pending investigations into his reason for bringing his marines to Bangkok without orders.[121] Vice Admiral Sangwon was also absent, for he had fled with Pridi.

THE MANHATTAN REBELLION, JUNE 29, 1951[122]

The Thai navy was an old and prestigious military institution that had long rivaled the army's prominence. The navy enjoyed royal favor from its inception. Its first commander was the second king in Rama IV's reign and subsequent commanders were princes of high rank.[123] The navy's social prestige and the highly

---

[117] Samut, *26 Kanpattiwat,* pp. 458, 459. These forces reached Bangkok the next day after the fighting had ceased and Pridi had fled.

[118] Sarit became famous after this affair and was given the position of Commander of the First Army for his work.

[119] Samut, *26 Kanpattiwat,* pp. 472–489. Sarit ordered investigations after he came to power and the real culprits were brought to trial.

[120] According to Professor Lauristan Sharp, those tanks were delivered in early 1948 and were United States Army surplus from the Philippines.

[121] Thahan was relieved of all duties at the end of the year. Eighty naval officers challenged Phibun to fire them first.

[122] A good account of this can be found in Thai Noi (pseud.), *Kabot 29 Mithunayon* [June 26th Rebellion] (Bangkok: Odeon Store Press, 1951).

[123] *Nawikasat,* XXIX (1965), pp. 1–4.

technical nature of the navy's armaments attracted sons of the aristocracy. The naval officers' corps had a historic sense of aristocratic pride, aloofness, and technical superiority that colored its relationship with the army.[124]

In 1932, certain members of the navy joined in the revolution.[125] Subsequently, perhaps mainly because of its rivalry with the army, the navy supported Pridi as a way of preventing total army domination. During the war, many naval officers joined the Seri Thai cause, and the relationship between Pridi and the navy flourished.[126]

As we have seen earlier, important naval officers backed the Seri Thai attempt to retaliate against the army's coup of 1947. Luang Thamrong, Luang Sangwon, and Admiral Thahan were all key naval officers who openly supported Pridi. The removal of these men from the naval hierarchy was a direct threat to the power of the navy, for it was now open to penetration by the army. The abortive Pridi coup of 1949 brought to the surface the intense rivalry between the army and the navy. The post-coup solidarity celebration was only an artificial remedy and a postponement of further conflict. It was apparent that neither side was fooled, for when the so-called Manhattan Rebellion broke out (as explained later), both sides were ready to use harsh and violent tactics. As the senior navy officers had been eliminated after the Palace Coup, naval leadership fell to radical young officers who wanted to regain the navy's pride. The restraint and cool calculation of the experienced Pridi, Luang Sangwon, and Admiral Thahan gave way to the more direct and violent methods of the young Manhattan Rebellion leaders.

These young men badly misjudged the real intentions of their enemies, however. The coup leaders believed that if they took Phibun as hostage, they could force the government and the army to capitulate. They did not see that preserving Phibun's life was a low priority to the army compared with its desire for a monopoly of power.

On June 29, 1951, Phibun attended the transferring ceremonies for an American-donated dredge named the *Manhattan*.[127] In full view of the diplomatic corps and other Thai officials, Phibun was accosted by a group of armed navy men led by Lt.

---

[124] A 1967 study by Police Colonel Chue Chanphen of the opinions of preparatory military cadets revealed that almost 47 percent of the naval cadets saw the navy as providing opportunities for academic advancement, compared to less than 1 percent among the army cadets. This indicates that the navy was known for its "modernistic" outlook toward military science and technology, while the army mainly attracted candidates interested in other aspects of military service, such as political advancement. See Chue Chanphen, "Opinions of Preparatory Military Cadets and Their Selection of Service Branch" (MA thesis, National Institute of Development Administration, Bangkok, 1968), p. 70.

[125] Nai Honhuai (pseud.), *Thahan Rua Wan Pattiwat Yai* [The Navy during the Important Revolution] (Bangkok: Thai Kasem Press, 1948). This book deals with the navy in the 1932 Revolution.

[126] Ibid. Among the naval officers involved in the 1932 revolution were Luang Sinthu, Luang Thamrong, Luang Sangwon, Admiral Thahan, and Luang Suphachalasai. All of these men were involved with Pridi and the Seri Thai. Likely explanations for why they joined Pridi and the Seri Thai are: first, their long association with Pridi since 1932; second, they were not involved in direct negotiations with the Japanese and thus had more freedom of movement; and, third, Pridi and the civilians needed the support of the navy as an ally to balance the power of the army, and so they cultivated navy officers.

[127] Thus the name *Kabot* Manhattan (Manhattan Rebellion).

Commander Manat Charupha.[128] Over the navy's radio, a new government was announced by the coup leader, Captain Anon Puntharikapha, who further ordered all naval units to converge on Bangkok to fight with government troops and to wait for further orders from Admiral Luaug Sinthu, the navy's commander-in-chief.[129] Phibun was transferred by navy landing craft to the flagship *Si Ayutthaya.* However, forces commanded by Sarit and Phao quickly routed naval units that attempted to capture strategic points on land. Before long, the rebels were confined to their stronghold in the *Si Ayutthaya.*

Despite the broadcast of a taped Phibun message asking the army to exercise the utmost caution and prudence, the army prepared to put into effect its drastic plans for purging the navy. Negotiations deadlocked because both sides threatened to use force to achieve their purposes. The next morning, while Phibun was still aboard the *Si Ayutthaya,* the army, the police, and the air force attacked. The army, under the direction of Sarit, used three-inch cannons to bombard naval installations. Air force planes attacked gasoline dumps and strafed naval positions. They also bombed the stationary *Si Ayutthaya* and sank it. Phibun escaped from the sinking ship and swam to safety. With the destruction of the flagship, the naval forces lost hope and hostilities quickly ended.[130] Luang Sinthu's indecision and failure to issue orders following the capture of Phibun also deprived the coup leaders of the reinforcements that they needed to fight the army.

The Manhattan Rebellion marked the entrance of the air force into Thai politics. The air force elite comprised mainly army officers, for this branch of the armed forces was formed only in 1947 and did not have its own academy until 1953.[131] (Rivalry between the army and the navy had been apparent even in this matter, for the navy had developed its own planes and recruited its own fliers.) The police fought on the government's side because of Phao's leadership, which earned him the position of police chief after the coup attempt was suppressed.

With the defeat of the rebels, the army was able to accomplish two things—the elimination of naval opposition, and the reduction of the navy to its bare essentials. The Coup Group ordered the dismissal of the top naval brass together with all those whom it suspected of having taken part in the ill-fated rebellion.[132] The four important personalities who emerged from the suppression of the rebellion, who came to be known as the *si thahan sua* — or the "four tiger soldiers" (Phin, Phao, Sarit, and Air Chief Marshal Fuen Ronnaphakat)—were responsible for the systematic stripping down of the navy to its barest bones.[133] Through government decrees, the navy suffered a massive reorganization imposed upon it by the army. It was

---

[128] Samut, *26 Kanpattiwat,* pp. 531, 532.

[129] Ibid., p. 532. Luang Sinthu, a long-time associate of Pridi, wavered at this juncture and thus helped determine the failure of the coup. The coup leaders were counting on their *fait accompli* to force the whole navy to join in the melee. For English translations of Anon and Manat's personal accounts, see Thak, ed., *Thai Politics,* pp. 594–673.

[130] The fatalities included 17 military personnel, 8 police officers, and 103 civilians. More than 500 people were wounded, and the country lost fifteen million baht in property damage. Moreover, the navy's most powerful man-of-war was sunk.

[131] Royal Thai Air Force, *Wan Kongthap Akat* [Air Force Day], 1952.

[132] *Prakat Samnak Nayok Ratthamontri* [Announcement of the Prime Minister's Office], July 2, 1951. Also see Ministry of Defense, directive no. 114/11999, July 2, 1951.

[133] Thai Noi, *Kabot 29 Mithunayon,* pp. 483–487. The four had written a joint letter to the prime minister demanding the reorganization of the navy.

restricted to sea operations and was deprived of its control of land territory. According to a ministry of defense directive, all navy circles and navy *changwads* (provinces) were transferred to the army.[134] In other words, responsibility for peace and order, as well as political influence in the provinces of Samutprakan, Samutsakhon, Samutsongkhram, Chanthaburi, Chonburi, Rayong, and Trat, which had earlier been under the navy's jurisdiction, were given to the army. With this accomplishment, the army now monopolized territorial command of the whole country. The navy's headquarters was moved out of Thonburi to Samutprakan, to keep it far from the seat of power in Bangkok. The navy's battleship department, hitherto stationed in the Chaophraya River, was moved to Sattahip and renamed *Kong Rua Yutthakan*. The list of dismantled and disbanded naval and marine battalions and other strategic offices was quite extensive. The reorganization was thorough and crippling to the navy.[135] The navy's air section was "given" to the air force, and—yet another humiliation—the navy's prestigious musical band was transferred to the control of the armed forces headquarters. Weapons and armaments of the dismantled naval units were also appropriated by the army. The navy was allowed to maintain only a minimum level of manpower, while the rest of its men were distributed among the victorious army, air force, and police. The shakedown and division of spoils was complete. The army's competitor was reduced to impotency, for even buildings formerly occupied by the navy were divided up.

We have now seen how the army was able to eliminate and undermine the civilian political leadership after the end of World War II. The 1947 coup was a bold bid by the army to re-enter the ring. Thereafter, it proceeded to engage in a systematic and thorough whittling down of the Pridi/Seri Thai group, as well as crippling the navy, an action justified by the abortive coups of 1949 and 1951. The army was now "top dog," but it still had to submit to parliamentary limitations imposed by the 1949 Constitution, which stated that army officers could not legally become members of parliament or cabinet ministers. But having eliminated all potential opposition, the army turned to dealing with the unresponsive parliament and the limits imposed by the constitution.

Sarit's education in Thai politics coincided with this period of political instability and the growing power and success of the army. Sarit's first major command position in Bangkok was the critical one, as it launched him into the thick of the Thai political struggle. His experience in the 1947 coup, the Palace Coup, and the Manhattan Rebellion showed him the supremacy of force in the solution of political problems. In the next chapter, I discuss Sarit's continuing political education, namely, how he learned to deal with a parliament that "limited" the freedom of action of the Coup Group.

---

[134] Ministry of Defense, directive no. 170/12926, July 16, 1951.

[135] Under the directive, eighteen departments and battalion-size units were dismantled. The hardest hit was the marine corps.

CHAPTER TWO

THE TRIUMVIRATE (1948–1957)

Phibun's return to political leadership in 1948 marked the beginning of his second tenacious grip on the office of prime minister of Thailand. Nonetheless, his position was different from what it had been four years earlier. He was no longer in supreme command of the army; neither did he dominate the Coup Group. The bombing of the *Si Ayutthaya,* while he was still aboard, was in itself a good indication of Phibun's relative unimportance to the emerging young and aggressive leaders within the Coup Group. To them, Phibun was useful but ultimately expendable.

The fact that Phibun was able to maintain his position as prime minister from 1948 to 1957 gives testimony to his seasoned ability to play one faction against another—as well as to his success in seeking support from outside the Coup Group itself. Phibun's political longevity can be attributed in part to the fact that the Coup Group's young leaders were busy consolidating their respective power bases and building up their socio-political status. Once accomplished, the elimination of Phibun would appear both plausible and appropriate. Thus, Thai politics from 1948 to 1957 can be said to have been influenced by these three factors: the Coup Group's young leaders' attempts to consolidate their political positions; Phibun's search for an alternative power base; and signs of an emerging struggle within the Coup Group for political supremacy.

The forcing out of Khuang Aphaiwong in 1948 (described in the previous chapter) was not an outright coup d'état. It was a strange political event, for while parliamentary democracy was technically maintained, force was used to push aside the legally elected government.[1] In addition, the new prime minister, Phibun, was openly designated by the Coup Group, a body outside the parliamentary system that had no legal rights under the constitution to act the way it did. Thus the Thai political system was, at that point, dual in structure. That is, there existed a constitution, a parliament, and a cabinet responsible to parliament—alongside a dominant extra-legal structure represented by the Coup Group.

An uneasy accommodation between the two structures existed from 1948 until the end of 1951. Parliament, with its limited powers, was still a reality and efforts were made by Phibun to penetrate and co-opt as many MPs as possible through bribery and mild persuasion. But the politics of this period showed the characteristic weaknesses of this parliament—lack of party solidarity,[2] opportunism, and excessive

---

[1] See Chapter One. One suspects that it was because Phibun was still conscious of his tainted international image and, perhaps, also because he remembered his own historical role in bringing "democracy" to Thailand, that parliament was allowed to exist. Furthermore, in 1948 Phibun badly needed the support of the United States, and this would be less easy to obtain if parliament was overthrown.

[2] Thai parties at this point did not have a mass organization or base. Parties were loose associations of MPs in parliament who joined together for various reasons, many of which were personal and opportunistic (as we shall see later).

personal ambitions—all of which facilitated the Coup Group's growing penetration. All the same, it was not until the Radio Coup (also known as "Silent Coup") of November 29, 1951, through which the Khuang Constitution of 1949 was replaced by the old 1932 version, that the Coup Group felt confident of its grip on parliament.

After the military coup of 1947, force became the political common currency in an unprecedented way. After the coup against Phraya Mano in 1933, government authority had rested upon the letter of the constitution and no further coups occurred. The coup of 1947 marked the beginning of a new political era in which constitutionalism declined as a source of political legitimacy. Force became the ultimate weapon, for even the so-called liberals (Pridi and the Seri Thai people) attempted to use it. Perhaps the spirit of militarism, the cult of leadership, and the emphasis on national and military prowess that were main themes of Phibun's wartime policies also had their effects on young military officers. The 1947 Coup Group certainly had no balancing civilian component, unlike the 1932 Promoters. Thus parliament necessarily had less legitimacy, and the search began for new nonparliamentary bases of legitimacy.

PHIBUN AND A HOSTILE PARLIAMENT, 1948–1951

When Khuang was forced out and Phibun became prime minister, the Coup Group faced a hostile parliament. Perhaps guided by Thai and Buddhist concepts of moderation, and certainly urged on by political expediency, Phibun tried to get the backing of parliament through political means. Persuasion and bribery were used to lure parliamentary leaders into accepting ministerial portfolios.[3] The relative ease with which this was accomplished indicated that party solidarity was not strong enough to restrain personal ambitions and individual animosities.

Phibun's first post-war cabinet, formed on April 8, 1948, was a reflection of the Coup Group's attempt to gain public credibility and acceptance. Phibun and Luang Chatnakrop were the only prominent members of the Coup Group holding ministerial positions. Phibun was both Prime Minister and Minister of the Interior. Luang Chat retained his previous job of defense minister. A minor member of the Coup Group, Colonel Nom Ketinut, was given the position of Deputy Minister of Agriculture. The rest of the cabinet was composed of Phibun's close friends, such as Lt. General Mangkon, respected bureaucrats (old aristocrats), and members of parliament. The most interesting feature of this cabinet, however, was the number of ministers without portfolio. Of the nine members in this category, eight were MPs.[4] Two of the eight were supporters of the 1947 coup.[5] Three were MPs from the Issara

---

[3] Phibun tried to persuade Khuang and members of his cabinet to join the new government so that Phibun's regime would appear more acceptable to the people as well as to the international community's major powers. Khuang and the former ministers refused, forcing Phibun to turn to MPs who were in opposition to Khuang. See Frank C. Darling, *Thailand and the United States* (Washington, DC: Public Affairs Press, 1965), p. 66.

[4] *Banthuk Phonngan khong Ratthaban Chomphon P. Phibun Songkhram rawang Ph. S. 2491–2499* [An Account of the Achievements of the Government of Field Marshal P. Phibun Songkhram, 1948–1956], Government Printing Office, Bangkok, 1957, pp. 1, 2. Cabinet appointed April 15, 1948.

[5] Nai Worakanbancha was an acknowledged financial backer of the 1947 coup; Khemchat Bunyaratthaphan was a close associate of Luang Kat.

(Independent Party) and two were nominal Democrats.[6] Liang Chaiyakan, head of the Prachachon (People's Party), which had acted as opposition to the Khuang government, was the only MP who received an influential portfolio—deputy minister of the interior. For a short period Kukrit Pramote, a leading Democrat, was also given the post of deputy minister of commerce, but he resigned over the issue of a salary raise for MPs.

After the promulgation of the Khuang Constitution in 1949, partial elections were held in nineteen provinces to elect an additional twenty-one representatives.[7] The elections gave the government more supporters, yet to retain the support of its MPs the Coup Group had to concede still more cabinet positions to them. Phibun's new government, which was formed on June 28, 1949, reflected this shift.[8] While Phibun controlled the ministry of defense, the MPs upgraded their status from ministers without portfolio to definite assignments at ministries. Six of the seven MPs in the previous cabinet were given ministries. (Only one became a full minister; the others were appointed as deputy ministers.) Also, a prominent former Democrat MP from the Northeast, Thep Chotinuchit, was appointed minister without portfolio after he left the Democrat Party to form his own Ratsadon (Citizen's) Party, which backed Phibun's government.

Cabinet assignment was done according to a rough quota formula. This Phibun-designed quota system is documented by Samut Surakhaka, who speculated that there were three basic considerations at stake.[9] First, MPs who defected from the Democrat Party had to be given ministerial portfolios or positions as secretaries to ministers. Second, members of the Coup Group and those whom Phibun saw as having special qualifications must be assigned key jobs. Third, members of parties that belonged to the Sahaphak,[10] or United Front, which backed Phibun, had to get two cabinet positions per party. This basic scheme for the division of spoils was not followed to the letter and thus it became the source of much haggling and friction between the Coup Group and its parliamentary supporters.

The cabinet formed on June 28, 1949 consisted of twenty-five members in all. Phibun himself controlled defense and foreign affairs in addition to being prime minister. Of the other twenty-four members, twelve were from four parties, each of which received its quota; the rest were appointed. Five belonged to the Thammathipat Party, which was formed by Luang Wichit Wathakan in an attempt to provide Phibun with his own party. (It was headed by Lt. General Mangkon, Phibun's close associate since 1932.) Liang Chaiyakan's Prachachon Party received three positions and the Independent Party two, while the other two went to former Democrats. The Thammathipat Party received the most favorable treatment, being in a way the Coup Group's own party. This division of the spoils led to criticisms by

---

[6] Because of personal ambitions, these five MPs sacrificed party affiliation for cabinet appointments.

[7] *Constitution of Thailand, B.E. 2492* [1949]. Article 87 stipulates that there shall be one representative to every 150,000 persons in one province. Previously, one MP represented 200,000 persons. Hence elections were held to adjust to this new constitutional requirement.

[8] *Banthuk Phonngan,* pp. 4–6, Cabinet appointed June 28, 1949.

[9] Samut, *26 Kanpattiwat,* pp. 500, 501.

[10] Sahaphak, or United Front, was a coalition of parties in parliament that supported Phibun for political gains, such as cabinet positions and other privileges. It was also known as the "Phibun Forever" group.

members of the Prachachon, which actually held a majority of seats in the Sahaphak.[11] Members of the Prachachon Party thought that they should have received more cabinet positions, or at least the ministerial secretaryships that were instead allotted to seven Democrat turncoats.

Phibun's coalition government faced its first test in July when the Democrat Party tried to maintain its hold over its members by calling for a vote of confidence on the government. It threatened to expel those nine members who had joined Phibun's government if they did not vote with the party against Phibun. After long debates over the qualifications of three ministers,[12] no conclusion was forthcoming until the presence of Phao was announced.[13] Phao was greatly feared by all MPs after the recent assassination of the four Seri Thai former ministers.[14] Needless to say, parliament gave the government its stamp of approval by a count of 63 to 31.

A word on the nature of Thai parties at that time is perhaps in order here. Thai political parties were not mass parties. Rather, they were parliamentary clubs where personal interests and individualities determined party structure. Seats were won through local popularity and prominence, rather than on political platforms. Principle and ideology were not the underlying foundations of parties. Authority was not formally hierarchical, but pyramidal in nature, and thus its basic characteristic was heterogeneity and fragmentation. Figure I illustrates this phenomena.

Figure I
Authority Relationships in Thai Parties

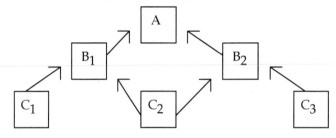

The authority relationships between the titular party leader represented by A and the various party members represented by B and C show A's lack of full control.

---

[11] After the elections of June 5, 1949, the composition of parliament and ministerial appointments was as shown below. The Thammathipat Party supported Phibun. Samut, *26 Kanpattiwat*, p. 498.

Party	MP	Minister	Secretary to the Minister
Democrat	40	2	7
Prachachon	31	3	
Issara	14	2	
Thammathipat	12	5	
Independents	24	2	

[12] The ministers in question were Lt. General Mangkon (close friend of Phibun), Khemchat (Kat's associate), and Liang (head of the Prachachon).

[13] Liang allegedly telephoned Phao, requesting him to come and make his presence felt. See Samut, *26 Kanpattiwat*, pp. 505, 506.

[14] See Chapter One on the assassination of the four Seri Thai ministers. Phao's presence was intimidation enough to convince nine Democrats, then, to vote against their own party.

Party regulations and sanctions were nonexistent or inoperative. A had to rely upon his personal contacts with each individual to maintain party solidarity. While A's relationship to B_1 and B_2 might be direct and strong, its connections with C_1, C_2, and C_3 were usually indirect and weak. Members at the C level often joined A's party mainly because of friendship with members at the B level rather than through any attraction to A. The lack of consistent horizontal and vertical links generated by ideology and tight organization weakened party solidarity even further. Party groupings were thus the result of periodic overlaps of political interests. When interests changed, there were corresponding shifts in party affiliation and unity. In this respect, unless A could provide party members with jobs and monetary support, A would be unable to hold the ruling party together.

The fragmented nature of Thai political parties is further illustrated by the behavior of the nine Democrats who put personal ambitions above party loyalty. Another good indication was the breakdown of the Prachachon. After receiving only three cabinet jobs, the Prachachon called for a meeting of the Sahaphak to air its grievances. A group of Prachachon members also threatened to resign to form a new party, attacking Liang as incompetent.[15] Liang himself threatened to resign as party head.

The breakup of the Prachachon appears to have been a political scheme designed by Phibun. In his first cabinet, Liang had been given the job of deputy minister of the interior while Phibun himself was minister. Since Phibun did not supervise day-to-day work in the ministry, Liang got quite a free hand. Through his control of the interior department, Liang was able to attract many followers to his party and he used his position to influence the outcome of the elections of 1949. However, Liang himself was well aware of his tenuous position, for he said:

> … politicians are like birds sitting on a tree. The tree is analogous to the political party. When the tree bears lots of fruits, i.e., plentiful money and privileges, MPs will leave their parties and join it.[16]

Phibun's second cabinet marked the eclipse of Liang's "tree." Lt. General Mangkon was appointed minister of the interior and Liang was instructed not to act independently without Mangkon's authorization. Since Mangkon was head of the Thammathipat Party, this party now became the most luscious tree around.

Phibun would have preferred to deal with only one party, the Thammathipat Party, of whose loyalty he was assured. After the breakup of the Prachachon had been engineered, meetings of the Sahaphak were referred to by Phibun as Thammathipat Party meetings. Those who did not object to the label received monetary bonuses.[17] However, the Prachachon did not totally disintegrate; it merely gave rise to two splinter parties. Of the fourteen members who resigned, some joined the Thammathipat Party, while others banded together to form the Chatsangkhom (National Socialist Party), led by Colonel Banyat, a Coup Group member. This small

---

[15] "Incompetence" here refers to the Prachachon's inability to snag more ministerial appointments for its members, although it was the largest party in the Sahaphak. Though Liang got the position of deputy minister of the interior, he felt that the Coup Group had been unjust in dividing up cabinet appointments. Samut, *26 Kanpattiwat,* pp. 506, 507.

[16] Samut, *26 Kanpattiwat,* p. 511.

[17] Ibid. Samut maintains that funds were obtained through illegal opium trading.

party with its ten members split again six months later and the Ratsadon Party emerged under the guidance of Thep Chotinuchit, a former Democrat. Both parties continued to support Phibun.[18] Party formation appears to have been a useful tactic for obtaining cabinet appointments. To join the Thammathipat Party was not a profitable move for ambitious MPs, however, because that party already had five ministerial posts—more than its fair share. The logical move was to form a new party, which could then bargain for cabinet representation in return for its support.

THE RADIO COUP OF NOVEMBER 29, 1951

The political configurations prior to the coup of 1951 were indicative of the instability of the Coup Group's control of the cabinet and parliament. Basically, five groups could be discerned. The first was composed of important members of the Coup Group who chose to hold on to their official jobs and were not directly involved in parliamentary politics. These were people like Phin, the Commander-in-Chief of the Army; Sarit, the First Army Commander; Phao, the Director General of the Police Department; and Fuen, the Commander-in-Chief of the Air Force. The second group included members of the Coup Group who left their regular jobs in the armed forces to take part in politics as well as several MPs who supported the 1947 coup. Such men were Banyat[19] who headed the National Socialist Party; Major General Sawat; Nai Worakan; and Khemchat. Also included in this group were men personally close to Phibun, such as Mangkon, head of the Thammathipat Party. The third component of the political spectrum comprised the other members of the Sahaphak who, for personal gains, supported Phibun after the coup. These men belonged to the Prachachon, Ratsadon, and Issara parties and were the most difficult for Phibun to control. The fourth group was Khuang's Democrat Party, which acted as an unofficial parliamentary opposition. The fifth category included members of the senate who had been elected earlier by a Democrat-controlled house.

Friction within the Sahaphak between those belonging to the Coup Group and the other political parties constantly threatened the organization. The row over ministerial assignments and favoritism within the Sahaphak described earlier is an example. The relationship between the factions was also in constant jeopardy because of the blunt manner in which certain members of the Coup Group expressed their ideas in public. It was difficult for military officers to grasp the intricacies of political bargaining, and so their remarks became a source of embarrassment for Phibun. For example, Major General Banyat, head of the National Socialist Party, said in an interview with the press that there were only three parties, which really

---

[18] For studies of the development of Thai political parties, see Khachatphai Burutphat, *Kanmuang lae Phakkanmuang khong Thai* [Thai Politics and Political Parties] (Bangkok: Odeon Store Press, 1968); and Chaowat Sutlapha, *Phakkanmuang* [Political Parties] (Bangkok: Sahasayam Phatthana Press, 1968).

[19] Maj. General Banyat Thephasdin na Ayutthaya was Sarit's second in command of the First Regiment during the 1974 coup. Cremation Volume of Sarit Thanarat [Cabinet edition], p. 41. His party was called Chatsangkhom, not to be confused with Sarit's Chatsangkhomniyom Party, formed in 1958.

backed the Phibun government: the National Socialist Party, the Thammathipat Party, and the Agriculturalist Party.[20]

Reaction from the other parties within the Sahaphak was immediate and vehement. Liang's *Prachachon*, Pathom Phokaeo's Independent Party, and Thep's Citizens' Press Party sent a joint letter to Phibun demanding Banyat's resignation from the cabinet. The letter was worded in the most scathing and derogatory terms:

> Although fancying himself a politician, his [Banyat's] brashness, bordering upon ignorant pride, exposes him as nothing but a novice. If there were to be mentally incompetent people within the government and the Sahaphak, there is no doubt that your [Phibun's] government will become tainted. We therefore urge that this ignoramus of a politician be booted out of the cabinet immediately.[21]

Civilian politicians in the Sahaphak continued to try to dam the advances of the Coup Group into the political arena. In 1951, a law was passed to make the Railway Corporation an autonomous government enterprise and positions were open for members of its board of directors.[22] Conflict arose between the Coup Group's choice of Major Praman Adireksan over the objections of Prasert Sudbanthat, the deputy minister of communications. Prasert objected because Praman was already the director of the Rapid Transportation Organization.[23] When Praman was appointed despite Prasert's strong objections, the latter resigned. He criticized the Coup Group's meddling in the affairs of the communications ministry and said that he was unable to tolerate such a "comedy" any longer.[24]

In other instances, however, the Coup Group had to give in to the demands of the MPs to obtain assurance of their continuing support. One source of headache and bitterness to the Phibun government was the political pressure exerted by the Isan MPs, whose momentary regional solidarity, cutting across party affiliations, gave them bargaining leverage. On December 21, 1950, Liang called a meeting of all MPs from Isan to ask them to demand at least twenty million baht for the development of the Northeast.[25] Subsequently, the Isan MPs formed the "Isan Camp" in parliament, which was determined to become involved in the drafting of all money bills concerned with allocations for development. A memo was drafted, signed by thirty Isan MPs, and presented to Phibun, demanding a share in the development funds that would be applied to the Isan region. Phibun received the memo with outward

---

[20] Press interview, Bangkok, August 25, 1951. This occurred prior to the 1952 elections. The Agriculturalist Party (Kasikammakon) was only "agriculturist" in name. Nai Worakan was its head, and Admiral Luang Yutthasat was among its more prominent members.

[21] Quoted in Samut, *26 Kanpattiwat*, p. 542.

[22] *Phraratchabanyat Kanrotfai haeng Prathet Thai, B.E. 2494* [Thai Railway Decree, 1951]. *Ratchakitcha*, vol. 68, section 40, 1951, p. 1.

[23] The Rapid Transportation Organization was a government enterprise that handled land transportation, trucking, and busing. The rivalry, however, went deeper, for the two were contesting the lone seat to parliament from Saraburi and both wanted the Coup Group's support.

[24] *Sayam Samai*, June 17, 1951.

[25] Samut, *26 Kanpattiwat*, p. 559. For the historical basis of Isan regionalism and the relationship between the central government and the northeast region, see Charles F. Keyes, *Isan: Regionalism in Northeastern Thailand*, Data Paper No. 65 (Ithaca, NY: Cornell Southeast Asia Program, 1967).

calm and promised to allot twenty million baht for Isan's development. Phibun's action gave the Coup Group a short "reprieve." Phibun himself was publicly praised at a Sanam Luang rally by the Isan MPs.

Playing on their collective bargaining strength, the thirty MPs now petitioned Phibun to dismiss three ministers, namely Major General Banyat, General Mangkon, and Lt. General Phao P. Boriphanyutthakit.[26] Their reason for this bold demand was that the three were not MPs of the first category, that is, elected by the people, but rather were only appointed MPs. Furthermore, Isan MPs belonging to the Sahaphak threatened to withhold their support for Phibun until he reorganized his cabinet. Faced with this crisis, a compromise was devised where the ministers of communications and education resigned and two Isan MPs were given those jobs.[27]

Although this was a momentary success for the civilian politicians, their actions deeply annoyed the Coup Group, which came to realize that, as long as the 1949 Constitution was in force, it would have to deal with the Isan MPs and other MPs in the Sahaphak at a handicap, for the constitution restricted its power to maneuver.[28]

The Coup Group's parliamentary weakness is also apparent when one examines the actions of the senate with regard to government proposals. A case in point was the failure of the passage of a government bill on new election procedures. Phibun wanted soldiers and policemen to be able to vote in districts where they were stationed, but the senate argued that they should vote at their domiciles. The senate, it seems, wanted to prevent block voting by troops who could be instructed to line up and vote as their commanding officers saw fit. So the senate defeated Phibun's bill by a vote of 37 to 7.[29]

The Coup Group also came under censure by the senate for its purge of the navy following the Manhattan Rebellion. The senate met on October 27, 1951 to question the government's harsh action against the navy and especially the unfortunate sinking of the *Si Ayutthaya*. The debate was heated, and the senate characterized the government's sinking of the flagship as rash and excessive. Air Chief Marshal Fuen was present during the questioning and was angered by the senate's reprimands. On October 30, after more attacks from the senators, Phibun countered by stating that harsh measures had been needed to unify the armed forces against the growing dangers of a communist plot. He continued by saying that, even as the senate was meeting, the police had unearthed a plan for a communist takeover the very next day, and that army and police forces were on the alert. Parliament was already "surrounded" to ensure the lawmakers' "safety."[30] This was an outright threat to the senate, cautioning its members to step lightly upon the interests of the Coup Group.

---

[26] Lt. General Phao P. Boriphanyutthakit is not to be confused with Police General Phao Siyanon, one of the main 1947 coup leaders.

[27] General Phraya Thephasadin, the Minister of Commerce, and Lt. General Sawat, the Minister of Education, had been in poor health, and thus their resignations were easy to procure. Sawat was, however, an important Coup Group member and was thus elevated to Assistant Prime Minister. Pathom Phokaeo was given the commerce portfolio, and Liang became education minister. *Banthuk Phonngan*, pp. 7, 8.

[28] *Constitution of Thailand, B.E. 2492*, Article 93, section 5 prohibits government and military officials on active duty from entering elections.

[29] *Raingan Kanprachum Wutthisapha*, November 2, 1951. The senate had the power to delay bills for one year.

[30] Samut, *26 Kanpattiwat*, p. 553.

Another source of annoyance to the Coup Group was the growing militancy of university students, especially at Thammasat. Thai versions of the Stockholm peace movement, which demonstrated against the use of nuclear armaments, emerged in the early 1950s. A Thai peace committee was formed, headed by an MP from Pattani and a Buddhist monk, with the goal of gathering as many signatures as possible to support the peace movement.[31] This movement met with support from Thammasat students who organized their own Student League for Peace in June 1951. The students deplored the fact that more government money was expended for war and on the armed forces than for education. A manifesto was presented to Phibun and the king. The government struck back, however. The students involved were interrogated by the police and, subsequently, seven of them were suspended for one year for "being involved in politics."

During this politically volatile business, the Manhattan Rebellion took place on June 29, 1951, and Thammasat University was occupied by Pridi and used as his headquarters. After the rebels were routed, soldiers occupied the campus and it was converted into an army barracks. The ministry of defense even attempted to purchase Thammasat from the government. The students countered by offering to outbid the army for Thammasat and demanded that the soldiers from Saraburi vacate the classrooms. The students showed no respect for Lt. General Sawat, the newly appointed rector, who cautioned the students in typical military style that he was not to be treated lightly. The situation was getting out of hand when the students ignored Sawat and marched to parliament to protest Thammasat's "occupation." Phibun was more diplomatic when he met the students. He seemed to show respect for the students, and called them his children. He assured them that he would return Thammasat to them shortly. Indeed, this was accomplished in October, one month before the Radio (Silent) Coup.

Phibun's inability to fully control the Sahaphak MPs, to engage the senate under the 1949 Constitution, and to contain the rising militancy of the students acted as a rationale for still another coup d'état. This came in the form of a radio announcement on November 29, 1951, suspending parliament and abrogating the 1949 Constitution in favor of the 1932 edition.

The radio announcement gave several reasons for this new seizure of power.[32] First and foremost, the international situation and the communist threat were mentioned. Communists were allegedly infiltrating parliament and the cabinet, and no matter how hard the government tried to solve this problem, it could not do so within existing constitutional limits. The coup d'état was carried out mainly in order that the 1932 Constitution could be reimplemented to facilitate changes and the improvement of prevailing political conditions.[33] The announcement was made in the name of the army, the navy, the air force, the 1932 promoters, the 1947 Coup Group, and patriots who wanted to preserve the ideals of nation, religion, the house of Chakkri, and constitutionalism. It is interesting to note here that, for the first time, the communist threat (both internal and external) was used as a major justification for a coup d'état.[34] A national executive council was formed consisting of nine senior

---

[31] Ibid., p. 573.

[32] Pla Thong, *Phakkanmuang*, p. 190. Also see Chit Wiphathawat, *Phao Saraphab* [Phao Confesses] (Bangkok: Phrae Phitthaya Press, 1960), pp. 6–15, concerning the announcements.

[33] *Proclamation No. 1*, November 29, 1951.

[34] The development of domestic communist organizations had been weak. In 1946, the Central Labor Union (CLU) was formed, allegedly backed by Pridi supporters. Initial Thai leadership

officers—three each from the army, the navy, and the air force. The most important members were Sarit and Phin from the army. While not officially a member of the council, Phao was given charge of internal peace and security in his capacity as director general of police.[35] Political gatherings were banned and political parties accordingly ceased to function.[36]

As parliament was dissolved after the coup, an appointed senate came into existence under the 1932 Constitution.[37] This body acted as the legislature until elections could be held for members of the lower house. Phibun's new cabinet was given the expected unanimous approval by the senate. The 1932 Constitution did not bar the participation of civil servants or active military officers in either the cabinet or parliament. Hence we find that Phibun's cabinet was composed of men simultaneously holding two types of job—bureaucratic and political. An examination of the two cabinets formed on June 28, 1949, and December 8, 1951, gives a clear indication that the coup was planned precisely to end the Coup Group's dependence on civilian MPs of the Sahaphak and to increase its grip on the cabinet and parliament.

Table 1
Cabinet Members and Affiliations

Position/Deputies	June 28, 1949	December 8, 1951
Prime Minister	Field Marshal Phibun (1932/1947)	Field Marshal Phibun (1932/1947/1951) Gen. Phin (1947/1951) Air Vice Marshal Muni (1951)
Defense	Field Marshal Phibun (1932/1947)	Field Marshal Phibun (1932/1947/1951) Rear Admiral Luang Sunawin (Thammathipat/1951) Lt. Gen. Sarit (1947/1951)
Interior	Lt. Gen. Mangkon (Thammathipat)	Maj. Gen. Banyat (1947/1951) Police Lt. Gen. Phao (1947/1951) Lt. Gen. Det (1951)
Foreign Affairs	Field Marshal Phibun (1932/1947) Phote (expert)	Nai Worakan (1947/1951)

soon fell into the hands of the Chinese, who represented the majority of the rank and file. The CLU joined the World Federation of Trade Unions in 1949, and it became influenced by Chinese Communists. See David A. Wilson, "Thailand and Marxism," in *Marxism in Southeast Asia*, ed. Frank N. Traeger (Stanford, CA: Stanford University Press, 1959), p. 82. After the 1951 coup, Phibun's government cracked down on suspected Chinese communists and closed down the *Chuan Min Pao*, a Chinese newspaper, on communist charges.

[35] Wilson, "Thailand and Marxism," p. 82.

[36] *Proclamation No. 5*, November 29, 1951.

[37] Khachatphai, *Kanmuang*, p. 199. The senate was mainly composed of officers of the armed forces and police. There were a few civil servants in that body. Also see *Proclamation No. 2*, November 29, 1951, and Withetkorani (pseud.), *Khwampenma haeng Rabob Prachathipatai khong Thai* [History of Thai Democracy] (Bangkok: Phanfa Phitthaya Press, 1968), pp. 1387–1393, which shows a list of the appointees. Out of the 123 appointees, 106 were either police or military officers.

Finance	Prince Wiwatchai (expert)	Maj. Gen. Phao P. (expert)
	Sawat (Issara)	Maj. Gen. Prayoon (1932)
	Nai Worakan (1947)	
Education	Maj. Gen. Sawat (1947)	Gen. Mangkon (Thammathipat)
		Air Vice Marshal Luang Cherd (1951)
Communications	Lt. Gen. Phraya Thephasdin (expert)	Air Marshal Fuen (1951)
	Pathom (Issara)	Rear Admiral Luang Chamnan (1951)
		Col. Praman (1947/1951)
Justice	Phra Manuphan (expert)	Phra Nittitham (expert)
	Kemchat (1947)	
Commerce	Maj. Gen. Phao P. (expert)	Luang Wichit (Thammathipat)
		Col. Siri Siriyothin (1947)
Agriculture	Phra Chuang (expert)	Rear Admiral Luang Yutthasat (1951)
	Fuen (Prachachon)	Police Col. Lamai (1947/1951)
Industry	Sukich (Thammathipat)	Sukich (Thammathipat)
Public Health	Phraya Borirak (expert)	Phraya Borirak (expert)
	Nom (1947)	
Without Portfolio	Maj. Gen. Plod (Thammathipat)	Khemchat (1947)
	Luang Sunawin (Thammathipat)	
	Capt. Prasert (Thammathipat)	
	Col. Banyat (1947)	
	Luang Atthaphon (Prachachon)	
	Khun Khongrit (Democrat)	
	Thep (Democrat/Ratsadon)	

Source: Compiled from *Banthuk Phonngan*, pp. 4–6, 10–12.[38]

A brief glance at the two cabinets reveals that while the June 28, 1949 cabinet was bottom heavy, the December 8, 1951 cabinet was top heavy. This is to say that while the December 8 cabinet found Phibun sharing the critical ministries with other Coup Group members, the June 28 cabinet did not reflect the Coup Group's real power. Also, the June 28 cabinet had seven ministers without portfolio while the December 8 cabinet had only one.

For the first time, deputy prime ministers were appointed in the December 8 cabinet. Control of the defense ministry was also divided up and power shared with other members of the Coup Group. Whereas in the 1949 cabinet there were six members of the 1947 Coup Group, the 1951 government had ten. It is also clear that after the 1951 coup, no former members of the Sahaphak (except the Thammathipat Party) received cabinet appointments.

Another consideration behind the coup, as Frank Darling points out, was the expected return of young King Bhumibol from Switzerland in late 1951.[39] This would be the first time that the king would take up residence in the country since his

---

[38] The reason why the cabinet of June 28 was chosen over Phibun's April 8, 1948 cabinet was that Phibun's cabinet had been put together after Khuang was ousted, at a time when political lines were not too clearly demarcated. The June 28 cabinet was chosen because it was formed after the elections of 1949 and reflected the consequent political configurations. The cabinet of December 8, 1951 (with readjustments on December 11 and 15) was similarly chosen over the interim November 29, 1951, cabinet.

[39] Darling, *Thailand and the United States*, pp. 91–94.

brother's death. The Coup Group leaders were afraid that the king might become the instrument of the old royalist-inclined senate, which would urge him to exercise his prerogatives as stipulated under the 1949 Constitution.[40] Thus the coup was timed to coincide with the king's return and to present him with a fait accompli.

Hence, by early 1952, the Coup Group held full sway over the government as well as the country's legislature. The senate was already completely appointed by the Coup Group.[41] The lower house fell under its control after the 1952 elections. Since political parties were defunct, candidates had to run independently. The Coup Group fielded many candidates and backed them with financial support.[42] Opposition candidacies were negligible in number for Khuang, and the Democrats boycotted the elections, claiming that they were immoral.[43] The eventual estimated division of seats was as follows: Pro-government—85 seats; Independents—9 seats; and Opposition—29 seats.[44]

INTERNATIONAL CONSTRAINTS AND INFLUENCE OVER THE RISE OF THE MILITARY

The resurgence of the military to political leadership in Thailand cannot be viewed solely from within the framework of domestic Thai politics. International constraints and influences were important factors in the military's post-war entrenchment in Thai politics. Darling feels that the initial failure of the United States government to support Sir Josiah Crosby's post-war recommendations regarding the reorganization of the Thai armed forces marked the ultimate doom of any post-war liberal government.

> The most serious weakness of American intervention in these negotiations was the failure to support the British proposal to reduce the power and prestige of the Thai armed forces as previously recommended by Sir Josiah Crosby. This move was to have profound repercussions in post-war politics in Thailand. A unique opportunity for the Western democracies to weaken the authoritarian political tradition by reorganizing the armed forces and discouraging military interference in politics was thereby neglected.[45]

Sir Josiah Crosby, who had been the British Minister in Bangkok prior to the war, had recommended that Thailand be treated as an enemy state and that the country be liable for punishment.[46] He had wanted some kind of supervision of the country, probably by a British-led delegation, and had urged the Allies to impose sanctions on

---

[40] Article 30 allows the king to delay the passage of a bill by refusing to endorse it. Articles 78 and 79 allow the king to dismiss any cabinet member, or the whole cabinet, through royal decree.

[41] Withetkorani, *Khwampenma*, pp. 1,387–1,393.

[42] Pla Thong, *Phakkanmuang*, p. 201. Phao was the government's campaign organizer and fundraiser.

[43] Chit, *Phao Saraphab*, p. 39.

[44] Darling, *Thailand and the United States*, p. 118. Estimate obtained from Prince Chula Chakrabongse, "Siam's Anti-Communist Role," *Standard*, May 22, 1954.

[45] Darling, *Thailand and the United States*, pp. 43, 44.

[46] Sir Josiah Crosby, "Observations on a Post-War Settlement in Southeast Asia," *International Affairs* (July 1944), p. 362. From Darling, *Thailand and the United States*, p. 40.

the Thai armed forces similar to those used on Germany and Japan. He had also expressed the view that liberal democracy in Thailand could not be implemented if the powerful army was not decisively weakened.[47]

The United States, on the other hand, relying on the advice of old Thai hands such as former Ambassador Dr. Kenneth Landon and Abbot Moffat, was suspicious of any British attempt to reestablish itself as an influential power in Thailand.[48] The Americans viewed Crosby's demands as an excuse for continuing interference in the domestic affairs of Thailand. Anti-colonial feeling, then on an upsurge in US political thinking, played its part—with many Americans wanting to see the United States as a liberator and not as a suppressor of the self-determination of small countries.

We have seen how, in view of the United States' moderate stance on a post-war settlement for Thailand, Seni Pramote was the natural choice for prime minister in 1945. He was believed to have some influence with the US authorities because of his wartime collaboration with them. The Thai government exploited the differences between the United States and Great Britain to whittle down the demands made upon their country. Darling reveals that extensive British demands were mitigated by the friendly attitude of the United States and by US pressure on Britain to tone down its claims.[49]

Thus the structure of the Thai armed forces was, in the end, not too greatly damaged except for the weak efforts of the post-war civilian governments to cut back the army. With the benefit of hindsight, one can suggest that a coup such as that of November 1947 was inevitable since the essentially unreconstructed army, accustomed to power, would continue to demand a major share of the political cake, if not the whole thing.

Changes in international circumstances and in international power configurations after 1945 made a military takeover in Thailand an increasingly plausible adventure. As Western Powers became more and more concerned with the Cold War and the communist threat in Asia and Eastern Europe, they became less and less interested in the struggle between liberalism and authoritarianism in the non-Western world. A stable, strong government was seen as essential, regardless of the type of regime. In 1946 the United States was already providing military aid to Greece and Turkey, and loud concern was being expressed over the fate of China and other Asian countries. By 1948—when Czechoslovakia fell to the communists, China's Chiang Kai-shek was clearly faltering, and communist guerrillas were rapidly expanding their strength in Vietnam and Malaya—Thailand, relatively free from any viable communist force, was naturally seen as a possible stronghold that might impede the advance of the "communist menace." American opinion increasingly saw authoritarian right-wing regimes as acceptable partners in the fight against communism. As a result of these developments, the first Phibun government

---

[47] Sir Josiah Crosby, "The Failure of Constitutional Government in Siam," *The Asiatic Review* (October 1943), p. 420. From Darling, *Thailand and the United States*, p. 41.

[48] Darling, *Thailand and the United States*, p. 42. Also from an interview with Professor Lauristan Sharp.

[49] Ibid., p. 43. Among the things the British wanted were: compensation for property losses; a monopoly of foreign trade; the right to station military forces in the country; the right to reorganize the armed forces; and a monopoly of commercial airline operations in Bangkok. In short, the British were looking forward to a commercial domination of the country as well as the right to use Thailand for strategic military purposes.

was quickly recognized by the United States on May 3, 1948, and other countries followed suit.[50] Darling writes:

> Thus almost by coincidence the two years of liberal government in Thailand had coincided with the two-year transition in the foreign policy of the United States from the hope of peace and freedom in the early post-war period to a policy emphasizing peace and security in the new era of Communist aggression.[51]

With this shift in United States interests, Phibun saw his opportunity to remain in power. His control of the army had been taken over by Phin and the more forceful Sarit. Phao, too, was a rising political leader in his own right with the support of the police force. Phibun realized that he had no strong committed internal backing. To strengthen his tenuous position and make himself indispensable, he turned to foreign policy for salvation. After 1948, Phibun increasingly voiced his fear of the communist threat and moved Thailand closer to the United States. United States military and economic assistance in turn bolstered Phibun's position vis-à-vis the internal power structure and the Thai public at large.

Hence, when the remaining vestiges of civilian (conservative–royalist) elements within parliament were eliminated, the move was justified by the need for a more powerful executive to stem the tide of communist activities within the country. A month before the 1951 coup, Phibun had gravely informed a somewhat skeptical parliament that the police had unearthed a communist plot to overthrow his government.[52]

The Emergence of the Triumvirate

The early 1950s saw the maturation of two important personalities emerging from the 1947 Coup Group: Phao and Sarit. The domestic political scene was relatively calm following the various coups of 1947 to 1951, and Phao and Sarit were given the opportunity to build up their political prestige and power—thanks in part to the flow of aid from the United States, which Phibun had managed to generate. While Phao controlled and improved the police force, and also managed Phibun's post-1951 domestic political machinery, Sarit bided his time by getting rich and gathering supporters within the army, which he was to control after Phin's retirement. Phibun, on the other hand, searching for new bases of power, launched upon programs of closer identification with the United States, reinforced traditional concepts of legitimacy, sought a popular base through electoral support, and generally attempted to balance off the power rivalry between Phao and Sarit.

The parliament formed after the 1952 elections was heavily pro-government—as might be expected, since the reinstituted 1932 Constitution made half of parliament's seats appointed positions. To provide a structure for its parliamentary supporters,

---

[50] Ibid., p. 66.

[51] Ibid., pp. 67, 68.

[52] See David A. Wilson, *Politics in Thailand* (Ithaca, NY: Cornell University Press, 1962), pp. 28, 29. Largely for foreign policy reasons, anticommunism became a keystone of government policy. By the end of 1952, a wide roundup of suspects took place, which included the arrests of writers, intellectuals, young military officers, and several Chinese. Also, an "anticommunist act" was rushed through parliament.

and to sidestep the issue of political party formation, the Coup Group convened periodic meetings of its backers who were known collectively as the Sapha Nittibanyat, or Legislative Committee. In actual fact, it was the government party caucus that met to map out plans regarding the passage of bills. MPs were informed of and directed in their respective roles in parliament so that they could "perform" according to prearranged plans. This privileged group met at the Manangkhasila House, the government guesthouse, and received special compensation for their trouble.[53]

The organizing genius behind this group was Police General Phao, who turned to parliament to supplement his power. In his attempt to build a political following, Phao engaged deeply in the opium trade to amass enough money to "lubricate" his political machinery. Phao also saw to it that no other political groups were to be organized to rival his "committee." In a 1954 speech attacking the proposal of some MPs that political party legislation be enacted, Phao stated that parties were unnecessary and that a bill to regulate political parties would infringe upon the freedom of the MPs themselves.[54] He said that the difference between a democratic system and a communist one was that in the former, individuals could speak out without the aid of a party.[55] He reasoned that a law regulating political parties would limit the freedom of MPs for, according to the 1932 Constitution, parties could be formed without any limitations as long as they did not conflict with existing laws. He did not mention the fact that, after the 1951 coup, political gatherings were still banned under a Coup Group directive.

Phao, who was still in his early forties, was an ambitious man.[56] He was a capable organizer and administrator, but his views of domestic and international politics were unrefined. Everything he deemed communist he detested and everything he detested was labeled communist. Phao was raised and trained by the army but, because of political circumstances after the 1948 coup, he was transferred to the police department as the Coup Group's controlling agent there. Phao's rapid rise to fame was further enhanced by his marriage to Phin's daughter.

Under Phao, the police force expanded quickly, as he wanted to create an alternative power base outside the army (with which he was now no longer connected). After 1947, and the various attempts of other factions to capture power, force had become the acknowledged key to political success. Phao understood this perfectly and thus proceeded to build up the police as his own military force. The chain of command was tightened and esprit de corps among police officers was strengthened, through Phao's personal influence. To all appearances, the police force was to be turned into a second army. Since police officers had daily public duties to

---

[53] Pla Thong, *Phakkanmuang,* p. 206. The author contends that members of the legislative committee received a monthly allowance of 2,000 baht, as well as travel privileges to Europe and permission to import cars tax free. To finance this, Pla Thong felt that funds were taken directly from the national budget, government monopolies, and Phao's opium profits.

[54] Ibid., p. 214.

[55] Ibid.

[56] Chit, *Phao Saraphab,* p. 679. Chit had personally interviewed Phao in Geneva after the latter's exile. Phao confessed that his harsh actions were prompted by his own ambition— *khwamyakpen yai*—literally, "the desire to be big." For an account of Phao's (and Sarit's) involvement in the opium business to finance Phao's political career, see Alfred W. McCoy, *The Politics of Heroin in Southeast Asia* (New York, NY: Harper and Row, 1972), particularly pp. 136–145.

perform and did not have as much free time for exercises and indoctrination as did army recruits, it was difficult for Phao to create a truly army-style solidarity among his men. But he tried his best and came up with his own tight-knit group of officers-cum-bodyguards.

Phao's corps of followers was known as *asawin,* or "knights."[57] They were police officers who were singled out by Phao for the good work they had accomplished on his behalf. These "knights" could be recognized by the gold or diamond rings which Phao bestowed on them. They were even given special retainers by Phao. These men did Phao's dirty work and helped establish what several Thai writers have referred to as a "police state." In later years, Phao tried to shift the blame for this on to Phibun, but it is clear that extensive police brutality was committed under Phao's personal direction.[58] At its height, the police force had close to 43,000 men, a number large enough to stand as a serious rival to the army.

The United States had also been good to Phao.[59] It supplied the Thai police with tanks, armored cars, planes, helicopters, boats, and modern firearms.[60] The police even had their own paratroop division and the only paratroop training school in the country.[61] Another source of assistance was the CIA-affiliated Sea Supply Company, which trained Thai police in the art of guerrilla fighting.[62] Phao's public reason for

---

[57] *Asawin* means "the horsemen." George Bradley McFarland, *Thai–English Dictionary* (Stanford, CA: Stanford University Press, 1944). The word comes from two Vedic deities, twin sons of the sun or the sky. "They are ever young, handsome, bright, ... agile, swift as falcons."

[58] Chit, *Phao Saraphab,* p. 681. Phao told Chit that he was only Phibun's agent and did what he was ordered. This is hard to believe, for Phao could do what he pleased by then. Phibun had little real power.

[59] Darling, *Thailand and the United States,* p. 114.

[60]   **American Expenditures in Thailand: 1952–1955**

US Fiscal Year	Technical Cooperation (in dollars)	Economic Aid (defense support)
1952	7,200,000	--
1953	6,500,000	--
1954	8,800,000	--
1955	4,600,000	29,700,000

See Darling, *Thailand and the United States,* p. 103. Darling says that the money spent in direct support of the armed forces was a classified secret. However, another source reveals that military grants to Thailand were as follows:

US Fiscal Year	Military Grants (in millions of dollars)
1946–54	$111.2
1955	$40.8
1956	$43.4
1957	$26.2

John D. Montgomery, *The Politics of Foreign Aid* (New York, NY: Praeger Co., 1963), p. 283. In the period 1946–54, 85 percent of military aid was obligated in fiscal year 1953 and 1954. This coincided with the rapid development of both the police and army.

[61] With the help of the Sea Supply Company, Phao founded the first paratroop training school for police personnel in 1951. See *Wan Kongthap Bok, 2497* [Army Day, 1954].

[62] Chit, *Phao Saraphab,* p. 654. Little information is available regarding the Sea Supply Company and the extent of aid it provided the police.

such an extensive force was that it was necessary for communist suppression campaigns. This claim was perhaps made to please his American backers and to reduce army resentment. In reality, however, it was used mainly for political repression, and private gain, as we shall see below.

To finance his political machine in parliament as well as his personal followers in the police force, Phao had to resort to opium trading. It was an open secret that Phao's "knights" were involved in drug markets. In many cases, rewards were actually offered for the seizure of opium that slipped through Phao's monopolistic fingers.[63] While Phao's opium trade gave him the most returns, he also was involved in other businesses. Riggs's extensive study on the subject reveals that Phao was on the board of directors of no fewer than twenty-six companies.[64] His Swiss bank account was also legendary: after his exile in 1957, he was still able to live in style in Geneva, even hiring an English chauffeur.[65] Phao also took along with him two of his loyal "knights" and their families.

Phao's penetration of the political arena was the most extensive of any member of the Coup Group. He was its most dynamic worker and organizer, and his star rose rapidly after 1953. He held the positions of Police Chief, Deputy Minister of Defense, Deputy Minister of Finance, and official spokesman of the government in parliament. He was a feared personality because of his "security and intelligence" powers. At one time, he headed the cabinet's Political Affairs Bureau, which was in charge of investigating political dissenters.[66] He also headed a special committee to look into communist infiltration of the civil service.

Under Phao's guidance, the Criminal Investigation Division and the Crime Suppression Bureau acted with Gestapo-like harshness. Political agitators and people suspected of being anti-government (and hence "pro-communist") were arrested. Although no full accounting of those affairs has been made, a number of infamous cases did come out after Sarit's takeover. Only then was what had long been suspected factually substantiated. The execution of the four former Seri Thai ministers has been described earlier, but other cases of police brutality and atrocities emerged after Phao's eclipse.

Phao's unconventional methods for suppressing crime foreshadowed the methods he would be willing to use against enemies of the regime. Shortly after the Radio Coup, Bangkok newspapers carried a news item stating that seven bandits had been killed while planning a holdup. The incident occurred at a temple while the bandits were allegedly making their plans. They were not arrested, but summarily shot by the police. Parliament, although composed only of appointed senators, was shocked at such tactics and Phao was questioned over this new police method of killing suspects even before any crime had been committed. Phao replied that the police discovered (later) that all seven had police records and were wanted for many previous crimes.[67] The elimination of Phao's enemies followed a similar pattern.

---

[63] Samut, *26 Kanpattiwat*, pp. 515, 571. On one occasion, the police seized five tons of opium at Lopburi. When the contraband arrived at police headquarters in Bangkok, the opium turned out to be mud. A switch had occurred in transit while the opium was in police custody.

[64] Fred W. Riggs, *Thailand: The Modernization of a Bureaucratic Polity* (Honolulu, HI: East–West Center Press, 1967), p. 269, also see pp. 242–310.

[65] Chit, *Phao Saraphab*, p. 654.

[66] Darling, *Thailand and the United States*, p. 115, maintains that the CIA was involved in investigations and giving advice.

[67] Chit, *Phao Saraphab*, p. 58.

Force and violence were used to get rid of personal and political enemies. The dirty work was usually carried out by Phao's "knights," who acted to get the chief's approval and his gratitude (expressed in terms of monetary and status rewards). While the violent tactics of the police were well known and talked about, those actions were condemned only at the gossip level. Official investigation was impossible, for the crimes were committed by the police themselves. (Some of these cases did come to court immediately after the 1957 coup.)

For example, during the confusion of the 1949 Palace Coup, a personal enemy of Phao was indirectly implicated with the Pridi people. This man, Police Colonel Banchongsak Chippensuk, a police officer on inactive duty, was killed while "resisting arrest."[68] Colonel Banchongsak's name had been suggested by the rebels for the post of director of metropolitan police without his prior consent. After the suppression of the Seri Thai/Palace Coup, Colonel Banchongsak was to have been arrested. However, while he was in custody in his house, he was shot and killed.

Subsequent investigations in 1958 revealed that while Banchongsak was director of police in Lampang, he had been involved in intercepting and investigating opium shipments. Phao was behind these drug ventures, although he was not yet deputy police chief. Phao had sent one of his prototype *asawin*, Police Lieutenant Annop, to Lampang to supervise the opium operations. Colonel Banchongsak did not cooperate but instead tried his best to obstruct the opium traffic. In a later confrontation, after Phao became Deputy Director-General of Police and Banchongsak was promoted to Director of Metropolitan Police in Bangkok, the two had exchanged unkind words; at the time, physical violence was only prevented by the intervention of Luang Kat.[69]

Evidence produced at the 1958 investigation pointed out that Phao had ordered Banchongsak's arrest but not his execution. Phao's *asawin* (Annop) had overreacted in an attempt to please Phao. Phao was angry when he learned of the murder and is supposed to have remarked sadly that he was sorry that it all happened. He had instructed another of his men to bring Banchongsak in for questioning, but Annop went instead, perhaps to pursue a personal grudge. Phao even referred to the deceased as *Phi Banchong*.[70]

Other political murders by the police were cleared up when the government prosecuted several police officers implicated in the deaths of Phon Malithong and Phong Suwannasin.[71] The incident occurred on March 24, 1954, when the two were strangled, then thrown into the Chaophraya river, "Mafia style"—their bodies weighed down by concrete posts. Phon was an MP from Samutsakhon Province who had constantly reprimanded Phao in parliament for the police chief's unsavory activities. He had earlier been arrested on suspicion of involvement in the 1949 Palace Coup, but no evidence was found to support conviction. Many times in parliament Phon had berated Phao in front of the assembly and even rudely pointed at Phao's face. Phon's friends and relatives had warned him of the dangers of his bravery, but Phon had shrugged it off by saying that he was doing it for the good of

---

[68] San Aya [Criminal Court], Case no. (black) 1952/2501 and Case no. (red) 1551/2502. Black numbers refer to preliminary hearings and red numbers to the actual case on trial. There was no official notice put out for Banchongsak's arrest.

[69] Annop was the arresting officer who shot Col. Banchongsak while the latter was shaving. See testimony in San Aya, Case no. 1551/2502.

[70] Although he showed formal respect, Phao's sincerity was questionable.

[71] San Aya, Case no. (black) 2682, 2683/2501, and Case no. (red) 1691/2502.

the nation and that he was already advanced in age and death did not scare him. The police had been observing him constantly and various spies had been sent to keep an eye on his activities.[72]

One of the spies was Phong, a civilian police informer. According to testimony in the trial, Phong had revealed to Phon that the police had asked Phong to plant communist documents in Phon's house. Phong wanted some money so that he could retire to the south. Instead of agreeing to the blackmail, Phon reported the incident to Phao. Annop, who was in charge of the affair, was furious at Phong's treachery and Phon's audacity. Later Annop and Phon exchanged angry words. On the day of the crime, Phon was summoned to police headquarters for interrogation by Annop, and was never heard of again. Subsequent government investigation found out that both Phon and Phong were strangled and thrown into the river. Phon's car was also dismantled and parts scattered into the Chaophraya River to conceal evidence of the victims' whereabouts.

The most grisly political crime committed by the police was the elimination of five men, three of whom were former Seri Thai members accused by Phao of being communists. The disappearances of Tiang Sirikhan, Chan Bunnag and Lek Bunnag (brothers), Phong Khiewwichit, and Sanga Prachakwet were tied to police work in December of 1952. In 1958, fifteen defendants were charged with murder and concealing evidence during a government investigation.[73]

Tiang was a well-known Seri Thai from Isan. He was involved in the planning of the Sahaphan Rat Laemthong. In 1948, together with other Isan Seri Thai colleagues, he was arrested but later released.[74] His ties with Pridi and the Seri Thai movement were strong. Tiang was also the founder of the Sahachip Party, in 1946, which supported Pridi.[75] He was elected to parliament on February 26, 1952. After the elections, Phao approached Tiang and former members of the Sahachip Party, asking them to support the Phibun regime.[76] These MPs agreed, provided that their former party platform of the establishment of cooperatives be included in the government's policy and that the government refrain from accusing them of being communists. When Phao agreed, Tiang and his friends joined the legislative committee despite the fact that Phao had already eliminated other Seri Thai leaders in the sensational murder of the four former ministers. The Tiang-Phao cooperation did not last long, for it appears that Phao was determined to weaken the Sahachip MPs by getting rid of Tiang.

The Bunnag brothers had a long history of conflict with Phao, dating from the time when Phao was Phibun's personal aide. In 1942 the brothers were working at Chalerm Krung Theater, in Bangkok. One day their car was splashed by Phibun's limousine as it passed by. Its occupants shouted "hey" and laughed, not knowing that Phibun was in the other car. They were arrested and brought before Phibun, who allegedly challenged the brothers to fisticuffs. Phibun was angry because the

---

[72] Again, Annop was in charge.

[73] San Aya, Case no. (black) 2628/2501 and Case no. (red) 1542/2502.

[74] See Chapter One.

[75] Khachatphai, *Kanmuang*, pp. 176–181. The Sahachip Party advocated the socialist sentiments that were voiced in Pridi's Economic Development Plan.

[76] Chit, *Phao Saraphab*, p. 216. Chit estimates that there were about twenty members of the Sahachip group who were elected.

brothers did not accord him due respect as their *phunam,* or leader.[77] Later, Phao took up the harassment and forced the Bunnags out of work.

The brothers then went to work in the film industry on their own. Their first job was to help make the soundtrack for Pridi's English-language movie, *Chaophraya chang phuek* ("King of the White Elephant").[78] Their acquaintance with Pridi flourished and they later worked for the Seri Thai. After the war Chan was appointed senator but was ousted after the 1947 coup. Subsequently, the brothers were always interrogated whenever rumors of a coup cropped up.

Chan and Tiang became good friends during their Seri Thai stint. After the war, Tiang asked Chan to take in Phong Kiewwichit as an apprentice in the movie business. Phao had been eying Tiang and Chan for some time. Finally, in December 1952, the police acted. Chan, Lek, and Tiang were accused of being party to a coup attempt planned with "foreign backing" in October 1952 and the three were thoroughly investigated. Their final interrogation occurred in December, and the three, together with Phong and Sanga (Tiang's chauffeur), were never seen nor heard of afterward.

Tiang foresaw his impending doom and had told his MP friends to question Phao if he disappeared. At first, Phao denied any knowledge of the whereabouts of Tiang. But a few days later, at the legislative committee's meeting, he informed the members that Tiang was a communist and that he had fled to Victoria Point, in Burma, to escape arrest. Following that announcement, newspapers began to run articles on Tiang, who was rumored to have surfaced in various parts of the country. One particular account showed him in a picture with Ho Chi Minh, although the picture was undoubtedly retouched.

Evidence brought out during the trial revealed that the five were strangled and then transferred to Kanchanaburi, where they were crudely cremated and buried. An excavation of their graves produced enough personal belongings to confirm their families' worst fears. An interesting incident was brought out during the trial. Those involved in the murders later held a party, where Phao appeared and doled out 30,000 baht to each of the noncommissioned officers and police privates involved.[79] They were then cautioned not to speak out and to use the money to build new houses for themselves. The reward given to Phao's *asawin* was not disclosed.

Such police brutality no doubt intimidated the MPs and others who were dissatisfied with the regime. It was through such tactics, together with bribery, that Phao was able to control his political machine. Phibun and Sarit seemed happy to stay in the background and allow Phao to eliminate potential and real opposition. It was through these extreme methods that Phao helped maintain regime stability. While Phao was spreading his influence and control through repression and the expansion of the police force, Sarit and Phibun tried to organize their own power bases to counterbalance Phao's bid for political supremacy.

---

[77] The incident occurred during Phibun's advocacy of the *phunam* cult. The national slogan then was *Chua phunam, chat phonphai*—"Trust the leader and the nation will escape danger." See San Aya, Case no. (black) 2628/2501 and Case no. (red) 1542/2502.

[78] This story, written by Pridi in English and produced in English as a movie, never had wide circulation. The purpose of the movie is still unclear, and its true significance has not been ascertained. For further research, consult Pridi Phonomyong, *The King of the White Elephant* (Bangkok: University and Political Science Printing Press, 1940).

[79] A defendant testified that there were approximately thirty noncommissioned officers and privates present. See testimony in San Aya, Case no (red) 1542/2502.

SARIT VERSUS PHAO

Phao's rival for future political domination was Sarit, a tough army commander of the same generation. Like Phao, Sarit was raised and trained within the army organization from his early school days. Both were trained within the country and were not exposed to direct Western influence. Sarit's rise to fame coincided with his participation in the 1947 coup and the suppression of the 1949 and 1951 rebellions. It is most likely that his meteoric rise was assisted by Phibun, who wanted to counteract Phao's power and that of his father-in-law, Marshal Phin. At the beginning, Sarit appears to have been a good soldier and loyal to Phibun. His expressed abhorrence of politics was well known, and many observers did not view him as a politician, as they did Phao. Even American authorities saw Sarit as a "rugged and dour army officer to whom they paid considerable respect."[80]

Phibun's trust of Sarit can be surmised from Sarit's rapid promotion, his inclusion in the cabinet, and appointment to the lucrative position of the head of the Government Lottery Bureau. Within eight years of the 1947 coup, Sarit achieved the illustrious rank of Field Marshal.[81] At forty-seven, he was the youngest marshal of the post–1932 era. In between those years, he was first promoted to Vice Admiral and Air Vice Marshal in 1952,[82] and later in 1955, he received the ranks of Admiral and Air Chief Marshal.[83] He started his political career in 1951, when he became Deputy Minister of Defense, a position he retained for the next five years. He took over the army's top position on June 24, 1954, after Phin retired.

During the early 1950s, Sarit was not deeply involved with politics and parliamentary bickering, as was Phao. This period witnessed the maturation of Sarit as a leader and the establishment of his political machine in the army. Sarit's proudest achievement at the time was the development and reorganization of the army into a modern fighting force. The Royal Decree of July 30, 1951 was a turning point in the future of the Thai army.[84] It marked the Americanization of the Thai army. Sarit wrote that since the Thai army was receiving aid from the United States and cooperating in many international exercises, it was imperative that the army should be modernized along American lines.[85] Sarit was also proud of his 1954 trip to Washington, DC, during which he negotiated more military aid for the armed forces.

---

[80] Darling, *Thailand and the United States,* p. 117.

[81] Sarit was promoted to Field Marshal on January 1, 1956. Cremation Volume of Sarit Thanarat (Cabinet edition), p. 54.

[82] Sarit's promotion to the ranks equivalent to his own in the navy and air force was a means by which military leaders rewarded themselves for meritorious service. Ranks in other service branches were conferred for two main reasons: first, as a reward for real contribution (military service); second, as a means of placating high-ranking officers whose direct promotion was not possible for various reasons. For example, a full general who wanted to retire as a marshal but could not do so because the appointment of too many marshals would degrade the rank's importance was given a high rank in another service. Sarit's promotion in 1952 appears to have been for services rendered during the repression of the Manhattan Rebellion.

[83] Cremation Volume of Sarit Thanarat (Cabinet edition), p. 54.

[84] *Phraratchakrisdika Chat Rabieb Ratchakan Khong Kongthap Bok nai Krasuang Kalahom* [Royal Decree for the Organization of the Army within the Defense Ministry], July 30, 1951. *Ratchakitcha*, vol. 68, section 45, 1951, p. 1.

[85] See Sarit Thanarat's article in *Wan Kongthap Bok, 2496,* no pagination.

The Thai army developed its organization rapidly after 1951. The government's decision to send troops to Korea helped bring this about.[86] This international cooperation with the United States in Korea increased the need for the Thai army to adapt itself to the American model so that it could effectively synchronize its operations with the US effort. Adoption of the American model, incorporating the necessary management personnel to handle the new technology and armaments, which the United States gave to the Thai armed forces, "modernized" the Thai army. The size of the army was greatly increased, and many new regiments and battalions were formed. The army's educational institutions were also improved and enlarged to help train military officers for their new roles in the "modern" army. Especially in 1952, a large number of army officers were sent to the United States for training. To oversee the rising complexity of the army, the Thai general staff department was reorganized along American and British lines.[87]

Although Phin was Commander-in-Chief of the Army until 1954, he did not concern himself too deeply with its development.[88] Instead, he and his sons-in-law were more interested in getting rich. Sarit was thus given quite a free hand to mold the army in ways he found appropriate. He was also able to maneuver his own followers into positions of responsibility and consolidated his hold over the First Army (which he still commanded) and the powerful First Division, stationed in Bangkok. The First Division was Sarit's old command and he saw to it that his supporters—General Thanom, General Praphat, and General Kris—held key positions in it. Because of Phin's involvement in business, a preoccupation that diverted him from his commitment to the army, the internal affairs of the army were left in the hands of the more dynamic Sarit, who, in 1954, took over complete control.

Sarit, however, was engaged in a two-pronged approach to the building up of his political organization. The army's 1952 reorganization brought unit commands in Bangkok under the control of the First Army, which Sarit directly commanded. So that he would have the means to "support" his followers within the army, Sarit got control of the profitable Lottery Bureau in 1951. The following year, he secured a seat

---

[86] See Phin Chunnahawan's article in *Wan Kongthap Bok, 2496,* no pagination.

[87] See Sarit Thanarat's article in *Wan Kongthap Bok, 2496,* no pagination.

[88] After the 1947 coup, Phin became Commander-in-Chief of the Army, but his concern for internal army affairs appeared to be secondary to his desire for material gain. His political ambitions were not clear (unlike Luang Kat's) and he was not active in the Phibun regime's political organization, which was run by Phao, Phin's son-in-law. Phin's main interest after 1947 seems to have been invested in the Thahan Samakhi Organization, a business arm of the Veterans' Organization. Under Phin's direction, this organization became involved in the rice trade when, in 1947–1948, the Northeast Rice Millers' Association became shareholders. The Thahan Samakhi soon got control of the northeast line freight cars, which transported rice to Bangkok. (See Skinner, *Chinese Society in Thailand,* pp. 346, 347.) Phin was assisted in his various business ventures by his other sons-in-law, namely, Colonel Praman Adireksan, Colonel Siri Siriyothin, and Colonel Lamai Utthayananon. At the time of the 1947 coup, only Lamai had command of troops (in Lampang), but he was soon transferred to the police department. In 1951, Siri became Deputy Minister of Commerce and Praman Deputy Minister of Communications. By 1954, Siri got the position of Economic Affairs Minister and Phao became Deputy Minister of Finance. In 1957, Phin became Minister of Agriculture, with Lamai as his deputy minister, while Siri controlled the Ministry of Cooperatives and Praman had charge of the Industry Ministry. In effect, Phin and his sons-in-law got control of key positions in the cabinet to facilitate their business concerns. An apparent example of the use of their office for personal gain was Phin's involvement in the lumber scandal, discussed toward the end of this chapter.

on the governing board of the Veterans' Organization. In addition to this, Sarit sat on the boards of directors of no less than twenty-two private corporations and government-controlled enterprises, such as the Northeast Gunny Bag Industry, the Thai Financial Syndicate, and the Thai Economic Development Company.[89]

While Phao and Sarit were building their respective political organizations, Phibun tried to maintain his own legitimacy on the basis of personal leadership, cultural revitalization, and identification with the United States. More and more, Phibun realized that Phao was gaining control of the government's party machinery while Sarit tightened his grip on the army. This left Phibun with little or no organization to support his position. However, his unique status of being the only prominent national leader remaining of the 1932 Promoters was an asset, which helped maintain him as arbiter between Phao and Sarit.

The first program launched by Phibun to generate public interest and support was the establishment of a ministry of culture. In 1942, Phibun had instigated a similar program when the National Council on Culture was founded. Following the Radio Coup of 1951, Phibun went one step further by elevating the council on culture to the status of ministry in 1952.[90] Phibun himself became the ministry's first chief.

Under Phibun's direction, cultural and spiritual development was emphasized, an interesting contrast to Sarit's later emphasis on economic development. He dispatched cultural cadres to the schools, organized radio programs, circulated pamphlets, and even had mobile cultural units go out and indoctrinate people on the finer points of Thai culture and social behavior.[91] The general content of the teachings, lectures, and messages published in pamphlets harped on the age-old theme of filial piety and the dangers of communism. The duties of a good citizen were to believe in the principle of respect for elders; sons and daughters should listen to their parents, and the parents should love their children.[92] Popular radio soap operas were ordered not to present programs that were sad, or to depict illicit love affairs, broken homes, and the like, which Phibun felt would make the people depressed and neglect work.[93] Programs were to emphasize filial piety, nationalistic themes, and national security. The message conveyed over the public air waves was that communism was the number-one public enemy, so that Phibun's anti-communism and pro-Americanism points of view would become accepted, vital ingredients in the public's view of proper Thai politics. Attempts were also made to use the *likae,* or traditional folk opera, to propagandize against communism to the peasants.[94]

Phibun's cultural revitalization program embraced the arts as well as religion. Thai music and other art forms were revived, and attempts were made to elevate the

---

[89] Riggs, *Thailand,* p. 269.

[90] *Banthuk Phonngan,* p. 183. Phibun remained Minister of Culture until 1955, when Admiral Luang Yutthasat took over. Madame Phibun soon became deeply involved in cultural revitalization. However, observers generally agree that the programs of the ministry were really aimed only at the official elite and their wives.

[91] Ibid., pp. 183–186.

[92] See footnote 79. Phibun's attempts to reinforce traditional social values were met with cynicism and amusement by many people. Phibun's scheme appeared to be a piece of propaganda, intended to convince the public to accept him as a leader and father figure, one who loved his people and whom they should respect and obey.

[93] Chit, *Phao Saraphab,* p. 125.

[94] Ibid., p. 130.

social status of performing artists. Plays, too, were written and presented to the public to educate them further along the lines that Phibun wanted, especially with the idea that Phibun was a "father" to the people, rather than just a *phunam* (leader) as before. One good example of this was Phibun's attempt to make the public think of him as a latter-day Ramkhamhaeng. To this end, he sponsored the production of a play, written by one of his own supporters, entitled *Anuphab Phokhun Ramkhamhaeng,* or "The Power of Phokhun Ramkhamhaeng."[95]

Phibun also tried to make himself the *de facto* patron of Buddhism. He was deeply engaged in the restoration of national monuments, temples, and shrines. Under his direction, statues of Phraya Phahon and King Taksin were erected.[96] This last move might have been interpreted as a slight to the ruling royal house, for Phahon had been a 1932 Promoter, while Taksin was the founder of Thonburi, a Thai king who many felt had been put to death unjustly by the founder of the Chakkri dynasty. Phibun seemed to be competing with the king by developing alternative sources of legitimacy, such as Ramkhamhaengism, patronage of the arts and religion, his status as a 1932 Promoter, and his tributes to non-Chakkri charismatic leadership (Takinism).

Phibun's most elaborate maneuver in this area was his self-portrayal as the champion for Buddhism. According to his government's statistics, a very large number of temples received financial assistance for improvement and restoration during his term.[97]

From the figures listed below, we can detect two distinct peaks—1951 and 1956. One explanation for this pattern may be that Phibun's position was especially weak during those two years. In general, expenditures were heavier from 1952 to 1956, however, perhaps as a way of counteracting the growing importance of Phao and Sarit. 1956 was also a year of preparation for the 25th Centennial Celebration of the Buddhist Era. While Phibun's support of Buddhism was made nominally on behalf of the king, a closer examination of the celebration plans does not bear this out.

---

[95] *Banthuk Phonngan,* p. 194. The play tried to demonstrate to the people that it was essential the nation be guided by a father figure—a traditional Thai concept. *Phokhun* means "highest father," a term used to refer to Thai kings of the early Sukhothai period. Lacking the power bases of Phao or Sarit, Phibun tried to use this concept to ensure his own legitimacy. The play itself was written by Luang Wichit Wathakan, in 1954, while he was ambassador to Switzerland. See Luang Wichit Wathakan, *Anuphab Phokhun Ramkhamhaeng* [The Power of Phokhun Ramkhamhaeng] (Bangkok: Rungruangtham Press, 1954). In the play, Ramkhamhaeng speaks lines such as "There are no big shots or lords in Sukhothai; there are only fathers and children [*pho kap luk*]." "Sukhothai has no king [*chaokrung*], it has only father [*pho*], father of the city [*phomuang*], and highest father [*phokhun*]." *Anuphab Phokhun Ramkhamhaeng,* p. 6. According to the message of the play, the country was strong and prosperous because it had a great and understanding *phokhun* who mingled with the people. It is interesting to note that Sarit later used this concept too, and even more extensively than Phibun. For the English version of the play, see Thak, *Thai Politics.*

[96] *Banthuk Phonngan,* p. 193

[97] Ibid., 186, 197. Professor Lauristan Sharp told the author that the villagers at Bang Chan were aware of that Phibun had funded and helped restore a number of temples (*wat*), but believed nevertheless that he was trying to compete with the king, which was unacceptable to them.

Table 2
Number of Temples Restored, 1948–1956

Year	Number of Temples Restored
1948	15
1949	56
1950	312
1951	1,117
1952	40
1953	123
1954	164
1955	413
1956	1,239

As far as can be ascertained, the planning of the Twenty-Fifth Centennial Celebration was a Phibun-directed operation, during which the king's role as the nation's religious leader was given lip service, nothing more. Rather than honor the throne's traditional link to Buddhism, the government effectively designated the regime as the official sponsor of the national religion. A government announcement stated that:

The Thai believed in the Buddhist religion since time immemorial and has received great benefit from its faith in Buddhism. Governments of the country in all ages have respected Buddhism as the national religion. On this august occasion, the government plans to hold a special celebration so the people can take part in the festivities.[98]

The king played no real part in planning the event, which was handled by trusted friends of the prime minister.[99]

Celebrations called for the establishment of a Buddha Monthon,[100] the initiation into monkhood for 2,500 young men, the casting of 2,500 golden Buddha images, and other festivities. In an attempt to bolster his status, Phibun invited Burma's premier, U Nu, as his personal guest.[101] U Nu and party were to later go to Ayutthaya to visit the restored ruins and the people of Ayutthaya, whom the Burmese had "wronged" in 1768. This was Phibun's way of showing the people that he was the nation's leader who could act independently of the throne in trying to erase animosities between

---

[98] Finance Ministry, "Ruang chernchuan ruam kankuson nai Nganchalong 25 Phutsatawat doy chuaikan borichak ngern raidai nung wan [Invitation to donate a day's income to charity during the 25th Centennial Buddhist Celebrations]," in Krom Kansatsana [Department of Religion], *Ngan Chalong 25 Phutsatawat* [25th Centennial Buddhist Celebrations], May 12–18, 1957, p. 25.

[99] Those heading committees were people like Phao P., Sawat, Mangkon, and Madame Phibun. Praphat from the Sarit camp was only later appointed vice chairman of the main committee.

[100] In constructing a Buddhist Center, Phibun finally satisfied ambitions he had conceived during wartime. In 1944, Phibun was rebuffed by parliament over this issue, which led to his resignation as prime minister.

[101] Krom Kansatsana, *Ngan Chalong*, p. 61. U Nu and his wife were Phibun's guests. Madame Aung San, the wife of the assassinated founder of modern Burma, was also Phibun's guest. Phao invited Bo Khin Muang Gale, U Nu's finance minister.

two ancient adversaries. The king's absence from many of the ceremonies spoke for itself,[102] and many in Ayutthaya viewed U Nu's visit with contempt. It was felt that the prerogative for righting an ancient conflict was properly the king's, and that such power should not appropriated by a commoner like Phibun. Rumor was that when U Nu came to Ayutthaya, the city would be covered with darkness and ghostly wailing would be heard—thereby indicating the displeasure of the Ayutthaya ancestors.

Phibun's final source of potential legitimacy came from his position vis-à-vis the United States. After assuming the premiership in 1948, Phibun immediately jumped on the American bandwagon of fighting the "international communist conspiracy."[103] He declared that Thailand was increasingly the target of communist intentions, and he proceeded to seek American economic and military assistance. The United States government supported Phibun's position by offering more aid and seeking out his cooperation.

The outbreak of the Korean war, in June 1950, provided a good opportunity for Phibun to raise his prestige in the eyes of the United States government. He abandoned the traditional Thai foreign policy of flexibility and aligned the country with the United States (as he had once allied it with Japan) by offering in July 1950 to send troops and rice to war-torn Korea.[104] The US government was most grateful to Phibun, for Thailand was the first Asian country to offer concrete assistance to the American venture made in the name of the United Nations. Phibun's unabashed pro-Westernism brought forth American praise and support; the latter particularly enhanced his position domestically, since many leaders thought him essential in acquiring future American aid. At this juncture, Phibun's ties with the United States were definitely an advantage and strengthened his political position vis-à-vis Phao and Sarit.

Immediately following Phibun's commitment regarding the Korean conflict, the United States government responded with the Fulbright educational exchange agreement and the more important Economic and Technical Cooperation Agreement, signed on September 19, 1950.[105] Ambassador Stanton's speech on the occasion of the signing made it clear that this was a political payoff. Stanton said that the American people wanted to assist the Thai people because of their belief in freedom, and that this and their "whole-hearted support of the United Nations have won the admiration of the American people."[106] With American support, the World Bank also agreed to give Thailand a loan for development projects. On October 17, 1950, less than a month after the signing of the economic assistance pact, the two

---

[102] Although scheduled to appear at a main ceremony, the king remained at his summer palace at Hua Hin "because of a cold." His absence was perceived by farmers as a slap at the "militarist" (pseudo-Buddhist) government leaders. From an interview with Professor Lauristan Sharp.

[103] *New York Times*, August 31, 1949, as cited in Darling, *Thailand, and the United States*, p. 70.

[104] *New York Times*, July 23, 1950, as cited in Darling, *Thailand, and the United States*, p. 78. Phibun was alleged to have said that he would cooperate with any power that would win in any international conflict

[105] See Darling, *Thailand and the United States*, p. 79. Also see *The Bangkok Post*, September 19, 1950.

[106] Darling, *Thailand and the United States*, p. 79.

governments signed an "Agreement Respecting Military Assistance."[107] This agreement provided for armaments assistance as well as training for Thai military officers in the United States.

The intensification of the Cold War and United States support for Thailand led Phibun to align himself still closer to the United States. Indeed, the success of Phibun's regime in the late 1940s and early 1950s depended on his ability to attract American economic and military aid, World Bank loans, and the benefits of international trade. Anti-communism thus became a lucrative foreign policy for Phibun to pursue. The Indochina conflict and the defeat of the French in 1954, together with Peking's formation of the "Thai Autonomous People's Government" in Southern Yunnan[108] in January 1953, gave Phibun concrete cause for seeking even more American aid. When the Southeast Asia Treaty Organization was hastily organized as a deterrent against communist expansion in the region, Thailand became an eager partner in this American-concocted venture, which in reality was a means to establish South Vietnam as a *de facto* entity.[109] SEATO emphasized the need for its members to build up military and police forces to maintain internal security; this was probably the organization's most significant effect on Thailand's domestic government. Domestic politics from 1951 to 1955 were generally quite lackluster. The period was marked by an intensification of military/police rule and the strengthening of ties between the United States and Thailand. The Constitution of 1952, which amended that of 1932, provided a legal framework through which the Coup Group maintained power. It now controlled both the executive branch of government and the legislature, and various laws were passed designed to ensure a still firmer grip on the country. For example, an Emergency Law was passed in February 1952 that provided the government with wide powers of arrest and press censorship.[110]

By November of that same year, a stringent "anticommunist" law was approved by parliament by an almost unanimous vote.[111]

PHIBUN THE DEMOCRAT, 1955–1957

Phibun's actions after 1955 indicate that he was aware of the fact that his authoritarian regime, by alienating the citizenry, was slowly working in favor of his potential adversaries, Phao and Sarit. The prime minister began to look for new ways to curb Phao's power and to bolster his own position. His world tour to the United States and Europe seem to have convinced him of the practical merits of popular elections and legitimacy based upon the people's mandate.

For almost thirty years, Phibun had not observed firsthand political developments abroad, and his trip in April of 1955 seems to have got him thinking

---

[107] *The Bangkok Post,* October 17, 1950. Ambassador Stanton said that the agreement was not for American military purposes, as there was no provision for the establishment of bases, such as those in the Philippines.

[108] Donald E. Nuechterlein, *Thailand and the Struggle for Southeast Asia* (Ithaca, NY: Cornell University Press, 1965), p. 112.

[109] George McT. Kahin and John W. Lewis, *The United States in Vietnam,* revised ed. (New York, NY: Dell Publishing Co., 1969), pp. 61–63.

[110] *Ratchakitcha,* vol. 69, section 16, 1952, p. 278.

[111] See Wilson, *Politics in Thailand,* pp. 28, 29.

about how he could further enhance his own position at home. Darling has insisted that Phibun's subsequent attempt at restoring democracy was the result of the influence of his American experience.[112] But I suspect that one trip could not change a person drastically, particularly an experienced politician like Phibun. Darling is closer to the mark when he notes that the U.S. government originally invited Phibun to visit the United States to give him moral support and world exposure to compensate for his domestic weakness within the triumvirate. Phibun took his cue from this. During his three weeks in the United States, Phibun did not fail to stress the communist threat and the fact that Thailand—under his guidance—was on the side of the democratic states.[113] When he spoke before the Far East–American Council of Commerce and Industry, he declared that Thailand belonged in the camp of the free democratic nations.[114] Phibun ingratiated himself with the US Congress by telling the American lawmakers that he was trying to implement full representative government and that Thailand would "always be on your side."[115] The United States tour brought about a fair amount of praise for Phibun and earned him a reputation as an astute leader of the Free World.

The official Thai political style underwent a transformation after Phibun's US tour. The former *phunam* now turned to democracy and representative government as the solution to maintaining the political stability of his regime while strengthening his own position vis-à-vis Phao and Sarit. Phibun announced upon his return that he would run for an elected seat in the assembly in 1957. He also personally convinced parliament to pass a Political Party Bill.[116] Democracy became the central theme of Phibun's public addresses, and he delivered a most revealing speech before naval cadets shortly after his return from Europe. He told the cadets that soldiers should not be involved in politics and should not be engaged in trade; power should come from popular elections, and that, in general, force and coups d'état were no longer in style.[117] At a later date, Phibun even declared that a coup d'état now was to be considered a coup against the king and the establishment of a republic.[118]

Phibun's appeals for democracy were backed by certain innovations that he had observed during his world tour. Like his earlier wartime policies of insisting on the wearing of hats, pants, and skirts, the use of business cards, and the kissing of wives before going off to work, Phibun's new programs were also simplistic borrowings of Western institutions and concepts. Whereas the former programs were designed to make the nation modern and prosperous, his post-1955 programs were designed to make the premier politically more impressive.

---

[112] Darling, *Thailand and the United States*, p. 138.

[113] Ibid., p. 139.

[114] Ibid., p. 140.

[115] Ibid.

[116] *Phraratchabanyat Phakanmuang* 2498 [Political Parties Act, 1955] in *Ratchakitcha*, vol. 72, section 77, 1955, p. 1. Article 18 lowered the voting age to twenty, and educational requirements were eliminated. Phao did not object this time. It may be conjectured that Phao was not ready to break away from Phibun, and that he must have felt that his power vis-à-vis Sarit was not yet adequate. Also, unlike Phibun, Phao did not have the full support of the United States.

[117] *The Bangkok Post*, July 19, 1955, in Darling, *Thailand and the United States*, p. 142.

[118] *The Bangkok Post*, August 19, 24, 1955, in Darling, *Thailand and the United States*, pp. 142, 143.

Press conferences were introduced, and these elaborate affairs were held every Friday. Members of his cabinet were sometimes forced to attend. Phibun felt that he could use the press to bring his regime closer to the public and make it appear more democratic. Censorship was now relaxed, and the press was allowed to study the achievements and work of various cabinet ministers. (Phibun evidently hoped that the press would expose the corruption of his rivals.)[119] To supplement press conferences, political rallies and meetings were allowed, and Sanam Luang was designated as the Thai Hyde Park. But whereas England's Hyde Park was really designed only as a place to give eccentrics the opportunity to let off steam, the Thai Hyde Park was taken seriously as a legitimate place to articulate and hear different points of view. Phibun even ordered government officials to pay attention to the suggestions of the speakers at Sanam Luang.

Sanam Luang became the platform for opposition politicians to air their grievances and to "wash the Coup Group's dirty linen" in public. Like his introduction of press conferences, Phibun's decision to allow open discourse at Sanam Luang was basically another scheme to discredit his rivals, especially Phao. Indeed, Phao became the figure most often subjected to criticism in this arena. At first, he did not know how to react to this. On one occasion he was forced to swear that he had no part in the various political assassinations, and that his sudden acquisition of vast wealth had been a natural process.[120] Phao agreed to take an oath that said that, if he had lied, let him not achieve prosperity in this life and the lives to come. But having learned the ropes through his appearances at Sanam Luang, Phao then used that venue to criticize and discredit Phibun by hiring speakers to attack Phibun. Seeing that his plan had backfired, Phibun again banned public meetings and the weekly press conferences became more rare.[121]

To implement his plan for elections, Phibun had to whittle down Phao's influence. While Phibun still needed Phao for his organizing abilities, Phibun had to bring Phao under control. He had seen how Phao had manipulated the legislative committee to his own advantage. To counteract this, Phibun envisioned a larger government party that would include more of his own friends and supporters. His first move against the growing influence of Phao was through cabinet reshuffling. On August 2, 1955, Phibun assumed the powerful post of Minister of the Interior,[122] and three days later relieved Phao of his position as Deputy Minister of Finance.[123] Phin was also relieved of his position as Deputy Minister of Defense.[124]

---

[119] Pla Thong, *Phakkanmuang*, p. 223.

[120] Prachuab Thongurai, *Sin Yuk Mut* [End of the Dark Ages] (Bangkok: Akson Borikan Press, 1957), p. 163.

[121] Pla Thong, *Phakkanmuang*, p. 229.

[122] *Banthuk Phonngan*, p. 22. Vice Admiral Luang Sunawin, the Interior Minister, was transferred to the Ministry of Cooperatives. Phao was Deputy Minister of the Interior as well as Deputy Minister of Finance.

[123] Phao was then in the United States negotiating a loan.

[124] *Banthuk Phonngan*, p. 22. For the first time, Thanom Kittikachon was appointed to the cabinet as Deputy Minister of Cooperatives.

ELECTIONS OF FEBRUARY 26, 1957[125]

The passage of the 1955 Political Party Bill gave rise to a proliferation of political parties, more than twenty-five in all. The government's legislative committee was transformed into the Seri Manangkhasila Party, a name derived from the place where they had usually held meetings, to which the word *seri* (free) was added. The party had Phibun as the head, Sarit as deputy chief, and Phao as secretary general. Sarit played no significant role in preparing for the elections and generally allowed Phao to run the show. (Sarit's reluctance to engage in party politics at this point was probably a precautionary move so that he would not be associated with Phao's strong-arm tactics.) The government's major rival was Khuang's Democrat Party, which rallied royalist/conservative elements to contest Phibun's leadership. Phibun was the only member of the triumvirate to run for a seat in Bangkok.

The February 1957 elections were very lively, with heated contests in Bangkok. Although the Seri Manangkhasila Party won seven seats to the Democrat's two in the city, the latter won a moral victory. Khuang, a popular local vote-getter, led Phibun in vote counts until tampering resulted in Phibun's victory.[126] The results of the elections were as follows:[127]

Table 3
February 26, 1957, Election Results

Party	*Seats in Parliament*
Seri Manangkhasila	85
Democrat	28
Seri Prachathipatai	11
Thammathipat	10 (pro-Phibun)
Economic Front	8 (Isan MPs)
Chatniyom	3 (pro-Sarit)
Hyde Park	2
Issara	2
Independents	13

The press and the Democrats protested the government's tampering with votes and its use of hoodlums to intimidate voters and candidates. Because of rising public resentment regarding Phibun's "democratic" practices, he reverted to the use of proven repressive methods. A state of emergency was declared, and Sarit was appointed Supreme Commander of military forces to maintain order. The attempt to build a new legitimacy was clearly not a success, and signs that the regime was in decline now began to appear often.

---

[125] See A. Pickerell and D. E. Moore, "Elections in Thailand," *Far Eastern Survey*, XXVI (June–July, 1957), pp. 92–96, 103–111.

[126] Sarit refused to order his troops to vote for the Seri Manangkhasila. Pla Thong felt that this was one reason why the government had to tamper with ballot boxes. *Phakkanmuang*, pp. 272, 273.

[127] See Withetkorani, *Khwampenma*, pp. 1,407–1,416; and Khachatphai, *Kanmuang*, p. 258.

As long as Phibun's position had seemed secure, the triumvirate survived, but as Phibun weakened, opportunities for the other two men to act alone became increasingly possible. The Sarit coup of 1957 was the logical outcome of this process.

The Phibun regime's power declined rapidly after the general elections of February 26, 1957 (the results of which notably increased public discontentment).[128] Hitherto there had been no effective leader to take advantage of such discontent. But now the students, the press, the disenchanted public, and certain politicians discovered a leader in the person of Sarit.

Students were deeply angered by the rigged elections, and the flag at Chulalongkon University was flown at half-mast to mourn the passing of democracy. Students also called a meeting to plan a protest rally against the government. On March 3, 1957, Phibun responded by declaring a national emergency and giving Sarit responsibility for peace and order.[129] Rumors were spread that the communists were instigating the disturbances.[130]

Sarit's sudden popularity with the students and the press developed out of his position as supreme commander of the military forces during the brief emergency. At a convocation at Chulalongkon University to plan for the rally against Phibun, Sarit had appeared and spoken frankly with the students. His delivery style and decisive manner gained their fancy. He cautioned the students not to do anything rash. When queried about the elections, Sarit replied, "If you ask me directly, I will say that they were dirty, the dirtiest. Everybody cheated."[131] By this stroke, Sarit was able to dissociate himself from the corrupt tactics of the government of which he was deputy leader. Regarding the students' request for protection during their planned demonstrations, Sarit said that he would not stand in their way. Thus the students got the tacit support of Sarit, whom they saw as an honest man who could protect them against Phao's police and hired goons.

To many observers at that time, there were more and more signs that the government was losing its power. It was as though the cosmic forces had turned against Phibun. In Thai popular thinking, the events that followed the dirty elections were seen as foreboding signs of doom, or *lang hayana*.[132] The psychological impact was significant, for it prepared people for the final fall of Phibun. Hence, when Sarit took over, his accession seemed almost inevitable and no surprise at all.

---

[128] Previous elections in Thailand had not received great publicity and fanfare. They were basically honest, and the government did not exercise overt intimidation. Thus the tactics deployed by Phao to threaten voters and tamper with the balloting were very noticeable when compared to past events.

[129] *Sayam Nikon*, March 3, 1957. It may be speculated here that the appointment of Sarit was a Phibun scheme to lower Sarit's growing public popularity. Sarit was known for his harsh tactics in maintaining order (e.g., the methods he used in suppressing the Palace and Manhattan Rebellions). Perhaps Phibun and Phao wanted to see Sarit order his troops to fire upon the demonstrators and thus make him a public enemy. However, Sarit was able to use this opportunity for his own gain by telling his troops to refrain from hurting the people and, in general, supporting their opinion that the elections had been dirty. Martial law lasted from March 2 to March 12.

[130] *Sayam Nikon*, March 3, 1957. After March 3, care was taken to stress that "foreign elements" had been involved and that a national emergency was declared for this reason. In fact, declaring a national emergency was the only way to prevent further political disorder on the part of the students and others.

[131] Ibid.

[132] This expression came up frequently during discussions of the fall of Phibun in 1957.

The stability of a regime is a function of many factors. One of these is effectiveness, particularly in a period of crisis. Seymour Lipset defines "effectiveness" as the actual performance of a political system, that is, the extent to which it satisfies the basic functions of government as defined by the expectations of most members (or perhaps the most relevant sectors) of the society, and particularly the expectations of powerful groups within the society that might threaten the system. In the Thai case, for example, an "effective" government would have to meet the military's expectations.[133]

Phibun's short outburst of liberal practices gave the public a sudden chance of venting long-suppressed resentment of the regime, and thus opened the door for Sarit to side with them against the corrupt and repressive activities of Phao. Sarit was in a good position to do so, for we have seen how, after 1951, regime repression was mainly carried out by the police and not the army. His sense of public backing made him bolder in dealing with Phibun, who was forced to concede more positions to Sarit's supporters in the post-election cabinet. Thanom became Sarit's deputy in the defense ministry, while Praphat, another Sarit protégé, was appointed Deputy Minister of the Interior. To counterbalance the growing power of Sarit, Phibun had to give control of the Interior Ministry to Phao.

At this point, four vital issues (described below) arose more or less concurrently to rattle the Phibun government. The first two revealed the ineffectiveness of the government in solving an immediate problem and the plan of some leaders to use their positions in government for financial profit on a vast national scale. The other two crises were political in nature, for they brought into question the authority and legitimacy of the regime itself.

THE ISAN CRISIS

One of Isan's worst droughts occurred in 1957, the same year that Phibun's government was floundering under public pressure. There was a great exodus of people from the Northeast into Bangkok, but this phenomena did not seem to disturb the government. In fact, the regime seemed to regard this migration into the capital as something natural, a phenomenon that acted as a safety valve to ease peasant discontent.[134] Marshal Phin, who was Minister of Agriculture, said that migration into the capital and the eating of frogs and lizards by Northeasterners were common things, nothing to be worried about.[135]

The newspapers felt very differently. *Sayam Nikon* reported that hordes of locusts had descended upon Mahasarakham to devour the crops and that in other areas this problem was complicated by severe drought.[136] Other obvious signs were also

---

[133] Seymour M. Lipset, "Some Social Requisites of Democracy," *The American Political Science Review* LIII (March, 1959): 86.

[134] See Samuel Huntington, *Political Order in Changing Societies* (New Haven, CT: Yale University Press, 1969), pp. 279, 280. Huntington feels that peasant migration into the cities is an alternative to peasant revolts, for by moving to the cities, the peasants in general raise their standards of living. This view does not pay too much attention to the reasons for such rural displacement. It prescribes a remedy but does not diagnose the sickness.

[135] *Sayam Nikon*, August 15, 1957.

[136] *Sayam Nikon* August 1–5, 1957.

present. At Hua Lamphong railway station in Bangkok, so many refugees poured in daily that students and monks had to set up emergency help stations.[137]

The government's foot-dragging was obvious. Only on August 10 was the deputy minister of agriculture sent to Isan to survey the situation by helicopter—and he found little wrong. In the meantime, opposition MPs and Isan representatives who had not been "bought off" by the government met and planned to face the prime minister with certain basic demands. Representative Bunkhong Bunpetch spoke at the Phramaen Grounds (Sanam Luang), accusing the government of catering to a few rich families while ignoring the need for true national development. Another deputy threatened that Isan would revolt if the government refused to help. The Democrats, on the other hand, pledged to give financial assistance and sponsored two fund-raising movies, appropriately entitled "Political Hooligan" and "Nation in Confusion."[138]

Annoyed at this criticism, the government sent Phin to Isan for another look.[139] Again, the survey was done by air; the government used planes from the Department of Rice Affairs to do a quick study. The results of the Phin survey were published and his findings dryly served out to add fuel to the disenchantment of the Isan representatives, the opposition parties, and the students. The government report was as follows: 40 percent of Isan's farm land was in "good" condition; 50 percent was in "fair" condition, as these plots had been planted with rice only thirty days behind the seasonal norm; and the remaining 10 percent was classified as "satisfactory," where planting was merely forty to fifty days behind schedule.[140] To compound the insult, the government hinted that the communists were responsible for exaggerating the predicament and had urged the people to flock to Bangkok. What the report implied was that there was no crisis in Isan, since all the land was at least in satisfactory condition. This unrealistic survey by air was a crude attempt by the government to avoid responsibility and discredit opposition charges, while at the same time blaming the communists for the crisis.[141] The final solution was typical of the Phibun regime. It tried to bribe Isan MPs by allocating fifty-three million baht to be divided equally among fifty-three Isan representatives.[142]

THE LUMBER SWINDLE

Before the government could live down its inept handling of the Isan crisis, its credibility was again cast into doubt. With plans to construct the Bhumibol Dam in Tak province, an opportunity opened up for a lumber swindle on a very large scale. According to a press release from the World Bank on August 20, 1957, Thailand was awarded US$66,000,000 for Project Bhumibhol. The plan called for the building of a dam five hundred feet high on the Ping River in Tak. Two hydroelectric plants were to be constructed. The project was to last six years and be completed by 1963. The

---

[137] *Sayam Nikon,* August 20, 1957. Student leaders from seven universities and normal colleges pledged their support for the refugees.

[138] *Sayam Nikon,* August 11, 1957.

[139] *Sayam Nikon,* August 15, 1957. The government finally took official notice.

[140] Thai Noi (pseudo.), and Kamon Chantarason, *Waterloo khong Chomphon Plaek* [Waterloo of Field Marshal Plaek] (Bangkok: Phrae Phitthaya Press, 1957), p. 23.

[141] *Sayam Nikon,* August 23, 1957.

[142] *Sayam Nikon,* August 17, 1957.

loan was a long-term one, which would be repaid over a twenty-five year period, the first payment falling due six years after the contract was signed. This meant that the plan called for the dam to pay for itself after completion.

Since this agreement was made soon after the Isan famine, a number of MPs resented the loan incurred by the initiative.[143] Their complaint was that the interest rate was 5.75 percent per annum, or approximately seventy-two million baht per year. The opposition used the slogan "one million baht in three days" to accentuate their opposition. However, because of respect to the king, the plan for the dam was not too harshly debated, although some deputies did stage a walk-out in protest. But things did not stop there.

Thiem Khomkrit, Director General of the Forestry Department, was suddenly forced to resign, and charges of administrative incompetence were leveled against him. Ordinarily, this would have gone unnoticed, but Thiem decided to put up a fight to defend his own integrity. The press had become more outspoken since the inauguration of the "new Democracy," and Thiem felt that he could bring his case to the public. Thiem went to the press and aired his grievances.[144] As it happened, many of his subordinates had already visited Sarit to appeal for help, evidence that helps explain why Thiem was willing to act so boldly. His followers said that only Sarit could act judiciously.[145] Thus, even the bureaucracy had begun to consider Sarit as a court of appeal, hoping he could force the government to initiate reforms.

Thiem proceeded to reveal the sinister background behind his dismissal. He said that some powerful figures in the government wanted to establish a "Forestry Company of Thailand," which would merge with all other private wood-product companies, thus monopolizing the lumber and teak industries. Thiem declared that Phin was behind the project and that when the other companies refused to cooperate, Phin made plans to suspend all forestry licenses. Thiem, as the official directly responsible, had refused to implement those suspensions.

The plan to establish the Forestry Company of Thailand also involved the Bhumibhol Dam Project, for the people wanted to capitalize on the cutting of timber in areas to be flooded by the dam. Thiem said that the trees in those areas were some of the best in the country, and whoever got the rights to market them would earn at least one thousand million baht. Thiem revealed that an early application for a license to cut timber in the soon-to-be-flooded area had been submitted by Rasmi Wantawirote, acting on behalf of the Seri Manangkhasila Party.[146] Rasmi's application had the personal endorsement of Phin, and it included instructions to issue the required papers without any delays. Thiem refused to cooperate, and as a result was dismissed. Because Thiem managed to bring these scandals out into the open and because he could rely on Sarit's tacit support, the government was forced to back down. Government evidence against Thiem was mysteriously misplaced, and his case was dropped. Sarit accused the government and the Seri Manangkhasila of attempted corruption. He told the press:

---

[143] *Sayam Nikon*, August 29, 1957. A few deputies spoke at the Hyde park gathering, criticizing the government for incurring debts while Isan was starving.

[144] *Sayam Nikon*, August 6–14, 1957.

[145] Ibid.

[146] Rasmi was a lumber magnate and supporter of the Seri Manangkhasila. The press expressed surprise that a civilian had obtained information about the Bhumibhol Project and the ways in which the construction of the dam would affect particular areas. *Sayam Nikon*, August 11, 1957.

... all of us, no matter whether we are speaking of the Coup Group, Manang [Seri Manangkhasila], or the government, if we do not perform well in this "lumber incident," we would not be able to face the people again.[147]

A move was even launched in parliament to impeach Phin for incompetence and improper use of his powers to dismiss a public official.

GENERAL DEBATE

As in 1947, when the Thamrong government was shaken by mounting parliamentary opposition and the army cited that disruption to justify its coup d'état, Phibun's government came under heavy fire from the assembly on August 29, 1957. At first, a debate resulting in a vote of confidence was planned, but opposition leaders were not able to obtain the necessary one-third signatures required. In the end, they were forced to be satisfied with a general debate and public questioning of the government under Article 75 of the 1932 Constitution (revised 1952).

The planners were led by Sanguan Chantharasakha, Sarit's half-brother, who had formed the Sahaphum (Unionist) Party to support Sarit in parliament. Five opposition parties were involved in the affair, and the nine issues selected for confronting the government were divided up among them. The issues were peace and order (Sahaphum), economic instability (Democrat), poor foreign relations (United Front), educational underdevelopment and poor living standards (Free Democrat), poor economic development (Economist Party), and corruption, incompetent ministers, and the government's antidemocratic practices.[148] Those involved in the challenge made a request to broadcast the debates over the radio, but the government would not permit it. At first, many ministers refused to face the parliament. Their reluctance prompted the press to remark:

... a government that thinks it is governing on behalf of the people should not be afraid of any discussion ... The constitution states that the government has the right to prevent questioning "only concerning affairs which should not be made public because it involves the security of the nation." The issues raised pertain to matters of administration and not national security. The most important point that the government should keep in mind is that the security and interest of the nation and the government are not the same; the government is not the nation.[149]

The most incriminating and certainly the most emotional issue centered around Phao and the accusations that he was contemplating the arrest of the king and that he supported a paper that ran news items criticizing the king. Luang Atthaphonphisan accused Phao of also bringing in gold bullion and counterfeit money—which was then distributed to the police by the Sea Supply Company—amounting to four hundred million baht, part of which was used to finance the *Thai*

---

[147] *Sayam Nikon,* August 9, 1957.

[148] This debate was recorded in its entirety by Singhakhom (pseud), *Sakfok Ratthaban Nai Plaek* (Grilling Plaek's Government) (n.p.: n.p., n.d.).

[149] *Sayam Rat Weekly,* August 18, 1957.

Seri paper, which ran stories criticizing the king and all royalty.[150] Luang then proceeded to read off some of the paper's headlines, which he had brought along as evidence. He noted that *Thai Seri* ran captions and headlines such as *Chao Phayong* [Royalty Dares], *Chao Lang Sasana* [Royalty Snubs Religion], and *Chao Cha Tai Hong* [Royalty Would All Die]. Reading further, Luang Atthaphon told the assembly that the paper had accused members of the royal family of planning to overthrow the Coup Group, and that it attacked the king and Sarit for feigning sickness in excusing themselves from attending the 25th Buddhist Centennial Celebrations.[151]

A far more serious charge was leveled against Phao by Phian Bunnag (Sahaphum Party). He claimed that at a meeting of the Seri Manangkhasila Party, Phao had accused the king of giving 700,000 baht to the Democrat Party[152] and had suggested that the king should have been arrested together with other cabinet ministers during the earlier declaration of national emergency.[153] Later, Phian was forced to withdraw those statements as hearsay, but the damage had been done. Phian's "Perry Mason-ite" tactics helped further arouse public resentment against Phao.

SARIT'S BREAK WITH THE PHIBUN REGIME

The fate of the Phibun regime was settled in August 1957. While it was trying to weather the Isan crisis, the lumber scandal, and the general debate, a far more important development was shaping up. This was Sarit's breakaway from the Seri Manangkhasila Party and the Phibun cabinet.

Phibun's intransigence and complacency in the face of crisis seriously aggravated the situation. Instead of trying to find a working solution with his main adversary, Phibun announced that government ministers should not engage in business while in office. He asked for their resignations. This was an attempt to weaken the position of Sarit, who was gaining popularity with the press, the public, and in parliament. Phibun wanted to expose Sarit's business connections as well as deprive him of his lucrative position as head of the Lottery Bureau.

However, to Phibun's dismay, Sarit was able to exploit this situation by resigning from his position as Defense Minister on August 20, 1957, allegedly to protest the government's inability to institute the reforms that he had urged. Together with Sarit, such key army officers in the cabinet as General Thanom, Deputy Minister of Defense and commander of the powerful First Army; General Praphat, Thanom's second in command and Deputy Minister of the Interior; and Air Vice Marshal Chalermkiat, Deputy Minister of Agriculture, also resigned. Attempts by Phibun to woo them back failed.

In an interview with the press, Sarit said that the resignations had been precipitated by differences of opinion with the government and for "reasons of health."[154] Khuang, leader of the Democrat Party, said that Phibun was fooling

---

[150] Singhakhom, *Sakfok*, p. 48. Luang Atthaphonphisan was a former member of the Prachachon Party. At this time, he was probably affiliated with the Sahaphum party.

[151] Ibid., pp. 49, 50. The paper prayed that "all those royalty should die" for not attending the festivities.

[152] Ibid., p. 59.

[153] Ibid., p. 60. The authenticity of these statements is questionable, for they were designed to discredit Phao and the Phibun regime.

[154] *Sayam Nikon*, August 22, 1957.

himself when he remarked that the resignations of Sarit, Thanom, Praphat, and Chalermkiat would not affect the stability of his government. Khuang added that when one of the main pillars of the government has fallen, the structure was bound to crumble soon.[155]

The press took up Sarit's cause and supported his reason for resigning. Anon wrote in his column in the *Sayam Rat Weekly* that Sarit's resignation was commendable in that it created political pressures on the government. He noted that the public had had hopes that Sarit would generate reforms when he joined the Phibun cabinet after the "dirty" elections. The press believed that since Sarit had promised the people that he would personally insure that the Phibun government paid attention to the their wishes, having failed, it was right that he should resign. Thai Noi wrote:

> The government usually does things contrary to the popular will ... Field Marshal Sarit promised the people before he joined the cabinet of Phibun that the government would reform many things which the people demanded and for which Phibun had given his word. But now five months have passed, and the government has not implemented the reforms that the public called for. Therefore, Sarit had to resign.[156]

Sarit's resignation was supported by forty-six deputies of the second (that is, appointed) category. In identical letters of resignation from the Seri Manangkhasila Party, they stated that, as appointed deputies, their responsibility was mainly to act as tutors to the elected MPs and thus they should not belong to any party. In the event that their party should lose in the elections and become the opposition, they felt that it would not be right that they should work in opposition to his majesty's government.[157]

It became apparent that, by the end of August 1957, Sarit had gained the moral support of the public and that his support in parliament was growing. On September 13, Sarit presented the army's ultimatum to Phibun. It was signed by fifty-eight army officers who demanded that the government resign immediately and that Phao be relieved of his position as director general of the police department. In this state of confusion, Phao and Phin tendered their resignations to Phibun, who refused to accept them.

The public reacted favorably to Sarit's ultimatum. On September 15, 1957, a Hyde Park gathering was staged to attack Phao and the Phibun government. The crowd grew in numbers and then marched to Sarit's house to show their support for the army's demands. Sarit was not at home, so the crowd proceeded to the government house, where an ugly mood developed. People stormed the gates and broke into the compound and from there they made speeches. The demonstrators then returned to Sarit's house, where the army chief was waiting to address them. Sarit said:

---

[155] Thai Noi and Kamon, *Waterloo*, p. 13.

[156] Ibid., p. 3.

[157] Ibid., p. 114.

In the name of the army and deputies of the second category, I have conducted my activities based upon the popular will and the interests of the people—your coming here gives me moral support to continue. [158]

The next morning, Sarit fulfilled that promise. The well-oiled army machinery staged a blitzkrieg coup d'état. Within less than an hour the army was able to capture all strategic points. Police headquarters were secured, and the anticipated counter-attack from Phao's commandos never materialized. The Sarit forces used white arm bands, a sign of purity, to identify themselves. The code for the exercise was traditional—*Rerkdi Thanarat* (Good Auspices Thanarat).

Phibun panicked and left the country immediately. Phao, on the other hand, turned himself in to Sarit and requested that he be allowed to go into exile in Switzerland.[159] Sarit was reported to have told Phao that the coup was staged to save Phao's life, for many people hated him.[160] Within twelve hours, Phao was escorted to a plane bound for Europe. The triumvirate had dissolved. Sarit was in complete control of the country.

---

[158] *Sayam Nikon*, September 17, 1957.

[159] It is still puzzling that Phibun chose to flee while Phao turned himself in to the coup leaders. Phibun was a crafty politician and perhaps wanted to escape, to bide his time for a comeback. Phao, on the other hand, acted as expected. Phao showed his *nakleng* form (i.e., daring qualities) and was not afraid to face Sarit. Marshal Phin, Phao's father-in-law, was not involved in this political struggle. By this time, Phin was more concerned with his business ventures, and Sarit left him alone. (See also footnote 91 in this chapter.)

[160] Thai Noi and Kamon, *Waterloo*, p. 180.

CHAPTER THREE

THE SEARCH FOR POLITICAL LEGITIMACY

SARIT'S POLITICAL EXPERIENCE

The ten years between 1947 and 1957 gave Sarit a firsthand view of Thai politics in action. The use of force in the various coups of 1947, 1948, 1951, and 1952 showed that force as a means to power was highly feasible and had become an accepted feature of Thai political life. After 1951, the Coup Group's hold on power came to rest on two pillars, i.e., the armed forces (excluding the police) and Phao's political machine.

While Phao, as we have seen, controlled the police and was responsible for the suppression of opposition to the regime, he was also in charge of keeping the government's parliamentary political machinery working smoothly. Sarit, on the other hand, had merely to maintain the loyalty of the army, including those military officers who were appointed by the regime to the senate. Two financial empires were also created: Phao's based in the opium trade and Sarit's in the Lottery Bureau. The difference in the position of the two men was that Sarit had relatively little to do with coping with the volatile civilian backers of the regime and had the relatively easy task of maintaining solidarity within the military. It was only after Sarit assumed power in 1957 that he encountered the difficulties of trying to reconcile the different interests and demands of his civilian parliamentary backers.

It appears that at the time that Sarit made his move in 1957, he did not have a clear idea of how to run the country. His assumption of power occurred in circumstances that called for a "charismatic" person to change an unpopular government but not an unpopular system. Public resentment was not aimed at the parliamentary system *per se* but rather at the regime's corrupt practices and hypocritical approach to the elections of 1957.[1] Thus, when Sarit staged his coup d'état and ousted the Phibun regime, he acted as a "savior" statesman who wanted only to purify the system by getting rid of its corrupt members. It was only after a year's attempt at governing under the old system that Sarit realized that he could not operate freely and fulfill his goals. He then proceeded to stage Thailand's second "revolution"[2] to create a political system ideal for his purposes, as well as one readily understood by the public.

Sarit's coup of September 1957 was a popular one, and he used this popularity for short-run legitimizing purposes. Before we turn to his emerging political

---

[1] General elections had been held in 1933, 1937, 1938, 1946, 1948, and 1952. These had been relatively uneventful and "clean" in contrast to the February 1957 one.

[2] Sarit considered his coup d'état of October 20, 1958 a *pattiwat*, which can be loosely translated as "revolution." *Pattiwat* has a special meaning in Thai and is not to be confused with Western theories of revolution. What this meaning was will be discussed later.

philosophy and his ideas concerning political legitimacy based upon traditional concepts of the state, it is useful to examine his initial (1957) claims to legitimacy in the eyes of the public.

Basically, these claims were four: that he had approval by the throne, close identification with the "popular will," active support by the students and the knowledgeable public, and his own "charismatic" personality.

Although politically weakened by the coup of 1932, the Thai monarchy continued to maintain widespread popular legitimacy. When Rama VII abdicated in protest against the People's Party's failure to implement democracy, the Phahon government felt too insecure to eliminate the throne. Fearing widespread public resentment, it designated the young Ananda as his uncle's heir. Even Phibun did not dare attack the monarchy openly.

Sarit understood this situation very well. Immediately after the coup, he went to see the king to inform him of his actions, and the king provided him with a document appointing him Defender of the Capital. Although the king probably had no choice but to comply, the ease and lack of conflict with the throne facilitated Sarit's legitimization in the eyes of the public. At an interview with the press on September 17, 1957, Sarit stated that "I am the Defender of the Capital and can give orders in accordance with the law because it is the royal command."[3] He and Thanom had met with the king and related the events that had forced them to act, and the king had given them his support. Sarit told the newsmen that he had the original copy of the royal appointment in his safe and could produce it to satisfy the press of the legal authenticity of his powers.[4]

At the same September 17 press conference, Sarit also stressed his identification with the needs and desires of the public. The tone and content of his reply to press inquiries parallels Weber's famous "call" to charismatic leadership.[5] Sarit said:

> . . . I do not feel at all glad at the actions taken. Necessity and the popular will demanded this . . . Our actions were precipitated by two reasons: that the government should resign, and that Phao should also resign from his position as Director-General of Police. Our aims were these two reasons, which the people clamored for. The people and the press had always reminded me never to retreat and that I should make them [demands] successful. Now they are achieved.[6]

He went on to say that the coup was carried out not so much by a coup d'état group, but by a common citizen, meaning himself, who was comparable to an "old boy," that is, a former student and member of the former government. The government had not been "good," for it had governed without paying attention to the demands and the needs of the public.

---

[3] *Sayam Nikon,* September 18, 1957.

[4] A photocopy of the document was distributed to the various newspapers. The document approved the actions of Sarit and was signed by the king.

[5] See Max Weber, *The Theory of Social and Economic Organization* (New York, NY: The Free Press, 1969), p. 359. Weber wrote that the basis for claim to charismatic legitimacy lies in the "conception that it is the *duty* of those who have been called to a charismatic mission to recognize its quality and to act accordingly. Psychologically, this 'recognition' is a matter of complete personal devotion to the possessor of the quality, arising out of enthusiasm, or of despair and hope."

[6] *Sayam Nikon,* September 18, 1957.

Much of the public concurred with this claim. Many writers maintained that the aim of the Sarit coup was to preserve democracy. In the preface of *Waterloo of Field Marshal Plaek,* Thai Noi and Kamon Chantarason wrote that Sarit executed the coup on behalf of the people, who were identified as the moving force behind democracy.[7] They said that public opinion and the popular will still had power, which permitted those with good intentions toward the nation and the people justly to exploit the strength of the army to eliminate the government in the name of the people. The authors quoted Abraham Lincoln's statement that when the people had no more confidence in their government, they had the right to drive the government out. Thus the vague understanding of democracy by the general public as being equivalent to a concept of popular will, an understanding devoid of concrete ideas about the proper processes of change, further facilitated the rise of Sarit to legitimate power and helped establish him as the representative and agent of the people and a force working for democracy.

Another source of legitimacy played up by Sarit was the active support he received from the students, the knowledgeable public, and most of the press.[8] In various demonstrations and speeches at Hyde Park, students and political leaders affirmed their support.[9] Sarit's initial policy towards the press was to solicit their support by refusing to enforce censorship and urging them to provide him with advice. When asked about the possible dissolution of the assembly, he replied that he did not know what to do and that he lacked command of legal procedures. He than urged the press to write their opinions on the matter and to convince him and the public of the right course of action. He said that the press had educated him on national affairs and thus had prompted him to stage his coup d'état. Thus, when Sarit dissolved the "dirty elections" parliament, his actions were initially seen as fulfilling the demands of the press and public. It was only after Sarit's second coup d'état in 1958 that he reversed his policy of allowing press freedom; heavy censorship as well as repression were then used against the news media. After 1959, Sarit had a more secure vision of the future course of his regime and "education" by the press was no longer needed.

---

[7] Thai Hoi and Kamon, *Waterloo.* In the preface of this book, which was published immediately after the coup, the writers state: "We welcome the statement of Field Marshal Sarit, the Supreme Military Commander, who said that he did not have any ambitions in his actions but that the popular will [*mati mahachom*] had forced him to do so. If he would keep his word, at least we would have the hope of achieving full democracy in this near future."

[8] *Sayam Rat,* September 4, 1957 reported that Sarit used forty million baht from the Lottery Bureau to fund a smear campaign. It appears that public support for Sarit was more of a negative reaction to the Phibun regime and Phao's activities. The reported spontaneous demonstrations urging Sarit to act were perhaps staged by Sarit and his supporters. Sarit controlled his own newspaper, and after the coup the circulation of that publication increased. Interviews by the author with certain people who were involved in the student demonstrations revealed that some leaders, especially students from Isan, had received money from Sarit as support for their political activities.

[9] See Chapter Two. After returning from his trips to America and Europe in 1955, Phibun allowed people to make public speeches at Sanam Luang, which became known as the Thai equivalent of the English Hyde Park.

THE PHOTE SARASIN CABINET: SEPTEMBER 20–DECEMBER 26,1957

Whether the coup of September 17 could have been avoided by timely concessions to the Sarit camp is debatable. It appears that, at the beginning, Sarit had only wanted the Phibun cabinet to resign and perhaps hold new elections. Phao was also to be forced out of power. However, for reasons that are not fully clear, Phibun gambled on the support of Phao, on support from the MPs of the first category, and on the sanctity of the constitution. He told Sarit and army leaders that he would refuse to resign and that he would trust his future to parliament. He informed the army leaders that in his lifetime he had only staged one revolution/coup d'état, and was not planning to do so again. A few days before the coup, Phibun called a meeting of his cabinet and members of his party in parliament and informed them that his cabinet would not resign under any circumstances.[10] He thus gave the army no choice but to follow through with its threat. Phibun's unwillingness to dismiss Phao stemmed from the fact that his position depended largely on keeping Phao and Sarit balanced off against each other. Furthermore, his control of parliament was based on Phao's machine there.

Sarit told the press later that he had had no choice. Since "peaceful persuasion" had failed to bring about change in the government, force was necessary to achieve what the public demanded. He remarked piously that he had wished Phibun would return from exile in Cambodia so that he could pay his respects to the former premier and ask him to remain quiet. He would gladly provide "guards" for Phibun to insure his safety. Phibun in turn cabled in a message to military command headquarters stating that "for the well-being of both sides, I decided to make a personal sacrifice and leave the country."[11]

Immediate house cleaning by the new ruling group was put into effect. On September 18, an announcement was made that the Constitution of 1932 (revised in 1952) was to be enforced with four exceptions—parliament was to be dissolved; elections for MPs of the first category were to be held within ninety days; no more than 123 MPs of the second category would be appointed to act as a national assembly until elections were held; and the Defender of the Capital (Sarit) was to be given the power to appoint a new cabinet.[12] Appointment and promotions of police officers were temporarily suspended, except that Police Lt. Colonel Sanga Kittikhachon (General Thanom's brother) would be elevated to the position of deputy commander of the Crime Suppression Division.[13] The high commands of the air force and the navy were also changed, and Sarit's supporters were appointed to positions of responsibility.[14] Sarit did this because he did not want to see a replay of

---

[10] *Sayam Rat*, September 15, 1957. An impasse was reached, for the two sides now took firm stands. Phibun refused to resign, while the army and MPs of the second category insisted that he resign together with his cabinet.

[11] *Sayam Rat*, September 19, 1957. By September 26, Sarit had changed his mind and said that it was not appropriate for Phibun to return. Pridi would also be arrested if he came back. *Sayam Rat*, September 26, 1957.

[12] *Sayam Rat*, September 20, 1957.

[13] Ibid.

[14] *Sayam Rat*, September 21, 1957. Field Marshal Fuen and Luang Cherdwuthakat, the Commander-in-Chief and Deputy of the Air Force, respectively, were relieved of their duties, and Air Marshal Chalermkiat, a very close friend of Sarit, was appointed Air Force Chief. Air Marshal Bunchoo Chantarubeksa was appointed Chief of Staff of the Air Force, while Air Chief Marshal Thawee Chulasap was promoted to become Deputy Chief of Staff of the Armed

the 1951 Manhattan attempted coup, where the navy challenged the power of the army and the 1947 Coup Group. He also did not want the police to challenge the army's monopoly of the use of force. Sarit's supervision of the police later became more direct after the October 20, 1958 *pattiwat*, when he himself assumed the position of Director-General of the Police Department. General Sawai, who was appointed police chief in 1957, became President of the Constituent Assembly in 1958.

In line with previous public statement that their actions were done for the people and not for themselves, Sarit and Thanom told the press that they were not ambitious and would not accept the premiership. Thanom told newsmen that:

> It was the understanding within the military circle and among MPs [who supported the coup] that it was not proper for a military officeer to assume the position of Prime Minister. That position should be given to a person whom the people genuinely liked.[15]

The only conditions the new leaders stipulated in the choice of a premier were that he should be able to work closely with the armed forces, that he should have an impeccable record of honesty, and that he should be respected by the international community.

Six names were put forward by the military committee and the MPs of the second category who were currently acting as parliament. These were: Chaophraya Sithammathibet, Phraya Siwisanwacha, Khuang Aphaiwong, Seni Pramote, Nai Worakanbancha, and Phote Sarasin. The first two were respected aristocrats; Khuang and Seni represented conservative/royalist elements, as well as being the leaders of the Democrat Party, which had acted as the main opposition party in parliament during the Phibun regime; Nai Worakanbancha belonged to the Seri Manangkhasila Party, but had had close ties with Sarit since the 1947 coup; Phote Sarasin was a respected lawyer and diplomat who had recently returned from an ambassadorial assignment in Washington to assume the post of Secretary-General of SEATO (Southeast Asia Treaty Organization).

While the first two on the list were well-respected, their candidacies were handicapped by age and their sociopolitical backgrounds. Khuang and Seni were poor choices, for they represented a minority in the previous parliament. Sarit had made a statement before the coup that it was not only the Seri Manangkhasila Party that had cheated in the elections—"everybody cheated." Hence it would have been odd for Sarit to allow Khuang or Seni to form a government when the military had just eliminated Phibun and Phao on the grounds of unethical conduct during the elections. Nai Worakan was a strong choice, though compromised by his former connections to the Seri Manangkhasila Party and his known association with the military leaders. The new elite wanted someone who was neutral so it could

---

Forces. Field Marshal Luang Yutthasatkoson was replaced by Admiral Luang Chamnan as Navy Chief. General Sawai Sawaisaenyakon became the new Police Chief, with Lt. General Prasert Ruchirawong as his deputy. Upon assuming command, Sawai told the press that there would be a transformation in the police force to make it a public-oriented organization and to eliminate the police's capacity to pose a threat to the armed forces, which should prevent any future armed struggle between the police and the army. Of the 120 appointed members of the Senate, only three were police officers. See Withetkorani, *Khwampenma*, pp. 1422-27, for a list of the appointees.

[15] *Sayam Rat*, September 21, 1957.

demonstrate to the public that it had not acted out of self-interest. Thus the choice of Phote Sarasin was most appropriate. Phote was a very wealthy man in his own right and therefore unlikely to become involved in corruption in office, which could embarrass the military leaders. He was also internationally known and respected. Phote was best suited for the purposes of the military. He could normalize relations with foreign governments as well as satisfy domestic requirements.

For all intents and purposes, the Phote Sarasin cabinet was an interim government meant to obtain the continued support of foreign governments as well as supervise the upcoming elections of members of the lower house.[16] Phote's cabinet was composed of men chosen by the new Coup Group. While Lt. General Thanom controlled the Defense Ministry, Maj. General Praphat saw to the affairs of the Interior Ministry. Of the twenty-nine members of the cabinet, fifteen were military officers from the new ruling group. Two important members of the Sahaphum Party were also given appointments in the Phote cabinet.[17] With the appointment of a cabinet, Sarit's role as Defender of the Capital lapsed, and he was subsequently appointed Supreme Military Commander of the Armed Forces, leaving the challenges of establishing internal and external normalization to the Phote government.

It was a delicate situation on both fronts during this time. The domestic mood concerning Thailand's foreign commitments was in a state of ferment. There was clear evidence that the public had been displeased with the Phibun regime prior to its downfall because of its close relations with the American government. (This "displeasure" was partly engineered by the Sarit camp in cooperation with the royalist conservatives in an attempt to discredit the regime.) Speakers at the Hyde Park demonstrations had attacked Phibun for following the lead of the United States in international affairs, and Isan MPs suggested that the country should trade with Communist China.[18] The chief spokesman of the royalist conservatives, Kukrit Pramote, was involved at this time in a government suit publicly accusing the American ambassador, Max Waldo Bishop, of interfering in Thai politics. Sarit himself indicated that he was not opposed to trade with Communist China and felt that Thailand should not rely mainly upon the help of the United States.[19] Student leaders from the major universities had wanted to travel to attend the Moscow Youth Festival; when the Phibun government seemed reluctant to let them go, newspaper reports suggested that the government's stand had been determined by American pressure.

When the Phote government assumed office, it had to make public concessions in the beginning to this anti-American trend. Phote made a statement that the government was not against anyone traveling to Communist China, but he warned that if anything happened to these travelers, the government would be in no position to help.[20] Lt. Gen. Chitti Nawisathien, Deputy Minister of Economic Affairs, also

---

[16] Phote's role was thus similar to the one played by Khuang in 1947.

[17] These two were Sukich Nimmanhaemin, the party chief, and Sanguan Chantarasakha, Secretary of the Sahaphum, who was also Sarit's half-brother. The Sahaphum was organized after the February 1957 elections by MPs who supported Sarit.

[18] Eight Isan MPs elected to parliament in 1957 belonged to the Economist Front, which advocated trade with all countries, including Communist China.

[19] Darling, *Thailand and the United States*, p. 162. This was a political gesture to gain the support of the students and Isan MPs.

[20] *Sayam Rat*, September 27, 1957.

indicated that the government was not opposed to trade with Communist China.[21] The United States appeared concerned with these developments, indeed with Sarit's assumption of power. On September 20, three days after the coup, Ambassador Bishop went to see Sarit and offered the support of the United States government. Sarit informed the ambassador that he was willing to receive aid, so long as it had no strings attached, to develop the armed forces and improve living conditions and to accept other types of assistance that would benefit the people directly.[22]

While public sentiment against a pro-American alliance was evident, and Sarit had earlier voiced his support for trade with Communist China, he nevertheless realized that his government needed financial support from the United States. The armed forces also had to rely upon continued American assistance. Thus, Phote Sarasin was entrusted with the responsibility of assuring the United States that Thai foreign policy would not undergo major changes, and that Phote would shoulder the blame (in domestic circles) for the government's intended drift away from the anti-American line.

Another task of the Phote cabinet was conducting elections for members of the lower house. To establish that Sarit's coup was credibly disinterested, a neutral and independent government was needed to oversee the elections and to prevent a replay of the February elections, which had been marked by violence and unethical conduct on the part of the government party. Maj. Gen. Praphat, a close associate of Sarit, was appointed Minister of Interior with responsibility for organizing fair elections. This he did, and the clean elections held in December won wide public, as well as royal, approval. Sarit himself made appearances on public media to remind all parties to be honest. When he was queried by the press at a polling station, Sarit replied that the elections would show to all that the military was not above the law and that the choice of a new Prime Minister rested entirely with parliament.

The results of the elections were as follows:[23]

Table 4. December 15, 1957 Election Results

Party	Seats in Parliamant
Sahaphum	44
Democrat	39
Economist	6
Free Democrat	5
Seri Manangkhasila	4
Chatniyom	1
Hyde Park	1
Independent Party	1
Independents	59

Although statistically the Sahaphum, the government party, held a majority over other political parties, the Democrat Party had essentially won the elections. In the major cities, the Sahaphum candidates were routed. No government MP was elected

---

[21] *Sayam Rat,* September 28, 1957.

[22] *Sayam Rat,* September 22, 1957.

[23] See Withetkorani, *Khwampenma,* pp. 1428-38. for the list of MPs elected. Note the large number of independents. These MPs were mainly former Seri Manangkhasila members.

from Bangkok and Thonburi.[24] Out of the nine seats contested in Bangkok, eight were won by Democrats and one by an independent; the Democrats swept all three seats in Thonburi. In Chiengmai, where the Sahaphum Party chief, Sukich Nimmanhaemin, led a strong delegation to contest the seats, only he himself was elected, along with two Democrats and two independents. While the elections did not give the government party a clear majority in parliament, it did give the Military Group moral prestige, for it could now claim that it had acted in good faith and had complied with public demands for fair elections and the continuation of democratic practices.

However, like previous ruling groups, the military leaders wanted a comfortable, if not complete, control of parliament. Thus, six days after the elections, a new party was formed known as the Chatsangkhomniyom Party (National Socialist Party), with Sarit himself acting as head, Thanom and Sukich as deputies, and Praphat as party secretary. This party was to attempt to win over former Seri Manangkhasila Party members who had been elected to parliament as independents. This move was necessary because the Sahaphum had earlier refused to accept Seri Manangkhasila MPs into its ranks. By forming the Chatsangkhomniyom Party, Sarit was able to bring Sahaphum MPs and other MPs together.

THE FIRST THANOM CABINET: JANUARY 1–OCTOBER 20, 1958

It is still unclear why Phote refused to continue on as prime minister. In an interview with the press a few days after the elections, Phote told newsmen that he would refuse the premiership on the grounds that his obligations to his country had been fulfilled.[25] It could be speculated that Phote did not agree with the formation of the military's Chatsangkhomniyom Party and did not want to be a puppet of the Military Group. Khuang criticized the formation of the new government party, labeling this new development as the inauguration of a period of group rule (*khanathipatai*).[26] Sarit's decision to consolidate his parliamentary backing also did not receive instantaneous approval from members of the Sahaphum, which hitherto acted as Sarit's political arm in parliament. They did not want former members of the Seri Manangkhasila in the new government party. Thirty-six Sahaphum MPs signed a petition of protest to Sarit, stating their objections. However, they pledged that they would continue to support him.[27]

The Military Group was not ready to assume political leadership and wanted time to observe developments further. Phote's decision to resign in late December was unwelcome news. Attempts by army leaders to convince Phote to continue in his office failed, and a leadership crisis developed, aggravated by the fact that Sarit himself was still convalescing in Bangsaen, a seaside resort outside Bangkok. The only solution seemed to be to let Thanom assume the position of Prime Minister. To

---

[24] Assuming that Sarit was popular in the capital, it is surprising that his party fared so poorly. A plausible explanation is that voters still chose MPs based on the strength of their personalities, and no prominent member of the Sarit coup group ran for an elected seat. Democrat candidates were, however, well-known and seasoned politicians. More studies on Thai voting behavior are still needed.

[25] *Sayam Rat*, December 19, 1957.

[26] *Sayam Rat*, December 24, 1957.

[27] *Sayam Rat*, December 25, 1957.

effect this, Sarit sent a tape recording to a meeting of the Chatsangkhomniyom Party asking the members to choose Thanom as Prime Minister. Thanom accepted the responsibility reluctantly, telling the press that he did not want to be a professional prime minister and that if he could not achieve his set goals, he would promptly resign.[28] It was apparent to all that Thanom was only a stand-in. Even the new premier-designate himself accepted this fact and said that after he had put together a cabinet, he would go to see Sarit and ask for his approval. The king also sent flowers to Sarit and prayed for his quick recovery.

If Thanom was reluctant to take over the reins of government, it was quite understandable. While his cabinet included eleven members from the Military Group, there were six from the Sahaphum, several independents, and three former Seri Manangkhasila MPs.[29] Since the start, the Military Group had had to rely upon the support of these groups to achieve political effectiveness in parliament. Like previous governments, the new leadership tried to consolidate its parliamentary backers into a single workable organization—the Chatsangkhomniyom Party—but it faced the same difficulties and limitations that had been confronted by its predecessors.[30]

The first few months of the Thanom government were marked by internal strife within the Chatsangkhomniyom. Some former Sahaphum members refused to dissolve their old party in favor of the new one, which would include former Seri Manangkhasila MPs and other independents. The Sahaphum itself was divided between those who agreed with Sarit that the Sahaphum should be dissolved and others who insisted that it should continue to function within the Chatsangkhomniyom, which they saw as a compromise and a coalition party. The independents and former Seri Manangkhasila members were also jealous of Sahaphum MPs, who received a larger share in cabinet positions. Thanom was ill-equipped to handle these developments, for he did not have the forceful character of Sarit, and it was accepted by all, including Thanom himself, that Sarit had the final say on all political matters. Since Sarit was still resting at Bangsaen, all he could do was to try to convince his followers that they should cooperate with each other. The news of his pending trip to the United States for major surgery at Walter Reed Army Hospital only served to make matters worse for the Thanom government.

Three days after Sarit left for the United States, Thanom's government faced its first crisis: the resignation of its Minister of Justice, who left because he was accused of nepotism by certain members of the Military Group for hiring his son-in-law as his personal secretary.[31] Thanom did not know how to react, and could only complain to the press that he himself wanted to resign.[32] He was also unable to prevent the

---

[28] *Sayam Rat*, December 28, 1957.

[29] *Sayam Nikon*, January 3, 1958.

[30] Phibun and Phao had to spend much time and money to win assurances of support from the Sahaphak (United Front, 1949–1951) and the Sapha Nittibanyat (Legislative Committee, 1951–1957). See Chapter II. Sarit would soon face a similar predicament.

[31] *Sayam Nikon*, January 26, 1958.

[32] *Sayam Nikon*, January 28, 1958. In an attempt to strengthen its hold over the country, the Military Group instigated a major reshuffling of positions in the armed forces. The most noticeable change was the promotion of Praphat to Commander of the First Army in Thanom's place. Praphat was known for his rather straightforward, tough style. He was not as subtle as Sarit or Thanom and had a reputation for being a strong-minded person with ruthless inclinations.

resignation of twenty-six Sahaphum MPs from the government party and had to face opposition from members of his own party, who resented the cut in the education budget and the increase in the military budget.[33] Thanom's government was also pressed by several MPs to enact a law to curb illegal spending of the Lottery Bureau funds after news was published that the bureau had sent three million baht to Sarit for his medical treatment.[34] At this juncture, rumors circulated in the press that Sarit had expressed his desire to resign from the government party since he had spent more than fourteen million baht already on the party and all he had got in return were headaches.[35]

A major test for the Chatsangkhomniyom and the popularity of the Thanom government came towards the end of March 1958, when partial elections were held in five provinces, namely: Bangkok, Thonburi, Kalasin, Roi Et, and Ubon.[36] The election results proved to be a major setback for the Thanom government, for out of the twenty-six seats available, the Democrats garnered thirteen compared to the Chatsangkhomniyom's nine. Especially in Bangkok and Thonburi, the government party was soundly defeated despite heavy campaigning by military leaders. The elections were, however, conducted in correct fashion, a fact confirmed by the king's praise for the government's honesty.[37] To alleviate the military's anxiety, the king approved the promotion of over fifty generals, with Thanom especially singled, for the king personally conferred the rank of full general on the prime minister.[38] The Military Group's frustration came out in the press when an urgent meeting was called by the military leaders to determine why the government party had fared so poorly. An urgent report was sent to Sarit informing him of the election results.

Again Thanom told the press that he wanted to resign.[39] However, the results of the elections were not the only headache that the Thanom government had to contend with. The budget for fiscal year 1958 posed another problem for the weakening government, for the government-proposed budget showed a deficit of over 2,200 million bath. In an attempt to reduce this deficit, the government proposed to raise taxes on certain commodities such as gasoline, cement, and other imported goods. This tax proposal attracted heavy criticism from the press and the opposition parties, as well as from certain quarters within the Chatsangkhomniyom itself. Under this pressure, Air Marshal Chalermkiat was quickly dispatched to the

---

[33] *Sayam Rat,* February 21, 1958.

[34] *Sayam Rat,* March 18, 1957 and March 20, 1957. During Sarit's absence, his half-brother, Sanguan, was in charge of the Lottery Bureau.

[35] *Sayam Rat,* March 27, 1958.

[36] The elections were held in accordance with the Constitution of 1952, which contained a clause stating that, after five years, MPs of the second category had to draw lots to choose which of them would resign in favor of MPs of the first category. The basis for computing the number of MPs who would resign was conditional upon the government's determination that a certain province had reached a literacy level such that the number of citizens who had passed primary schooling was over half of the number of the electorate in that province. The quota of MPs in these provinces would then double. Hence, there was to be an election for nine MPs from Bangkok, three from Thonburi, three from Kalasin, four from Roi Et, and seven from Ubon. As a corollary, the senate would be reduced in membership by twenty-six.

[37] *Sayam Nikon,* April 2, 1958.

[38] Ibid.

[39] *Sayam Nikon,* April 16, 1958.

United States to confer with Sarit. Thanom told the press that he would resign immediately upon Sarit's return to Bangkok.[40]

Chalermkiat returned from the United States with a recorded message from Sarit to the MPs in the Chatsangkhomniyom, urging them strongly to lend their support to the government.[41] But despite Sarit's pleas, Thanom's government continued to suffer attacks from MPs in parliament and strife within his party. In an attempt to bolster Thanom's position, Sarit made a surprise visit to Bangkok on June 27. Parliamentary opposition leaders had planned a session during which they would question and essentially challenge the government; it only failed at the last minute, when thirteen MPs withdrew their support. Newspaper rumors suggested that these MPs were bribed by Sarit, who himself unabashedly told newsmen that the MPs withdrew out of "respect" for him.[42] One of the MPs who backed out of the opposition's plan to challenge the government revealed that Sarit had threatened him, saying that unless he complied with Sarit's request, the latter would be forced to use "de Gaullism."[43]

During his short stay in Bangkok, Sarit became impatient with the press and warned them that they should not interfere by exaggerating news regarding the affairs of his party. He also stated that he had not been home for even two days when the *Issara* paper accused him of being involved in the heroin trade. He warned that he would not be responsible if soldiers got out of hand and paid a visit to the newspaper office to express their anger.[44] True enough, the newspaper was visited by a group of soldiers who destroyed a few printing presses. After this show of force, Sarit left for England to rest. But Thanom's government received only a short breather at this juncture. The sensitive issue of the Phra Wihan Temple (see below, Chapter Five) received wide publicity, resulting in a public demonstration against the Cambodian embassy and announcements by Praphat that he would let the temple fall into Khmer hands. Thanom was at the end of his rope. Again he threatened to resign, but the Military Group urged him to stay on and told him to take a two-week rest.[45] An emergency was declared in seven provinces bordering Cambodia; six ministers resigned from the Thanom government; and Sahaphum MPs threatened to leave the government party over the issue of "favoritism." In this confused political situation, Thanom seemed quite at sea. To save the situation from deteriorating any further, Sarit quietly returned from England and called a meeting of the Military Group on October 19, 1958. The next day, Thanom resigned as prime minister and Sarit staged another coup d'état, as the public had expected him to do all along.

---

[40] *Sayam Nikon,* April 22, 1958.

[41] *Sayam Rat,* May 4, 1958.

[42] *Sayam Rat,* July 3, 1958.

[43] *Sayam Rat,* July 5, 1958.

[44] *Sayam Rat,* July 6, 1958

[45] *Sayam Nikon,* September 4, 1958.

THE *PATTIWAT* OF OCTOBER, 20, 1958

Sarit's coup d'état of October 20, 1958 is important in Thai political history, for it marked the beginning of a new political system that endured until very recently.[46] The significance of this coup, which its leaders called a *pattiwat* (revolution), has not been fully appreciated by scholars, whether Thai or foreign. Sarit's rule has been characterized as a dictatorship, as benevolent despotism, and as military rule. However, if one examines the basis for this "revolution" and tries to understand the thinking of its instigator, one realizes that the political system imposed upon Thailand by Sarit and his followers can be said to be "revolutionary" in the sense that it tried to overthrow a whole political system inherited from 1932, and to create one that could be described as more "Thai" in nature. However, before we can appreciate this change, it may be useful to examine briefly the political leadership style of Phibun to provide a basis for comparison with Sarit's innovations.

Phibun was Thailand's prime minister from 1938 to 1944, and from 1948 to 1957. It makes good sense, therefore, to divide his tenure, and his style, into two separate phases. Phibun's first period in power can be characterized as an attempt by the People's Party to use constitutional democracy as the legitimizing principle of political leadership.[47]

The People's Party was represented as the group that would bring democracy to Thailand. Propaganda and public indoctrination were conducted to educate the people on the merits of democracy as practiced by modern and civilized countries. Thailand had to become civilized and up-to-date and thus must accept democratic practices.

Phibun himself, however, is best remembered for his strong nationalism and his programs designed to make Thailand a powerful state. When he became defense minister in 1934, he began to promote such concepts as *phunam* (leader), *chatniyom* and *ratthaniyom* (nationalism and state-ism), *wirachon* (heroes or people conducting their lives in a style closely related to the Japanese concept of *bushido*, the Samurai's warrior code), and militarism (modernizing the army and strengthening the armed forces).[48]

Phibun's early political ideology was dual in nature. While, on the one hand, he acknowledged constitutionalism as the state ideology, he wanted to promote nationalism and state-ism and the concept of a national leader similar to that current at the time in Nazi Germany and Fascist Italy. The culmination of Phibun's political leadership came in the proclamation of *ratthaniyom* as the state ideology. The government declared in 1940 that, in order to guarantee and protect the achievements of the regime,

---

[46] Following student demonstrations in October 1973, the Thanom government resigned and a civilian government was formed. The period of open democracy lasted three years, and ended when a civilian authoritarian regime was installed, backed by the military. It lasted a year and was replaced by a military government that promised to allow free elections to be held by 1979.

[47] Col. Luang Phibunsongkhram, *Pathakhatha Ruang Kanborihan Ratchakan Phaendin* [Speech on National Administration], Bangkok, November 18, 1934. Phibun refers to the government as *ratthaban ratthathammanun*, or "constitutional government."

[48] For accounts of the work of Phibun, see Charun, *Chiwit Kantosu khong Chomphon P: Khunsuk phu rai Phaendin* [Field Marshal P.—Warrior without a Country] (Bangkok: Phatthana Kanphim Press, 1964).

. . . the Thai people should build new characteristics to conform with the new [political] system. Because of this, the government must be interested in building progress to conform to the monumental work that it has strived to achieve.[49]

The announcement pointed out that it was easy to protect the political structures because laws could be passed to safeguard them. However, laws by themselves were useless as tools to build progress, and the government must devise other means to affect this change: the program to be known as *ratthaniyom*.

Similar to the concept of constitutional democracy advocated and implemented in 1932, the concept of *ratthaniyom* was a foreign product that Phibun tried to import for use in Thailand. He attempted to give the new concept Thai historical roots by stating that *ratthaniyom* was similar to the traditional concept of *phraratchaniyom* (royalism), the only difference being that now loyalty should be directed primarily not to the king, but to the state, which was established through the consensus of the masses.[50] *Ratthaniyom* was to become the popular tradition *(praphaeniniyom)* of the country. All Thais who wanted national progress must honor and comply with this new ideology.

Phibun was quite popular with the public during the first phase of his rule. However, the actual workings of *ratthaniyom* confused many people. The marshal directed that in order for the country to be modernized, the people must *look* modern and civilized. Thus he urged people to dress like Europeans, prohibited the chewing of betel, encouraged the use of business cards, and suggested that husbands kiss their wives before going off to work. In a public address on the occasion of National Day, 1943, Phibun expressed his pride that Thai now *looked* good. A progressive state must have progressive people who dress properly, he said, and this was why the government had spent time and energy convincing the people to do so. He continued,

> I have seen in our society today, [something] that has made me happy ... proper dresses and correct manner are no different from other civilized countries ... In the past, it was seldom that one heard the remark "I saw a well-dressed lady." One only heard "I saw a beautiful [face] lady." But now, men remark after coming back from any social affair that "I was lucky today because I met a lady who wore a skirt and hat ... gorgeous shoes. She was as beautiful as any lady from any other country.[51]

In this respect, Phibun differed fundamentally from Sarit, who insisted that cultural and political innovations should be viewed in the light of Thai tradition and culture.

Nevertheless, Phibun's *ratthaniyom* was similar to Sarit's *pattiwat* insofar as both were means for achieving or maintaining national solidarity, expressed in terms of *samakhitham* or *watthana phatthana*.[52] Phibun wanted to build up popular loyalty to

---

[49] Krom Khotsanakan, *Pramuan Ratthaniyom* [State-ism], Bangkok, April 17, 1940, no pagination. Italics added.

[50] Ibid.

[51] Luang Phibunsongkhram, *Khamprasai Wan Chat* [National Day Speech], Bangkok, June 24, 1943. Italics added

[52] Phibun used the term *watthana*, Sarit used *phatthana*. Both these words mean "progress" and "development." *Samakhitham* means "moral solidarity" and "cooperation."

the nation-state, and the programs inherent in *ratthaniyom* were geared towards this goal: the changing of the name Siam to Thailand, the adoption of a national anthem, the emphasis on economic nationalism, the elimination of distinguishing terms such as "Isan Thai," "Muslim Thai," "Central Thai," "North Thai" (everybody would now be known as "Thai").[53] By Sarit's time, this battle had largely been won, and Sarit was more concerned with the political divisions in the nation.

A striking resemblance between Phibun's early political style and that of Sarit is apparent if we consider the manner in which both stressed personal leadership. Despite Phibun's exposure to Western democracy, he was certainly affected by the concept of the benevolent and all-powerful despot, which has deep roots in Thai politics. Phibun consciously promoted a leadership, or *phunam,* cult, which was reflected in his slogan, "believe in the leader and the nation will escape danger." At the same time, Phibun's leadership cult was clearly influenced by Western models, as evidenced by his fascination with fascism and the Fuhrer concept. Sarit, on the other hand, did not outwardly advocate a leadership cult as such; rather, he created such a cult through active demonstration. When Sarit spoke of leadership, it was in terms of traditional paternalistic ideas, whereby the nation figured as the family and Sarit took on the role of father.

Phibun consciously wanted to mold Thai society to meet international standards and thus insisted that the people adopt Western clothing and manners. Phibun wanted the regime to determine what the culture of the nation should be, and he took steps to organize a Cultural Ministry to realize this goal. Sarit, on the other hand, wanted to maintain a conservative lifestyle for the Thai people and insisted that Thai society should be governed by the concept of *riaproy* or orderliness. Sarit's social programs were designed to make society conform to a conservative social ethic loosely defined as proper Thai social conduct.

As we have noted earlier, Phibun's return to political leadership in 1948 saw him initially attempt to reimplement the *phunam* cult. But because conditions had changed and Phibun was saddled with two younger rivals, his political position was not strong enough for him to be successful. Consequently, he fell back upon his early commitment to constitutional democracy as a basis for legitimizing power. He had to abandon his *phunam* claims and invoke his role in the 1932 Revolution as a justification for continued leadership. The failure of his "constitutional government" and the corruption of his regime gave Sarit a chance to stage a coup d'état in 1957 and drive Phibun from office. In 1957–1958, Thanom (under Sarit's direction) tried to govern with Phibun's apparatus. They found it increasingly unsatisfactory. The "revolution" of 1958 was instituted, as Sarit put it, so that political concepts borrowed from the West could be reexamined and re-Thai-ification implemented.

An excerpt from Sarit's biography found in his Cremation Volume published by the cabinet is a good starting point for analyzing the workings of his new political system. After attempting to shore up Thanom's government by his surprise visit to Bangkok from the United States, Sarit left for London in July of 1958 to recuperate from his surgeries at Walter Reed Army Hospital. According to the Cremation Volume:

---

[53] Krom Khotsanakan, *Pramuan Ratthaniyom,* no pagination. The government chose the army's entry in the national anthem contest as the winner. Also see, Chaloemtiarana, *Thai Politics,* especially the dialogue between Nai Man and Nai Khong.

Using London as a base, Sarit went on study tours of many [European] countries ... While in London, more and more unpleasant news reached him. This was due to the fact that after the coup d'état of September 16, 1957, there was no attempt to alter the form of government and administration. There still existed a parliament, political parties, a free-press system that could criticize the government, and there were labor unions that could go on strike whenever they were unhappy with their employers. Although the government tried to function to the best of its abilities, it could not do its work properly owing to these adverse political mechanisms. The worst aspect was the desires of MPs to become cabinet ministers and political appointees. They threatened to leave the government party and establish new opposition parties.

As leader of the 1957 coup, Sarit received such troubling news from home with great concern. At this point, Sarit admitted that there was no way to redeem the situation unless the political system were altered, and a constitution suitable for Thailand devised. Therefore, he invited the Thai ambassador to the United States, Thanat Khoman, and the Thai ambassador to Switzerland, Luang Wichit Wathakan, to bring several constitutions of other countries to discuss with him. It was concluded that there must be a revolution [*pattiwat*] in Thailand to implement political mechanisms suitable for the administration of the country, and that a coup d'état [*ratthaprahan*] would not solve any problems.

At that moment, Prime Minister Thanom Kittikhachon sent a representative to London to urge Sarit to return to Thailand. Consequently, Sarit decided to return secretly to the country and landed at Don Muang airport on October 18, 1958 at 4:00 pm. The next morning, he conferred with Thanom and other leading members of the government [also Military Group]. They all agreed that "revolutionary" methods must be used and that "major surgery" was needed to solve the nation's problems.[54]

The Military Group's frustrations and subsequent actions parallel previous events in the political history of the country. After the military coup of 1947, the Coup Group attempted to engage in politics by forming its own party, an action that invariably involved trying to build a coalition of various parliamentary factions. It was difficult for the military leaders to generate genuine solidarity within the political machinery, however, and internal squabbles became a source of headaches for the ruling military elite. Their attempts to play party politics also cost them heavily, for bribery became a major instrument for control. The 1947 Coup Group's Sahaphak, or United Front Party, proved costly to run, as well as frustrating to keep intact. Thus the Silent or Radio Coup of 1951 was staged in an attempt to get rid of "troublesome" MPs who had demanded more privileges and more money. The dissolution of the Sahaphak led to a new coalition of MPs known as the Sapha Nittibanyat, or Legislative Committee, which in turn became the Seri Manangkhasila Party. Again the Coup Group had to spend large sums and rely on political patronage to keep this group together. Again the Coup Group, especially Phao, indulged in illegal and corrupt tactics to raise funds to keep party members happy, and they used repressive methods to clamp down on opposition factions in parliament. The Coup Group's involvement in parliamentary and party politics was

---

[54] Cremation Volume of Sarit Thanarat [Cabinet edition], pp. 65, 66.

a major source of grief and was one factor that finally led to the split in its own leadership and the eventual downfall of the triumvirate.

The Sarit coup of September 16, 1957 came about through circumstances that precluded immediate radical changes in the political system. It was ostensibly staged to save the country from a corrupt and unpopular government, not an unpopular system. It also appears that the Sarit clique had not yet formulated any definite ideas on national administration and thus had to rely temporarily on old political practices. In essence, the Sarit group initially fell into the same pattern that Phibun and Phao had developed. The Seri Manangkhasila was replaced by the Military Group's Chatsangkhomniyom Party, again a conglomeration of various factions that supported the Military Group but were antagonistic towards each other. Sarit and Thanom found it hard to keep the group together and had to resort to the same tactics that Phibun and Phao had practiced: bribery and intimidation. Government administration became bogged down by the attempt to please all factions. As military officers who were used to having their commands and wishes carried out by their subordinates, Sarit and Thanom found it intolerable that they were forced to comply with demands of civilian MPs because of political necessity. This frustration led to the Sarit coup of October 20, 1958 which paved the way for the "major surgery" promised.[55]

Immediately following the coup, political parties were banned, and the constitution set aside.[56] Mass arrests were made of suspected communist sympathizers and of newspaper editors.[57] In the meantime, political gatherings of more than five persons were banned.[58]

Sarit immediately called a meeting of the Revolutionary Council[59] to find ways to gain public support. Among the schemes devised were: a reduction in electricity rates; the provision of free tap water; the holding of Sunday Flea Markets in various areas to provide cheap commodities for the public; a reduction in price of iced coffee, sugar, and charcoal; an increase in the number of protected professions for Thai nationals from thirteen to twenty-seven; and a directive to the navy to search for cheap coconuts to sell to the public. As a result of this kind of example, and perhaps also because they were pressured, other organizations offered to lower their prices as

---

[55] It appears that Sarit's personal experience influenced his political metaphors. After the "major surgery" at Walter Reed improved his own condition, he suggested that the nation undergo "major surgery" to give it new life and vitality.

[56] Khana Pattiwat [Revolutionary Council], *Prakat khong Khana Pattiwat Chabab thi 8, Chabab thi 3* [Proclamation of the Revolutionary Council No. 8, No. 3], October 20, 1958. Proclamations of the Revolutionary Council could be found in Police Lt. Sathien Wichailak, comp., *Ruam Prakat khong Khana Pattiwat Chabab thi 1 thung Chabab sutthai* [Collection of Proclamations of the Revolutionary Council from number 1 to the last] (Bangkok: Nitiwet Press, 1967). Subsequent references to the proclamations of the Revolutionary Council would be written as *Prakat khong Khana Pattiwat No.* [ ], [date].

[57] See *Sayam Rat,* October 22, 1958. Thirty-one persons were arrested on October 21, among them two politicians, MP Khlaew Norapat from Khonkaen and Police Capt. Chiep Amphunan, a former Pridi supporter; eight newsmen; and twenty-one civilians, including eleven Chinese. Twelve more persons were later arrested, including four newsmen, one teacher, MP Thep Chotinuchit from Srisaket, and five persons who had returned from a visit to China.

[58] *Prakat khong Khana Pattiwat No. 13,* October 23, 1958.

[59] After the October 20, 1958 pattiwat, the Military Group (Khana Thahan) was transformed into the Revolutionary Council (Khana Pattiwat).

well, giving Sarit's regime a benevolent aura. The Telephone Organization asked Sarit whether it could reduce telephone rates to help the public and assist the cause of the revolution. Railway rates were reduced and school tuitions were decreased.

Within a span of two months, Sarit was able to establish the tone of his regime: the immediate needs of the public were to be achieved regardless of cost. The various arrests, the closing down of bookshops, the banning of political parties, the crackdown of labor unions,[60] the decisive action taken against arsonists,[61] the arrests of hooligans, balanced by the reduction in prices of commodities and other benevolent despotic actions, were meant to demonstrate to all that the new regime was indeed "revolutionary" and that things would now "get moving."

On the international front, the US State Department immediately issued a statement that the political changes in Thailand would not affect Thai-United States relations.[62] Three days after the coup, Thanat Khoman, the Thai ambassador in Washington, returned to Bangkok and reported to Sarit that the United States sympathized with him and understood the need for security and stability, conditions which Sarit's actions promised to make possible.[63]

The king himself issued a statement to the Revolutionary Council reminding the leaders that they should act faithfully for the good of the people and the nation.[64] Sarit, meanwhile, had sent a message to the king assuring him that the institution of the monarchy would be one of the perpetual pillars of the Thai nation:

In this revolution, certain institutions must be changed. However, one institution that the Revolutionary Council will never allow to be altered is the institution of the monarchy representing the nation as a whole. The Revolutionary Council will stand firm in preserving this system, and we have promised the people in various proclamations regarding this point. I would like to give your majesty personal assurances that the new constitution will preserve this particular feature.[65]

An official explanation of the actions taken by the Revolutionary Council was given in Proclamation No. 4. It stated, first, that the growing internal menace of communism was undermining the basic foundations of the state by attempting to "uproot the monarchy, destroy Buddhism, and overthrow institutions of all types which the Thai nation cherished."[66] Second, several parties had made a sham of the

---

[60] *Sayam Rat,* November 19, 1958. Four labor unions were banned.

[61] In November, two fires took place at a market place. Sarit personally interrogated the suspects who were Chinese and concluded that they had set fire to their own shops to get insurance money. He promptly ordered their public executions.

[62] *Sayam Rat,* October 23, 1958.

[63] *Sayam Rat,* October 26, 1958.

[64] Samnak Ratchalekhathikan [Royal Secretariat], Document No. 2183/2501, October 21, 1958

[65] Kongbanchakan Khana Pattiwat [Revolutionary Council Headquarters], Document No. 8/2501, October 20, 1958. It is likely that the king was informed of Sarit's coup and gave his approval, for very soon a law granting amnesty to those engaged in the October 20, 1958 affair was signed by the king. *Ratchakitcha,* Vol. 76, section 41, 1959, p. 1. By contrast, it has been rumored that the king refused to grant amnesty to Thanom and the group that staged the 1971 coup.

[66] *Prakat khong Khana Pattiwat* No. 4, October 20, 1958. Perhaps Sarit felt that he was not in a position to be able to ignore the demands of certain MP s and students who wanted trade and

constitution and democracy through their selfish manipulations of the system. Their abuse of the privileges and liberties provided for by the constitution had obstructed national progress, created rifts within the nation, and made people enemies of each other, conflicts that threatened to bring about the eventual disintegration and collapse of the nation. These national ills could not be solved by the mere act of replacing the government. Things were so basically wrong that a major transformation was required.

According to the Proclamation, the country faced external threats in addition to these internal maladies. By this, the Revolutionary Council meant the deteriorating situation in Indochina and the growing animosity between Thailand and Cambodia. To be able to face these threats, new ways had to be devised to "create stability for the nation, based upon firm principles of democracy and a system of economics and society suitable for the survival of the nation and the Thai people."[67]

A new constitution was clearly a necessity. The Revolutionary Council was not essentially against the parliament or the government. It realized that the government and parliament had tried their best to function within the limitations imposed by western democracy; hence it was the *system* that must undergo transformation.

The Revolutionary Council outlined four fundamental principles it would uphold: basic human rights as determined by the United Nations; the integrity of courts of law; the honoring of international obligations; and the indivisibility of the king and the Thai nation.

Why Sarit believed that the pursuit of these aims required a transformation of the Thai political system, and why he saw these changes as "revolutionary," requires analysis at this point. We shall proceed to scrutinize more closely Sarit's thinking on politics, political stability, Thai social structure, and the like—that is, his political philosophy as a whole.

SARIT'S POLITICAL PHILOSOPHY

Western scholars have dealt only superficially with the role of Field Marshal Sarit Thanarat in the modern political history of Thailand. The most prominent of these scholars, David Wilson, was not much concerned with Sarit as a person nor indeed with any other individual Thai leader. He was more interested in discovering "recurrent patterns of institutional behavior[68] and the underlying structural bases of the Thai political system. Fred Riggs, on the other hand, was interested in the formation of cliques and the relationships between them.[69] Using another approach, Frank Darling explored the impact of American foreign policy and the interaction between Thailand and the United States in trying to understand the workings of modern Thai politics.[70] By contrast, Thai authors have emphasized the leader's personal ambitions and the intrigues by which he achieved and retained power. While these various approaches are all useful and enlightening, they fail to explain

---

diplomatic relations with China. In 1957, influenced by political considerations, he had expressed no objections to such trade. His need for American support may have also encouraged him to shift his stand.

[67] Ibid.

[68] Wilson, *Politics in Thailand*.

[69] Riggs, *Thailand*.

[70] Darling, *Thailand and the United States*.

fully the thrust behind the dynamic changes in Thai politics after 1958. For these reasons, I propose to tackle the problem from another angle.

A major assumption here is that Sarit, more than any other person in the modern period, set the pattern of present-day politics in Thailand. While it would be rash to assert that Sarit was a man who had a clear "vision" of how to reorganize the Thai socio-political system, he did have certain set ideas about politics, and these came to have a decisive effect on Thai politics. These rough-hewn notions of how the country should be organized politically and socially are the best guides to understanding the full range of programs in their totality, however strange some of them may seem by themselves.

In this context, it is vital to bear in mind that, while most of the leading members of the 1932 Revolution had some training abroad, the 1958 Coup Group were mostly "indigenous products."[71] Sarit's generation did not have the opportunity to study abroad because of the economic depression of the 1930s and the lack of government support. It was only after 1952, and the reorganization of the army along American lines, that the military again sent officers to study abroad. Even here, American aid clearly played the central role in providing the necessary financial assistance. Liberalism and democracy were thus largely alien principles to the new military leaders, whose only frame of reference was Thailand. Furthermore, their observation of politics had always been from a commanding vantage point, and they became uneasy when politicians exerted pressures from below with which they were supposed to comply under the rules of the post-1932 political system. While recognizing the fact that the Revolution of 1932 and the advent of constitutional democracy had given military officers the chance to rule the country, they were nevertheless imbued with traditional authoritarian notions of political leadership based mainly on patron-client relationships. The failure of the 1932 Promoters to bridge the ideological gap between Western concepts of democratic rule and traditional ideas of politics, and to develop true political parties, led to the perpetration of a system of government heavily relying on authority, personal relationships, and clique politics.[72] The various constitutions drafted were legal documents constructed to enforce each new status quo, though lip service was paid to democratic principles and Western concepts of constitutionalism for legitimizing purposes (mainly abroad).

While the Sarit Interim Constitution of 1958 could be said to have been no different from its predecessors in that it was meant to confirm the new *status quo,* it nevertheless attempted to shift the basic concepts underlying the Thai state from Western values to Thai notions of government.

What these notions were can be gleaned from Sarit's speeches. Sarit was an accomplished speaker in the Thai sense. At times, he was brief and explicit, while on other occasions he was eloquently long-winded. His speeches, however, revealed that he was essentially an intuitive thinker, not an ideologue. No single document

---

[71] See Thawat Mokaraphong, "The June Revolution of 1932 in Thailand: A Study in Political Behavior," PhD dissertation, Indiana University, 1962. All but two members of the 1932 Promoters had received foreign education.

[72] As we have seen, political parties were not even established until after the promulgation of the 1964 Constitution.

therefore fully represents his philosophy of state. One has to piece the picture together from a careful analysis of his speeches and some secondary sources.[73] Sarit is usually seen in the literature as a practical solver of concrete problems. He is described by observers as a "dour army officer," an "opportunist," and so forth. Thus Sarit's capacity for abstract thought has been badly neglected by scholars. I myself feel, however, that it was precisely his abstract conceptions regarding the basic foundations of the state that were the most important in shaping his policies.[74]

In Sarit's view of the national political order, it is possible to distinguish three basic elements. First and foremost, politics must be based upon indigenous principles of state—*lakkanmuang Thai*. Foreign ideals had to be discarded, and Thai ideals restored to their traditional centrality. This idea was succinctly expressed by Sarit's international spokesman, Thanat Khoman, who said shortly after the 1958 coup that

> ... the fundamental cause of our political instability in the past lies in the sudden transplantation of alien institutions onto our soil without careful preparation and, more particularly, without proper regard to the circumstances that prevail in our homeland, the nature and characteristics of our own people—in a word, the genius of our race—with the result that their functioning has been haphazard and ever chaotic. If we look at our national history, we can see very well that this country works better and prospers under an authority—not a tyrannical authority, but a unifying authority, around which all elements of the nation can rally. On the contrary, the dark pages of our history show that whenever such an

---

[73] The materials used in this section include Sarit's speeches, found in one of his Cremation Volumes published by the cabinet: *Pramuan Sunthoraphot khong Chomphon Sarit Thanarat, Ph.S. 2502-2504, 2505-2506* [Collected Speeches of Field Marshal Sarit Thanarat, 1959-1961, 1962-1963], II vols., Bangkok, March 17 1964; (hereafter referred to as *Pramuan Sunthoraphot*) and the various proclamations of the Revolutionary Council. Another revealing document is the speech made by Thanat Khoman, Sarit's Foreign Minister, in 1959 before a meeting of the American Association in Thailand. For that speech, see *The Bangkok Post*, March 10, 1959. Also of special interest is a rather curious compilation of lectures delivered over the army radio "20" in 1965, two years after the death of Sarit. Although they were broadcast after Sarit's death, these lectures were an attempt to educate the people on the finer points of the Sarit *pattiwat* system, which Thanom had continued to follow. The lectures entitled "*Prachathipatai baeb Thai* [Thai Democracy]" tried to discredit the ideas of Western democracy brought to the country by the 1932 Promoters. I justify the use of these documents on the grounds that they sought to formalize what Sarit had said in his various speeches. While there are continuities of thought between what Sarit personally said and what appears in the lectures, discontinuities also do exist and must be acknowledged. Deviations from the Sarit political philosophy appear to be immediate readjustments by allies of the new Thanom regime, adjustments necessitated by the crisis that Sarit's embezzlement of government funds had created. The lectures were allegedly authored by a civilian expert, although no one has openly admitted to writing them. Another source of interest is a book entitled *Nayobai thuapai khong khana Pattiwat* [General Policies of the Revolutionary Council] (Bangkok: Wit-thayakon Press, 1966), which uses the radio lectures as primary material. The full title of the book when it was first released was *Botkhwam ruang Prachathipatai ru Nayobai thuapai Khong Khana Pattiwat* [Articles on Democracy or the General Policies of the Revolutionary Council], which leads one to think that the two are the same.

[74] An important analysis made along these lines was the pioneering article by Toru Yano, "Sarit and Thailand's Pro-American Policy," *The Developing Economies* VI (September 1963): 284-299

authority is lacking and divisive elements are set into play, the nation has been plunged into one disaster after another.[75]

In direct censure of the previous system, Sarit himself said:

> If you recall the condition of the country prior to the revolution [1958], you will observe clearly that there were severe divisions, intrigues ... and the desire to destroy each other ... Subsequently, the government of that period [Thanom] was forced to resign and admitted that it could not function correctly. Therefore, the revolution's first plan is to ... rebuild national solidarity. Because of this, I have relied upon the principle of *Samakhitham* [moral principles of solidarity] as the first principle [*lak*] of the task of the revolution.[76]

Social and political divisiveness was seen by Sarit as the byproduct of the Western system of government. In emphasizing *lakkanmuang* Thai, Sarit maintained that although the Interim Constitution of 1958 was short and had very few articles, it nevertheless followed

> ... the traditional Thai concepts of state. The prevailing conditions in the present parliamentary system differs from normal parliamentary practice in the fact that there are no popularly elected MPs. But I assure you that, regarding the protection of the interests of the people, goodwill toward the people, and the desire to develop the nation, the members of the Constituent Assembly are not inferior to MPs of any previous parliaments. We work with honesty, scholastic competence, and just decision-making that is not under the influence of any private party and does not have to demonstrate personal heroism for purposes of future elections, I can guarantee that present members of the Constituent Assembly labor under an oath of loyalty to the people.[77]

The Revolutionary Council under Thanom's guidance further articulated the goals of Sarit in the implementation of "Thai Democracy." Its spokesman told the public that:

> The Revolutionary Council wishes to make the country a democracy ... and to be able to bring this about, it must correct the mistakes of the past ... The revolution of October 20, 1958 abolished democratic ideas borrowed from the West and suggested that it would build a democratic system that would be appropriate to the special characteristics and realities of the Thai. It will build a democracy, a Thai way of democracy.[78]

However, the people were reminded that:

---

[75] *The Bangkok Post,* March 10, 1959.

[76] Sarit Thanarat, "Khamprasai nai Wan Chat [National Day Speech]," June 24, 1959, in *Pramuan Sunthoraphot*, I, p. 16.

[77] Sarit Thanarat, "Khamprasi nai Wan Ratthathammanun lae Wan Sitthimanuchon [Speech on Constitution and Human Rights Day]," December 10, 1960, in *Pramuan Sunthoraphot* I, p. 301.

[78] Army Radio "20," August 17, 1965, in *Prachathipatai baeb Thai* (Bangkok: Chokchai Thewet Press, 1965), p. 65.

In studying democracy, one should not forget the important principle that knotting the outer skin of democracy is inadequate, one must also understand the "meat."[79]

This was to say that, while democracy in all its forms appears superficially similar, if one dug deeper into the meaning of individual systems, then one would understand the subtle, but basic, differences between the various forms. Leaders prior to 1938 were alleged to have put the emphasis on the skin and not the meat, and it was the purpose of Sarit and the Revolutionary Council to bring into prominence the real meat in Thai democracy.

In a more colorful passage, the speaker said:

Let us hope that our democracy is like a plant having deep roots in Thai soil. It should grow amidst the beating sun and whipping rain. It should produce bananas, mangoes, rambutans, mangosteens, and durians; and not apples, grapes, dates, plums, or horse chestnuts.[80]

Another regime source stated that:

... the major principles of democracy established at that time [1932] were taken from the West, from England and France. Although there were many changes, those changes were made within the framework of Western democracy. Therefore, they were merely minor changes and could not be said to have been "revolutionary."

The Revolution of "October 20," although involving changes within the democratic system and not a change from democracy to another system, entails the transformation of the style and type of democracy. That is to say, it encompasses the overthrow of Western democracy and creates a democratic system suitable to the special conditions of Thailand.[81]

The new leaders believed that the relationship between the executive and legislative branches of government dictated by Western systems of democracy was inapplicable to the Thai setting, since it promoted neither stability nor governmental effectiveness.[82] The Revolutionary Council felt that:

There are still people who believe that anarchy is democracy. They say that "to be able to speak freely is truly Thai" ... Furthermore, the conflict between political parties unfettered by proper rules of conduct, to the point of fisticuffs in parliament, the prostitution of newsmen and politicians ... were sure indications of anarchy.[83]

Furthermore:

---

[79] Army Radio "20," August 11, 1965, in *Prachathipatai baeb Thai,* p. 40.

[80] Ibid.

[81] *Nayobai thuapai,* p. 3. This revolution was compared to De Gaulle's takeover and Ne Win's coup.

[82] Army Radio "20," August 31, 1965, in *Prachathipatai baeb Thai,* pp. 93-101.

[83] Army Radio "20," August 11, 1965, in *Prachathipatai baeb Thai,* p. 38.

In the democratic political party system of Thailand, we find key problems that must be resolved. The question is how to make party conflict beneficial to our democracy ... One way is to stipulate in the constitution that there should be executive supremacy over parliament. This would mean that elections would not greatly affect the formation of new governments. [84]

The choice for political leadership should (theoretically) depend upon the wishes of the king, who could designate cabinet members regardless of party affiliation. The government would then be truly the nation's government and not that of any particular party.

In line with this argument, the Revolutionary Council insisted that it represented the general aspirations of the people. It was sure that it had found a correct theory of representation based upon traditional ideas that could be readily understood by the public and would thus provide political stability for the country. [85] To wit:

The building of democracy in all aspects has been successful, leading to political stability. This is because the government of the Revolutionary Council has various instruments that consolidate the ideas of the people which it can employ when administering the country. For example, elections have helped indicate the desires of the people. The ability of the present system to gather public opinion to direct the national administration and thus enhance political stability is a good indication that the present system, which separates executive power from the legislative branch, has practical benefit for the Thai people. That is to say, the present system is able to represent the wishes of the Thai people. The concept of the people's sovereignty does not mean that the people directly exercise legislative, executive, or judicial power, but the concept implies that these powers should represent the aspirations of the nation ... Therefore, "sovereignty of the people" is not merely nice-sounding words, but is reality. [86]

Again:

"How would we know then what system is suitable for Thailand?" We could find out from ... examining the actual functioning of the system. Democracy is the best system in the world, for it is the only system that can facilitate progress and happiness for both nation and people. Thailand is an underdeveloped country ... thus the happiness of the people depends on national development in various fields ... To be able to modernize, many factors are involved, but the most important one is political stability. "What then is the most important factor for political stability?" It is democracy. [87]

---

[84] Army Radio "20," September 1, 1965, in *Prachathipatai baeb Thai*, p. 112.

[85] The king could appoint those who really wanted to work for the national interest.

[86] Army Radio "20," August 31, 1965. The elections in question probably refer to previous ones. It is not clear what the instruments for gathering public opinion involve. One can only speculate that they involve government reports and surveys, information gathered by local administrators, Sarit's personal study tours, and the like.

[87] *Nayobai thuapai*, pp. 66, 67. Democracy here refers to "Thai democracy," which is based upon a Thai theory of representation and democracy grounded in the Thai social system. Ibid, p. 18.

Thus, to the Revolutionary Council, truly Thai political principles were political stability, proper social behavior *(Khwam riaproy),* and strong executive leadership that would "represent" the popular will and national development. One Thai writer, expressing what he felt was the Thai political ethos regarding government, wrote, in the same vein:

> The Thai people in general do not wish to have a part in national politics. They wish only for a leader who has *khuntham* [moral responsibility] and ability. This is because a majority of the people feel that the power to rule belongs to the monarch who has moral and intellectual gifts from birth and to the *chao nai* [master] who have *bun wasna* [merit]. The social division between the ruler and the ruled is absolute ... and the two classes could never be equal in any way. [88]

Out of this conservative concept of social hierarchy, the second feature of Sarit's political philosophy emerges. He believed that the nation could not be kept in order by a vertically divided system of political parties but should rather be based upon a horizontal division between ruler and ruled. An examination of Sarit's terminology in detail shows this very clearly. He saw the state organized into three strata—*rat/ratthaban* (government/nation), *kharatchakan* (bureaucracy), and *prachachon* (people)—very much as the traditional Thai monarchs had done. The ideal norm of national order necessarily involved definite rules and regulations concerning the nature and proper conduct of the *rat/ratthaban, kharatchakan,* and *prachachon.*

As we have seen earlier, the role of the government was quite clear. It represented the popular will and would direct the destiny of the nation. The government (executive branch) was supreme, and all major policy-making would be its responsibility since it naturally knew what the people wanted. Government was to be benevolent, and its main task was to provide political stability and maintain national solidarity. As Sarit had said, his government would rely upon the concept of *samakhitham* as the basis for rule.[89]

Regarding the bureaucracy, Sarit's views were based upon traditional concepts as well. In an address to local government officials, he said:

> Our ancient Thai concept of government considered local officers [*chaoban phan muang*] to be the ears and eyes of the government. This ancient saying "ears and eyes" [*tang hu tang ta*] does not only involve "ears and eyes"; ancient administration also has the position of *khaluang tangchai* [king's governor], which

---

[88] Anan Changklip, "Kanplianplaeng Rabob Kanpokkhrong khong Prathet Thai [Political Change in Thailand]," MA thesis, Thammasat University, n.d., p. 54. Also on this subject, see Sujin Thangsubut, *Juton Rabob Kanmuang Thai* [Weakness of the Thai Political System] (Bangkok: Thailand Social Science Association Press, 1971); and Phaiboon Changrian, *Laksana Sangkhom lae Kanpokkhrong khong Thai* [The Social System and Thai Politics] (Bangkok: Thai Watthanaphanit Press, 1971). Also of special interest is a research effort made by faculty members of the Political Science Faculty, Thammasat University, on the subject: *Laksana bangprakan khong Sathaban Sangkhom Thai thi penuppasak to Kanpokkhrong Rabob Prachathipatai* [Some Aspects of Thai Social Institutions that are Obstacles to the Implementation of Democracy], Thammasat University, 1972.

[89] Sarit Thanarat, "Khamprasai nai Wan Chat," June 24, 1956. *Samakhitham* translates loosely as "moral standards of cooperation and solidarity."

means that the governor has to be the heart of the government in the remote areas. [90]

It is the same in this period, especially in the time of the revolutionary government, in which I hold the position of prime minister. I feel that you are my ears, eyes, and heart, which I have given to the people. The well-being of the people is my heartfelt concern. I ask you to represent my heart, which wants to give love and concern for the people. Help me hear, help me see, and, most important, help me think of the ways to bring happiness to the people. Always remember that you are my *khaluang tangchai*, representing my heart. My heart is honest and loves the people, and thus you must love and be honest towards the people.

In short, the national bureaucracy had to become loyal servants of Sarit's benevolent despotism. It constituted a class in the ruler category and must be loyal to the demands and goals of the government and its political leader. It was to gather information for and administer the policies of the government. It was to reflect the benevolent authority of the regime, serving the people within the framework set down from above. Sarit believed the bureaucracy should be uniform in thought and action, that it should have *samakhitham* within itself, and it should be " socialized /educated" to see things from the viewpoint of the government.[91]

Regarding the people in general, Sarit felt that, at least for the time being, they should remain agrarian in outlook and condition, leaving the government to look after their material needs. The masses should be contented to remain on the land and go about their daily tasks in an orderly and proper manner. Social mobilization should be minimized, for it caused the disintegration of traditional institutions and values. The revolutionary government alone should plot and direct the course of modernization. Sarit's various slogans, which were constantly appearing over the radio, on television, and on large billboards, stressed his idea that progress and modernization could only come to a stable three-tiered society; progress and modernization were expressed in terms of having enough to eat, a place to live, and work to do.[92]

In a revealing statement, Sarit said:

Another chronic problem—which had brought worries and grief to the government for some time—was the problem of the pedicabs. It was a small matter that the pedicabs obstructed traffic and were eyesores in the capital. The major consideration involved was the question of young men from the rural areas numbering in the ten thousands who had left agricultural productivity in favor of the unproductive profession of pedicab driving. This was detrimental to our national economy. Furthermore, the pedicab profession destroyed health: according to the Interior Ministry, pedicab drivers in the end become opium

---

[90] Sarit Thanarat, "Khamklao nai Kanpedprachum Phuwaratchakan Changwad lae Phubangkhapkan Tamruad Phuthonkhet [Opening speech at the Conference of Governors and Regional Police Chiefs]," March 16, 1960, in *Pramuan Sunthoraphot* I, p. 147.

[91] This aspect of Sarit's game plan will become clear later on when we deal with the socialization of top bureaucrats at the National Defense College.

[92] These slogans invariably involved the themes of "running water, bright lights, good roads, and regular jobs."

addicts in large numbers ... It is widely held in political science theory that the advent of rural population movements into the capital is a sign of social deterioration.[93]

Also, pedicabs were signs of improperness (*mai riaproy*) in Thai society and must be gotten rid of. Sarit wanted to see these men return to the land. Accordingly, in 1959, pedicabs were abolished in the capital. To help pedicab drivers reorient themselves back to their agrarian heritage, the prime minister organized *nikhom chonnabot* (rural communities) and provided them with government loans to start a new life of "agricultural productivity."

Lastly, Sarit viewed the state in paternalistic terms. In many of his speeches, Sarit referred to the country as a large family and to himself as the father of that family.[94] "The nation is like a family.[95] If any family has quarrels, has no unity, that family cannot be happy." In a speech made in 1959, Sarit said:

> In this modern age, no matter how much progress is made in political science, one principle in the traditional form of Thai government which still has utility and must be constantly observed is the principle of *phoban phomuang* [father of the family and father of the nation]. The nation is like a large family—provincial governors, vice-governors, and district officers are like the heads of various families. Local administrators must keep in mind that the people under their jurisdiction are not strangers, but are sons and daughters, brothers and sisters, nieces and nephews of a large family. Poverty, happiness, and problems that the people experience are family problems which the parent/father must look into closely and "rule" through love and mutual goodwill ... Whenever we obtain the confidence of the people, their love and respect befitting the head of a family, then we can consider ourselves good administrators. We have heard stories of some administrators whom the people so loved as a father that when they were transferred, the people would cry. They truly were good administrators.[96]

"The Prime Minister is the father of a large family,"[97] Sarit once remarked; and in addressing a group of *kamnan* (commune heads) from the Northeast, he tried to make clear to them his views on the organization of the state. Sarit believed that the *kamnan* was a Thai construct that epitomized how the old and the new could be most usefully combined:

---

[93] Sarit Thanarat, "Khamprasai nuang nai Wan Khroprop Pi haeng Kantang Khanaratthamontri [Cabinet Anniversary Speech]," February 10, 1960, in *Pramuan Sunthoraphot* I, pp. 127-28.

[94] In this model, the king had no formal place. However, one gathers that the king was seen as the symbolic representation of the nation, and his major political role was to choose the prime minister, who would act as the "father" responsible for the welfare of all members of the Thai "family." See Introduction.

[95] Sarit Thanarat, "Khamprasai nai Wan Chat," June 24, 1959, in *Pramuan Sumthoraphot* I, p. 15.

[96] Sarit Thanarat, "Khamklao Pedkanprachum Paladchangwad lae Naiamphur thua Ratcha-anachak [Opening Speech at the National Conference of Vice-Governor and District Officers]," April 27, 1959, in *Pramuan Sunthoraphot* I, p. 31.

[97] Sarit Thanarat, "Sunthoraphot nai Phithipedprachum Pathomnithet Nganphatthanakan Thongthin [Opening Speech at the Conference on Local Development]," October 24, 1960, in *Pramuan Sunthoraphot* I, p. 255.

... the *kamnan* is an important link in national administration. He is close to the people and government. He represents the blending of traditional and new concepts of government. The Thai traditional concept of ancient government upholds the principle of father ruling children. We called our kings *phokhun*, which connotes the "highest" father. Next came *phomuang*, which refers to the governor. Below this was the *phoban*, meaning the *kamnan* and *phuyaiban*. In the end we find the *phoruan*, or head of households.

Even today, although the system of government is different and one does not use the word the word "*pho*" as before, I still hold on to our ancient Thai traditional concept of father "ruling" children.[98]

More precisely, Sarit delivered a concrete lesson to a group of *anthaphan* (hooligans) on the occasion of their release from jail. He informed them that:

I do not hate you. For even though you are hooligans or whatever, you are my compatriots. I have always maintained that the nation is like a large family. Be it because of *bun* [merit] or *kam* [demerit], I happen to have the responsibility of being the head of the family at this moment. I have extended to all my goodwill, but if any person in this household creates trouble for the whole, it is my duty to stop this person. The reason why I have had you arrested and incarcerated is to make you good people again.[99]

From the speeches we have examined, it is clear that Sarit basically relied on what he saw as traditional concepts of statecraft and tried to apply them concretely.

But it would be perhaps unfair to label Sarit simply as a political reactionary. We must view his ideas in terms of an attempt to develop a workable alternative to the political trend set after 1932. For Sarit believed that his return to old concepts of government was a *means* that would propel the nation toward modernization. He never failed to point out the fact that his assumption of power in 1958 was not a coup d'état (*ratthaprahan*) but a revolution (*pattiwat*). He said that if he had only wanted to become prime minister, he did not have to take power, since Thanom had already resigned and he could have assumed the premiership without resorting to drastic measures.[100] He had had to stage a revolution so that the old system of government could be changed, enabling the nation to gather its strength and devote all its energies to development. Yet it appeared to him that, before modernizing, a developing country must realize the rules that form the natural basis for national existence and make them obligatory elements of governance.

We may ask here: "What was it then that Sarit wanted to create in Thailand?" Although it is not easy to answer this question, we can make some educated conjectures from examining his speeches and actions and the relationship between

[98] Sarit Thanarat, "Khamklao Pedprachum nai Kanobrom Kamnan 4 Changwad Phak Tawanokchiengnua [Opening Speech at the Briefing Conference of Commune Leaders from Four Northeastern Provinces]," August 7, 1961, in *Pramuan Sunthoraphot* I, p. 437.

[99] Sarit Thanarat, "Owat lae Khamklao Pidkanobrom anthaphan [Reminder and Closing Speech before the Release of Hooligans]," September 6, 1960, in *Pramuan Sunthoraphot* I, p. 215.

[100] *Prakat khong Khana Pattiwat No. 2*, October 20, 1958. This announcement stated that the action of the Revolutionary Council had the approval of the outgoing government (the Thanom cabinet).

them. While not going into detail at this point, we can say that it appears Sarit's ultimate aim was the establishment of a modernized state that would realize the "fundamental values of the Thai people," values that could be best expressed in the three ideals of king, religion, and nation. In his concept of the modern Thai state, the king was to be revered as symbolizing the spirit of the people, their past, and their tradition; Buddhism was to be embraced by all as the source of social morality and ethics. As both king and Buddhism were taken as absolute values, ideological claims that slighted these values must not be allowed to invade the country. The Sarit coup of 1957 could be seen, in part, as an attempt to stop criticism against the throne.[101] The Interim Constitution reflected Sarit's wish that the king be revered and above the law—the king could do no wrong.[102] The early arrests of suspected communist sympathizers and the harsh repression of the Isan plot led by Khrong Chandawong grew out of Sarit's view of communism as posing a fundamental threat to king and religion. The government's announcement regarding the execution of Khrong stated that the accused had advocated the overthrow of Buddhism and the monarchy, as evidenced by Khrong's declaration that the king and monks would be subjected to labor in factories following a communist revolution.[103]

Sarit's idea of national well-being was defined in terms of wholesomeness, dignity, properness, and resourcefulness. Progress was represented in terms of environmental cleanliness *(khwam sa-ad)*, properness of things *(khwam riaproy)*, and material well-being. Sarit once remarked after traveling to inspect the North that people there were progressive *(charoen)* because their villages and houses were clean and very proper.[104] Thus Sarit's concern with economic development was mingled with an obsession with cleanliness, purity and discipline.

On the practical side, Sarit was a born problem-solver. His instinctive ideas were always tempered by a concern to solve problems with skill and dispatch. Paradoxically, this meant that, far more than Phibun, he tried to be scientific in overcoming his problems, showing considerable respect for modern scholarship and technology. He was able to exploit the knowledge of qualified people by according them more participation in government than hitherto. Sarit was very proud of the fact that he was the only Thai prime minister ever to have recognized and accorded scholars great respect. However, scholarship appeared valuable to him only if it was useful and efficient.[105]

---

[101] See Chapter Two. Phao's papers had allegedly criticized the king and the royalty for not joining in the Twenty-Fifth Buddhist Centennial Celebrations in 1957.

[102] *The Interim Constitution of Thailand,* 1959. Article 3 stipulates that "The person of the King is sacred and inviolable."

[103] Prime Minister's Office, *Prakat Samnak Nayokratthamontri* [Announcement of the Prime Minister's Office], May 31, 1961.

[104] Sarit Thanarat, "Khamklao Pedkanprachum Paladchangwad," April 27, 1959. "When we talk about progress, being civilized, and culture, we talk about how this country is more progressive than that country ... What is our standard of measurement? I think that our standard of measurement, or the most concrete standard of judgment, is cleanliness, and things being in their proper stations [*khwam penrabieb riaproy*]." *Pramuan Sunthoraphot* I, p. 4.

[105] Sarit Thanarat, "Khamklao Pedprachum Phatthana Nakborihan runthi 1/2504 [Opening Speech at the Conference of Administrators, group no. 1/2504]," February 6, 1961, in *Pramuan Sunthoraphot* I, p. 339. Sarit told his audience that Confucius should be admired for his idea that the most important factor in national administration was the principle of "using the right person."

Sarit's initial view of international relations appears to have stemmed from his traditionalist view of national interests. His goal in reorganizing the country was to create a government responsive to *actual conditions* and to provide *strategic leadership*. He paid great attention to modernizing the bureaucracy and making plans for regional development, not only to broaden his power base but to fulfill national development goals. In his opinion, political stability was the most important prerequisite for a profitable foreign policy. Sarit was basically opposed to the old Phibun foreign policy, which had become an end in itself. In accommodating Thailand's foreign policy to international events for personal advantage, Phibun had sacrificed the country's independence. Accommodation to international politics was necessary, but only as a means to national ends. Thus United States–Thai relations were viewed by Sarit with utilitarian logic as an instrument for developing national power.

To summarize, Sarit's ideas of representation were conceived in a Thai mold. Sarit felt that political order in Thailand would never be made secure by implementing foreign theories of representation, as Thailand had not produced the type of person who could make such concepts work. He was a realist in that he thought that objective social facts had to be considered in developing a political ideology. But he was a romantic in his emphasis upon the stability of a traditional-style social system, however well administered. Because Sarit believed that the culture of a nation was far more important than foreign theories, he emphasized the concept of the nation as a family and his own role as father of that family.

Sarit's thinking clearly had its limitations, which can be briefly pointed out. One major weakness involved his relationship with the United States. Although Sarit's foreign policy was based upon his idea of a national interest defined in terms of technical and regional development, the risk of becoming dangerously entangled in the international interests of the United States was left unresolved. It was doubtful whether Sarit ever thought carefully about how to resolve conflicts between the national interests of Thailand and those of the United States. In practice, heavy reliance on American aid pushed Thailand further and further away from a real capacity to form an independent foreign policy. It is possible that Sarit's failure to confront this problem effectively resulted from his own sense of proper behavior; he had once reminded the Thai people that they should trust the United States and that Thai *khuntham,* or moral behavior, censured the act of *na wai lang lok,* which referred to the hypocritical practice of being "two-faced."[106] Here "national interest" has given way to simple ethics.

Secondly, the principle of representation that Sarit used as the basis for political stability contained elements that were incompatible with the actual process of social change. His own modernization plans, which emphasized technological and social development, were likely to create their own dynamic processes which would eventually challenge Sarit's concept of the proper social order. While Sarit remained alive as the omnipotent autocrat, he was able to keep his system going, but as society progressed and lesser leaders took over, the conflict between prescription and reality became ever more apparent.

---

[106] Sarit Thanarat, "Khamprasai nuangnai Okat Wankhroprop 10 Pi haeng Kanlongnamtoklong Ruammu kap Saharat Amerika naithang Setthakit lae Wichakan [Speech on the 10th Anniversary of the Signing of the United States–Thai Treaty of Technical and Educational Cooperation]," September 19, 1960, in *Pramuan Sunthoraphot* I, p. 222.

The Ramkhamhaeng stone inscription discovered by Rama 4. The story of Ramkhamhaeng animated the notions of *phokhun* as the ideal traditional leader. Luang Wichitwathakan embellished this idealism in his play *Anuphab Phokhun Ramkhamhaeng* (The Prowess of Phokhun Ramkhamhaeng) written in 1954.

CHAPTER FOUR

IMPLEMENTATION OF THE SARIT SYSTEM: PERSONAL LEADERSHIP

Most Thai and Western writers agree that the government of Marshal Sarit was generally successful: while he was dictatorial and repressive, Sarit was nevertheless an exceptional man who was able to capture the fancy of the public. They also seem to recognize that the man had a certain personal style of leadership that was quite Thai in character. One thing which these writers generally fail to grasp, however, is the basis upon which Sarit fashioned this personal style of leadership: his fascination with what he saw as the traditional Thai political order.

The following brief review of the traditional sociopolitical organization of Thai society is intended to show the fundamental components of the traditional Thai political world that Sarit was brought up to understand and later tried, in part, to restore. It is doubtful how far Sarit comprehended the complex causes of the various structural changes that occurred in Thai politics since the time of Sukhothai. But there is little doubt that he saw himself as an inheritor of this tradition, even if he interpreted it in a basically ahistorical and eclectic fashion.

Sarit's paternalistic style of leadership was modeled mainly on the concept of the father–children (*pho–luk*) relationship made famous by the Ramkhamhaeng inscription of Sukhothai.[1] King Ramkhamhaeng (1276-1317) is reputed to have been the erector of a stone platform (*Phrathaen Manangkhasila*) that was used by Buddhist monks to deliver sermons for the public. On other occasions, Ramkhamhaeng himself would occupy the stone platform to listen to the petitions of his subjects as well as discuss matters of state with his officials. A section of the inscription reads as follows:

> ... when it was not a day for sermons, Phokhun Ramkhamhaeng, the King of Sisatchanalai and Sukhothai, would sit on the stone platform and allow the public and officials [*fung thuai lukchao lukkhun*] to talk about the affairs of state.[2]

.

---

[1] George Coedes, *Prachum Sila Charuk* [Collection of Inscriptions], vol. I (Bangkok: Ho Phrasamut Wachirayan, 1924), pp. 53, 54.

[2] Prayun Kanchandun, *Khambanyai Prawat Kanpokkhrong Chan Prinya Tho* [Lectures on Political History for the MA Level], Thammasat University, 1956. The people had equal rights and were referred to as *luk*. Thongbai Wongchettha, "Prawat Kanpokkhrong Samai Krung Ratanakosin [Political History of the Ratanakosin Period]," MA thesis, Thammasat University, 1962, p. 5. Note that Ramkhamhaeng's example was also used to demonstrate that democracy had roots in traditional Thai politics: the name of his platform was applied to Phibun's political party, the Seri Manangkhasila.

Ramkhamhaeng's father, Phokhun Si Intharathit, the first king of Sukhothai (r. 1237 to about 1270), already ruled according to the principle of *pho–luk*. The principle called for the elevation of a qualified *phoban*, or household leader, to the position of *phomuang*, or father of the city, and if he was really able, he could eventually become *phokhun*. When Si Intharathit became king of Sukhothai, he retained his title of *phokhun*, as did his son. The right to rule was then based upon a person's *kharma*, or what is known in Thai as the *thotsaphiratchatham* (Ten Kingly Virtues). An inscription found at Nakhom Chum reveals that:

> ... the *khun* who leads a life governed by *tham dang an*, that *khun* would *kin muang* for a long time. Whoever acts contrary to the *tham* [dharma] could not exist for long.[3]

An authority of Thai political history stated:

> [In] the Thai concept of administration, the king is honored as the father of all the people ... The father is the head of his family ... Many families join together to become the *ban*, or village, under the leadership of the *phoban*. Those under his responsibility were called *lukban*. Many *ban* join together to become the *muang* [city]. If the *muang* is under the authority of a *phomuang prathet rat* [autonomous *phomuang*], its leader would be called *khun*. Many *muang* join together to become a country under the rule of a king, which the ancients called *phokhun*. The various officials were then called *lukkhun*. Therefore, we see that the method of Thai administration followed the manner of a father looking after his children, or as it is called in English "paternal government," which is employed as the principle of administration in Siam even until the present time.[4]

Sukhothai declined rapidly after the death of Ramkhamhaeng in 1317 and was soon overshadowed by the new kingdom of Ayutthaya, founded in 1350 by a ruler of U-Thong.[5] James Mosel maintains that the advent of Ayutthaya marked the beginning of present-day Thailand and that the Ayutthayan period laid down the

---

[3] See Anan Changklip, "Kanplienplaeng Rabob Kanpokkhrong khong Prathet Thai [Political Change in Thailand]" (MA thesis, Thammasat University, 1965), p. 26. *Tham an dang* refers to the ten kingly virtues, *thotsaphiratchatham*, to be found in the teachings of Buddha. These were charity, morality, liberality, rectitude, gentleness, self-restraint, non-anger, non-violence, forbearance, and non-obstruction. *Kin muang* literally translates as "eating the city," which implies that the *phomuang* derives his income from the control of the *muang*.

[4] Prince Damrong, *Laksana Kanpokkrong Prathet Sayam tae Boran* [Ancient Siamese Administration], a speech delivered before the Samaikhayachan Samakhom, Bangkok, October 8, 1927. In his speech, Prince Damrong talked about administration in various periods, from the Sukhothai to the Ratanakosin (Chakkri) era. He particularly dealt with the evolution of the concept of *pho–luk* rule through the reformations initiated by Trailok and the Chakkri kings. I do not mean to imply that political references to sources of this type were totally correct. They are used to illustrate the understanding of Sarit's generation of leaders concerning the traditional Thai socio-political order, which became the basis for Sarit's political philosophy.

[5] For an intriguing study of the formation of Ayutthaya, see Charnvit Kasetsiri, "The Rise of Ayutthaya" (PhD dissertation, Cornell University, 1973). This work was subsequently published by Oxford University Press, 1976. See Charnvit Kasetsiri, *The Rise of Ayudhya: A History of Siam in the Fourteenth and Fifteenth Centuries* (Kuala Lumpur and New York, NY: Oxford University Press, 1976).

four basic foundations of the Thai political system—a new concept of kingship, shifting from *phokhun* to *devaraja*, an administrative structure based upon centralization and specialization of functions, a personally based feudalism, and a new social order built upon intensive hierarchization.[6]

The Thai political system of the Ayutthayan period underwent a grand transformation after the third conquest of Angkor Thom, perhaps in 1431, when a large number of Khmer courtiers and Brahmans were brought to the Thai capital. The rulers of Ayutthaya, particularly King Boromatrailoknat (Trailok) learned a great deal from these Brahmans. The Thai concept of leadership based upon the father–son relationship gave way to a Hindu-Khmer concept of divine kingship, although this notion was adapted to fit particular Thai Buddhist ideas whereby the king was viewed not as a reincarnated Hindu god but as a future Buddha or Boddhisattva.

Subsequently, the Thai king became an absolute monarch surrounded by court Brahmans whose main functions were to devise rituals and ceremonies to render the king mysterious, magical, and remote. The people were transformed conceptually from children to servants and slaves of the throne. New taboos prohibited his subjects from even approaching or addressing the king directly. The elaboration of court language further widened the gap between the throne and the people. Affairs of state thus became the monopoly of the king and court, and the masses were expected only to pay taxes, do corvée labor, and join armies during times of need.

The innovations of Trailok in the 1450s had great repercussion on the social foundations of the Thai state. Whereas the Thai nation prior to his reign was a loose conglomeration of principalities ruled by local *phomuang* and *chaomuang*, Trailok's attempt to create a centralized bureaucracy left a legacy that persisted into modern times. So important was this change that recent scholars have depicted traditional Thailand as a "bureaucratic polity."[7] It was from the time of Trailok's era that the Thai social system began to be considered a three-tiered pyramid made up of king/country, *kharatchakan* (bureaucracy), and the common masses (*ratsadon*).[8]

A Sukhothai style of feudalism based upon the control of land and the people occupying those lands changed into a feudalism based upon the control of people through a pyramidal system of patrons and clients.[9] The patrons were known as *nai* or *munnai*, and their clients were designated as *phrai*, or freemen. The *that*, or slaves, constituted a category of people inferior to these.

Trailok's reorganization involved developing a graded hierarchization of society. From the royal princes down to the lowly *that*, status and dignity were determined by the amount of *sakdina* ("control over fields") that each man had. The original idea of the *sakdina* appeared to be determined by the capacity of a person to utilize land. Thus a *phrai*, for example, could not control more than twenty-five *rai* of land (2.5 *rai* = 1 acre). Even a slave received a *sakdina* of five *rai*. The highest commoner official received a *sakdina* of from 15,000 to 20,000 *rai*. Eventually, the *sakdina* not only

---

[6] James N. Mosel, "Thai Administrative Behavior," in *Toward the Comparative Study of Public Administration*, ed. William J. Siffin (Bloomington, IN: Indiana University, 1959), p. 284

[7] Riggs, *Thailand*. William J. Siffin, *The Thai Bureaucracy: Institutional Change and Development* (Honolulu, HI: East West Center Press, 1966); James Ansil Ramsay, "The Development of a Bureaucratic Polity: The Case of Northern Siam" (PhD dissertation, Cornell University, 1971).

[8] Sarit's view was based upon this division. Even to the present time, government announcements invariably begin with greetings to the *kharatchakan* and *prachachon* (citizen, as opposed to *ratsadon*, or subject).

[9] Mosel, "Thai Administrative Behavior," p. 287.

designated how much land a person controlled[10] and how many people were under his jurisdiction, but also denoted social status, for by the reign of Rama V land grants had been abolished, so that the *sakdina* had merely honorific value.[11] But the idea of a "bureaucratic" vertical classification of the entire population persisted.

King Trailok was also responsible for the creation of somewhat functionally specialized administrative organs known as *Krom*, the precursors of modern ministries. There were four important *Krom* during the time of Trailok—*Muang* (city), *Wang* (palace), *Khlang* (treasury), and *Na* (fields). The various *krom* were subdivided into smaller *krom* (departments), *kong* (divisions), and *mu* (sections), staffed by royal princes at the top and lower down by people from the *nai* class.[12] The *phrai* automatically *belonged* within the *krom* to which his *nai* was assigned. Thus bureaucratic and feudalistic controls were combined through the *krom* system. Patronal status and bureaucratic power were thus inseparable.

The basic socio-political system founded by Trailok persisted down into the Ratanakosin (Bangkok) period, though important changes were made, particularly during and after the reign of King Mongkut. The idea of kingship as *devaraja* gave way to a more strongly Buddhist-related concept of the righteous monarch. King Mongkut (1851–1868) once again encouraged people to come and pay respects to him whenever he ventured out of the palace, and many taboos, such as the prohibition against looking at the king's face, had been abolished even before his time.[13] It could be said that with Mongkut, the Thai kings moved back towards a more Sukhothai concept of leadership compatible with the Buddhist idea of kingship. King Mongkut or one of his sons would appear at the palace wall four times a month to give alms to the poor and to receive petitions from the people.[14] From this, we can surmise that the cult of *devaraja* was losing its influence and a principle that approximated the old *pho–luk* idea was reemerging.[15]

The bureaucratic innovations implemented during the reigns of Mongkut and Chulalongkorn, known as the Chakkri Reformation, adapted the system started by Trailok to meet the pressures exerted by the Western powers in their quest for colonies in the East. By the end of Chulalongkorn's reign (1910), the old *krom* had been transformed into European-style ministries, in some cases headed by commoners. Royal officials were turned into salaried civil servants, though their appointment still remained in the hands of the king. Local administration became increasingly bureaucratized as local leaders became civil servants and were subjected to rotation from locality to locality.

---

[10] Akin Rabibhadhana, *The Organization of Thai Society*, Data Paper No. 74 (Ithaca, NY: Cornell Southeast Asia Program, 1969), p. 23.

[11] Mosel, "Thai Administrative Behavior," p. 289.

[12] Akin, *The Organization of Thai Society*, p. 24, points out that the Thai *krom* and its organization could be viewed as analogous to a military hierarchy in which the large *krom* was equivalent to the division, the smaller *krom* the regiment, the *kong* the battalion, and the *mu* the platoons. He further states that the Thai word for minister—*senabodi*—originally meant an army general.

[13] This taboo was abolished during the reign of Rama II.

[14] Royal Proclamations of 1856, 1858 in *Prachum Prakat Ratchakan thi Si* [Collected Royal Proclamations of the Fourth Reign], 1851–1857, pp. 263, 264.

[15] See Joseph B. Kingsbury and Robert F. Wilcox, *Introduction to the Principles of Public Administration in Thailand* (Bangkok: Institute of Public Administration, Thammasat University, 1961), p. 22.

The creation of a modern state based upon rational bureaucratic administration allowed the rise of a new Western-educated elite in the various ministries. The royal policy of sending bright young students abroad created a commoner intelligentsia that was increasingly troubled by the inconsistency between absolute monarchy and modern administration. The Revolution of 1932 was an attempt by this new elite to resolve that inconsistency. With the advent of constitutionalism, the role of the throne became mainly ceremonial. Constitutionalism brought an end to the *devaraja* cult, and the monarch was relegated to being a figurehead, a symbol of the nation's traditions and integrity. Power, however, moved no further down than to the bureaucracy, civil and military, and the social structure as a whole did not change much. The old three-tiered division remained: only the power of the king and princes was reduced.[16]

SYNTHESIS AND FORMULATION OF SARIT'S POLITICAL PHILOSOPHY

Sarit's understanding of the traditional Thai sociopolitical order we have described was greatly influenced by Luang Wichit Wathakan.[17] An official indication of this debt can be found in Sarit's Cremation Volume, which mentions that Sarit

---

[16] After the abolition of slavery, the *phrai* and *that* became subjects (*ratsadon*). After 1932, the *ratsadon* became *prachachon* (citizens).

[17] *Anuson Phraratchathan Pluengsop Phon Tri Luang Wichit Wathakan* [Cremation Volume of Maj. Gen. Luang Wichit Wathakan], Bangkok, August 16, 1964. Luang Wichit was born in 1898 in Uthaithani Province of a business family. His early education was in local temple schools. Between the ages of thirteen and twenty, he became a novice and subsequently a Buddhist monk and was known for his academic achievements. In 1910, he received a diploma from Rama VI for achieving the fifth grade in the study of Pali. Upon leaving the monkhood, Luang Wichit joined the Foreign Ministry as a clerk. During his spare time, he went to attend classes at the Law School, but his studies were interrupted when he was sent to Paris. While in Paris, Luang Wichit pursued his legal studies at the University of Paris, but again his work toward a law degree was interrupted, as he was transferred to London.

While in London, his career as a writer flourished, and he published the first of his numerous books on a very wide variety of subjects. After the Revolution of 1932, he wrote two political pieces entitled *Kanmuang Kanpokkhrong khong Krung Sayam* [Politics and Administration of Siam] and *Khana Kanmuang* [Political Groups]. At the early age of thirty-five, he was promoted to the position of Director-General of the Protocol Department in the Foreign Ministry.

Because of his friendship with Pridi and Phibun, Luang Wichit was selected to head the new Fine Arts Department in 1934; in that post, he diligently carried on the pioneering work of Prince Damrong. It was in his capacity as Director-General of the Fine Arts Department that he presented his first play, *Lued Suphan* [Suphan Blood], which was a great success and established Luang Wichit as a playwright. From that time on, he began to deliver speeches on nationalistic and political subjects. Some of his topics included "The Culture of Sukhothai," "The Loss of Thai Territory to France," "Thai Racial Relations with Khmers," "The Thai Nation will be Victorious," and "Good Things in Isan." In all, he authored more than fifty plays, many of which were on nationalistic themes, recalling the past greatness of the Thai and how their ancestors had fought hard to maintain their independence and national unity.

Luang Wichit eventually became Minister of Education and Minister of Foreign Affairs during the Phibun wartime regime and then ambassador in Tokyo until the surrender of Japan at the end of World War II. After his arrest by the Allies and release from prison, Luang Wichit turned to writing again. He wrote thirteen serious books dealing with subjects such as history, religion, political psychology, Thai research works, and the control of mind over matter. Aside from his plays, speeches, and serious books, Luang Wichit was well-known for his songs, which were sprinkled with patriotic motifs, as well as dozens of novels.

summoned Luang Wichit to London in 1958 to discuss his future course of action.[18] There is additional unofficial evidence to indicate that Luang Wichit played an influential role in Sarit's political development.[19]

It is a curious fact that while Luang Wichit was never really powerful politically, he helped shape the approaches of the two most influential military leaders of the modern period, Phibun and Sarit. Under Phibun, Luang Wichit acted as an instrument of the state in writing propaganda against the French and the local Chinese and in pushing irredentist nationalism. During the war, he acted as Phibun's ambassador in Japan. When Phibun returned to power after 1948, Luang Wichit was again asked to join the government. In 1951, he was appointed Minister of Finance and later transferred to become Minister of Economic Affairs.[20]

In Chapter Three, we saw how Phibun tried to use the *pho–luk* concept, which concerns the traditional Thai relationship between a father and his children, in his attempt to gain legitimacy in the face of challenges from Phao and Sarit. One source cited in that discussion was a play written by Luang Wichit entitled *Anuphab Phokhun Ramkhamhaeng*, which was an attempt to recreate, in simplified form, the essence of Ramkhamhaeng's greatness and the traditional concept of Thai leadership.[21] The play represented Luang Wichit's latest ideas about the type of Thai leader who could guide the country to become great and prosperous. In the play, Ramkhamhaeng was portrayed more as a very able leader than as a monarch and presented as a caring father of his people whose his benevolence was appreciated by all. He ruled with compassion and decisiveness, and his officials were told to treat their subordinates as their own children. The benevolent paternalism of Ramkhamhaeng was likened to that of a father who has the interests of his children at heart and whose actions, no matter how severe, are carried out in good faith. Because of this, the king, or *phokhun*, could never become a tyrant. Under the *pho–luk* principle, the benevolence of the *pho* was axiomatic and an intrinsic part of the leader's nature.

According to Jitlada Sirirat, who interviewed Khunying Praphaphan, Luang Wichit's wife, Sarit had long known of and respected Luang Wichit for the latter's wisdom and ability to write nationalistic plays.[22] In a letter dated June 13, 1956, Sarit was already remarking that the army needed a scholarly person like Luang Wichit to help direct the future course of political action in Thailand.[23] Another important letter, dated September 5, 1958, was written by Sarit in London shortly after he returned from Bangkok to try to bolster the position of the Thanom government. In

---

[18] See Chapter Three.

[19] Correspondence between the two men pre-dates their 1958 meeting in London. Evidence suggests that the two kept in touch as early as 1955, when Luang Wichit was ambassador to Switzerland. Jitlada Sirirat, who has done research on the subject, informs me that Luang Wichit's letters laid out plans of action for Sarit that included irredentism as well as *pattiwat*. Letter from Jitlada Sirirat, dated February 27, 1974.

[20] Luang Wichit returned to the diplomatic service in 1953 and became ambassador to India and later to Switzerland.

[21] Luang Wichit, *Anuphab Phokhun Ramkhamhaeng*. This play was written in Switzerland and first presented in Bangkok in June 1954. An English translation can be found in *Thai Politics, 1932-1951*, ed. Thak Chaloemtiarana (Bangkok: Social Science Association of Thailand, 1978), pp. 744-794.

[22] Jitlada Sirirat, correspondence dated March 17, 1974.

[23] Ibid.

that letter, Sarit asked Luang Wichit to help him draft an economic development plan to cover finance, transportation, education, and other aspects of public policy.

The most vital piece of evidence showing Sarit's reliance on Luang Wichit is a letter dated September 28, 1958, sent from London.[24] In this letter, Sarit asked Luang Wichit to draw up a plan for his *pattiwat*, including the drafting of all proclamations that would be announced after the coup d'état. On the question of a constitution, Sarit wrote:

> I have an aspiration to make a permanent constitution that would endure like the constitutions of England and the United States. This might be too high a hope. However, in principle, should one not set lofty goals rather than mediocre ones? When we have decided to engage in an important enterprise, we should be brave enough to take action, and we should hold true to our convictions. Furthermore, having an able general staff officer like *khun luang* [Wichit] has made it easy for me to make decisions true to the model of a good commander-in-chief.[25]

He also outlined some of his concerns about future domestic development. The monarchy should have no political power but merely play a role of symbolic importance. A unicameral parliament would be best to facilitate the passage of legislation. He criticized what he believed was the basic characteristic of Thai politicians, that is, "more talk than action." He asked Luang Wichit to devise a way to enable the government to make quick decisions and suggested that perhaps there should be a clear division between the executive and legislative branches of government. By this Sarit meant that parliament should exercise the least possible control over the cabinet.

Two weeks prior to his return to Bangkok to stage his coup d'état, Sarit wrote Luang Wichit (on October 4,1958), giving him an outline of his plans. He told Luang Wichit that:

> I have asked Air Marshal Chalermkiat Watthanangkun, the commander-in-chief of the Air Force, to come to see me in secret here at London to inform him of my decision and plans so that we can coordinate our work here with the work of those in Bangkok. Thus, when I go back, we could immediately act.
>
> Please come to see me. We must also be sure that whatever we do, we should not disturb His Majesty the King.[26]

Thus, when Sarit returned to Bangkok on October 19, 1958, Luang Wichit accompanied him. Luang Wichit was appointed Deputy Director of the Revolutionary Headquarters (Civilian Section) after Sarit staged his coup. He was also the Chairman of the Revolutionary Council's Committee for Educational Planning. In December of that year, he reached the mandatory retirement age, but

---

[24] Ibid.

[25] Ibid.

[26] Ibid. The plan involved: first, the resignation of the Thanom government; second, announcement of a coup d'état in the name of the *Khana Thahan* (Military Group) and the people, with the support of the Thanom government; third, announcement of the appointment of a national protector of the situation; fourth, announcement of the formation of a government of the Revolutionary Council; fifth, appointment of a Constituent Assembly.

Sarit kept him on special duty as Assistant to the Prime Minister (*Palad Banchakan*), whose responsibilities were to advise and assist Sarit in national administration and policy planning. Luang Wichit was a member and head of many committees established by the Revolutionary Council in its attempt to revolutionize the country. In his capacity as Assistant to the Prime Minister, Luang Wichit wrote many of Sarit's speeches, and it was known by those close to Sarit that the prime minister relied heavily upon his advice. When Luang Wichit was finally hospitalized for heart trouble—indeed, until his death—he continued to work feverishly to fulfill the wishes of the demanding Sarit. The importance of Luang Wichit to Sarit was demonstrated by the announcement that, in memory of Luang Wichit, the post of Assistant to the Prime Minister would be abolished.[27] Apparently Sarit could not or would not find a replacement for this trusted adviser.

The nature of Luang Wichit's influence on Sarit can be suggested from the themes in some of his writings before the 1958 coup and in the wordings of the announcements of the Revolutionary Council.[28] In 1952, he had written a book entitled *Kusalobai Sang Khwam Yingyai*[29] in which he outlined the various means through which a leader could be assured of a position in history. He pointed out that when one referred to greatness, one usually meant political greatness, which could be obtained through two basic routes: achieving independence or making a revolution. Luang Wichit wrote the following words, which became quite well-known when the Revolutionary Council's pronouncements echoed them:

> ... we should make it clear that we cannot confuse revolution with coup d'état or rebellion. The work of a revolution not only means the changing of leadership, but involves changes that are important to the lives and thoughts of the people— the changing of the social system, the economic system, the path of education, together with the changing of people's habits toward something that is better than before.[30]

Luang Wichit's fascination with revolution was not something new. Writing in 1959, he said:

> Readers will notice that the word *pattiwat* [revolution] appears throughout this book. This is not new or inserted recently but was written and talked about since twenty years ago. It goes to show that I have been fascinated by the idea of

---

[27] *Phim Thai*, August 17, 1962.

[28] Thai Noi (pseud.), *Buanglang Kanmuang Yuk Sarit* [Politics of the Sarit Regime] (Thonburi: Krungthai Press, 1965), pp. 16, 17. Thai Noi asserted that Luang Wichit was the key to Sarit's decision to stage a *pattiwat*. The author said that Luang Wichit convinced Sarit that parliament and the constitution must be abolished and that Thailand had to be ruled by only one individual. He advocated "dictatorship" under a democratic form of government based upon traditional Thai concepts of state. Luang Wichit also wanted to delay the promulgation of a new permanent constitution so that development plans could be pushed through without having to face any political opposition.

[29] Luang Wichit Wathakan, *Kusalobai Sang Khwam Yingyai* [The Path Toward Greatness] (Bangkok: Watthanawibun Press, 1952).

[30] Ibid., p. 285.

revolution for some time already, and have dreamt that I would be able to witness a true revolution in our country. [31]

By contrast, prior to 1958, Sarit had little real idea of how he wanted to run the country. The idea of revolution thus seems to derive from the direct influence of Luang Wichit.

Along with the idea of revolution, another concept outlined by Luang Wichit that left its mark upon Sarit's leadership was the notion that Thailand should be ruled by a man who believed in the principle of *pho–luk* as the guiding model for political leadership. We have noted how most of Luang Wichit's plays and some of his novels were written with nationalistic themes based upon traditional history and ideas, particularly his interest in a "Sukhothai" style of leadership as portrayed in the play *Anuphab Phokhun Ramkhamhaeng*. This conception was reflected in the pattern that Sarit later fashioned for his own style of leadership, as evident, for instance, in his exhortations that Thailand's administration should use the traditional concepts of *phoban phomuang* and in his portrayal of himself as the father of the nation.[32]

Perhaps if Sarit had lived in ancient times, he would have founded a new dynasty as the new *phokhun*, or even as an absolute king. But given the situation he faced, the installation of a new king was out of the question. Thus, to overcome this obstruction, it proved essential for Sarit to accept a dualistic type of leadership, in which the king still existed as the physical representation of the sovereignty of the Thai nation and its glorious past, while Sarit was to become the actual leader, or *phokhun*. Sarit's genius seems to have lain in his ability to reconcile the two concepts and to use the throne to enhance his own position. While demonstrating his allegiance to the throne, Sarit still could operate as *phokhun*. Thus, while operating within the existing parameters of state, he introduced subtle changes to Thailand's political organization. Sarit's regime was to be a paternalistic regime, imagined after the model of Ramkhamhaeng, yet it would operate within the system of constitutional monarchy that had evolved after 1932.

SARIT *AS PHOKHUN*: HELPING THE CHILDREN

The *phokhun* model demanded a continuing flow of direct personal benevolent interventions on behalf of the *phokhun*'s "children." Sarit's determination to respond directly and personally to popular needs (or what he saw as such) was evident from the start. A flood of decisive interventions followed rapidly after the *pattiwat*.

Electricity rates were ordered lowered almost within days of the coup.[33] In the Bangkok-Thonburi area, where potable water was in short supply, Sarit decreed each family be given three hundred *pip* (large buckets) free of charge each month.[34] Telephone rates, railway rates, and tuition in schools were also reduced in response to these initiatives.[35]

---

[31] Luang Wichit Wathakan, *Anakhot* [The Future] (Bangkok: Kasem Bannakit Press, 1959). The above paragraph was part of the preface to the new printing of his book.

[32] See Chapter Three.

[33] *Sayam Rat*, October 26, 1958.

[34] *Sayam Rat*, November 6, 1958.

[35] *Sayam Rat*, November 13, 15, 16, 21, 1958.

The Revolutionary Council announced that the municipal government had been ordered to abolish certain taxes, license fees, and charges for official services. Medicine and health care would be dispensed free of charge to needy families at hospitals. Social workers and student nurses were instructed to visit poor families to help treat illnesses and assist in childbirth. The proclamation also directed the municipal government to provide free textbooks for poor students enrolled in the thirty schools under its jurisdiction.[36]

Sarit also proposed to limit working days for civil servants to five, to provide extra pay for those with more children, and to establish credit funds for lower grade civil servants so that they could borrow money more easily.[37] Buses were to take the place of the slow and cumbersome trams in the capital.[38]

To help cut food prices, Sarit ordered new markets opened, modeled on the Sunday flea market usually held at Sanam Luang, where merchants and tradesmen could bring their goods directly to the people without involving middlemen in the transactions. These open-air markets selling both foodstuffs and clothing were set up on government land, and only nominal fees were charged for the participating merchants. Prices consequently were relatively low by comparison with regular shops.[39]

Aside from opening new market sites, Sarit decreed the retail price of coffee be reduced from 70 satang to 50 satang per glass. Iced black coffee is a very popular beverage in Thailand, and the price reduction for this item was meant to illustrate Sarit's interest in the smallest domestic needs of the people.[40] (However, the effectiveness of the order was circumvented by wily merchants, who made glasses smaller, put less coffee in their brews, or added more ice to their drinks. To satisfy their habitual thirsts, the public had to resort to ordering "special" iced coffee, which was sold at the old price.) Furthermore, in response to Sarit's appeals, the Association of Rice Merchants agreed to reduce the price of rice in many of the association-controlled shops.[41] Besides rice and coffee, coconut is essential for preparing the curries Thai families eat daily. To show that all parts of Thai society were pitching in to "revolutionize" the country, Sarit ordered the navy to search for cheap coconuts and bring them to sell to the public at cost.[42] And to fulfill demands for more recreational facilities, Sarit announced that the United States would provide a loan of 83,000,000 baht for the construction of four new theaters.[43]

Although these programs were short term, and many were never actually implemented, the way in which they were announced and publicized created a general atmosphere of change and generated considerable enthusiasm for the benevolent paternalism of the new *phokhun*.

---

[36] Note the emphasis on the family as the relevant social unit.

[37] *Sayam Rat,* November 16, 1958.

[38] *Sayam Rat,* November 18, 1958.

[39] *Sayam Rat,* November 4, 5, 1958. Yet these markets later closed down because of insufficient public support.

[40] *Sayam Rat,* November 5, 1958. The prices of sugar, charcoal, and pork were also ordered reduced. *Sayam Rat,* November 14, 1958.

[41] *Sayam Rai,* November 14, 1958.

[42] *Sayam Rat,* December 12, 1958.

[43] *Sayam Rat,* February 4, 1959.

SARIT AS *PHOKHUN*: MAINTAINING *KHWAM RIAPROY* IN THE FAMILY

Thai writers particularly have tried to analyze Sarit's hatred for *anthaphan* (hoodlums), opium, uncleanliness and social impropriety by looking into his past. They found precedents for his crackdown on the *anthaphan* in a personal experience in 1929, when, as a newly commissioned lieutenant, he personally shot and killed three leading *anthaphan* at Sanam Pao in Bangkok.[44]

His obsession with cleanliness and proper social behavior related to his personal lifestyle. He was described by a former fellow officer as a person who valued beauty, who dressed in clean and well-pressed clothes, washed his face many times a day, had his hair always combed, and acted with social propriety (*riaproy*).[45]

Undoubtedly, Sarit's personal experiences and preferences contributed to his public activities, but one should not put too much emphasis on these factors. As we have seen, the *pattiwat* of 1958 was intended to try to rid the nation of evil foreign influences contaminating Thailand's social purity. Sarit wanted to create a social atmosphere that would be conducive to his leadership, an atmosphere characterized by proper development and modernization. In a speech quoted above, he expressed his opinion that the cleanliness and proper appearance of a village or town meant that the people in it were progressive and modern.[46] It appears that he believed that any attempt to achieve national modernization and progress must start by insuring that the nation's citizens are in the correct state of mind; in this approach, he resembles a father who, when attending to his children's upbringing (their "development"), believes that this undertaking must begin with proper moral education.

Immediately after the coup of 1958, Sarit ordered that the *anthaphan* who infested the urban areas be arrested and reformed. The Revolutionary Council's Proclamation No. 21 stated that the *anthaphan* were a menace to society and the common people and that eliminating them would help promote the happiness of the people.[47] While mass arrests and interrogations resulted from the Proclamation No. 21, Sarit felt this was not enough. He saw to it that accused hoodlums were sentenced not merely to thirty-day detentions, as had been typical, but were also enrolled in reformatory institutions established under the provisions of Proclamation No. 43.[48]

This blanket authority was employed to clear the cities of petty criminals as well as to intimidate young people into adopting a more "traditional" social life. People with long hair, tight pants, and flashy clothes, which were then in vogue in the United States and had found their way to Thailand, were arrested as *anthaphan*. Sarit ordered the weekly dance at Lumpini Garden closed on the grounds that it was bad for the youth.[49] He also instructed the police to detain youths who frequented night spots. Rock and roll music was banned from government parties, and the police were told to be on the look out for illegal dancing of the "twist" in public places.

---

[44] Thai Noi (pseud.) and Rungrot Na Nakhon, *Nayok Ratthamontri Khon thi 11 kap 3 Phunam Pattiwat* [The Eleventh Prime Minister and the Three Leaders of the Revolution] (Bangkok: Phrae Phitthaya Press, 1964), p. 16.

[45] These were the words of General Sanit Sanityutthakan Thaiyanon in the Cremation Volume of Sarit Thanarat [Cabinet edition], p. 26.

[46] Sarit Thanarat, "Khamklao Pedprachum Palachangwad," April 27, 1959.

[47] *Prakat khong Khana Pattiwat No. 21*, November 2, 1958.

[48] *Prakat khong Khana Pattiwat No. 43*, January 10, 1959.

[49] *Sayam Rat*, March 8, 1961.

The program for social purification involved a few thousand people who were arrested and sent to reformatory schools, many of whom were puzzled by their arrest.[50] The effect on the public, however, was great, for it instilled fear of and respect for Sarit in the citizenry. The marshal viewed his role as the father of the nation who must reprimand and try to reform his errant children. He told his victims upon their release that he did not hate them, but had to act for the good of the "family."[51] As father, he was doing the nation a good turn, and he hoped that the former *anthaphan* would realize their shortcomings.

Prostitution also came under the personal purview of Sarit, who believed sexual solicitation encouraged crime. He ordered that all prostitutes arrested be reformed by sending them to institutions that would train them for new professions. Two institutions were specially established at Pak Kret and Ban Kret Trakan to treat and train prostitutes for new social roles. Sarit was also responsible for the passing of the Law Against Prostitution, BE 2503.[52] No less un-*riaproy* than prostitutes, in Sarit's eyes, were the *samlo*, or pedicabs, that cluttered and dirtied the streets of the capital. As Police General Prasert Ruchirawong, the director-general of the Police Department, puts it, the *samlo* raised the

> ... question of cleanliness of the country. Because of neglect of their former occupations [that is, rice farming], these laborers do not have proper dwelling places.... They sleep in temples or garages. Some areas, huts were constructed under bridges or on the side of roads as permanent homes which make the country dirty and not proper [*mai pen rabieb riaproy*].[53]

Sarit wanted these men, usually from the Northeast, to return to the village farms, back to what he considered their proper place and role in society.[54] For these reasons, he ordered a ban on *samlo* in the capital.

Sarit did much more to make the country look clean and proper. Roads were frequently swept, beggars taken off the streets,[55] stray dogs exterminated, lepers[56]

---

[50] Sarit Thanarat, "Owat lae Khamklao Pidkanobrom Anthaphan," September 6, 1960.

[51] Cremation Volume of Sarit Thanarat [Cabinet edition], p. 50. The following is a statistical breakdown of the number of persons affected by Proclamations Nos. 21 and 43.

Year	No. Arrested	30-Day Detention	To Reform Institutions
1958	894	261	633
1959	2,210	1,157	1,053
1960	1,015	236	779
1961	816	233	538
1962	1,353	515	838
1963	1,251*	341	852
Total	7,539	2,743	4,738

*This total includes 58 persons who were released after questioning.

[52] *Ratchakitcha*, vol. 77, section 89, November 1, 1960.

[53] Cremation Volume of Sarit Thanarat [Cabinet edition], p. 62

[54] Ibid. Statistics from 1953 to 1959 indicated that there were only 4,303 pedicab drivers who were indigenous to the Bangkok–Thonburi area, while 12,546 drivers were from the outer provinces who came to find jobs in the capital.

ordered arrested and sent to care centers,[57] and people were fined for littering. Sarit's credibility as *phokhun* was enhanced when he personally apprehended people whom he saw littering the streets. He directed the municipal authorities to crack down on houses where clothes were dried on balconies and plants grown in an unkempt and untidy fashion.[58] He ordered the municipal authorities to plant gardens and help beautify the cities by constructing fountains along public thoroughfares. New laws were passed to allow the police to arrest and fine offenders who transgressed against the Sarit campaign for cleanliness.[59] Sarit further asked people and officials of the government not to be overly annoyed by the many regulations imposed by his new initiatives, for he said that he was doing it for the good of the whole.[60]

Sarit's popularity was increased by his management of fire prevention and his executions of arsonists. Arson and fires have long been frequent phenomena in the major cities of Thailand, especially during times of economic depression. After the coup of 1958, many suspicious fires broke out. Prime Minister Sarit expressed deep concern for the plight of the fire victims, and, in an address to the people, he promised that:

> I have decided that prompt and decisive actions must be taken immediately, especially in the case of fires ... Therefore I am forced to act with ultimate decisiveness [*det khat*]. Whatever is right or wrong, I and I alone will take responsibility for carrying out policies that I deem most correct and which will lead to the happiness of the people. Please accept and take note of this. [61]

The test of Sarit's decisiveness (*det khat*) came on November 6, 1958.[62] A Chinese merchant in Thonburi had hired an unemployed laborer to set fire to his shop so that he could collect on his fire insurance. The amateur arsonist was quickly apprehended as he fled the scene of the crime. After extensive interrogation, Sarit ordered the Chinese merchant to be executed immediately. Addressing the public to inform them of his decision, he said:

> I have no alternative but to act in the manner that I have described to you before. I will do anything to achieve happiness for the people, regardless of the consequences.
> The fire that erupted on November 6 of this year has been thoroughly investigated by myself and the police. We all agree that there is no doubt that the fire was the result of a selfish individual.
> Therefore, I now order the execution of this person to pay for the *kam* [Karma] which he had committed. Again, I would like to inform my Thai

---

[55] *Sayam Rat*, February 21, 1959.

[56] *Sayam Rat*, January 9, March 6, 1960. Soldiers were also ordered to help clear the city of stray dogs.

[57] *Sayam Rat*, March 1, 1961.

[58] *Sayam Rat*, March 1, 1961.

[59] *Sayam Rat*, September 13, 1959. Police reported that within three days, 5,000 baht were collected in fines.

[60] *Sayam Rat*, November 15, 1959.

[61] *Sayam Rat*, November 2, 1958.

[62] *Sayam Rat*, November 7, 1958.

brothers and sisters that decisiveness [*chiep khat*] is the only instrument that can help the nation achieve progress.

Whether it is just or not, I do not fear. I only hold on to the thought that with every breath I take, I think only of the happiness of all Thais. This is my highest wish which has led me to make this drastic decision.

I will assume sole responsibility if there is any. [63]

Another major fire occurred on November 7, again in Thonburi and in the same area. The arsonists were two Chinese brothers who were also attempting to collect fire insurance.[64] Sarit once more personally investigated the matter and ordered the public execution of the brothers. That same month, on November 27, fire broke out at a lumber mill in Bangkok. Sarit, who was making a tour of border areas, returned immediately to supervise the fire-fighting. The damage came to over fourteen million baht. In this case, foul play by the owner was ruled out, for his fire insurance only covered losses totaling three million baht. Sarit's investigation turned up a suspect who later confessed that he had set fire to the mill out of revenge for being fired from his job earlier. Because of the suspect's total disregard for the law and "non-cooperation" with the revolutionary government, Sarit ordered his execution.[65]

Yet a fifth arsonist would die the next month. On December 19, 1958, a fire broke out in Suphanburi which destroyed over four hundred houses. The suspected arsonist was a young Chinese who had operated a photo shop. Sarit flew by helicopter to interrogate the suspect at once. There was no obvious reason why the suspect would want to set fire to his own shop. Unlike previous cases, there was no question of insurance. However, after intensive grilling and questioning by the premier, the suspect "confessed" to the crime committed. The government announced that the fire was part of a larger plan by the communists to create confusion and subvert the morale of the public.[66] The suspected arsonist was executed on Sarit's order. He was shot at the site of the fire amid the victims who turned out to curse him and witness his death. This was the last person executed for the crime of arson.

It is interesting to note that the five who were executed were all Chinese. Through their executions, Sarit was able to gain favor with the Thai public who generally distrust the Chinese. There is no doubt that Sarit seized the opportunity to please the public as well as show them that he cared for their welfare. His decisiveness (*det khet/chiep khat*) was effective, and the majority of people commended Sarit for trying his best to curb the rash of fires. From that time on, Sarit saw to it that he was informed of any fires, large or small, so that he could personally go to supervise the fire-fighting. Night or day, sick or well, Sarit always appeared at fires. Thus his reputation grew as a result of his interest in fires, and the public appeared convinced that Sarit was a great leader in the tradition of *phokhun*.

---

[63] Chakkrawan Chanuwong, *M. 17 kap 11 Nakthod Prahan* [Article 17 and the 11 Executed Prisoners] (Bangkok : Chaichana Press, 1964), pp. 47–49.

[64] There are two conflicting accounts, although both agree that the amount insured was 220,000 baht. Chakkrawan maintains that the brothers had a dressmaking shop, while the account given by Police General Prasert in the Cremation Volume of Sarit Thanarat [Cabinet edition], p. 29, says that the brothers had set up a fake pharmacy shop that was not registered and had nothing in it when the fire broke out. For the Chakkrawan account, see ibid., pp. 61–69.

[65] Chakkrawan, *M. 17 kap 11 Nakthod*, pp. 80–88.

[66] Ibid., pp. 94, 95

SARIT AS *PHOKHUN*—IMPORTING HEALTH AND MORALS

Historical evidence shows that opium addiction has been a problem in Thailand at least since the time of Ayutthaya and maybe earlier. A law enacted in the reign of Ramathibodi I (U Thong) stipulated that the public was prohibited from smoking, eating, or selling opium.[67] The problem of opium persisted on through the Rattanakosin, or Bangkok, period, from the late eighteenth century to the present.

In 1803, Rama I decreed that those caught with opium would be punished by the confiscation of their property and confinement; the defendant's families and slaves would become the property of the realm.[68] Rama III decreed that opium found by the authorities was to be destroyed immediately. The opium confiscated was ordered burnt, and elaborate ceremonies presided over by monks attended the incineration of the forbidden substance. These affairs were called *kratham chapanakit phao fin*, or opium cremations.[69] Rama III's attempts to control trafficking in the drug were unsuccessful, however, because of the great profits to be had from the illegal opium trade. Accordingly, the government of Rama III began importing opium from India and selling it by auction to the highest bidders, who were called *nai akon*, or tax officials.[70]

In the reign of Rama IV, opium use was restricted to the Chinese community. Thais were not permitted to deal in or use opium.[71] From that time on, opium became associated with the rise of Chinese secret societies that tried to corner the opium market.[72]

After the Second World War, opium remained an official source of government revenue in Thailand, becoming a major source of corruption and power. We have seen how Police General Phao Siyanon used his control of the local opium trade to finance his political machine. But because of increased international pressures, the Phibun government finally agreed on August 3, 1955 that opium sales and use would be terminated by the beginning of 1956.[73] This deadline was later moved back a year, for the government argued that it could not find additional revenues to replace the money lost from opium taxes. Advisers from the United Nations were consulted, but their recommendations were only half-heartedly implemented.

---

[67] *Kotmai Waduai Laksana Chon Ph. S. 1903* [Law Pertaining to Banditry, 1350] in *Ruang Kotmai Muang Thai Chabab Mo Bradlae* [Thai Laws: Dr. Bradley Edition], vol. I (Bangkok: Dr. Bradley Press, 1896), p. 293.

[68] See *Pramuan Kotmai Ratchakan thi. 1*, Ch. S. 1166 [Compilations of Laws in the First Reign, 1804].

[69] Phracho Boromawongthoe Kromphra Sommutiamonphan, *Prakat Phraratchaphithi* [Royal Ceremonies], vol. II (Bangkok: Phim Thai Press, 1916), p. 26. Also consult *Prachum Phongsawadan* [Collected Chronicle], section 12, 1929, p. 37.

[70] Police Lt. Sathien Wichailak, comp., *Prachum Kotmai Pracham Sok*, vol. XVI, R.S. 116-117 [Collection of Annual Laws, 1898-1899] (Bangkok: Daily Mail Press, 1935), p. 486. *Prakat Khobangkhap Phasi Fin* R.S. 118.

[71] Siriwat Osathanukhro, "Fin kap panha Sangkhom nai Prathet Thai [Opium and Social Problems in Thailand]" (MA thesis, Thammasat University, 1960), p. 23.

[72] "Nithan Borankhadi [Historical Tales]," in *Anuson Phraratchathan Pluengsop Kromphraya Damrongrachanuphab* [cremation Volume of Prince Damrong], Bangkok, April 11, 1944. The copy used was one sponsored by Phibun.

[73] Cremation Volume of Sarit Thanarat [Cabinet edition], p. 32.

After the coup of 1958, however, the prime minister took matters into his own hands. He was determined to end opium sales and consumption immediately. The rationale behind this decision was complex. First, Sarit wanted to demonstrate to the people that he was not out to gain personal profit from opium in the manner of Phao and that he was sincere in his desire to eliminate the corruption represented by Phao's activities in the Phibun regime. Second, he expected this initiative to please the Western powers. In his public statements, he linked opium addiction to a subversive international communist scheme intended to undermine the economy and morale of countries in the Free World:

> ... our world is divided into two sides, namely; the Free World and the Communists. The Communists try all methods, good and bad, to destroy the Free World. One of the things the Communists use to try to destroy the Free World is opium. Because Thailand upholds the principle of democracy and is on the side of the Free World, there is no doubt that Thailand is an enemy of the Communists. Therefore, there is no question but that the Communists will try to use addictive drugs to subvert the Thai economy and the health of its people. [74]

But third, and not least important, Sarit saw ending addiction as part of his *phokhun* mission of moral uplift.

By the Revolutionary Council's Proclamation No. 37, opium consumption was declared illegal after January 1, 1959; from that time, the drug would only be administered to registered addicts. Opium dens would be permanently closed by June 30, 1959, and treatment centers would be established to help addicts through the withdrawal process. [75] Sarit announced to the people on June 30, 1959 that:

> Now, the designated time has arrived. The first minute after midnight on July 1, 1959 marks the ultimate [*det khat*] termination of opium consumption in Thailand. Therefore, July 1, 1959 is a historic day, for it is a day that inaugurates a new chapter, a new section, a new society in Thai history. We will now be able to state confidently that we are a civilized [*araya*] nation, and our national prestige will be unsullied by international criticism ... The sale and use of opium is illegal, and I maintain that it is a major crime and whoever resists will be severely punished. Alien offenders will be deported, and Thais will be marked as traitors who refuse to make sacrifices for the nation, which is equivalent to not cooperating with me personally, and I will therefore be forced to use severe repression. I can sacrifice even my life. I consider that opium is a national menace, and I will do anything to save the nation. [76]

As we can detect from the above passage, the prohibition of opium use and sale was imposed within the framework of creating a new society: offenders became enemies of the nation, as well as being likened to rebellious sons who refused to follow the wishes of their father, Sarit. The prime minister's words were uttered in the tone of a father lecturing his children, more than of a leader reasoning with his fellow citizens.

---

[74] Ibid., pp. 33.

[75] *Prakat khong Khana Pattiwat No. 37* December 9, 1958.

[76] Cremation Volume of Sarit Thanarat [Cabinet edition], p. 35.

As father, he saw no need to give lengthy explanations. His judgment was to be accepted by all.

Following this statement, at precisely 1 am that day, opium paraphernalia that had been collected throughout the country were ceremoniously "cremated" at Sanam Luang. Opium pipes destroyed in the inferno totaled 43,445.[77] To insure strict supervision and control, Sarit further established the Committee to Combat Addictive Drugs and created a special section in the Crime Suppression Division of the Police Department to deal with all types of illegal drug traffic.

Sarit personally took charge of the Committee to Combat Addictive Drugs, which was composed of the Chief of Police (Sarit)—acting as chairman—along with the Directors-General of the Customs, Interior, Revenue, Courts, and Social Welfare departments, the Deputy Undersecretary of Health, and representatives from the Foreign Ministry and the Tax Audit Bureau. This committee had the power to review cases involving drug trafficking and abuse in line with requests made by the United Nations and Interpol.[78]

Shortly after the banning of the sale and use of opium, a new drug emerged to fill the vacuum—heroin. Sarit was just as determined to discourage its manufacture and widespread use. He said on February 10, 1962:

> Frankly speaking, Communism is our worst enemy, which poses an internal as well as external danger ...
>
> A new subversive threat is heroin, which I, in my capacity as Prime Minister and Director-General of Police, must suppress severely.[79]

Earlier, in August 1961, Sarit had ordered the arrest of a Chinese man in connection with heroin production in Bangkok. After a personal interrogation by Sarit, who was convinced that the suspect was indeed guilty, the man was ordered executed. Aside from this case, periodic arrests were made of heroin producers, and at times Sarit himself directed the operations.

SARIT AS *PHOKHUN* — IMPOSING ORDER

The legal basis of Sarit's power to order executions and other activities of the *det khat* (absolutely decisive) variety was Article 17 of the Interim Constitution of Thailand, B.E. 2502, which stated:

> During the enforcement of the present Constitution, whenever the Prime Minister deems it appropriate for the purpose of impressing or suppressing actions, whether of internal or external origin, which jeopardize the national security or the Throne or subvert or threaten law and order, the Prime Minister, by resolution of the Council of Ministers, is empowered to issue orders or take steps accordingly. Such orders or steps shall be considered legal.

---

[77] Ibid., p. 36.

[78] Later, the Director-General of the Prisons Department and representatives from the Defense, Industry, and Education Ministries were appointed as additional members. In 1961, the Undersecretary of the Interior became the Committee's special adviser.

[79] Cremation Volume of Sarit Thanarat [Cabinet edition], p. 42.

All orders issued and steps taken by the Prime Minister in accordance with the provisions of the foregoing paragraph shall be made known to the National Assembly.[80]

This article is known in Thailand as "M 17," and the mention of its name evokes a mixed feeling of fear and reverence. While it is possible to view Article 17 as the basis for dictatorial power, it was also the modern legal basis for a *phokhun* style of leadership, which was key to Sarit's concept of political administration. Sarit as the head of the Revolutionary Council was the head of the national family and had to be able to enforce his will.

Hence, immediately after Sarit's second coup in 1959, parliament was dissolved, parties were banned, newspapers came under censorship, political gatherings were outlawed, and people suspected of being sympathetic to communism or opposed to Sarit's leadership were arrested and imprisoned. From 1958 to 1963, Sarit invoked Article 17 to order the execution of eleven persons. Five were executed for arson, one for producing heroin, one for leading a messianic uprising, and four on charges of communism. So far, we have dealt with the executions of the first six of these, who were convicted essentially on moral, rather than political, grounds. The last five were rather different.

Sila Wongsin was a peasant from Nakhon Ratchasima who fancied himself as a *phi bun*, or messianic leader with supernatural and magical powers.[81] He established his "kingdom" at a village in Nakhon Ratchasima, elevated himself to the position of king, and held sway over the two hundred villagers who resided within his "realm." When the District Officer of the area went to see him to question him regarding his so-called secessionist movement, the official was attacked and a few members of his party were killed. A police detail was then sent out to arrest *phi bun* Sila, who told his followers that they could not be harmed because of his magical powers. Fighting broke out, and in a short time the authorities were able to kill eleven of Sila's subjects and capture eighty-eight prisoners. Sila, his family, and eight disciples escaped, but were later captured near the Laotian border. He was personally interrogated by Sarit, who ordered that he be publicly executed in Nakhon Ratchasima.[82]

Sila came from the Northeast, an area with a rich history of opposition to the central government. Local political leaders made no exception for Sarit, even though his mother was from that region and many considered him a northwesterner. Of the other four persons executed on political grounds, two were charged with trying to spread communism and overthrow the central government; the other two were accused of being communists operating in Bangkok-Thonburi and Suphanburi.

Sarit's regime, as well as earlier governments, had often used accusations of communism or suspicion of communist sympathies to justify crackdowns on the political opposition. Immediately following the coup of 1953, over forty persons were arrested on suspicion of being communists; those arrested included politicians, students, journalists, and labor leaders.[83] In November of the same year, four labor unions were closed on the grounds that they only promoted division between

[80] *Interim Constitution of the Kingdom of Thailand*, 1959.

[81] *Sayam Rat*, May 31, 1959; and Chakkrawan, *M. 17 kap 11 Nakthod*, pp. 101-120.

[82] *Sayam Rat*, June 2, 1959.

[83] *Sayam Rat*, October 21 ff., 1958.

workers and management, as well as being instruments of communism.[84] In January 1959, the police arrested forty-seven persons in Sisaket on charges of planning a communist uprising.[85] Many of those arrested were teachers in schools owned by former MP, Thep Chotinuchit: namely the Thepwitthaya North, Thepwitthaya South, and Satriwitthaya schools. The authorities asserted that the suspects had planned to infiltrate these schools with communist propaganda.

The first major case involving the charge of communism was that of Suphachai Sisati.[86] He was accused of being the author and printer of leaflets that were circulated after the first Sarit coup of 1957. Suphachai had a degree in electrical engineering from Japan, had been to Peking, and had for a short period studied in Moscow. He was a member of the Communist Party of Thailand and was instrumental in forming the Thai Labor Council. While he was in custody following his arrest, the police were able to capture documents, firearms, and printing material at his hideout in Thonburi. After his arrest, he was interrogated personally by Sarit and then ordered publicly executed on July 5, 1959. Together with Suphachai, twelve other persons were arrested and imprisoned.

On May 6, 1961, the police arrested Khrong Chandawong and Thongphan Sutthimat in Sakon Nakhon on charges that they had been involved in a communist conspiracy. A hundred other persons were detained in that province and surrounding areas for involvement in Khrong's plans.[87]

Khrong Chandawong was a former MP from Sakon Nakhon who had been arrested and imprisoned in 1952 on charges of rebellion. He was released in 1957 in accordance with the mass amnesty to commemorate the 25th Centennial Celebrations of the Buddhist Era. After regaining his freedom, Khrong returned to the Northeast and began to lay the groundwork for future political plans. After the Kong Le coup in Laos in August 1960, Khrong seems to have become convinced that the Pathet Lao would soon have control of Laos. He proceeded to organize a secret society called Samakhitham (Solidarity) to educate people about communism.[88] Khrong also emphasized that people from Isan were not Thai, but Lao, and that the Isan region was formerly an independent Lao state until the Thais seized control. He called for the liberation of Isan from the central government, and for union with their brothers, the Pathet Lao.

For these activities, Khrong and Thongphan were sentenced to death. The announcement of their fate stated that:

> ... in accordance with the power invested by Article 17 of the Constitution, and the decision of the Cabinet, which met on May 30, 1961, the Prime Minister has ordered the execution of Khrong Chandawong and Thongphan Sutthimat to protect national security and the Throne. This is to be an example to prevent this

---

[84] *Prakat khong Khana Pattiwat No. 19*, October 21, 1958.

[85] *Sayam Rat*, January 20, 1959.

[86] Cremation Volume of Sarit Thanarat [Cabinet edition], pp. 66, 67; and Chakkrawan, *M. 17 kap 11 Nakthod*, pp. 121–153.

[87] *Sayam Rat*, May 11, 13, 14, 20, 21 and June 2, 6, 1961. Also see Chakkrawan, *M, 17 kap 11 Nakthod*, pp. 153–167. For a detailed account of Khrong's life and activities from a "rightist" view, see Khomsan Matukham, *Khrong Chandawong khaw khu khrai?* [Who is Khrong Chandawong?] (Bangkok: Phithak Pracha Co. Ltd., 1978).

[88] Chakkrawan, *M. 17 kap 11 Nakthod*, p. 157.

type of crime in the future. Police authorities have already executed Khrong Chandawong and Thongphan Sutthimat at Sawang Daendin District, Sakon Nakhon Province, on May 31, 1961 at 12.13 hours.[89]

The Khrong "conspiracy" was apparently taken seriously by the government, for arrests were continuously made after the execution of the convicted ringleader, and a clash between police and followers of Khrong took place in December where over ninety persons were reportedly arrested.[90]

The last person to be executed as a communist agent was Ruam Wongphan. Ruam was from Suphanburi Province and had been educated at Thammasat University. He was a former headmaster of a Chinese school and a member of Thai Democratic Youth League (Sannibat Yaowachon Prachathipatai haeng Prathet Thai), which was a front organization for the Thai Communist Party. In 1949, he had been sent to Peking for indoctrination and returned to Thailand in 1954. His duties were to organize peasant groups in the provinces of Suphanburi, Lopburi, Saraburi, and Kanchaburi. His movements had been closely watched by the police, and he was arrested on February 3, 1962 and summarily executed on April 24, 1962. Thirty persons were arrested in connection with Ruam's work.

SARIT AS *PHOKHUN*—VISITING THE FAMILY

Thailand can almost be termed a city-state: Bangkok completely dominates Thai society.[91] The wealth of the country is centered in the capital and immediate surrounding areas, while the standards of living in the other areas—North, Northeast, and South—are far below that of the metropolis. It is also a fact that people of the Central area tend to look down upon those from the outer provinces as country bumpkins. The Isan area is the poorest of all the regions of Thailand, and people from Isan bear the brunt of insults and social insults. Before Sarit, no government had sincerely considered the welfare of the Northeast region, and this neglect was most strongly felt by the people of Isan, who in fact constituted the majority of the Thai population. Thus, we find that during the parliamentary period, MPs from Isan were always the most critical of the government, and on many occasions they banded together to demand development funds for their region. We have also seen that, of all the regional politicians, leaders from Isan were the most militant and dedicated to the well-being of their constituencies. Thus challenges to "political stability" and "national unity" usually came from Isan.

---

[89] Samnak Khao, Samnak Nayok Ratthamontri [Press Agency of the Prime Minister's Office], May 31, 1961.

[90] Sarit ordered a raid on suspects in Udon, Nongkhai, Nakhon Phanom, and Sakon Nakhon. *Sayam Rat,* December 16, 1961. Fighting broke out between Khrong's followers and the police in Sakon Nakhon. Ninety-one persons were arrested during the raid. *Sayam Rat,* December 17, 1961. Sarit said later that he was tempted to apply Article 17 to the leaders arrested but decided to imprison them for the time being. *Sayam Rat,* December 19, 22, 23, 1961. Apparently Khrong's organizational efforts had some lasting effects. See Louis E. Lomax, *Thailand: The War that Is, the War that Will Be* (New York, NY: Vintage Books, 1967), pp. 6, 7. Lomax offers an account of an alleged interview with Khrong's daughter who had taken over her father's work.

[91] Jeff Romm, *Urbanization in Thailand,* An International Urbanization Report from the Ford Foundation, [1972].

Marshal Sarit, who had grown up in the Northeast, was well aware of this. While he advocated stern measures to suppress political dissension and ordered the executions of Khrong and Thongphan and arrested several Isan politicians, he realized that his government must look more closely into the needs and welfare of the outer provinces to demonstrate to the people that the Revolutionary Government was sincerely concerned with their problems. Also, the unstable situation in Indochina posed a threat to the security of the country; this meant that internal strife and parochial and regional animosities must be minimized and national unity be strengthened. Sarit's plan for national development thus became both an end and a means. It was an end insofar as the *phokhun* was supposed to look after the well-being of the whole nation/family. It was a means insofar as it guaranteed national unity in the face of external danger.

Sarit went about promoting national unity and political stability on two fronts. First, he made personal tours of the provinces to show that he cared for the people of all regions and wanted to see their actual living conditions with his own eyes. Sarit was the first national leader to make frequent inspection tours by land. Second, economic development and the fulfillment of the immediate needs of the people were to be tackled through a national development plan.[92]

Sarit made his first inspection tours in 1960. From March 28 to April 12, he visited Isan and the North. In his remarks to the people of Isan, he stated:

> I left Bangkok with the desire to inspect the living conditions of local areas with my own eyes so that it could be food for my thoughts ... and so that I would be able to provide happiness for the people ... [93]

Sarit told them that he would never forget their needs and asked them to remember that he also had roots in the region, his mother being a native of Nakhon Phanom. He attempted to explain his goal of national development and the two-phase National Economic Development Plan. He urged the people of Isan to be patient and work hard and to look after the well-being of their families, thus establishing a strong foundation that would be the basis for national development. He also asked them to keep in mind that national unity (*khwam samakhi nai chat*) was the most important principle that they should all consider. In a national broadcast, Sarit told his listeners that the reason for the trip was to "see for myself the true conditions of the country" and to find out the real needs of the people.[94] From this tour, Sarit became convinced that the two most urgent needs of the people were water and roads. In all his other speeches made after inspection tours, these two necessary conditions for development were always mentioned.

Next to Isan, the Southern border provinces figured as a potential and real trouble spot.[95] A week after he returned from Isan, Sarit traveled to the South. He

---

[92] Regional development councils were established to deal with the particular problems of different regions. Sarit himself chaired the Council for the Development of Isan.

[93] Sarit Thanarat, "Khamprasi dae Phi Nong Chao Isan [Remarks to the People of Isan]," April 12, 1960, in *Pramuan Sunthoraphot* I, p. 154.

[94] Sarit Thanarat, "Khamprasai nai Kanpaitruad Ratchakan Phak Isan [Remarks Regarding Inspection Tour to the Isan Region]," April 12, 1960, in *Pramuan Sunthoraphot* I, p. 158.

[95] Press reports on unrest in the South had been reaching Bangkok at an alarming rate, and Sarit wanted to make a tour to the South to demonstrate his concern as well as show political dissidents that he had his eyes on them.

noted that, along the way, water was abundant and the vegetation lush and green. Here, water was no great problem compared to communications difficulties. He found that the economy of the South was controlled by non-Thai—mostly Chinese, as well as some Muslims—and so he urged the local people to exert themselves harder. Distressed to learn that in the border areas the people did not speak Thai and that he had to rely upon interpreters to talk to the local inhabitants, he said:

> ... we should not blame anyone but ourselves. However, it is not too late, nothing is too late. Although it would be a late start, we must start and act without hesitation ... I would like to urge and incite you to consider your love for the Thai nation. Our nationalism should flow thick in our blood, especially in the period of this revolutionary government. You must persevere, you must work. I want my Thai brothers from Isan, the North, and South to pour to the South to settle and work there ... Bring down Thai blood and the love of the nation to spread there.[96]

He said that he would assist those who were willing to settle in the South by creating government-sponsored farming centers to help them get started.

In May 1961, Sarit made another tour of Isan and the Central region. On this trip, he became still more convinced that roads and a land-based communications infrastructure were the nation's economic life-line, as well as being vital to national security and administration. He promised to double his efforts at road building in the Northeast. In a speech to the nation after his return, he urged that Thais should first act as tourists in their own country, for that sort of exploration would help promote better understanding among the people of the different regions.[97] That same month, he went to visit the North and addressed the people over the radio, explaining to them the essential points of his national development plan.[98]

Aside from these major tours, Sarit made periodic sorties to the provinces to inspect border areas and special projects. During his trips, Sarit traveled by car whenever possible, and he had a penchant for trying out back roads and visiting remote areas. To demonstrate his hardiness and informal lifestyle, Sarit refused to stay overnight in government guest houses but chose instead to camp out and sleep in tents. Wherever he went, he tried to talk to people and to inquire about their immediate needs. He also insisted that he be taken to inspect the local marketplace for he believed this was the best indication of the prosperity of the locality. In sum, his inspection tours were meant to demonstrate to the public Sarit's fatherly *phokhun* concern with their needs.

---

[96] Sarit Thanarat, "Khamprasai nai Kanpaitruad Ratchakan Phak Tai [Remarks Regarding Inspection Tour to the South]," May 2, 1961, in *Pramuan Sunthoraphot* I, pp. 171, 172.

[97] Sarit Thanarat, "Khamprasai Phailang Kantruad Ratchakan 19 Changwad [Remarks Following Inspection Tours to Nineteen Provinces]," June 1, 1961, in *Pramuan Sunthoraphot* I, p. 394.

[98] Sarit Thanarat, "Khamprasai dae Phi Nong Chao Phak Nua [Remarks to the People of the North]," June 19, 1961, in *Pramuan Sunthoraphot* I, p. 404.

PATERNALISM OR DESPOTISM?

One question that naturally crops up in any study dealing with a political leader who wields absolute power is: was he paternalistic or despotic? The two categories are difficult to separate and define, however. While the term "paternalistic" connotes kindly, fatherly characteristics, it is nevertheless possible to be a despotic, as well as a benevolent, father. Despotism implies that the leader's actions are undertaken for his own gain and carried out with little or no concern for his subjects. However, judging whether or not a leader has acted as a "despot" frequently involves value judgments and relative perceptions rather than objective assessment. While the so-called "despot" thinks that he is ruling paternalistically, others may think that he is not.

We have noted how Sarit dealt with the question of the *anthaphan*, political dissenters, suspected communists, prostitutes, pedicab drivers, and opium traffickers, and we have seen that in his speeches Sarit always justified his actions by asserting that they would make the family "better" and reform those members who were errant and unruly. Sarit's tours of inspection were conducted in an informal, fatherlike manner, as though he wanted to get closer to his family to determine their true needs. Generally speaking, Sarit worked hard to be accepted as a benevolent paternal leader. The most striking aspect of this effort was his attention to small individual problems and his accessibility to low-level petitioners. Roads in the capital city were known for being in poor condition and neglected for long periods of time. Reacting to public demands and petitions in the press, Sarit ordered the municipal authorities to step up their schedule for repairing the roads. But, in addition, he was known to send personal notes to the Lord Mayor instructing him to fix certain roads immediately. His effectiveness was demonstrated to an appreciative public when, on one occasion, certain deteriorating roads in Bangkok were fixed within seven days after Sarit applied personal pressure.[99] On another occasion, Sarit learned of the plight of fruit merchants, who needed more outlets for the sale of their goods, and he personally went to inspect the fresh-fruit market and talk to the merchants. He then ordered the municipal government to open additional market centers to help the fruit-sellers.[100] He made a point of conducting personal appearances during fires and other natural calamities, and often intervened personally in unorthodox ways to get things going. For example, when available funds became scarce for welfare housing projects under construction in June 1961, Sarit ordered his brother, who was director of the Lottery Bureau, to provide the necessary amount to build the initial 1,339 houses as model homes. In January 1962, Sarit urged the municipal government to complete its welfare community program quickly and promised that funds from the Lottery Bureau would be made available if needed. In September, Sarit appropriated 150 million baht from the Lottery Bureau for the construction of these welfare communities.[101]

Thus we find that Sarit used his influence and his leadership in government to sustain and develop his personal political legitimacy. Convinced that the people would understand and accept his leadership style based upon the traditional concept of the *phokhun*, Sarit was able to win the respect and support of the public. His

---

[99] *Sayam Rat*, September and October, 1963.

[100] *Sayam Rat*, July 18, 1963.

[101] *Sayam Rat*, July 25, 1961.

interest in solving immediate problems and meeting small-scale but pressing daily needs indicated to the people that their prime minister was sincerely interested in their affairs. His obsession with cleanliness, orderliness, and morals received support from the public, who were able to witness drastic changes—cleaner streets, fewer hoodlums, beggars, dogs and prostitutes, and no more *samlo*. The decision to wage all-out war on the opium and heroin trades also brought fame to Sarit and earned him the respect of the public. His drastic treatment of arsonists and communist suspects increased the awe and fear in which he was held, but also increased his prestige as a *phokhun* who was ready to sacrifice his future well-being for the collective good of the national family.

The despotic nature of Sarit's rule has not been so far clearly assessed. Above, we have described the nature of Sarit's paternalism and noted that justifications for despotism are implicit in paternalism. However, on the political level, Sarit's style of leadership, which placed a premium on *khwam riaproy* and *sathiaraphab*, necessitated the elimination of "heterodox" elements that could upset the "orthodoxy" of the *pattiwat* system.

Professor Toru Yano analyzed this Thai style of arbitrary rule, which he found to have three distinct features.

> First, there is a Thai version of the concept of noblesse oblige. All Thai politicians share this particular Thai brand of paternalism. Second, there is the dark side of paternalism, the concept of freedom in power, which consists in the freedom to formulate at will one's style of rule, and the freedom to govern by the issue of orders (*khamsang*). The nature of this freedom is so perfectionistic as to remove all restraints from the arbitrary exercise of power. The third feature is the harsh exclusivity directed against non-Thai elements or heterodox elements incompatible with the rulers.[102]

Working from this analysis, one could view the harsh nature of the Sarit regime as the direct result of the leader's concern with heterodox elements that had to be eliminated. In most instances, the despotic policies and actions of Sarit were extremely repressive, and many of these alleged "heterodox elements" were suppressed. The examples we have seen so far include the execution of Chinese arsonists, the execution of Sila Wongsin for presenting a "heterodox" version of traditional religio-political leadership, and the elimination of communist agitators for introducing "heterodox" political ideology that ran contrary to the *pattiwat* philosophy.

Sarit's dealings with the Sangha could be viewed as another case in point. Traditionally, the Sangha had not played a significant role in the politics of Thailand. They had provided an indirect basis of legitimization for the Thai monarchy, but were never really active in national politics. Sarit was to change this in 1962, when the existing decentralized Sangha organization was reorganized to facilitate political control and penetration. Regulations that had shaped the Sangha of 1941 by dividing authority between the legislative, judicial and executive branches were replaced in

---

[102] Toru Yano, "Political Structure," in *Thailand: A Rice-Growing Society*, ed. Yoneo Ishii (Honolulu, HI: The University Press of Hawaii, 1978), p. 131. Sarit established this pattern of despotic rule by issuing a *khamsang huana khana-pattiwat* [order of the leader of the Revolutionary Council], which has become part of the modern pattern of leadership behavior.

1962 with a system governed by a more monolithic administrative-judicial hierarchy. This system negated the previous intent and inherent idea of democratic control that had been implicit in the 1941 law.[103]

Under the system as it was organized in 1941, control over the Sangha was diffused through three ecclesiastical executive councils, a structure that prevented the Supreme Patriarch from taking a decisive role in leadership. Furthermore, protracted disputes between the two major sects of the Sangha—namely, the Mahanikai and Thammayutnikai—came to a head in 1958, when the search for a new Supreme Patriarch threatened to grow heated and expand from a religious struggle to a fierce secular quarrel. The majority Mahanikai, which controlled about 90 percent of the temples in the country, were not happy with the stranglehold imposed by the strictly disciplinary (and royally connected) Thammayut sect, which held a disproportionate number of seats in the ecclesiastical councils. This tension was temporarily solved by Sarit, who used his influence to help elect a Supreme Patriarch who satisfied his own preferences.

Sarit's political authoritarianism was not ready to be compromised by a liberally organized Sangha that could effectively block his schemes to exploit the Buddhist order for *pattiwat*. At first, Sarit issued warnings that if internal disputes in the Sangha were not settled, his government would intervene. This threat was carried out with the issuance of the Buddhist Order Act of 1962, which in effect centralized the system under a Supreme Patriarch with vast authority. By this act, Sarit made the Sangha conform to his visions of authoritarian rule. Also, through this reorganization, Sarit was able to exploit the Sangha for the purposes of national integration and, more importantly, to enhance his regime's stability—a prerequisite for *phatthana*.[104]

Thus the church was reshaped in accord with the main line of Sarit's political orthodoxy. Heterodox elements were also suppressed. Two liberal-minded senior monks, Phra Phimontham and Phra Satsanasophon, were openly opposed to Sarit's attempts. They were subsequently charged for communistic and immoral crimes and brought before the courts after they were stripped of their high ecclesiastical positions.[105]

The least studied aspect of Sarit's despotism was his policy towards intellectual heterodoxy, which was perceived by the regime as an influence that undermined the stability of the *pattiwat* system. In the late 1950s, interest in democracy and liberalism in general had produced an atmosphere of hope within the intellectual community.

---

[103] See Mahamakut Educational Council, *Acts on the Administration of the Buddhist Order of the Sangha* (Bangkok: The Buddhist University, 1963), for details of the texts. Also see Yoneo Ishii, "Church and State in Thailand," *Asian Survey* VII (October 1968): 864-871, for a concise history of state control over the Sangha. Ishii also provided a schematic comparison of the two hierarchies.

[104] Monks were later used as political informants in the rural areas. Note the Thammathut movement.

[105] See Stanley J. Tambiah, *World Conqueror and World Renouncer* (Cambridge: Cambridge University Press, 1976), pp. 257-260. Phra Phimontham was sent to Lad Yao Prison and held for a period under suspicion of harboring communist sympathies. Although both monks were ultimately exonerated by the courts, they were not reinstated to their former positions. The case was ignored by the Sangha authorities until after October 14, 1973, when younger monks protested against this injustice (some even went on hunger strikes) and, in response, the Sangha authorities made some effort to rehabilitate the accused monks in preparation for their reinstatement.

This hope was coupled with militancy, especially when interest in liberal politics incited a person to resist the reality of authoritarian rule made clear by the actions of the police and military organizations.[106]

The *pattiwat* system purported to present society with a new political orthodoxy based on traditional political concepts, and, in doing so, promptly eliminated all vestiges of Western liberalism. Further more, radical students, newspapermen, and writers who questioned and analyzed society's problems along leftist lines were seen not just as troublemakers and dreamers, but as part of an international conspiracy fomented by the Communists to subvert all that is dear to the Thai nation. Therefore, not only were these elements dangerous to the stability of the *pattiwat* system, they fundamentally were threats to the existence of the Thai nation defined according to absolutist values honoring king, nation, and religion. Writers and intellectuals who adopted certain critiques from Western historicism, voicing concern for society's ills and interpreting them as the results of historical flaws or exploitation by the ruling class, were harassed, arrested, incarcerated, and sometimes executed. Invariably, they were labeled as communists. Thus a whole generation of intellectuals who expressed a deep social consciousness was eliminated; this action, in turn, stunted the development of political leadership and intellectual diversity in Thailand. For over a decade, intellectualism in Thailand was marked by mediocrity, blandness, and orthodoxy. Only when the generation that experienced the effects of the Vietnam conflict on Thai society appeared did the intellectual community begin to question and reject the established orthodoxy and began to search for historical roots of their newly acquired radicalism.

Some have argued that many of the radical ideas expressed in the late 1950s were not especially relevant to Thai society of that period. This is debatable. What is significant is that when these intellectual radicals were resurrected after October 1973, they became potent explanatory symbols of Thai society's problems—both in regard to the contents of their arguments and their own roles as symbols of intellectual suppression. The central ideas expressed in the writings of the 1950s reflected the rising concern of the new generation of intellectuals bent on trying to alleviate the plight of the oppressed and neglected stratum of Thai society, i.e., the peasant farmers. The intellectual euphoria following 1973 was marked by a thirst for new ideas diametrically opposed to the orthodoxy of the immediate past. In this atmosphere, the suppressed intellectual works of the Sarit period found a ready market and satiated the hunger of a radicalized younger generation. It created an intergenerational as well as intragenerational schism that became characteristic of post-1970 politics. The political polarization of Thai society grew out of a convergence of historical events: 1) the intellectual and political suppression of Sarit and his successors; 2) the effects of Sarit's *phatthana* policies and Thailand's involvement in the Vietnam fiasco; 3) and the emergence of radicalized political ideas challenging established orthodoxy and fueled by the resurfacing of heterodox precedents. Once the specter of Sarit's despotism had been reexamined and brought into a new perspective, the younger generation, allied with left-leaning Thai intellectuals, mounted campaigns to prevent its recurrence. The process of polarization and radicalization affected dedicated and highly politicized youths,

---

[106] As October 14, 1973 opened the Pandora's box of intellectual renaissance, later generations of scholars have been exposed and made aware of the crisis of intellectual repression that marked the Sarit regime.

whose advocacy of extreme political reforms sparked a backlash and led to the rejuvenation of established orthodoxy, which in turn led to tension and crisis, marked by the bloodletting of October 6, 1976.[107]

Sarit himself may not have foreseen nor anticipated the long-term effects of his intellectual suppression. By his actions, he had elevated the status and enhanced the mythic stature of repressed intellectuals and their works. It is doubtful, for example, that Sarit understood the true implications of the writings of the young Chit Phumisak, whose works were dismissed as being communist-inspired.[108] Chit was a graduate of the Faculty of Arts, Chulalongkon University. He was a scholar, linguist, historian, and newspaper man. His "crime" appears to have been his obsession with trying to explain the fate of the oppressed Thai peasantry and the social roots of Thai political repression. His most significant work, *Chomna Sakdina Thai* [The Face of Thai Feudalism], was first published in the *Nitisat* journal of the Law Faculty in 1957; that issue was quickly confiscated by the authorities.[109]

While Chit used the Marxist approach to study pre-nineteenth century Ayutthaya, his carefully argued and footnoted monograph became popular a decade and a half later precisely because of its unorthodoxy. It dealt with Thai society from the standpoint of the fundamental class conflict between the oppressed peasantry and exploitative ruling class. Of far more significance, it was critical, on an intellectual level, of the main pillar of Thai conservatism, i.e., the historical centrality, paternalism, and traditional legitimacy of the Thai monarchy. By raising doubts about the hitherto orthodox interpretation of history based upon the magnificence of the Thai kings, the study indirectly undermined and critically questioned the motives of the main pillar of Thai absolutist conservatism—the monarchy.[110]

Sarit's campaign against political heterodoxy was best exemplified by his extensive arrests of "communist suspects." Communism was seen simply as being diametrically opposed to king, religion, and nation. The Thai monarchy had a history of aversion to communism; it was appalled by the revolution in Russia, which toppled the Czarist rule, and, more recently, Rama VII had strongly objected to Pridi's Economic Plan as being inspired by Russian communism, which threatened to destroy Thai society. Also, the traditional Thai leadership had always condemned communism as being anti-religion; thus, any slight to religion and king was equated with communism, regardless of its real nature and isolated from its contextual

---

[107] For an analysis of this event, see Benedict Anderson, "Withdrawal Symptoms: Social and Cultural Aspects of the October 6 Coup," *Bulletin of Concerned Asian Scholars* IX (July-September 1977): 13-30.

[108] Chit was arrested in 1958 and sent to Lad Yao prison. Eventually the court withdrew all charges, and he was released in 1964. He was killed soon after by policemen in highly suspicious circumstances.

[109] Subsequently published. Somsamai Sisutphan (pseud.), *Chomna Sakdina Thai* (Bangkok: Chakkranukun kanphim, 1974). For the significance of Chit, see Suchat Sawatdisi, ed. *Chit Phumisak: Nakrop khong khon runmai* [Chit Phumisak: Warrior of the New Generation], (Bangkok: Social Science Association, 1974).

[110] It is not clear how the majority of the radicalized youth reconciled Chit's bold description of the Thai kings as nothing but "managers of property" with the still predominant reverence for the contemporary king. I suspect that they accepted Chit's analysis of the roots of oppression by the ruling class, which was now equated with the military-capitalist complex, and also accepted the demystification and humanization of the monarchical institution.

relevance.[111] As a foreign ideology having claims of universality, communism was perceived as a force that could undermine the integrity of the Thai nation. Thus anti-communism became a very potent policy of the Sarit regime, for not only did opposition to communism cloak the leadership in conservative respectability, establishing them as very "nationalistic" and "Thai," it also justified political repression on a scale never before witnessed by Thai society.

Not only were intellectuals imprisoned by the Sarit government; all elements in society perceived as deviating from established policy were quickly labeled "communist" and promptly arrested. In the process of this witch hunt, many took to the hills and joined the insurgent movement; several took refuge in the People's Republic of China. But most of the vast number of those arrested returned to normal life. Some would later openly identify themselves with the Thai Communist Party.

The group interned at Lad Yao prison was comprised of politicians, former cabinet ministers, labor leaders, newsmen, lawyers, monks, student leaders, civil servants, businessman, farmers, and even hill tribesmen. Of the thousands arrested throughout the country, about three hundred found their way to Lad Yao.[112] Most of the internees were critical of the Sarit regime, several were writers who took a critical view of Thai society and history, and others were implicated in the "secessionist" movement of Khrong Chandawong.

Under Sarit, the Anti-Communist Activities Act of 1952[113] was given more clout by the Revolutionary Council Proclamation No. 12, dated October 22, 1958. The Proclamation empowered the investigating authorities to detain suspects for the entire period of their investigation without having to comply to the time limits stipulated under law. This ruling applied also to cases that were pending before the proclamation was announced. Under this formula, the police arrested many for violating the law of 1952 and detained them for long periods of time without any formal charges being brought in courts of law. The proclamation was a political instrument, naked and pure.[114] Furthermore, the Revolutionary Council Proclamation No. 15 stipulated that cases concerning communist activities were to be referred to military tribunals under conditions of martial law.

---

[111] It is noteworthy that the Anti-Communist Law of 1969 revised the law of 1952 to stipulate that communist activities included "persuading others to lose faith in religion or engaging in activities that would destroy Thai customs; or persuading others to admire ideologies that stipulate cynicism or function in ways to make individuals lose faith in religion or the customs of the Thai people." This blanket clause could be easily manipulated to include all types of activities. In the Thanin period (1976-1977), no one was allowed even to criticize or point out flaws in Thai society.

[112] The best account of life inside Lad Yao recently surfaced. It was written by an internee, Thongbai Thongpao. See *Khommunit Lad Yao* [Lad Yao Communists] (Bangkok: Samnakphim khonnum, 1974), which describes in detail members of the political prisoner community and their daily activities, such as studying and playing games. Several were joined by their children. Judging from his description, the prison authorities were very lenient with them.

[113] For text see Chaloemtiarana, ed. *Thai Politics*, pp. 819–821.

[114] Several political detainees attempted to get the courts to declare Proclamation 12 unlawful, but the courts of law were too timid to take up the issue and handed down the verdict that Proclamation 12 "gave power of detention of those suspected of breaking the Anti-Communist Activities Act to the investigating authorities for the period needed to investigate their cases, and did not allow indefinite detention." It refused to address the issue of the limits of that investigating period (usually eighty-four days in the case of the most serious of crimes). Dika Court ruling no. 326-327/2505, Case of Manat Phrombun and others versus the State. The plaintiffs in that case had been detained for over four years.

Because the government had the power to detain suspects without preferring charges, reliable statistics measuring the numbers of these detainees are difficult to find. Many temporary detention centers were opened throughout the kingdom. We know that only the more serious cases were sent to Bangkok for closer scrutiny. The total number of persons detained and processed is estimated at over a thousand.[115] To prevent detainees from presenting their cases before civil courts, Sarit revised the Anti-Communist Act of 1952 in 1962 to make it more compatible with Proclamation No. 12. Under the new law, the detainees could register their distress with the Minister of Interior, who had the final deciding authority. By claiming this extrajudiciary authority, Sarit was able to exercise fully his despotic control over political dissent.

Thus, in summary, while we have noted that Sarit's leadership was based upon traditional concepts of paternalism, under the *pattiwat* system (as with past absolutist rule), that paternalism was also by nature despotic.

---

[115] This conservative figure is estimated from police testimony in the court hearing of the case of Bunthai Namprakai and seventeen other plaintiffs who charged the police with unlawful detention. San Aya case no. (black) kh 2/2505. The police revealed that, from 1958 until 1962, 1,080 persons had been arrested. Of these, 420 were charged before court; 186 were released; 286 cases had been investigated and completed; 4 suspects had died; 4 of the accused had been executed; 3 escaped; and 6 were referred to the Immigrations Department for action. Also see Thongbai Thongpao, *Khommunit Lad Yao.*

Pitching military tents and camping out during official visits to the countryside.

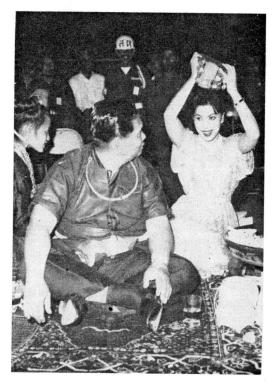

Wichitra playfully models a hill tribe headdress, official visit to
Maehongson Province, February 25-27, 1963.

Field Marshal Sarit Thanarat as "*phokhun*" visiting villagers in Phukheo District,
Chayaphum Province, April 18, 1962.

Sarit supervising fire-fighting in Bangkok, December 8, 1962.

The government incinerates opium-smoking paraphernalia at Sanam Luang, Bangkok, July 1, 1959 to mark the national ban on opium consumption.

Sarit personally interrogates prisoners implicated in the Ruam Wongphan communist plot, April 24, 1962.

Article 17 was invoked to execute alleged communists Khrong Chandawong and Thongpan Suthimat, seen here walking to their execution site in Sakon Nakhon Province, May 31, 1961. (Front cover of a book marking the fortieth anniversary of the political execution of Khrong Chandawong, published by the Political Development Institute, in 2001.)

Peasant leader Sila Wongsin captured in Laos and brought back to Nakhon Ratchasima for a public execution on June 2, 1959. Sila was a self-proclaimed *phi bun,* or holy man, who, with two hundred followers, established a separate kingdom in Nakhon Ratchasima.

Alleged communist Supachai Sisati was executed under Article 17 on July 5, 1959; Ruam Wongphan, accused of the same crime, was executed under Article 17 on April 24, 1962.

Sarit as "father of the nation" lectures re-educated hooligans about citizenship before setting them free (circa 1959).

CHAPTER FIVE

IMPLEMENTATION OF THE SARIT SYSTEM: MODERNIZATION AND THE IMPINGEMENT OF INTERNATIONAL POLITICAL FORCES

In the preceding chapter, we examined the basic foundations of the political system devised by Sarit. It was based upon political conservatism, dynamic personal leadership, and a rhetoric of national self-improvement through *pattiwat*. Sarit's regime tried to implement "traditional" concepts of political leadership seen as approximating Sukhothai paternalism and to stop giving lip-service to Western democratic ideas. To insure legitimacy over the long term, Sarit proposed that the task of his government was ultimately national development (*phatthana*). But the two ideas were of course intimately related.

SOCIOPOLITICAL LIMITATIONS ON THAI DEVELOPMENT

The *pattiwat* of 1958 was a movement to return the country to traditional notions concerning the foundations of state and government. Legitimacy was sought in the idea of approximating the norms of Sukhothai paternalism—*phoban/phomuang*. Sarit never tired of drawing the analogy between father/family and prime minister/nation. One of the most frequent statements made by the premier was that

> ... the Prime Minister is the father of the largest family. [He] has the greatest responsibility, and must oversee the happiness and welfare of his brothers and sisters. [1]

From this followed characteristically paternalistic principles of administration: the regime was to act as an authoritative father would and to make decisions independent of the wishes and desires of the public. While immediate needs of the public family would be attended to, long-term plans and policies were the special preserve of the regime.

Viewed in this light, development was there to enhance the regime's ability to function as a paternalistic system: the final goal of development and modernization was essentially to facilitate administration. Development in the political sense—a concept that might encompass expanding political participation, political mobilization, and the building of new political institutions—played no part in the Sarit regime's goals. But improvement in administrative articulation and

---

[1] Sarit Thanarat, "Sunthoraphot nai Phithi Pedprachum Pathomnithet Nganphatthanakan Thongthin," October 24, 1960, in *Pramuan Sunthoraphot* I, p. 255.

bureaucratic efficiency were very important aims. In part, this was because the image of *phokhun* was clearly not that of a politician.

Sarit's participation in and observation of Thai politics since 1947 (and perhaps earlier) had left him with a great distrust for politicians, whose rise he attributed to the implementation of Western-style democracy.[2] It is quite clear that Sarit did not view himself as a politician in the Western sense. Sarit saw such politicians as opportunists whose loyalty was to the ballot box and not to the state and nation. In this attitude, he was by no means unusual. Cabinet members tended to think of themselves as bureaucratic statesmen rather than as politicians, and resented prying from parliament. Government officials tended to look down upon politicians and MPs and despised the latter's meddling in affairs of state.[3] Ministers frequently complained that MPs obstructed their work and that national development was being held back by the criticism and the diverse views of politicians. As an army officer trained to command and to be followed, a leader who had achieved prominence through a series of coup d'états, Sarit was naturally inclined to believe in the superiority of the bureaucracy and government over parliament. In his opinion, planning and decisions should come from the top and regime programs should not be questioned.

Thus development in the context of the Sarit regime was generally confined to the social and economic sectors. But here too the implications of development were conservative in many ways. The prime minister once stated:

> Our prime objective is to strive to make the public aware and agree with the fact that the nation must develop, people must progress, and tomorrow must be better than today.[4]

His notion of modernization and development was largely conditioned by his generally conservative outlook of Thai society and polities. His obsession with *khwam sa-ad* (cleanliness), the concept of *riaproy* (properness), *khwam pen araya prathet* (being a civilized nation), as well as the concept of *phoban/phomuang*, shaped his ideas

---

[2] Chapters I and II describe briefly the extent of Sarit's political experience during the constitutional period after World War II. While the governments were relatively stable after 1951, the Military Coup Group to which Sarit belonged had to deal with civilian MPs and criticism from parliament which the governments did not appreciate. Sarit, as well as other military leaders, expressed the common Thai belief that politics (in the Western sense) was a dirty business. This notion, however, only referred to the politics involved in elections, etc. *Kanmuang* (state affairs) conducted by government leaders tended to be regarded as above parliamentary politics; and government ministers were seen as statesmen more than politicians. It appears that the presence of MPs as king's ministers was viewed by many as a denigration of such high offices.

[3] A possible explanation for this prejudice is the class background of the MPs as compared to that of the ministers. While a large number of elected MPs were bureaucrats or former bureaucrats, a sizeable number were businessmen and lawyers. Many MPs were from the strata of society which had traditionally been viewed by the bureaucratic elite as socially inferior. For a study of the background of MPs from 1933 to 1969, see Sethaphon Khusiphithak, "Ratsapha-Phumlang khong Samachik Saphaphuthaen Ratsadon Thai Run Ph. S. 2476-2512 [Parliament-Background of Thai MPs 1933-1969]," in Chai-anan Samutwanit, *Sat Kanmuang*, pp. 131–178.

[4] Sarit Thanarat, "Sunthoraphot nai Phithi Pedprachum Pathomnithet Nganphatthankan Thongthin," October 24, 1960, in *Pramuan Sunthoraphot* I, p. 255.

of the correct path for Thai development. These concepts will help us understand the constraints within which Sarit's National Development Plan emerged.

In a recent study of the problems of Thai development, Norman Jacobs concludes that Thailand has not developed, but rather modernized, because modernization means "the maximization of the potential of the society within the limits set by the goals and the fundamental structure (or form) of the society."[5] Jacobs contends that:

> Development, in contrast, is used to denote the maximization of the potential of the society, regardless of any limits currently set by the goals or fundamental structure of the society. In this view, development is an open-ended commitment to productive change, no matter what the consequences might be on existing goals or existing ways of doing things. For this reason, development is said to be dependent on a commitment to objectivity, that is, that innovation is accepted or rejected on the objective grounds of whether or not it contributes to maximizing the society's potential.[6]

Within this frame of reference, Sarit's government was clearly "modernizing." Yet clearly such a distinction would have made little sense to Sarit and his associates. The improvement of roads, irrigation, education, the outward appearances of villages and towns, cleanliness of houses and people, and proper social behavior all constituted development, or *phatthana*. They were means for "making better" a Thai way of life no less civilized (*araya*) than the life the West. The hardware of industrialized Western countries was to be adopted—including asphalt/concrete roads, electricity, technology, and so forth—but they were to be used within a Thai framework. Change was to be accepted, even encouraged, so long as it did not threaten the control of the governing elite and its role as protector of the Thai social and political morality.

In 1960, prior to the passage of the 1961 National Economic Development Plan, Sarit made a speech that revealed very well his understanding of what development (*phatthana*) entailed. He said:

> You have probably seen and were annoyed with my constant interest in development [*phatthana*]. I have acted in matters which some of you have advised against, saying that they are not the duties of the prime minister to spend time in overseeing the maintenance of city cleanliness, road problems, markets, river and canal problems, village welfare, public health, and activities of local government officials in the *changwad* and *amphur*. You have heard me complain about the inappropriate location of toilets and unsatisfactory sanitation. I may appear too particular, but I confess that it is my habit and personal ideals. Perhaps it could be a disease that I cannot tolerate impropriety [*mai riaproy*], and that I cannot ignore the livelihood of the people. I maintain that the elevation of the living conditions of the people is my ultimate task.[7]

---

[5] Norman Jacobs, *Modernization Without Development: Thailand as an Asian Case Study* (New York, NY: Praeger Special Studies in International Economics and Development, 1971), p. 9.

[6] Ibid., p. 9.

[7] Sarit Thanarat, "Sunthoraphot nai Phithi Pedprachum Pathomnithet Nganphatthanakan Thongthin," October 24, 1960, in *Pramuan Sunthoraphot* I, pp. 254, 255.

Sarit's concern with what some of his appointed experts saw as "details" reflected an idea of development in which macroeconomic change had only marginal place, and which focused on improving "Thai" life in its own terms.[8]

SARIT AND NATIONAL DEVELOPMENT: DOMESTIC CONSIDERATIONS

Before opening an analysis of Sarit's approach to development, it is important to note one major caveat. In matters of development, Sarit did not have as free a hand as in the domestic political sphere. Especially at the end of his life, American security concerns began to affect his development programs considerably. It is difficult to delineate what elements of his policy constituted "pure" Sarit and which represented Sarit's approach "plus American influence" in the matter of Thailand's development from 1958 to 1963. In general, the drafting of the National Development Plan made between 1959 and 1961 incorporated many of Sarit's original ideas. However, during its implementation, the plan was frequently readjusted out of consideration for the requirements of the United States government policy towards Southeast Asia. The turning point dividing what can be considered "pure" Sarit and Sarit "plus" appears to have come in late 1961, when the situation in Laos deteriorated. Although this date may appear somewhat arbitrary, it is useful for analytical purposes. After 1961, Sarit's programs were heavily affected by international circumstances. New emphases and priorities developed that became the basis for a "modernization" policy, which then did not change drastically, even after Sarit's death in 1963.

Sarit had made it clear to the public from the start that his revolutionary government was committed to national development.[9] He had once said that only 10 percent of the country could be considered developed and that the rest was in need of real attention. National development would be the task of his government and generations to come. In 1960 he noted that:

---

[8] A latter-day representation of this view is expressed by Professor Amon Raksasat (Dean of the Department of Public Administration, National Institute of Development Administration, which is responsible for training government officials), who has attacked the influence of Western theories of development and modernization. He has complained that "... our [present] goal for development is the imitation of Western countries, or in other words, if in this world only Thai society existed, we probably would not worry about the problem of whether our society is civilized or underdeveloped." See Amon Raksasat, "Boribun Sukhabot: Pratchaya lae Paomai khong Kanphatthana Prathet [Towards Prosperity and Happiness: Philosophy and Target of National Development]," in *Anuson Ngansop Nang Yen Huwanan* [Cremation Volume of Mrs. Yen Huwanan], Bangkok, March 13, 1972, p. 18. In this connection, also see Amon Raksasat and Khattiya Kannasut, *Thisadi lae Naewkhwamkhit nai Kanphatthana Prathet* [Theory and Thought on National Development], (Bangkok: n.p., 1970, revised edition). Like Sarit, Professor Amon has suggested that spiritual strength and morality should not give way to Western materialism. Economic indicators should not replace the idea of *kanyu di kin di* (good living, enough food to eat). He has reminded his readers of the Buddhist concept of inequality in *ayu* (age), *wanna* (status), *sukha* (health), and *phala* (strength). Thus, social and political reality should be considered determining factors when establishing the path of development.

[9] *Prakat khong Khana Pattiwat No. 11*, October 22, 1958. Point 4 stressed that the revolutionary government would "correct and improve the national economy to acceptable standards through the incorporation of democratic ideas suitable to the Thai system ... For this purpose, a national economic planning committee will be appointed." Furthermore, point 5 stipulated that the national economic plan would be a permanent one for future governments to follow as well, and, to insure this, the economic plan would be incorporated in the constitution, if possible.

Our important task in this revolutionary era is development [*phatthana*], which includes economic development, educational development, administrative development [*kanpokkhrong*], and everything else ... [Regarding] community development, I have noticed with great satisfaction that both government officials and the public have shown cooperation and unity, even in projects involving human labor such as digging, building, and repairing roads, digging and dredging canals, and improving and maintaining the cleanliness of the country. [10]

The various trips to the countryside that Sarit had carried out after 1958 strengthened his conviction that the rural population had two basic needs—water and roads. Sarit believed that, with the provision of these important ingredients, the country would be well on its way to development/modernization, that is, the *kanyu di kin di* of the people. In determining how these goals would be achieved, he was willing to listen to the experts, to whom, indeed, he gave the task of working out the national development plan.

In July 1952, the National Economic Development Board (NEDB) was formed to draft the country's first comprehensive development scheme. The board's task was made easier when the World Bank published the findings of research it had undertaken on behalf of the Thai government. [11] When the NEDB over a year later presented its final proposals—the First National Economic Development Plan, 1961–1965—it did not differ in substance from the World Bank recommendations.

The major development goals of the plan were as follows:

1. The primary objective of the National Economic Development plan is to raise the standard of living of the people of Thailand. This succinct statement appears to suggest a purely material goal, without regard to social\cultural and aesthetic values. But while material well-being may be an end in itself, it is also, and more importantly, a means to a further end, insofar as the achievement of this objective would enable all citizens to lead fuller, more creative, and happier lives. "Raising the standard of living" must, therefore, be construed in this wider sense.

2. The achievement of this objective requires that there should be an increase in the total per capita output of goods and services and that this increased output should be equitably distributed so that, to the extent possible, all citizens, and not merely a privileged few, derive benefit from it.

3. It is believed that in Thailand increased output will be most readily secured through the spontaneous efforts of individual citizens, fostered and assisted by Government, rather than through Government itself entering directly into the field of production. The key note of the public development programme is, therefore, the encouragement of economic growth in the private sector, and the resources of Government will be mainly directed to projects, both in the agricultural and non-agricultural sectors of the economy, which have this

---

[10] Sarit Thanarat, "Khamklao nai Kanpedprachum Phuwaratchakan Changwad lae Phubangkhapkan Tramruad Phuthonkhet," March 16, 1960, in *Pramuan Sunthoraphot* I, p. 146.

[11] International Bank of Reconstruction and Development, *A Public Development Program for Thailand* (Baltimore, MD: The Johns Hopkins Press, 1959).

objective in view. Over the next three years, the construction of irrigation works, the building and improvement of roads and other means of transport, the provision of inexpensive electric power, and other physical "infrastructure" projects will claim the bulk of Government expenditure. Agricultural extension and research, technical training, vocational education, and other projects to extend technical knowledge will likewise take a high share of Government investment. The use of resources for these purposes and other Government programs will provide means and opportunities for increased production and enable the private sector to expand on its own initiative. Government will also undertake to provide for the expansion of social services. [12]

Thus the salient points in the program included promotion of agricultural production, as well as industrial development, with a goal of raising the gross national product by 6 percent per annum. The plan also acknowledged the disparity between Bangkok and other cities and proposed to establish larger centers of economic and cultural activity outside of the capital area. The government emphasized that it would need to improve and expand the field and scope of public administration and local government agencies in order to be able to implement such an extensive program.

While the stated goals and policies of the Development Plan appear to be in line with accepted theories of development, a closer examination suggests that these goals could not be achieved. It is likely, in fact, that the stated goals and the real regime goals did not fully coincide. As has been pointed out earlier, Sarit was basically concerned with social and moral issues and the immediate daily requirements of the people. He abandoned efforts to spearhead economic and industrial development and permitted chosen experts to take over the leadership of those projects; these experts usually came from the bureaucracy or rich Bangkok elite. The conclusion that this broad initiative was more ideal than pragmatic seems borne out by the actual implementation of the National Economic Plan. The Plan basically had no clear and concrete long-term objectives. There was no vision in it of a change in the economic or social structure of the country. Employment targets and clear transmigration proposals that would shift population from rural to urban areas were nonexistent.[13] Industry was left to develop as part of the private sector, subject to the laws of a capitalist economic system. The government concentrated its attention and energies on the things that Sarit perceived to be important. These were the construction of roads, irrigation projects, education and health—in general, his approach focused on economic and social services. But it is probably correct to say that Sarit did not see their importance in abstract terms, as the improvement of Thailand's infrastructure, undertaken to facilitate macroeconomic development. Sarit appeared to be sincere in trying to fulfill immediate felt needs of the rural populace rather than satisfy long-term, statistically measured goals.

Because of Sarit's basic idea that the Thai social structure was based upon the three-tiered division of *rat/ratthaban, kharatchakan, and prachachon,* and his conviction that contented farmers were a necessary component of that structure, he tried to help

---

[12] National Economic Development Board, *National Economic Development Plan, 1961-1966, Second Phase 1964-1966* (Bangkok: NEDB, 1964), p. 9.

[13] Chatthip Nartsupha, *The Economic Development of Thailand, 1956-1965* (Bangkok: Phrae Phitthaya Press, 1970), p. 50.

the Thai farmer in the immediate tasks of planting and marketing rice and other agricultural products. As we have seen, after his first inspection tour of the Isan region (March 28 to April 12, 1960), Sarit came back to Bangkok with the renewed conviction that roads and water were the top priority needs of the area. He did not elaborate on the necessity of roads, merely saying that they would lead to modernization.[14] However, he explained the importance of water in the following manner:

> Water is a very important problem. I have noticed that in provinces where there is an abundance of water, the people in those provinces have bright faces, fresh and clean skins, and plants and food flourish, resulting in the prosperity of that province. [15]

The "moral" thrust he gives to his message when speaking about infrastructural development echoes the tone of his "ban the *samlo*" speech, noted above, in which he insisted that pedicab drivers should return to farming.[16] But he evidently wanted to convince farmers in general that their way of life was the respectable way and that they should remain happy and contented with their lot. This conservative view was well expressed at a lecture that Sarit gave to a group of young farmers (*yuwakasikon*) in early 1960. The premier said that:

> Agriculture is the surest way leading towards a free and stable [*mankhong*] life You can help yourself without having always to depend on others. To "establish yourself" [*tangtua*], agriculture is the surest way ... Although your house might be in a very poor condition, it is still a happy and peaceful place, for it is your own.
>
> In the past, we held the belief that the life of the farmer is a lowly lot, without any chance for progress or wealth. But now, conditions have changed immensely. The study of agriculture has progressed to the point where farming can produce wealth and happiness. The world has given agriculture more prestige; nations attest that farmers are the most important sector of society constituting the nation's backbone, the nation's nourisher ... The government, and myself in particular, have given great consideration to the farmer, we are improving and supporting agriculture by carrying out irrigation and water supply programs, by improving and creating transportation facilities, improving public health, and carrying out community development projects to increase the

---

[14] Sarit saw the presence of roads as signs of economic development and modernization. To wit, "this good and modern road [Sukhumwit Road, Bangkok] is [the sign] of economic development and the building of a new 'face' for the country, which should make us all extremely proud." Sarit Thanarat, "Khamklao nuang nai Kanpedthanon Sukhumwit thi Prapprung Mai [Remarks at the Opening Ceremonies for the Improved Sukhumwit Road]," June 15, 1960, in *Pramuan Sunthoraphot* I, p. 200. The road was widened and resurfaced with the help of American aid. The Sarit regime was interested in developing roads not only as a sign of modernity and economic development, but also for security reasons and to provide communication links between the government and the rural areas so that government services and controls could be more readily implemented.

[15] Sarit Thanarat, "Khamprasai nai Kanpaitruad Ratchakan Phak Isan," April 12, 1960, in *Pramuan Sunthoraphot* I, p. 159.

[16] Sarit Thanarat, "Khamprasai nuang nai Wan Khroprob Pihaeng Kantang Khanaratthamontri, February 10, 1960, in *Pramuan Sunthoraphot* I, pp. 127, 128.

return farmers earn from their labor. However, there are many farmers, and immediate results are not possible. There must be a comprehensive plan that will involve time and money. Nevertheless, it is my firm and unalterable decision that I shall to the best of my abilities continue to improve the livelihood of the farmer.[17]

It is in the light of these conservative aims, and in the light of Sarit's search for broad-based legitimacy, that the National Development Plan must be understood. To obtain the support of the elite and businessmen in the cities, industry and the private sector were left alone, and government assistance was provided when needed. The bureaucracy was pleased by the increase in national administration responsibilities that resulted from the plan. The masses were to have ample supplies of water and better transportation facilities so that their welfare would be improved. In the words of a rather disgruntled observer, "The plan implied only gradual progress, and demonstrated at least an unspoken commitment to static, rather than dynamic, change."[18]

Given these essential political aims behind the national development plan—aims focused on increasing the government's legitimacy and stability—it is easy to see why, as the international environment appeared to deteriorate after 1961, the emphasis in the plan shifted more and more to "security." This was especially obvious in the implementation of the regional and community development schemes which were a major component of the NEDB's plans. The growing influence of American money and technical/political advice resulted in the skewing of the early Thai community development programs towards rural "security" pure and simple.

---

[17] Sarit Thanarat, "Owat kae Samachik Yuwakasikon [Speech to Members of the Farmer's Youth Organization]," May 4, 1960, in *Pramuan Sunthoraphot* I, pp. 176–178.

[18] Chatthip, *The Economic Development of Thailand*, p. 51. Chatthip was thus largely correct in concluding that Thailand's economic development was driven by "services-led" growth, meaning that the development plan of 1961 emphasized infrastructural development and neglected the industrial sector. The government did indeed expend most of its financial resources on the building of roads, water projects, and community development. Yet despite the great improvement in the infrastructure, there was no corresponding growth in agricultural production. Because of this discrepancy, a balance-of-trade deficit developed as more money was spent on construction machinery and material without generating countervailing funds through greater agricultural exports. See Chatthip, Chapter III for details. Both Thai and foreign economists have analyzed economic development in Thailand. This writer must confess that he is in no position to add to these works. Economists, however, seem to agree that Thailand has undergone very little development in the field of heavy industry, and that the government's economic policies were conservative and not conducive to industrial development. While the exchange rate was stabilized and reserves increased from $334 million in 1960 to $672 million in 1965, the government made no attempts to utilize excess foreign reserves for industrial development. For further readings on the economic aspects of development in Thailand, see Chatthip, *The Economic Development of Thailand*; James C. Ingram, *Economic Change in Thailand, 1850–1970* (Stanford, CA: Stanford University Press, 1971); Robert J. Muscat, *Development Strategy in Thailand: A Study of Economic Growth* (New York, NY: Praeger Studies in International Economics and Development, 1966). Articles dealing with the economic aspects of the plan include Eliezer B. Ayal, "Thailand's Six Year National Economic Development Plan," *Asian Survey* II (January 1962); Vichitvong Na Pombejara, "The Second Phase of Thailand's Six Year Economic Development Plan, 1964-1966," *Asian Survey* V (March 1965). Also see Frank H. Golay, Ralph Anspach, M. Ruth Pfanner, and Eliezer B. Ayal, *Underdevelopment and Economic Nationalism in Southeast Asia* (Ithaca, NY: Cornell University Press, 1969), Chapter V.

Thus, the construction of roads and irrigation projects was increasingly made in response to official recommendations rather than in response to the needs of the local people.

Roads were designed to provide access for government officials and workers in "insecure areas." When the government decided which regions would receive development funding, priority was given to areas that seemed to pose security problems. Expenditures were more and more often allocated on an ad hoc basis, which contributed to the ineffectiveness of the planning administration. This change from a "welfare" orientation in development, which attempted to compensate backward regions of Thailand because of neglect by previous administrations, to a "security" orientation cannot be properly understood without a more detailed look at the growing impact of foreign policy on national development planning during the years in question.

FOREIGN POLICY AND NATIONAL DEVELOPMENT

Sarit's grand schemes for national development could not be implemented single-handedly. The Thai government did not have the money or the trained personnel to carry out the prime minister's programs. International aid and loans had to be sought from willing nations and international financial institutions.[19] Because of Thailand's cooperation with the United States since World War II and his own personal contacts, Sarit turned first to the United States for external support.

These close ties had really been cemented in the summer of 1950, when fighting broke out in Korea. On June 25, 1950, the United States decided to send troops to assist South Korea and seek United Nations backing for this initiative. Phibun immediately pledged support, and Thai troops were dispatched to Korea in September. The Thai government's reaction initially stemmed from domestic political considerations, most notably Phibun's concerns about his own situation. After his return to political leadership in 1947, Phibun's position was not very secure; he did not have a firm base of political support and had to compete with the two rising personalities—namely, Sarit and Phao. Accordingly, Phibun looked to the United States for personal support, hoping that he could remain in power by acting as broker between the United States and his rivals. He expected to get American financial aid and military supplies in exchange for close cooperation with the United States in international affairs. He also was convinced that by presenting himself as a true supporter of the United States and the Free World, he would gain international prestige that would strengthen his domestic position.[20]

For her support of the United States, and especially the American venture in Korea, Thailand received agreements regarding education, trade, technical, and military assistance from the United States. In July 1950, the Fulbright Agreement was signed by the two parties; it would enable Thailand to send promising students to

---

[19] For a discussion of the role of foreign aid and national development for Thailand, see Bunchana Atthakon, "Khwamchuailua chak Tangprathet kap Phatthanakan thang Setthakit khong Prathet Thai [Foreign Aid and Thai Economic Development]," Research Paper, Thai National Defense College, 1963. Also see Prawit Rattanarungsi, "Phon khong Khwamchuailua thang Setthakit lae Wichakan chak Tangprathet dan Kanphatthana Setthakit khong Prathet Thai [The Results of Foreign Economic and Educational Aid on Thai Economic Development]," MA thesis, Thammasat University, 1965).

[20] See Chapters I and II.

study at higher educational institutions in the United States. On September 19, 1950, one day before Thai troops were dispatched to Korea, the Economic and Technical Agreement was signed between Thailand and the United States.[21] This agreement provided for a financial aid program, which officially began dispensing funds to Thailand soon after. By October 17, 1950, the Military Assistance Act was concluded, under which the United States was to supply the Thai Armed Forces with modern weapons and help train Thai officers in the art of modern warfare along American lines.[22] At this stage, however, the United States was still careful to point out that these various treaties were not to be construed as a commitment by the United States to the defense of Thailand and that the United States did not intend to use Thai land for military purposes.[23]

From 1950 to 1954, the Thai government learned that it could play upon the fears of its wealthy partner, using the line that native communists were plotting to overthrow the friendly Phibun regime and establish a leftist regime in Thailand. The "unearthing" of communist plots by Phao in 1952 and the subsequent arrests of several hundred Chinese were indications of this trend. It culminated in the passage of the Anti-Communist Act of 1952, which empowered the Thai government to arrest and detain opposition figures tagged as communist sympathizers and also served to demonstrate the sincerity of the nation's anti-communism.[24] At the same time, external developments did cause the Thai leaders some real apprehension. In January 1953, Peking's announcement of the formation of the Thai Autonomous People's Government in Yunnan was interpreted as an act of propaganda aimed against the Phibun government. Later in the spring, the Viet Minh-supported establishment of the Free Lao Government also served to alarm the Thai government.

The United States during this period was actively supporting the French effort in Vietnam and viewed the fears of the Phibun regime with sympathy and interest. The subsequent defeat of the French at Dienbienphu and the intention of France to seek a political solution to the Indochina problem was viewed by American authorities with real alarm. The Geneva Conference of April 1954, which settled the Korean and Vietnamese disputes, was perceived as a political defeat by the Americans. Consequently, the American delegation both refused to sign the agreements and made a unilateral declaration that it would treat any violations of the agreements as a serious threat to international peace.

The withdrawal of the French from Indochina in 1954 and 1955 resulted in a major expansion of the American role.[25] Following the disappointment at Geneva, the Manila Conference was quickly convened in September 1954. The United States

---

[21] For the text of the treaty, see *Pramuan Khwamtoklong waduai Khwamruammu thang Setthakit lae Wichakan, Ph.S, 2493—2504* [Economic and Technical Cooperation Agreements, 1950–1961] (Bangkok: Prime Minister's Office Press, 1961), pp. 57-86. The treaties are in both Thai and English.

[22] Ibid., pp. 87-98.

[23] US Department of State Bulletin (October 30, 1960), p. 703.

[24] G. William Skinner, *Leadership and Power in the Chinese Community in Thailand* (Ithaca, NY: Cornell University Press, 1967), p. 355.

[25] The United States had recognized the Cao Dai government in 1950 and offered it American economic and military aid. From that time until 1954, the United States became increasingly involved in the affairs of Vietnam, and after the Geneva Conference it assumed a major role in advising and influencing the government of South Vietnam.

was now ready to make a military commitment to the security of Southeast Asia, as it had not been at the Baguio meeting in 1950.[26] Thailand was happy to follow the American lead, obtaining in return a formal commitment to her national security through collective defense backed by American firepower. The Southeast Asia Treaty Organization (SEATO), while it was the subject of a less firm United States commitment than the North Atlantic Treaty Organization (NATO), was unabashedly an American-dominated group, established primarily to support United States policy in Indochina. The United States was convinced that, through SEATO, it could, to a certain extent, justify any intervention against the spread of communist influence in Indochina.[27]

The signing of the SEATO agreements marked the high point of Phibun's foreign policy program, for he was able to obtain a commitment (admittedly limited) from the United States for the security of Thailand. Also, as a result of Thailand's support of SEATO, economic assistance to the country increased. Financial and technical aid grew from $6.5 million in 1952–1953 to $8.8 million in 1953–1954; for the next fiscal year, this amount shot up to $36.3 million.[28]

Phibun's growing commitment to the United States immediately came under some pressure. In 1954–1955, Moscow and Peking had initiated a new policy of "peaceful coexistence" and were moving to relax Cold War tensions. In addition, the prospect of another Korea or Berlin was unappetizing, especially to the smaller, newly independent states that wanted to find ways to bridge the gap between East and West. As a result, twenty-nine nations met at Bandung in April 1955 to discuss possible Afro-Asian alliances of small developing states that hoped their alliance might act as an independent force for peace.

At the Bandung Conference, Thailand was assured by China that the latter did not have any aggressive intentions regarding Thailand and that the Autonomous Thai Government in Yunnan was a domestic affair that had no international implications.[29] The "Spirit of Bandung" influenced opinions back home, and the Thai government came under some criticism domestically for aligning itself so closely to the United States under SEATO and for carrying out previous repressive acts against the Chinese and political dissenters in 1952–1953. Yet Thailand's political leaders did not fully trust the giant Communist nation they were being encouraged to approach.

---

[26] The Baguio Conference was held in the Philippines in May 1950. It was attended by Australia, Ceylon, India, Pakistan, Indonesia, the Philippines, and Thailand. While the United States was not an official participant it had hoped that the meeting would result in a collective effort against the spread of communism in Asia.

[27] See George Modelski, ed., *SEATO: Six Studies* (Melbourne: F. W. Cheshire for ANU, 1962). Secretariat of the Manila Conference, *The Signing of the Southeast Asia Collective Defense Treaty,* Manila, September 8, 1954. SEATO later provided Presidents Johnson and Nixon with legal grounds for American intervention in Southeast Asia independent of controls from Congress. See George McT. Kahin, "Cutting the US out of SEATO," *The Republic,* CLXIX (October 13,1973), pp. 18–21.

[28] See footnote 69 in Chapter II.

[29] Russel H. Fifield, *Southeast Asia in United States Politics* (New York, NY: Frederick A. Praeger, 1963), p. 246. Also, for a more detailed study of the relations between Thailand and China prior to the Bandung Conference and the period immediately following, a study that traces the decline of goodwill between the two countries, see David A. Wilson, *China, Thailand, and the Spirit of Bandung* (Santa Monica, CA: the Rand Corporation, 1962). Chou En-Lai invited the Thai government to send a delegation to visit Thai areas in southern China, but the invitation was not accepted.

Indications that the West European Powers were contemplating rapprochement with the Soviets and the Chinese at the 1955 Geneva talks made the Thai leaders very uneasy.

The consequence was a brief amelioration of the Thai government's anti-Chinese policy. The traditional Thai concept that recommends a government try to maintain balance in foreign policy matters, expressed by the saying *"yiep rua song khaem"* (placing both feet on both sides of a ship's hull to avoid capsizing), again came into practice. Phao's relentless efforts to arrest and investigate "communists" (mostly Chinese) were halted when Phibun relieved him of that authority. More mainland Chinese goods were permitted to enter the country and the government reversed its policy and permitted businessmen to carry on trade with China. It was also during this time that the government tacitly allowed Thai delegations to visit Peking.[30]

During the period 1956-1957, Marshal Sarit, who had earlier supported closer ties with the United States, mainly for military reasons,[31] began to waver and suggested that trade with China was perhaps good for the country. He also gave verbal support to those who wanted to travel to China and Moscow. Probably he was not happy with the United States government for supplying his rival, Phao's police, with modern weapons and funds, an act which he viewed as undermining the army's monopoly over arms and its political supremacy. To discredit the Phibun regime, Sarit also played up to the students and the various peace groups by proposing a shift to a foreign policy more independent of control by the United States.

However, after assuming power from Phibun and Phao in 1957, Sarit proceeded to appease the United States and actively sought its support. The immediate appointment of Phote Sarasin, Secretary-General of SEATO and a believer in the alliance with the Americans, as caretaker prime minister was a good indication of this. As prime minister, Phote immediately announced that Thailand's foreign policy would not change and that she would continue to support SEATO and seek American aid. Shortly after this, suspected communist sympathizers were arrested and leftist newspapers were shut down. In return, in 1958 the United States approved a Development Loan Fund for Thailand that raised the total economic aid program for 1958-1959 to $58.9 million, which more than doubled the amount given the previous year.[32]

Sarit's regime made it very clear that an exchange was involved and that Thailand was acting as a freer agent than hitherto. Donald Neuchterlein wrote that:

---

[30] The most publicized of these visits was one led by MP Thep Chotinuchit in 1956. This delegation of Isan socialists was cordially received by Mao Tse-tung and other Chinese leaders. Upon their return, the Peking travelers were detained, questioned, and then released. An account of this episode was recorded by a member of the group, and the government seemingly allowed it to be circulated. See Khlaew Norapati, *Yiam Pakking* [Visiting Peking] (Bangkok: 1957).

[31] Sarit helped negotiate the military assistance pact of 1950 and was a major moving force behind the reorganization of the Thai armed forces along American lines in 1951.

[32] Statistics and Reports Division, Office of Program and Policy Coordination, Agency for International Development, "United States Overseas Loans and Grants and Assistance from International Organizations, Obligations and Loan Authorization, July 1, 1945–June 30, 1967," March 29, 1968.

This assertiveness became particularly pronounced when Tanat [*sic*] Khoman was brought back early in 1959 by Sarit from his assignment as ambassador to the United States and was appointed Minister of Foreign Affairs. He represented a "new look" in Thai diplomacy which sought to bring Thai foreign policy more into accord with the views of other Asian nations and to avoid the charge made by some neutral nations that Thailand was a satellite of the United States. In this respect Sarit's policy seemed to be more appealing to the Thai educated class than was the Pibun [*sic*] policy from 1950 to 1954.[33]

Yet the basically pro-Western thrust of Sarit's foreign policy remained strong and was further accentuated when China abandoned its peaceful coexistence stance, gave more public support to North Vietnam, and stepped up its propaganda against the Thai regime.[34] Nonetheless, Thailand's entanglement with the United States remained relatively loose until the onset of the Laotian crisis and the intensification of the Vietnam war in 1960–1961.

THE LAOTIAN CRISIS—DEEPER ENTANGLEMENT

Based on both history and ethnicity, Thai leaders considered Laos to be closely related to Thailand. Parts of Laos had been loosely bound under the administration and influence of Bangkok until 1893, when the French forcefully wrested the eastern provinces of Laos away from Bangkok's control. Ethnically, the valley-dwelling people of Laos are of the same race and stock as many Thais, sharing a similar language with North and Northeastern Thais. Laos and Cambodia have traditionally been treated by Bangkok rulers as buffers between Thailand and the powerful Vietnamese Kingdom of Annam and, to a lesser extent, as cushions against Chinese hegemony. Optimally, any Bangkok regime would prefer that the Laotian government be on friendly terms with Thailand, and to guard this alliance, Thai leaders have usually designated themselves as elder brothers of their Laotian counterparts. Thus Laos has always been considered strategically important, culturally and ethnically related, and naturally situated within the Thai sphere of influence.[35]

By the 1950s, the possibility of establishing real political control over Laos was remote, and thus Thai policy was to prevent the establishment of any hostile leadership there. The way the Thai leaders viewed it, the main difficulty would come from Laotian groups allied with the Viet Minh who represented both ideological dangers and traditional Vietnamese ambitions. Immediately after the Geneva Conference of 1954 and the proclamation of Laos's independence, Bangkok tried to cultivate the Souvanna Phouma government by removing transit charges on Laotian imports, exchanging military and civilian good-will missions, opening air services

---

[33] Donald Neuchterlein, *Thailand and the Struggle for Southeast Asia* (Ithaca, NY: Cornell University Press, 1965), p. 1.

[34] Wilson, *China, Thailand, and the Spirit of Bandung*, pp. 8 ff.

[35] Phibun tried to reestablish Thai hegemony in Laos and Cambodia in 1940 and 1941 through collaborating with Japan. He forced the French briefly to relinquish part of the two kingdoms to his government. For accounts of this, see the propaganda writings of Luang Wichit Wathakan, such as *Thailand's Case*.

between Bangkok and Vientiane, and providing training in Bangkok for Laotian military and police officers.[36]

However, owing partly to changing domestic circumstances, the prevailing "Spirit of Bandung," and because of the terms of the 1954 Geneva Agreements concerning Laos, Souvanna Phouma soon moved to seek a permanent solution to the problem of finding a way to accommodate the Pathet Lao in his government.[37] After a short consultation trip to Peking in 1956, he returned to Vientiane and announced that his government would now make way for the inclusion of several Pathet Lao representatives.[38]

On November 12, 1957, an agreement was signed between the Laotian government and the Pathet Lao, providing for a coalition government to include two Pathet Lao officials, one of whom was Prince Souphanouvong, the prime minister's half-brother. The Pathet Lao agreed to return the two provinces under their control to the government, disband their fighting forces, and establish a legal political party called the Neo Lao Hak Xat (Lao Patriotic Front).[39]

Meanwhile, the Sarit coup had taken place in Thailand in September and the military regime observed the situation in Laos with concern. To show Bangkok's displeasure, the border was closed for a short period to remind Vientiane that Thailand could put an economic stranglehold on Laos.

Nonetheless, Pathet Lao influence on the Lao Assembly grew steadily.[40] This caused a reaction from the rightists in Laos. Faced with rising opposition to the Pathet Lao among government officials and powerful army officers[41]—who with encouragement and backing from the CIA formed the Committee for the Defense of the National Interest (CDNI)—Souvanna Phouma decided to resign on July 23, 1958.[42] He was replaced by Phoui Sananikone, an anti-communist from an old and

---

[36] Yet the basic policy thrust remained the same. The Phibun government's support of the Vientiane regime had, from the start, been in line with the United States policy. In 1951, the United States had concluded an agreement promising technical and financial aid with both the French government and the then pro-French Royal Laotian government, partly in response to the presence of a leftist government under Souphanouvong and the Pathet Lao in northern Laos since 1950. See Arthur J. Dommen, *Conflict in Laos: The Politics of Neutralization* (New York, NY: Frederick A. Praeger, 1967), p. 36. The agreement was signed on September 9, 1951 and provided the basis for initiating American aid to Laos. The establishment of SEATO in September 1954, which extended security guarantees to Laos, increased Thai and United States involvement in the country, contrary of the spirit of the July Geneva Agreements, which had called for an independent and neutral Laos. This was before Souvanna Phouma moved toward an even more neutral stance. Most of Laotian imports have to pass through Bangkok.

[37] For an account of this situation from a right-wing perspective, see Sisouk Na Champassak, *Storm Over Laos: A Contemporary History* (New York, NY: Praeger, 1961), pp. 40 ff.

[38] The Geneva Conference recognized that the Pathet Lao controlled two Laotian provinces in the north—Phong Saly and Sam Neua. This gave legal recognition to the existence of the Pathet Lao as a political force,

[39] *New York Times*, November 13, 1957.

[40] Supplementary elections on May 4, 1958 gave nine seats out of twenty-one to Pathet Lao representatives.

[41] The Royal Lao Army was organized and financed entirely by the United Slates for the purpose of providing favorable political leadership. See Dommen, *Conflict in Laos*, pp. 99–101.

[42] Ibid., p. 111. Also see Charles A. Stevenson, *The End of Nowhere* (Boston, MA: Beacon Press, 1972), pp. 64, 65. Stevenson writes that the CIA was deeply involved in promoting the CDNI as a political force in contradiction to the American ambassador's policy of supporting Souvanna Phouma.

prominent Lao family. Phoui's government closed ranks with the CDNI, and Laos moved closer to the West by promoting friendly relations with Thailand, South Vietnam, and Nationalist China. Thus in a short time, neutralist Laos became pro-Western. Marshal Sarit was particularly pleased with this development since his cousin, General Phoumi Nosavan, was Defense Minister of Laos.

In July 1959, Pathet Lao forces tried to capture Sam Neua after the government ceased all efforts to accommodate their party politically. Premier Phoui immediately sought United Nations' intervention. By October, reports came in that the Viet Minh were actively supporting the Pathet Lao and had crossed into Laotian territory. While the Laotian government opted for a United Nations investigation, the United States issued a strong warning to the communist powers that they were playing with fire.[43] The Thai government, on the other hand, called for an emergency session of the SEATO council and was able to obtain a collective warning directed at the Viet Minh.

While Sarit wanted direct SEATO intervention, the major powers in SEATO—namely, the United States, Britain, and France—pushed through a resolution in the United Nations Security Council calling for an investigating team to observe the extent of Viet Minh penetration into Laos.[44] The UN representative did not find evidence of Viet Minh forces in Laos, and it was widely speculated that either the whole story was a Vientiane fabrication or that the prompt reaction of the three SEATO powers had prompted a rapid Vietnamese retreat.

Because of political disagreements over cabinet allocations, Phoui was forced out by an army coup d'état led by General Phoumi in late December 1959.[45] Subsequently, after army-controlled elections in April of the following year, CDNI members won a majority of seats in the Laos Assembly.[46] While General Phoumi did not lead the new government, he retained his position as Defense Minister and was the acknowledged power behind the scene. Sarit was more than happy to have a pro-Thai government in Laos controlled by the army and his cousin, General Phoumi. The Bangkok press reported Phoumi's frequent cordial consultations with Sarit.

However, in August of 1960, while the Lao cabinet was preparing for the funeral of the king at Luang Prabang, an obscure army officer, Capt. Kong Le, seized Vientiane and persuaded Souvanna Phouma to take over the premiership once again.[47] The intentions of Kong Le have been the focus of much speculation. However, it seems clear that Kong Le was sincere in staging his coup to bring Laos back to a more neutral position in order to prevent further internal bloodshed.[48]

---

[43] US Department of State Bulletin (September 21, 1959), p. 414. Also see Stevenson, *The End of Nowhere*, pp. 73–83, for a comprehensive account of these developments.

[44] For a discussion of this, see Alan James, *The Politics of Peace-Keeping* (New York, NY: Praeger Publishers, 1969), particularly pages 200–206.

[45] Stevenson, *The End of Nowhere*, pp. 338, 339. The Appendix of this book has a chronology of events from 1954 to 1971. Dommen, *Conflict in Laos*, p. 27 asserts that the CIA supported Phoumi and the army in staging this coup.

[46] Dommen, pp. 144–148.

[47] Kong Le was considered to be one of the few battalion commanders in Laos who was not corrupt and who was able to hold the full loyalty of his troops. Earlier he had campaigned bravely against the Pathet Lao and was respected by his enemies.

[48] The elections were rigged by the CDNI-controlled government in a way that prevented Pathet Lao candidates from running. Dommen, *Conflict in Laos*, p. 129. The government

The Thai government was extremely concerned about the return of Souvanna Phouma to leadership. It did not want to see the 1956–1957 neutralist Pathet Lao coalition resurrected. It therefore proposed to SEATO that the situation in Laos was justification for intervention. However, the major powers were not totally in agreement concerning the proper path to follow. While all SEATO members publicly supported the idea of a neutral Laos, the British and the French wanted a solution that would give the Pathet Lao a substantial role in government. Washington, however, was very cool to the notion of a government incorporating communist elements and preferred a government led by Souvanna Phouma, backed by General Phoumi and the American-supported Royal Laotian Army. All parties recognized that only Souvanna Phouma could bring about enough agreement between the various factions to maintain a neutralist regime. Sarit viewed the cautious approach of the major powers as threatening the security of Thailand. He was poised to send troops to aid his cousin in an assault of Vientiane. To show his government's displeasure with the tardiness of the American reaction to the crisis, he ordered the Foreign Ministry to begin talks with the Soviet Union on the matter of cultural and economic exchanges.[49] Furthermore, the Thai-Lao border was again closed, which deprived Kong Le and Vientiane of needed food and fuel supplies.[50]

By early September 1960, the Thai press was openly questioning the ability of SEATO to intervene. It also attacked the Souvanna Phouma–Kong Le government for playing into the hands of the Pathet Lao.[51] On September 21, Sarit issued a statement warning the SEATO allies that Thailand would not wait passively if no action was taken by the organization. He asserted that Laos and Thailand had a unique and special relationship because of historical and ethnic ties. He predicted that if the situation was left to run its course, Laos would surely fall into the hands of the communists, which in turn would pose a grave security threat to Thailand. He was bitter at the Western powers for not driving Kong Le out of Vientiane, and he solemnly informed his countrymen that they should not stand idly by, but should be prepared to take the initiative and to "die fighting" against the communists.[52]

With Vientiane hard-pressed because of the lack of supplies, Souvanna Phouma was forced to seek a Soviet airlift of goods from Hanoi.[53] Phoumi's forces then seized Vientiane and drove Kong Le's troops out. A Laos Revolutionary Committee, formed along the Sarit model, took over the government on December 18, 1960. As a result, the situation in Laos was slowly developing into a major Cold War issue, swollen to a size out of proportion to the importance of the country itself. The decision of the Soviet Union to supply Souvanna Phouma and the Pathet Lao forces with food and

---

imposed higher educational standards for voting eligibility and used blatant gerrymandering tactics.

[49] Neuchterlein, *Thailand and the Struggle for Southeast Asia.* p. 178. It was clear that the Thai government was not sincere in its intentions to establish exchanges with the Soviet Union, and no agreements were reached.

[50] This was in support of General Phoumi, who was organizing troops in southern Laos and was being supplied covertly by the United States government.

[51] See for example, the editorials in *San Seri* (Sarit's paper), September 1960 and ff; *Sayam Rat,* September 23, 1960; *Kiattisak,* September 17, 1960.

[52] Ministry of Foreign Affairs, "Statement of His Excellency the Prime Minister on the Situation in the Kingdom of Laos, Bangkok," September 21, 1969. The text was in Thai, English, and French.

[53] US Department of State Bulletin (January 23, 1961), p. 114.

arms posed a major challenge to the United States policy of providing support to Phoumi and the Royal Lao Army. The newly inaugurated Kennedy administration was afraid that if the United States backed down, a "crisis of confidence" would occur among its allies, especially Thailand.[54] SEATO was immobilized, for despite strong Thai urgings, Britain and France insisted that a neutral Laos under Souvanna Phouma's leadership was the only possible solution.

By March 1961, Laotian government forces were faced with defeat at the hands of the Pathet Lao. To stabilize the situation, President Kennedy seriously considered sending troops into Laos and made a statement that the United States would never allow Laos to fall into communist hands.[55] As proof of his sincerity, a small contingent of marines was sent to Udon to supervise the supplying of arms to the Royal Lao Army. To avoid open conflict between the United States and the Soviet Union, the British proposed to reconvene the Geneva Conference to settle the future of Laos—to no immediate avail. Moscow insisted on a government led by Souvanna Phouma and including the Pathet Lao, while the United States wanted Laos to be truly "neutral"—i.e., friendly towards the West.

When it became eminently clear that the Pathet Lao forces were on the verge of taking the major Laotian cities, American policy became more firm. By this time, the Soviet Union had agreed to the British proposal that they should negotiate for a settlement at Geneva. At this point, Kennedy decided to settle the Laotian crisis at the negotiating table. Thailand was not happy with the developments, and Sarit threatened to boycott the meetings on the grounds that seven of the countries invited to attend did not recognize the new rightist Boun Oum government in Vientiane.[56]

The Geneva Conference was convened on May 16, 1961, and it soon became clear to all parties that a settlement depended upon an American-Soviet agreement, which indeed emerged in the form of a short communiqué between Kennedy and Khrushchev stating that

> The President and the Chairman reaffirm their support of a neutral and, independent Laos under a government chosen by the Laotians themselves, and of international agreements for insuring that neutrality and independence, and in this connection they have recognized the importance of an effective ceasefire.[57]

While not saying too much, the communiqué did pave the way for a settlement under the leadership of Souvanna Phouma with the cooperation of Phoumi and the Pathet Lao. Thailand had earlier proposed that membership in the International

---

[54] Roger Hilsman, *To Move a Nation* (Garden City, NJ: Doubleday & Co., 1967), chapters 9-12.

[55] US Department of State Bulletin (April 17, 1961), pp. 543, 544. Thanat Khoman acknowledged that that the sending of American troops at this juncture was agreed upon by both governments. However, the deployment of troops to Thailand in 1967 was initiated without cabinet knowledge and accomplished through secret agreements between the US government and high-ranking Thai military officers. See Thanat Khoman, "Thailand and Foreign troops," *Sangkhom Sat Parithat* [Social Science Review], XII (August 1974): 37-45. He also describes how, at first, the government was not very enthusiastic about the agreement.

[56] *New York Times,* April 29, 1961. *Bangkok World,* April 5, 1961. Speaking for Sarit, Luang Wichit expressed the Thai government's concern that its interests would be ignored and overwhelmed by a great power compromise. Despite talks of a boycott, the Thai delegation joined the meetings.

[57] US Department of State Bulletin (June 26, 1961), p. 999.

Control Commission for Laos be expanded to include Indonesia and Malaya, in addition to Canada, India, and Poland, but this found no support. At this juncture, the Thai government was increasingly bitter towards the United States for what it saw as American weakness and lack of commitment to the security of Thailand.[58] By the end of 1961, Thai-American relations were at a low ebb, and Thai leaders expressed their doubts about the effectiveness of SEATO and the commitment of the United States to the security of the area.

While negotiations continued in Geneva, Phoumi's forces were being driven back by Pathet Lao troops. In February 1962, the Pathet Lao forces advanced to the northwest town of Nam Tha, forcing government troops to flee into Thailand. Immediately, Sarit ordered troops to move out from Korat and Phitsanulok to the Lao border.[59] This troop mobilization was conducted without consultation with the United States or SEATO to show that Sarit had been serious when he had declared earlier that Thailand would act alone if necessary.

To appease Thai frustration, Robert Kennedy, during his visit to Thailand in February, reassured Sarit that the United States considered the security of Thailand to be vital to American interests.[60] Foreign Minister Thanat Khoman was also invited to Washington to discuss with President Kennedy the question of Thailand's security. The outcome of these talks was the issuance of the Rusk-Khoman joint statement, which in essence asserted that the United States regarded the security of Thailand with great interest and that the United States was prepared to resist any communist aggression and subversion that might endanger Thailand. Furthermore, the statement referred to American obligations under SEATO provisions, whereby action could be taken in accordance with each individual country's constitutional processes. However, in addition to the SEATO formula, reassurances were given to Thailand that:

> ... this obligation of the United States does not depend upon the prior agreement of all other parties to the Treaty, since this Treaty obligation is individual as well as collective.[61]

The joint statement was accepted by Sarit as the sign that the United States would come to Thailand's assistance in the event that SEATO could not act. In a radio speech to the public, Sarit again praised the United States for being a true friend.[62] From the American point of view, the Rusk-Khoman communiqué was issued to calm the Thai leaders, while attempts continued to get them to support the American-Soviet agreement that Laos should be led by Souvanna Phouma. Although it was never publicly revealed, it is most likely that a bargain had been struck between Rusk and Thanat. Shortly after their statement was made public, Thailand

---

[58] When Lyndon Johnson visited Bangkok in late May 1961, he was received coldly by Sarit. *The Bangkok Post,* May 31, 1961. It was reported that Vice-President Johnson suggested that American troops be based in Thailand for military operations in Indochina, but the idea was rejected by Sarit. If this is true, it could contradict the Thai belief that the United States was not ready to guarantee Thai security.

[59] *The Bangkok Post,* February 14, 1962.

[60] *Thai Foreign Affairs Bulletin* (February-March, 1962), p. 67,

[61] Ibid., pp. 5, 6.

[62] Sarit addressed the nation on March 10, 1962 alluding to the fact that the Thai leaders regarded the agreement as covering American support against an insurgency *within* Thailand and likened it to the American commitment in Vietnam.

agreed to the American solution to the Laotian dilemma and played down its support for the Phoumi-Boun Oum faction.

When Averell Harriman, the Assistant Secretary for Far Eastern Affairs, visited Sarit on March 21, 1962, the Thai leader was more open to American overtures. Harriman assured Sarit that the United States had plans that would insure the integrity of Thailand regardless of the deteriorating picture in Laos. He informed Sarit that pressure was being exerted upon the Boun Oum government and that the United States would not "support a government which does not follow the United States' policies."[63]

It became apparent by this time that the Lao army under General Phoumi would not be able to withstand any Pathet Lao offensive. Skirmishes in northern Laos had proven costly to the government forces. On April 15, 1962, as a demonstration of force, the SEATO nations staged a large military maneuver in Thailand involving 6,009 ground troops, 60 ships, and 100 planes.[64] Despite this action, Nam Tha in northern Laos fell to Pathet Lao troops on May 7, 1962. Five days later, Houei Sai was abandoned by government troops who retreated into Thailand without fighting. In response, Kennedy ordered American soldiers who had participated in the SEATO exercises to move up to positions along the Mekong river.[65] On May 17, 1,800 marines were dispatched to Udon near the Laos border. Other SEATO members reacted to the American example—Australia, the United Kingdom, and New Zealand sent token military contingents to Thailand to express their support for the American initiative.[66]

Having gained control of northern Laos and realizing that further consolidation might lead to outside intervention, the Pathet Lao now agreed to the coalition government proposed at Geneva. The routed Phoumi forces had no choice but to follow the dictates of its major backer, the United States.[67] Thus, on July 23, 1962, the Declaration of the Neutrality of Laos and the Protocol to the Declaration were signed by the fourteen nations at Geneva.[68] The new Souvanna Phouma cabinet formed after the signing of the Geneva accords was composed of nineteen members—eleven neutralists, four rightists, and four leftists. The Defense and Interior portfolios were held by neutralist members.

In spite of the government's growing acceptance of the situation, the Thai press—and especially Sarit's paper—revealed in editorials that they believed the "neutral" Laos government formed by these negotiations to be only a prelude to an eventual communist takeover.[69]

---

[63] *The Bangkok Post,* March 26, 1962. Harriman made it clear that the Phoumi-Boun Oum faction had to turn over the Ministries of Defense and Interior to Souvanna Phouma before any substantive settlement could be reached.

[64] *New York Times,* April 16, 1962.

[65] *The Bangkok Post,* May 15, 1962.

[66] See Hugh Toye, *Laos Buffer State or Battleground* (London: Oxford University Press, 1968), p. 184.

[67] Ibid., pp. 181–184. Sarit was assured by Harriman that the United States was ready to defend Thailand's national integrity. Sarit had confronted Phoumi at Nongkhai in Harriman's presence earlier in March, commanding Phoumi to concede to the demands of the United States that a coalition government for Laos was a necessity.

[68] A summary of the agreements could be found in Fifield, *Southeast Asia in United States Policy,* pp. 204, 205.

[69] *San Seri,* June 30, 1962. *The Bangkok Post,* July 24, 1962.

It is possible that Bangkok's increased sense of insecurity was fueled by deteriorating relations with Cambodia. Thai leaders have always been concerned with developments on Thailand's eastern frontiers. They have considered the Mekong boundary as one of the most vulnerable frontiers of the country and held the opinion that therefore Laos and Cambodia must be either friendly or indirectly controlled by Bangkok. Thus historically we find that Thai kings and Prime Ministers have tried to install friendly leaders in these regions.[70]

Relations between Thailand and Cambodia immediately after Cambodia gained independence in 1953 were cool, marked by minor incidents involving radio and press attacks, charges of cattle rustling and piracy. But no major conflict arose until the late 1950s. Prince Sihanouk was aware that the Thai government was not too happy with his leadership because during his brief exile in Bangkok in 1953 he was treated with cold reserve, and the Thai government seemed to have given support to Sihanouk's major political rival, Son Ngoc Thanh.[71] Shortly after his return from his spectacular trip to Peking in early 1956, Sihanouk was attacked by the Thai press for playing into the hands of the communists. Minor incidents followed, and Thailand closed her borders, preventing the flow of trade form Bangkok into Cambodia. Sihanouk claimed at this time that the Bangkok regime was supporting Son Ngoc Thanh and allowing him to use Thailand as a base for covert operations into Cambodia.[72] The final break between the two countries took place in 1958 over territorial rights to the famous Phra Wihan Temple.[73]

While negotiations were still in progress, and shortly before he was to come to Bangkok for talks with the Thai leaders, Sihanouk again visited Peking on August 14, 1958. In the course of this trip, the Cambodian government decided to recognize the Peking regime. This was viewed by the Thai authorities as an overt act of intimidation, and relations between the two countries rapidly deteriorated to the point where relations were broken off.

In summary, the instability of Laos after 1961 and the uneasy relationship with a Cambodia seen as open to Peking's influence annoyed and worried the Thai leaders. They seem to have been unaware that their own policies were viewed by their neighbors in a similar light and for similar reasons. This encouraged them to move still closer to the United States, abandoning much of the flexibility of traditional Thai

---

[70] This concern for the security of the Mekong boundary was reflected in Phibun's policy in the early 1940s, whereby Siemreap and Battambang were occupied. Although these two provinces were given back to Cambodia at the end of the Second World War, the Bangkok government continued to try to influence the domestic affairs of Cambodia.

[71] Roger M. Smith, *Cambodia's Foreign Policy* (Ithaca, NY: Cornell University Press, 1965), p. 48. Son Ngoc Thanh was a nationalist who advocated independence from the French and organized the Khmer Issarak.

[72] Ibid., p. 96.

[73] Particulars of the case are documented by Seni Pramote (the Thai counsel) in Seni Pramote, *Khadi Khao Phra Wihan* [The Khao Phra Wihan Case] (Bangkok: Prime Minister's Office Press, 1962). A comprehensive study made of the temple and the events following the 1954 Cambodian claim can be found in Prayad S. Nakhanat and Chamrat Duangthisan, *Khwammuang Ruang Khao Phra Wihan* [The Politics of Khao Phra Wihan] (Bangkok: Sansawan Press, 1962). For a very partial Thai account, see Siri Premchit, *Songkhram rawang Thai kap Khamen lae Prasat Khao Phra Wihan* [The Thai-Cambodian War and Khao Phra Wihan] (Bangkok: Phrae Phitthaya Press, 1959). Discussions of the conflict from the Cambodian standpoint can be found in Smith, *Cambodia's Foreign Policy*, and Michael Leifer, *Cambodia* (New York: Frederick A. Praeger, Inc., 1967), pp. 84-93.

foreign policy. The Thai government became increasingly dependent upon American support, and Thailand's role in the American security plan for Southeast Asia grew proportionally. While it had originally accepted the relatively passive role of receiving arms and economic aid from the United States, Thailand eventually began to prosecute American foreign policy aims for Indochina. As the country was influenced by international events, Thailand's own ambitions concerning national development became entangled in the concept of security and the future of Southeast Asia as conceived by Washington. While Sarit had initiated his *pattiwat* based on the assumption that his regime would try to develop the whole country for its own sake, the dependence upon the United States for military aid and later for security-related development made development increasingly the by-product of strategic security concerns. Plans for infrastructural development became subjected to the immediate security concerns of the government, especially in areas around bases used by the Americans. Response to the immediate needs of the rural populace was distorted by the strategic dictates of counter-insurgency preparation. Even the official raison d'être for national development shifted from a desire for national improvement to the need for security in the face of the developments in Laos, Cambodia, and Vietnam. Thus, as Sarit's National Development Plan called for more and more American aid and involvement, in the end, Thailand's national development became part and parcel of the execution of American Policy.

DEVELOPMENT AND SECURITY: DILEMMA AND COMPROMISE

As we have seen, when Sarit assumed power in 1957, one of his major overriding concerns was the search for a long-term legitimizing program. One major element in this program came to be *phatthana*, which initially meant simply paternalistic programs promising increased welfare in the rural areas. Roughly stated, this is what "pure Sarit" *phatthana* entailed. We must remember that Sarit conducted his tours to the Northeast, North, and South between March 28 and May 1, 1960, a time when Laos appeared to be safely under the control of right-wing elements. Phoumi had staged his coup in December 1959, and in April of 1960 the right-wing leadership had taken formal control of the Laotian government following the conclusion of rigged elections. Signs of serious trouble in Laos did not really emerge until January–March 1961, when Kong Le's and the Pathet Lao's forces threatened Phoumi's army.

Thus it is possible to suggest that Sarit's concern for "roads and water," which were reinforced by his inspection tours, represented the original core of his development aims. It is striking that in the National Development Plan one of the stated goals was to build public development projects "to cover as many areas of the country as possible."[74] As the situation in Laos deteriorated, however, government concern became much more narrowly focused on the provinces facing the eastern border, and particularly the northeastern region.[75] In 1961, Sarit headed a new special commission for developing the Northeast; a Northeast Development Plan was subsequently drawn up in 1962. There were no comparable plans made for the other regions.

---

[74] National Economic Development Board, *National Economic Development Plan, 1961-1966, Second Phase 1964-1966*, p. 12.

[75] See Chapter IV. Earlier, Sarit had indicated to Luang Wichit that he was not interested in irredentist adventures but wanted to concentrate on internal development.

But the broad shift of Sarit's *phatthana* from a national/domestic focus to a regional/strategic one was not only the product of the Thai government's worries about its neighbors. As the situation worsened for the United States in Indochina, the American government came to place more and more importance on Thailand in its plans for opposing communist power in mainland Southeast Asia. Compared to other countries in the region, Thailand was relatively stable and still free from any serious indigenous insurgent force. Should it be necessary to expand United States military involvement in Indochina, Thailand would be a good central basis of support and control.

The Thai government's requests for financial and military aid were therefore gladly met by the American government, which saw this aid as securing a loyal, stable, and grateful ally. In addition, by fulfilling the needs of the Thai government, the United States could exert its influence in the planning and implementation of aid programs to suit its military requirements. The more the Thai government could be convinced of the internal dangers posed by communist subversion in rural areas, the more tightly it would be tied into overall United States planning. The United States reinforced the Sarit regime's tendency to push for community development and rural pacification, now considered to be the key components of Thailand's national development. No less important was the fact that much of the US aid was directed to and through the Thai armed forces. The United States administration foresaw that, as the Thai military regime welcomed the supply of modern weapons and financial transfusions, it would necessarily become more dependent upon its benefactor. Furthermore, a sophisticated Thai army, alert to its rural counter-insurgency responsibilities, would be a most useful adjunct in a situation where the United States was politically vulnerable as a white power operating in a non-white Asian region.

We have noted that Sarit's early inspection tours in 1960 gave no indication of his overt concerns for internal security. His pronouncements were exclusively paternalist, expressed in a traditional manner, and they dealt mainly with social uplift and village beautification. Roads and irrigation needed to be expanded to increase production and make the farmers happy. This initial vision of more roads, better water supplies, and happier people turned out to be readily adaptable to American ideas about preventing internal unrest through community development and administrative control tightened by improvement of communications and bureaucratic infrastructures. One can see that while the National Economic Development Plan (1961–1959) incorporated measures perceived as important by the Sarit regime, the plan gave considerable room for maneuver to American policy-makers—to the point that, by the mid-1959s, while the interests of the United States and the Thai government converged, it was clear that the Americans were playing the senior partner role.

Statistics confirm that the initial concerns of the Thai government and the American authorities (who controlled IBRD, International Bank of Reconstruction and Development) were not quite the same. The recommendations of the World Bank survey and the proposals of the Thai development plan of 1961 differed on one important aspect, as shown by the table below.

Table 5.
Comparison of IBRD and the Thai Six-Year Plan, 1962
(in thousands of dollars)

	IBRD	Percentage	Thai	Percentage
Agriculture & Irrigation	255	9	542	28
Industry	50	2	267	14
Power	620	22		
Communications	1035	38	617	33
Social Welfare	483	17	346	18
Public Works	330	12	128	7
Total	2773	100	1900	100

Source: IBRD, *A Public Development Program for Thailand,* p. 25, and *National Economic Development Plan,* 1961-1966. The year 1962 is taken to show the initial emphasis of the Sarit scheme.

Particularly in irrigation, the Thai plan deviated greatly from the World Bank model.

Another good indication of the difference in American concerns for development as compared to the priorities of the Thai government is shown in Table 6, below. The figures clearly indicate that the United States was more concerned with strategic roads and communications, while the Thai government put more money into irrigation and social welfare.

Testimony offered by Ambassador Leonard Unger before the Senate Committee on Foreign Relations in November 1969 revealed that between 1954 and 1962, American military-related construction in Thailand, largely involving roads and bridges, had a cost totaling US$97 million, of which US$35 million came from the Military Assistance Program and US$62 million from the Economic Assistance Program.[76] Included in this initiative were the upgrading and construction of facilities at seven Royal Thai Air Force bases, ten Thai army camps, and other miscellaneous facilities of the Thai armed forces. Unger further revealed that:

The economic assistance program financed road work including the 450 mile long Friendship Highway between Bangkok and Nong Khai near Vientiane, about 100 miles of Route 12 in North Central Thailand, and more than 1,000 bridges scattered throughout Thailand. This road construction effort was primarily for economic development but improvement of overland lines of communication also contributed to the Thai self-defense capability.[77]

---

[76] US Senate, *United States Security Agreements and Commitments Abroad, Kingdom of Thailand,* November 1969 (Washington, DC: Government Printing Office, 1969), p. 613.

[77] Ibid., p. 614. See Appendix I for map and road planning.

Table 6
USOM Projects in Thailand, 1951-1962: Project Obligations
(in thousands of dollars)

	US	%	US Counter-part	%	Thai	%	Total	%
Agriculture/ Irrigation	13,132	9.5	14,906	10	13,357	28	41,395	12
Industry	5,348	4	4,200	3	1,348	3	10,896	3
Mining Prow	8,415	6	2,883	2	1,108	2	12,406	4
Communica- tions	70,631	52	92,044	65	8,083	17	170,758	52
Social Welfare	38,853	20	27,677	19	23,858	49	90,388	28
Community Development	448	0.5	987	1	593	1	2,028	1
Total	136,827	92.0*	142,697	100	48,347	100	327,891	100

Source: USOM, *Thai-American Economic and Technical Cooperation,* 1962. The Thai input was highest (40 percent) in Social Welfare ,which included Education, Public Administration, Police, and Health. Fifty-two percent of American funds were invested in road building projects. *8 percent is still missing in this total; it is unclear where it was allocated.

During the Laotian crisis of 1960, Kennedy sent in American marines to Nong Khai, and at the height of the crisis there were five thousand United States troops in Thailand. This experience indicated to American strategists the advantages of having land bases close to the theater of conflict. When the troops finally withdrew, American armaments were stored at Nong Khai in case the marines had to return in the future.[78] The feasibility of troop and plane deployment from Thai bases did not escape the notice of American policy makers, and one can only view the increase in military construction (roads, bridges, and base improvements) as a prelude of things to come.

During this same period, a community development program was implemented in Thailand, and that process provides us with another useful illustration of Thai and American perspectives and interactions concerning development. This program was financially backed by the United States, ostensibly to carry out Sarit's ideas of what the nation needed in order to achieve *phatthana*. Rural development programs were not new to Thailand, but little had been achieved.[79] In 1959, however, a National

---

[78] For a left-wing account of this affair, see R. H. Yadava, *Guests or the Masters: What the US Troops did in Thailand* (New Delhi: Three Friends and Associates, 1963).

[79] In 1939, a program of levying local taxes for local reconstruction was implemented, but was suspended during the Second World War. From 1942 to 1945, rural improvement committees were established at the local level to train leaders and solve problems having to do with marketing local goods. In 1951, Phibun tried to reinstate the rural improvement committees under a Rural Reconstruction Program, but the idea did not catch on. From 1956 to 1960, a national program of community development existed, but no real work was accomplished. See Ministry of Interior, "The Development of Community Development in Thailand," *Community Development Bulletin* II (April 1960), pp. 8, 40.

Community Development Plan was endorsed by the Sarit cabinet.[80] To supervise this plan, the Community Development Department was created in 1960; the department was heavily supported by the United States Operations Mission (USOM).

This community development program initially proposed to reach the village population and secure its loyalty through the extension of services. Development workers from the central government were directed to organize village clean-up campaigns and road repairs, items high on Sarit's list of the signs of development. [81]

After 1961, however, rural development in Thailand was "accelerated." Although the situation in Laos seemed to have stabilized, American and Thai leaders became increasingly concerned by the communist threat to the country's security and by the continued strength of the Pathet Lao. A study made by Ronald C. Nairn concluded that the Sarit government immediately reacted to the Laotian situation by stepping up community development work.[82] Curiously, however, Nairn did not allude to the fact that American concerns played a vital part in that shift of gears. This became quite apparent in 1962, when Sarit directed the army to engage in rural development programs by forming three army Mobile Development Units (MDUs), heavily financed by the United States. National development work was now to be spearheaded by the army in critical areas, while the remnants of the original program were to continue under the auspices of the Community Development Department.

The MDUs were overwhelmingly concerned with security problems. They engaged in short-term programs (fixing village roads, making improvements to sanitation and health, water supplies and propaganda) conceived as psychological operations to build village loyalties and as intelligence gathering missions.[83]

The ineffectiveness of MDUs is made quite clear from the following:

> Typically, in an operation of this kind, one or two vehicles appear in a village, team members seek out the *phuyaiban* [village headman] and school teacher, and hastily assemble a groug of residents at some central location. One or two officials will make a speech, a welfare man will distribute some clothing and

---

[80] Ministry of Interior, *The National Community Development Plan* (Bangkok: Ministry of the Interior, 1963).

[81] The Community Development Department proved a useful source of government patronage. It was capable of hiring approximately two hundred urban university graduates annually. By this method, the regime acquired additional support from a bureaucracy it helped create and sustain. Also, by co-opting young university graduates into government work, it tried to ensure that there would be less of a "floating intellectual" sector easily alienated from the regime because of a lack of jobs and the inaccessibility of politics as a means of redress for grievances. But because most of the community development workers were urban educated and young, community development programs had only limited success. Instead of using local people with technical skills who had proven to be more effective agents, the program sent out university graduates, who created friction with the local people. See Toshio Yatsushiro, "The Village Organizer," USOM publication, December 1974, p. 76. Because of the differences in social backgrounds, rapport between the villagers and student Community Development workers did not flourish. Far from generating local leadership, community development programs often revealed to the masses the incompetence of officials and the inefficiency of the bureaucracy.

[82] Ronald C. Nairn, *International Aid to Thailand: The New Colonialism?* (New Haven, CT: Yale University Press, 1966), p. 105.

[83] Lee Huff, *Observations on Mobile Development Unit-2 Operations*, Joint US-Thai Development and Test Center, June 1963, p. 2.

school supplies, and perhaps some booklets and pictures of the King, Prime Minister, and the Lord Buddha will be handed out. Then the party jumps back into the vehicles and bustles out of town as quickly as possible in order to rush to the next village.[84]

Such "shot in the arm" tactics did not generate the political support the government wanted. As long as the gifts were forthcoming, the people were grateful. But the programs introduced by the MDUs deteriorated immediately once the outside personnel left the village, for regular provincial authorities did not have the money or manpower to supervise or sustain MDU activities.

Also, the MDUs inadvertently politicized many of the peasants and awakened their awareness of their place in the Thai social order. Instead of generating centripetal forces in the rural community, the results of mobilization and politicization aroused centrifugal forces. Toshio Yatsushiro offers a somber picture of the effect of MDU activities:

> The concentrated and accelerated rural development program under the MDU organization is generating increasing bitterness and resentment among villagers of the few villages singled out for intensive development by the MDU. The consternation was particularly intense in a village visited that had no school and no year-round road connecting it with the outside world. A few years ago, this village was a hot-bed of communism. A government-favored community in this locality has good schools, good roads, and even electricity. In addition, it was recently awarded an amount of B 500,000 to improve an already good road that connects it to the main highway. The discontent that can easily spread among the "have-nots" and the ignored situated in close proximity to such a community can well be appreciated.[85]

The disparities that became evident in the process of development thus created much resentment.

Another program organized along these lines was the Accelerated Rural Development Program (ARD) which was similarly financed by American funds. According to Frank W. Sheppard, a former AID (Agency for International Development) director, the concept was:

> ... based on the assumption that bringing additional development resources to the villages could and would increase identification of the villager with his government.[86]

Capital inputs into the unmobilized sector were seen as the means of securing public support and regime legitimacy. The five prime goals of the ARD were: provide increased job opportunities; initiate development projects geared towards the

---

[84] Ibid., p. 7.

[85] Toshio Yatsushiro, "The Appeal of Communism in Northeast Thailand," USOM, *Community Development in Thailand* (Bangkok: USOM, n.d.), p. 5.

[86] Frank W. Sheppard, *Accelerated Rural Development Report* (Bangkok: USOM, n.d.), p. 2. Although ARD started to function after Sarit's death, it was the logical extension of the MDU program. The intensification of American participation in the fate of Vietnam and Laos skewed community development in Thailand further, binding it more firmly to military and security considerations.

demands of the people; coordinate various development projects; restore the faith and confidence of the people; and increase observations on territories threatened by outside subversives.[87] The program was thus two-pronged, that is, it was meant to generate legitimacy and to obtain information regarding threats to the regime.

The first priority of the program was the building of communications infrastructures. Ninety percent of funds would first be put into constructing roads in the sensitive areas. In the early period, when ARD first began work, few other projects were undertaken. Again, as in other development programs, there was no coordination between the various responsible agencies. A USOM report on the allocation of funds for new roads and for other development projects located along the planned roads reveals the following

> ... practically no worthwhile projects were apparent from these allocations. Village participation in planning through the *tambol* [commune] councils has not materialized. Integrated *changwad* [province] plans for accelerated rural development activities have not been effectively made.[88]

Before ARD construction work began, some roads did exist in the designated areas. However, these were impassable during the rainy season, when the farmers in any case are too busy in the fields to make much use of them. The new ARD roads, however, were designed for all-year use, essentially to provide penetration and mobility for the armed forces and the police. These roads would also be employed as supply routes to air bases which were being prepared for future deployment of United States planes over Indochina.[89]

Even in terms of the stated objectives of the ARD program, the road building was in many ways counterproductive. Initially, there were some positive economic impacts. A few villagers found short-term construction jobs, and a few local landlords were compensated for dirt fill or for laterite dug from their properties, which left depressions that were used later as fish ponds. A marginal increase in income near the ARD roads was also reported, and transportation costs dropped considerably for formerly isolated villages. However, prices of goods did not decrease significantly, while more consumer goods became readily available to compete for the villagers' small funds of cash.

There were many negative effects experienced by the villagers living along the ARD roads. The key problem was that the government failed to pay the farmers for valuable rice paddy appropriated for the roads. Land taken out of production for rights-of-way for the roads averaged 7.6 rai of paddy per kilometer of road, along with about 8.5 rai of unexploited forest land per kilometer.[90] In the first two years of road building, approximately 1,148 rai of paddy land worth 1,836,003 baht were appropriated without compensation.[91]

---

[87] USOM, *Second Joint Thai-USOM Evaluation of the Accelerated Rural Development Program*, I, July 1966, pp. 165, 166.

[88] Ibid., p. 72.

[89] Ibid., p. 33. A USOM survey showed that the villagers placed a low priority on roads, although they were not totally opposed to the program.

[90] Ibid., p. 55. 1 acre = 2.5 rai.

[91] Ibid., p. 237.

Farmers along the roads lost their lands and hence a part of their income without receiving compensation, though they were led to believe that they would be paid. The Thai government maintained that no funds were available for paying farmers, although there was compensation paid for land appropriated in urban areas.[92] To add insult to injury, taxes were raised two to seventeen times the previous rates on land situated near the ARD roads.[93] Funds raised through these taxes, which were not announced until after the completion of the roads, were supposed to be reserved for local development projects, but skepticism was widespread concerning this promise. Indeed, the main motivation for imposing the taxes seems to have been to pay for the costs and maintenance of the roads themselves, which amounted roughly to an average 503 baht annually per family living within four kilometers of the roads.[94]

Thus the economic impact was mixed at best. The combination of new taxes and soaring land costs—which increased to a reported 200 percent of their former value in three years—led to land speculation and growing absentee landlordism.[95] The withdrawal of land from agricultural production without adequate compensation also had damaging psychological effects on the rural population, which more than offset any savings they might have enjoyed from reduced transportation costs. Furthermore, without coordinated programs to help the villagers make use of the newly constructed roads to improve production to help pay the new taxes, the real economic position of those who were intended to "benefit" may well have declined.

The roads indeed increased the mobility of the police and the military. But although the frequency of visits by police teams, MDUs, and government officials certainly increased their presence, this presence did not generate much support for the government. Indeed their conduct reinforced the villagers' sense that steep hierarchical divisions separated officials from the common people.

Villagers had little or no opportunity to participate in planning for the roads. As planning and policy formation were still made exclusively in Bangkok, little local initiative was open to local communities. The results of a survey of Sakon Nakhon did "not suggest rapid progress on orienting planning toward those units [*tambol*, development councils] or towards the needs expressed at the local level."[96]

Too much emphasis was put on the problem of security. A large portion of AID funds was used for civil police administration aimed at increasing the number of provincial personnel and the efficiency of counter-insurgency work. The goal was to expand the police force by about twelve thousand men a year, to introduce a police presence at the *tambol* level, and improve strike force capabilities.[97]

But this "muscling up" of the police to increase the government's power to maintain law and order created new difficulties—the problem of defining who or what constituted an insurgency. For convenience and its appeal to political funding agencies, USOM and the Thai government, in most cases, listed all disturbances as

---

[92] *New York Times*, December 27, 1966.

[93] USOM, *Second Joint Thai-USOM Evaluation*, I, p. 174.

[94] Ibid., p. 207.

[95] Ibid., p. 208. Because of the rise in the land tax, farmers were forced into debt and usually had to forfeit their lands to moneylenders, who later profited by selling the lands for commercial use.

[96] USOM, *Impact of USOM-Supported Programs: Preliminary Report*, April 1967, p. 5.

[97] Ibid., p. 2.

communist-inspired. Thai police officials often acted on this assumption in a quite indiscriminate way. In the process, law enforcement paid less attention to mundane crimes such as theft and banditry, which in some cases even increased as a result. One report stated that:

> ... many farmers have lost faith in the *amphur* office's ability to protect them. Others are even afraid to report the thefts because the government cannot protect them from retaliation by the criminals. This is a rather strong indictment and realistically, no amount of movies, candy and speech-making can expect to overcome the resentment which has been built in the villagers' minds. [98]

Village attitudes towards the police are generally ambivalent at best. While Thai peasants sought security from thieves and terrorists, they grew perturbed by police behavior—brazen new demands for food and bribes, slow reactions to real security threats, and incompetence in catching thieves. For villagers, the police came to figure as the most obvious representatives of dishonest government officials, hungry for bribes. This development was indirectly revealed in an ARD evaluation report citing the great need for closer relations between the villagers and the police in order to "project an image to the rural population that the RTG [Royal Thai Government] is a benevolent, just, and effective government."[99] Indeed, when insurgents did approach villagers, seeking their support, one of their key promises was that they would end corruption and police abuse.[100]

INTENSIFICATION OF AMERICAN INVOLVEMENT

We have seen, then, that after 1961, the development policies of the Sarit regime became more and more focused on national security considerations and were heavily backed by American financial and technical assistance. What was started by Sarit continued to develop and intensify after the Marshal's death in 1963. The Thanom government, which became heir to Sarit's programs and policies, did not veer away from previous guidelines. The major difference was only in the extent and intensification of American interest in and influence on Thai politics. Thus, while American military personnel became increasingly involved in Vietnam, military aid to Thailand grew in the form of direct aid and the financing of communications infrastructures considered militarily strategic.

In FY 1963, total American aid to Thailand amounted to US$42.9 million. Of that total, US$7.3 million was dedicated to the Army Military Defense Program used for the construction of communications facilities, roads, housing, and training and base camp facilities. The Air Force Military Defense Program assistance amounting to US$8.1 million was used for operational and support facilities at Korat, Takhli, Ubon, Udon, Don Muang, Chiengmai, and aircraft control/warning communications installations at Khao Khieo.[101] The Navy Military Assistance Program used US$1.6 million to construct ammunition/cargo pier facilities at the Thai naval base at

---

[98] Huff, *Observations on Mobile Development Unit-2*, p. 68.

[99] USOM, *Second Joint Thai-USOM Evaluation*, I, p. 174.

[100] *New York Times*, December 25, 1966.

[101] US Senate, *United States Security Agreements*, p. 614.

Sattahip.[102] The additional US$25.4 million provided under aid funds were divided up as follows: communications facilities at eighteen scattered locations (US$12.9 million); security roads in north and northeast Thailand (US$9.7 million); base camp facilities (US$1.2 million); utilities at twelve scattered locations (US$0.7 million); and an addition of surgical facilities to a hospital at Sattahip (US$0.3 million). The rest was spent on small projects throughout Thailand.[103] It is quite clear that the Thai armed forces did not need such elaborate facilities; these construction projects could be only construed as preparations for supplying the needs of the modern American military machine.

The table below illustrates clearly the overall trends we have been noting.

Table 7
Timing/Fund Source of US Construction in Thailand (in millions of dollars)

Year	State/AID	MAP/MASF	MILCON	Other	Total
1954-62	62.4	35.1	—	—	97.5
1963	25.9	17.0	—	—	42.9
1964	0.2	4.1	—	—	4.3
1965	0.3	3.4	26.0	—	29.7
1966	0.1	3.9	196.0	—	200.0
1967	0.1	12.9	121.0	1.8	135.8
1968	—	2.5	21.8	—	24.3
1969	47.6*	1.8	4.9	113.4**	167.7

Source: US Senate, *United States Security Agreements and Commitments Abroad, Kingdom of Thailand*, November 1969, p. 621, includes US$46,600,000 for aid-financed LOCs, 1954-1969.
State/AID—State Department/Agency for International Development.
MAP/MASF-Military Assistance Program/Military Assistance Special Fund.
MILCON: Military Construction. LOC: Logistics and Communications.
**Communications program 1965–1968.

By 1964, the actual purpose of all the highway construction and other facilities became clear. In March, six F-100 planes were deployed to Takhli, and after the Gulf of Tonkin Incident, eighteen additional aircraft and a squadron of F-105's were stationed in Korat. By November, the F-100s were replaced by another squadron of F-105s at Takhli. By the year's end, there were seventy-five American aircraft in Thailand, with a ground-support crew of three thousand.[104] The next year witnessed the swelling of the American aircraft total to two hundred and air force personnel to nine thousand. The greatest increase in American forces occurred in 1966, when the aircraft total grew to four hundred and the ground crew increased to twenty-five

---

[102] Ibid.

[103] Ibid.

[104] Ibid., p. 615.

thousand. The first B-52s arrived at U Tapao air base in 1967. However, the bombing of North Vietnam and Laos from Thai bases had already begun early in 1965.[105]

Major United States support of Thailand's rural development phase followed closely in the wake of this escalation. Funds from the military aid program (MAP) were now used to support Thai counter-insurgency activities in conjunction with rural development schemes. Through MAP, the Volunteer Defense Corps was re-established. Although originally organized under a Royal Decree of 1954, it was abandoned in 1958 and only partly restored in 1962. This volunteer defense program was now seriously reactivated, with heavy American inputs of supplies, guns and ammunition, and financial assistance. Table 8, below, illustrates the post-1964 emphasis on community development.

Table 8
USAID to Thailand FY 1964 (in thousands of dollars)

	Amount	Percentage
Agriculture & Irrigation	793	7
Industry & Mining	184	2
Communications	89	1
Social Welfare	6,080	51
Community Development	4,645	39
Total	**11,791**	**100**

Source: USOM, *Thai-American Economic and Technical Cooperation*, 1965, pp. 13, 14. CD is subdivided into I MDU 42%; CD 5%; ARD 53%. As the percentages clearly indicate, rural development was closely tied to security.

Thus we have observed that while Sarit wanted long-term legitimacy and justification for his regime and found part of the answer in the National Economic Development Plan, its prospects came to depend largely upon American support and money. As a result of American interest in the fate of Southeast Asia— particularly the future of Vietnam—development in Thailand was subjected to ad hoc readjustments based on the changing views and needs of the United States.

As the Thai government cooperated more and more closely with the United States in the Vietnam war, and its stake in the outcome grew, concern for security and the smooth functioning of American/Thai bases shifted the focus of Thai development policies from welfare to control, from community development to the ARD, and from exercises in building government legitimacy to police actions against alleged communist insurgents.

---

[105] Ibid., p. 627. The American use of Thailand as an air base was not made officially known until March 9, 1967. In July 1964, the Thai government openly supported South Vietnamese and American foreign policy by pledging direct military support. In September, ten Thai pilots and a seven-man crew were sent to fly Vietnamese planes. Military support for the South Vietnamese government slowly increased with American promises of more aid and financial backing for a Thai expeditionary force to Vietnam. Ground troops were sent in September 1967, and this force eventually increased to two brigades totaling eleven thousand men. Ibid., p. 624.

Inspecting troops participating in the SEATO joint military "Operation Thanarat,"
Lopburi Province, June 11, 1963.

Sarit greeting Sir Frederick Scherger, the Australian military advisor to the
Southeast Asia Treaty Organization, October 1963.

Opening ceremony for the first national forest reserve established by Sarit
in Khao Yai, Nakhon Nayok Province, February 10, 1962.

CHAPTER SIX

THE ROLES OF THE BUREAUCRACY AND MONARCHY IN THE SARIT SYSTEM

In previous chapters, we have examined the activities of Sarit and his government in trying to obtain legitimacy among and control over the *prachachon* (people), the lowest tier of Thai society according to the three-tiered scheme he accepted. To strengthen his government further, however, Sarit worked to win the active cooperation of the upper two tiers, the bureaucracy and the throne. In order to obtain this cooperation, he tried various strategies for convincing these two institutions that his regime was sincere in its desire to develop the country, that it needed their support, and that offering such support would be in their best interests. In particular, the government tried to socialize top bureaucrats into recognizing the importance of national security for efficient development administration, and to harmonize their outlook with that of responsible military officials. To secure the support of the throne, the Sarit government gave the king far more public exposure than hitherto and increased both his official and his private duties. The regime wanted to show the nation and the monarchy that the government recognized the importance of the king and that, in essence, the regime's concern for security was largely based upon the need for the preservation of the monarchy.

Sarit's political vision of *rat/ratthaban—kharatchakan—prachachon* was not based upon a sudden revelation, but it was only during his tenure that the "formal" Thai political system came to approximate this model. Since the Revolution of 1932, which overthrew the absolute monarchy and installed constitutional rule in Thailand, the new political elites had, in fact, ruled on behalf of the bureaucracy while paying lip service to constitutional democracy. The close relationship between the government/cabinet and the bureaucracy had always been a reality in Thai politics after 1932. Wilson clearly appreciated this point when he wrote that:

> The ruling clique seizes the seats of power by a sudden coup and then uses these positions to establish and maintain its authority. But the constituencies of the members of the clique are the bureaucracy itself.[1]

While it is true that military cliques usually commanded the top leadership positions, the importance of the civilian bureaucracy could never be ignored by the ruling elite.

David Wilson's proposition that the Thai political elite has been drawn from the bureaucracy and, in turn, has reflected the interests of that bureaucracy rather than those of political groups or the general public is further strengthened by the

---

[1] Wilson, *Politics in Thailand*, p. 161.

exhaustive research of Fred W. Riggs.[2] Riggs suggested that, to test Wilson's proposition, the personal background of the men in the various Thai cabinets should be examined to determine the extent of the bureaucratic or, alternately, extra-bureaucratic backgrounds of cabinet members.[3]

According to Riggs's data, of the 237 men who served in Thai cabinets between 1932 and 1938, 184 were career officials, 38 non-officials, and 15 unclassified for lack of adequate information. Of these career officials, 109 were civilians and 84 were military men.[4] Furthermore, Riggs concluded that elected politicians played far less influential roles in government than did officials and coup members.[5] While an understanding of Thai politics would lead us to expect that military officers would be the most powerful and influential figures in Thai cabinets, Riggs's findings indicate that one should not underestimate the role of civilian officials, for "although military officers tend to gain greater power through participation in coups d'état, a relatively larger number of civil servants manage to hold office repeatedly in Thai cabinets.[6]

Various explanations for the close relationship between the cabinet and the bureaucracy (especially its top echelon)—a relationship clearly shown by Riggs's data—suggest themselves. The most obvious seems to be the lack of power centers or policy-making groups outside of the bureaucracy. In Thailand, political parties and parliament have always played secondary roles to the executive branch of government, which has manipulated or repressed them according to need and circumstance. Periodic coups and attempted coups by military and civilian groups have helped make the solid institutionalization of party and parliamentary system very difficult.[7] Because of the lack of any organized countervailing forces, the government elite have usually become the spokesmen for and instruments of the bureaucracy. While the political elite has acted in the interests of the bureaucracy by providing job security, status, and privileges, the bureaucracy in turn has carried out the programs of the elite. Without the bureaucracy's support, the regime in power has been helpless to implement its policies. But a powerful bureaucracy does not necessarily mean a united or an efficient bureaucracy. Bureaucratic supremacy can often degenerate into sterile infighting, fragmentation, routine, and inertia. Sarit's awareness of the problems posed by the Thai bureaucracy is clear. He moved rapidly to make himself its master, trainer and dynamizer.

---

[2] Riggs, *Thailand* pp. 311-356. Also see Uthai Hiranto, "Kanmuang nai Prathet Thai tam Thatsana khong Chao Tangprathet [Thai Politics in the View of Foreigners]," *Thai Community Development Journal* VII (November 1969): 33-44.

[3] Riggs, *Thailand*, p. 313.

[4] Ibid.

[5] Ibid. See table on page 315 in Riggs, *Thailand*. For a study of the military in parliament, see Chai–anan Samutwanit, "Botbat khong thahan nai kanmuang thai [the Military Role in Thai Politics]," *Journal of Social Sciences* (Chulalongkon University), XV (April-June 1978): 92-120.

[6] Ibid., p. 317.

[7] Cf. Samuel P. Huntington, *Political Order in Changing Societies* (New Haven, CT: Yale University Press, 1968). Huntington sees this as a form of political decay. However, he fails to recognize that his "decaying" process may be part of society's adjustment to new political forms better adapted for local political development.

MASTERING THE BUREAUCRACY

Sarit's first step was to arrange a drastic reorganization of the Office of the Prime Minister in order to centralize policy-making authority and control in his own hands. Ever since 1932, the position of prime minister had been the most powerful office in Thai politics. But Sarit changed the basic characteristics of the position from those generally typifying a first minister to those of a chief executive. As Wilson has pointed out:

> ... in the period of Field Marshal Sarit, changes, both legal and administrative, focused decisions on the Prime Minister, making the position uniquely potent and crucial. The Field Marshal was willing to take forthright action on a number of matters and both sought and had thrust on him organizational control over a wide variety of activities. During his tenure as Prime Minister, he served as the center of administrative dynamism. [8]

Soon after the *pattiwat* of October, 20, 1958, Sarit recognized the need to consolidate policy-planning and control within a formal structure subject to his personal supervision. The final proclamation of the Revolutionary Council on January 27, 1959, just prior to the promulgation of the Interim Constitution of January 28, already stipulated the need for a major reorganization of the Prime Minister's Office and gave Sarit the authority to carry this out as he saw fit. [9]

The promulgation of the Interim Constitution made Sarit's position as prime minister de jure, for section 16 stated that until a cabinet was appointed, the leader of the Revolutionary Council was to act as prime minister and head of the council of ministers. Furthermore, the constitution implicitly granted him full executive supremacy under Article 17, which stipulated that the prime minister had the power to issue orders to take appropriate steps for purposes of repressing or suppressing actions that might jeopardize national security, the throne, or subvert law and order. In line with his belief in the need to centralize executive power, Sarit cut back the number of cabinet ministers drastically and made his appointments from within the inner circle of his supporters. The previous practice, according to which the prime minister would name deputy ministers and ministers without portfolio, was not followed. [10]

A basic enabling act issued on February 14, 1959 prescribed the reorganization of the Office of the Prime Minister along the guidelines of Proclamation No. 57. [11] Besides giving the prime minister the power to appoint political officers to executive positions within the new executive office, the proclamation also transferred two important agencies to the Prime Minister's Office. First, the personnel and budget of

---

[8] David A. Wilson, *The United States and the Future of Thailand* (New York, NY: Praeger Publishers, 1970), p. 115.

[9] *Prakat khong Khana Pattiwat No. 517* January 27, 1959, section 4.

[10] While the distribution of political patronage to the bureaucracy through cabinet appointments was curtailed, Sarit used other avenues to achieve the same purposes: by handing out appointments to the Constituent Assembly, to newly created special agencies, and various planning boards, and by increasing the use of the National Defense College for prestige and status elevation.

[11] *Phraratchabanyat Chat Rabieb Ratchakan Samnak Nayok Ratthamontri, Ph,S. 2520* [Organization of the Prime Minister's Office Act, 1959], in *Ratchakitcha,* vol. 76, section 29, p. 1.

the Central Accounting Department of the Ministry of Finance were shifted under the prime minister's control and became part of a new Budget Office. In addition, the National University Council was changed to a National Educational Council, which became directly responsible to the prime minister.[12] The prime minister was also given the authority to serve as chairman of the Civil Service Subcommission, which had the duty of assisting the Civil Service Commission in its lawful functions. In actual practice, this meant that Sarit had the power to oversee the activities of all civil servants, and all important decisions regarding their futures would be scrutinized by him.

The February 14 reorganization had also provided the basis for streamlining the enlarged Prime Minister's Office. First, an assistant to the prime minister was appointed to act on behalf of the premier on administrative and policy matters;[13] secondly, a Budget Office was created within the Office to control administrative planning; thirdly, the prime minister and his appointed assistant now had exclusive control over all the components of the Office, whereas formerly control had been exercised by the premier and the cabinet jointly; and fourthly, under the enabling act, the prime minister could create, through official announcements, agencies and organizations directly subordinate to him and subject to his personal supervision. Armed with these powers, Sarit proceeded to consolidate his grip on executive leadership.

To coordinate and direct national economic development, the National Economic Council of the Prime Minister's Office was reorganized in July 1969 by adding the word "development" to its title and enlarging its membership.[14] Sarit became its chairman ex-officio. The National Economic Development Council was given broad responsibilities for economic studies and the collection of statistical information to enable it to make appropriate policy recommendations. It was also given the right to approve budget requests for development projects. A striking feature of the Council was its heavily academic membership: it contained forty-five experts in the field of economic development. This feature shows a notable aspect of Sarit's rule, namely the attempt to make effective use of Thailand's technical/academic elite and gain their political support in the process. In Sarit's own words:

> A new method in the revolutionary system is the prestige given to academicians/experts [*nak wichakan*]. In former times, academics received little status; economics was taken as common sense, and those who never studied economics could talk about the subject ... which led them to believe that they did not have to rely upon academic expertise. I have no such belief.[15]

---

[12] *Phraratchabanyat Sapha Kansuksa Haeng Chat, Ph.S. 2502* [National Educational Council Act, 1959], in *Ratchakitcha*, vol. 76, section 85, p. 1.

[13] *Palad Bancha*. Sarit appointed his political mentor Luang Wichit Wathakan.

[14] *Phraratchabanyat Sapha Phatthanakan Setthakit Haeng Chat, Ph.S. 2502* [National Economic Development Council Act,. 1959], in *Ratchakitcha*, vol. 76, section 69, p. 1.

[15] Sapha Phatthanakan Setthakit Haeng Chat, *Phaen Phatthana Setthakit Haeng Chat, Ph.S. 2504-2509* [National Economic Development Plan, 1961-1966], Bangkok, October 20, 1960, p. 6. Sarit was able to convince many dedicated technocrats to further his *phatthana* cause. He also appeared to be sincere in his dealings with them. See the experience of Dr. Puey Ungphakorn which he relates in Samnakphim laisu Thai, *Chiwit khong prathet* [The Life of the Nation] (Bangkok: Charoenwit kanphim, 1978), pp. 99-107.

In addition to making this type of flattering appeal, however, Sarit was careful to ensure firm control over the country's intellectual life. The National University Council Act of 1956 was amended in August 1959, transferring all the major universities to the Office of the Prime Minister.[16] At the same time, the National Education Council was given broader powers, which included review of university budgets and the need for founding, dissolving, or amalgamating the various universities. The Council also had the right to approve university curricula and matters dealing with the establishment or dissolution of academic faculties. With the universities under the prime minister's authority, Sarit could issue ministerial regulations in relation to the salaries, appointments, transfers, discipline, enrollment, and dismissals of university officials. In this connection also, the National Research Council Act was passed.[17] This Council was chaired by the prime minister and had the power to promote and coordinate research in all academic fields. An office was also established to provide permanence and continuity to the Council's work.

In September 1959, the National Security Council Act was promulgated to supersede the former Defense of the Realm Council.[18] In practice, these two councils did not differ greatly. The significance was in the change of name and the establishment of an operating office headed by a secretary-general appointed by Sarit.[19] To strengthen his position vis-à-vis the armed forces, Sarit also created the position of Supreme Commander of the Armed Forces, a political office he himself assumed.

Other adjustments and additions to the Office of the Prime Minister included the passing of the Budget Procedure Act, which contained a comprehensive statement of the basic budgetary processes and the powers and duties of the budget director.[20] On April 12, 1960, the Department of Administrative Inspection, created by Phibun to survey the conduct of public officials, was divided into the Office of the Complaint Committee and the Government Inspection Service.[21] Instead of maintaining constant surveillance of government officials, Sarit planned to control them through his budgetary powers and the Civil Service Commission.

Shortly afterwards, a Board of Tax Supervisors was organized to increase tax revenues, which were very low because of widespread tax evasion.[22] After its formation, the Sarit government made periodic announcements in the press, demonstrating the effectiveness of the Board by the large increases in taxes collected.

---

[16] *Phraratchabanyat On Mahawitthayalai pai sangkat Samnak Nayok Ratthamontri, Ph.S. 2302* [Transferral of Universities to the Prime Ministers Office Act, 1959], in *Ratchakitchka*, vol. 76, section 85, p. 9. The College of Education was not affected.

[17] *Phraratchabanyat Sapha Wichai Haeng Chat, Ph.S. 25o2* [National Research Council Act, 1959], in *Ratchakitcha*, vol. 76, section 102, p. I.

[18] *Phraratchabanyat Sapha Khwammankhong Haeng Chat, Ph.S. 2502* [National Security Council Act, 1959], in *Ratchakitcha,* vol. 76, section 92, p. 423.

[19] This was covered under the Prime Minister's Office reorganization law (No. 4) enacted on September 23, 1959.

[20] *Phraratchabanyat Withi Kanngobpraman, Ph.S. 2502* [Budget Act, 1959], in *Ratchakitcha*, vol. 76, section 98, p. 454.

[21] Reorganization Act No. 7, April 12, 1960.

[22] *Phraratchabanyat Truadsob Kanpattibat kiewkae Phasi lae Raidai un khong Rat, Ph.S. 2503* [Taxation and Other State Revenues Act, I960], in *Ratchakitcha*, vol. 77, section 31, p. 1. See page 10 for the formation of an Office of the Export Promotion Commission, also in the Office of the Prime Minister.

The Prime Minister's Office now had the ability to review and propose budgets, survey the conduct of officials, supervise education, and determine allocation of funds for development programs, along with wielding various other powers. But Sarit's mastery of the bureaucracy did not stem solely from his assumption of the prime ministership and his reorganization of the Office of the Prime Minister. He was also Supreme Commander of the Armed Forces, Commander-in-Chief of the Army, and Director-General of the Police Department. When the Ministry of National Development was established, Sarit became its first Minister. His concentration of power was thus quite comprehensive. All of this illustrates the pattern of his thought. In a report on the performance of the government, one finds the following:

> One phenomenon that has occurred following revolutions in most countries, and inmost times, which could almost accepted as part of the natural course of a revolution, is that once a revolutionary government has been formed, with the leader of the revolution established as prime minister, decision-making in general is carried out by the prime minister. This does not mean that cabinet members do not have the right to propose policies ... the special characteristic of a revolutionary government, where the revolutionary leader is the prime minister, is that policy initiatives are usually the responsibility of the prime minister. Therefore in the system of a revolutionary government which is manifested in our country today, nobody knows more than the prime minister about the order of priorities. No person has more responsibility in the division and timing of "work." Thus, it is imperative to delegate initiating powers to the prime minister as much as possible. [23]

But if Sarit drew the substance of power ever more tightly into his own hands, he was careful to distribute its forms among his new constituents. A good illustration of this is Sarit's handling of the "legislative" arm of government. The Interim Constitution of 1959 provided for the appointment of a Constituent Assembly to draft a permanent constitution for the country. In the meantime, this body was to act concurrently as the National Assembly, vested with the legislative power to enact laws.[24] While theoretically the king appointed the 240 members of this Assembly, in reality the Revolutionary Council determined its membership.[25] Article 10 stipulated that:

> On the completion of the drafting of the Constitution by the Constituent Assembly, it shall sit as the National Assembly to resolve whether the draft Constitution can be submitted to the King for Royal Signature prior to being

---

[23] Samnak Nayok Ratthamontri, *Raingan Khwamkaona khong Kitchakan nai Rob Pi thi Song haeng Kanpattiwat* [Progress Report of Activities during the Second Year of the Revolution], vol. I, Bangkok, October 20, 1960, p. 1. For further discussion of the supremacy of the prime minister, see Sawaeng Senanarong, "Khana Phuchuai thi Pruksa khong Nayok Ratthamontri [The Prime Minister's Advisory Group]," *Thai Journal of Public Administration*, 1 (January 1961), pp. 36–47. Choop Kanchanaprakon, "Nayok Ratthamontri Samai Pattiwat [The Prime Minister in the Revolutionary Period]," *Thai Journal of Public Administration* IV (July 1963): 1-18, and (October 1963), pp. 151-190.

[24] Article 6.

[25] Article 7.

promulgated. At such a sitting, the Constituent Assembly shall not make any amendment to the draft Constitution. [26]

This made it quite dear that the regime was appointing its supporters to the Assembly to draft a constitution strictly in accordance with its liking. Similarly, in its legislative aspect, the Assembly was to do no more than rubberstamp regime decisions. But the Assembly was not created simply to give formal legitimacy to Sarit's rule. He used his control over the appointment of members of the Assembly to extend patronage as payment for services rendered or for future support. We find that the overwhelming majority of members to this body were military and civilian bureaucrats. A breakdown of the Assembly appointed on February 3, 1959 reveals the following: of a total of 220 persons, there were 102 army officers, 26 navy officers, 24 air force officers, 18 police officers, and 50 civilian officials. It was noticeable that the army received the largest cut of this patronage. The huge army delegation included many middle-grade officers, while those from the other forces were all top brass.

SOCIALIZING THE BUREAUCRATIC ELITE

As pointed out earlier, the modern Thai political system has been described as a bureaucratic polity where the regime represents the interests of the bureaucracy, both military and civilian. Riggs and Wilson believed that because of the great number of bureaucrats in post-1932 Thai cabinets and because of the prevalence of patron-client relationships, cabinet members would act in the interests of their particular ministries. In other words, the Thai bureaucracy was a fragmented institution whose support for the regime was channeled through particularistic ties to specific representatives in the top echelons of the government.

The drawbacks of this type of system were reflected in repeated complaints about administrative inefficiency, corruption, nepotism, and general compartmentalization of interests, and about the lack of cooperation and coordination between the various ministries and departments within ministries. Bureaucratic obstruction as the result of jealousies, rivalries, and discontent with regime policies were commonly blamed as major obstacles to governmental efficiency. In addition, because of the steep pyramid of patron-client relationships, which tightly restricted the number of people at the top, broad-based bureaucratic participation in governmental decision-making on the national scale was low and the majority of bureaucrats suffered from what might be called a lack of a sense of efficacy. They saw themselves as administrators who could make no real contribution to national policy-making.

Following his *pattiwat* of 1958, however, the prime minister saw an urgent need not just to control, but also to mobilize and gain the enthusiastic support of the bureaucratic elite. He wanted also to create institutionalized linkages between the members of the bureaucratic hierarchies so that they would understand the importance of cooperation with each other to realize regime goals. Furthermore, since political leadership had long been in the hands of the military and there had long been something of a gulf between the military and civilian elites, Sarit saw an urgent need to narrow this distance and promote better mutual comprehension. His

---

[26] Article 10.

method was to broaden bureaucratic participation in policy-planning, although not in actual decision-making. To provide a sense of efficacy, particularly for the civilian elites, Sarit planned to expose them systematically to regime explanations of national priorities and to consult them on their opinions. They should also be encouraged to interact with one another on a direct personal basis.

This bureaucratic socialization program was mainly accomplished through the National Defense College, an institution officially inaugurated by Phibun in 1955.[27] By the process of subjecting bureaucrats to a common institution of learning, government propaganda, and personal contacts in a congenial setting, the Sarit regime was able to achieve a high level of elite bureaucratic solidarity. In this para-academic setting, the government could put forward its goals and solicit discussions from the participants. Their experience at the prestigious National Defense College raised the morale and sense of efficacy of the participants, as well as allowing them to establish personal contacts which could be used later to facilitate intra-bureaucratic cooperation and efficiency. Through socialization at the Defense College, Sarit was able to persuade most top echelon civilian bureaucrats of the urgency of national development and the linked problem of national security, which had to be handled primarily by the armed forces, supported by a loyal civil service. In the final analysis, it is clear that a major purpose of the socialization program was to try to convince civilian bureaucrats of the legitimacy of military supremacy in government.

---

[27] The National Defense College was actually the result of a long evolutionary process. A Council for the Defense of the Realm was first organized by Rama VI in 1910 and reorganized in 1917 under Rama VII. In 1944, the Council's membership was changed to include major military and civilian ministers, with the prime minister as chairman. Witthayalai Pongkan Ratcha-anachak, *Nangsu Prachampi Runthi 9, Ph.S. 2570* [National Defense College Yearbook, 9th Class, 1967], no pagination. The National Defense College was opened on Phibun's birthday, July 14, 1955 and Phibun became its first commandant, although the college was run by a director who has since always been an army general. At that time, the purpose of the college was described as follows: "The National Defense College is an institution of education and research in the field of national defense. It aims to coordinate national defense tactics between senior officials, both military and civilian, and to generate the appreciation and understanding of joint responsibility in defense, the organization of administration, and the maintenance of peace." *Rabieb Krasuang Kalahom waduai Witthayalai Pongkan Ratcha–anachak, PhS. 2498* [Ministry of Defense Regulation regarding the National Defense College, 1955]. Administratively, the college was (and is) located under the Ministry of Defense. The commandant of the institution was the Defense Minister, his deputy was the Chief-of-Staff of the Armed Forces, and the director was the Director for Education and Research from the General Staff Division of the Ministry of Defense. From these arrangements, it is clear that the college was controlled and operated by the military from the start. Admission to this prestigious institution was controlled by nomination and approval of the cabinet. Candidates were confined to military officers with the rank of Brigadier General or its equivalent, and to special grade civil servants. Courses usually ran for approximately ten months, with students attending classes from 9 am to 12 noon on Mondays, Wednesdays, and Fridays. They concurrently worked at their jobs and went to school. At the end of the course work, each student had to submit a research paper. The courses offered covered such topics as geopolitics, administration, and research, the United Nations and International Agencies, and international relations. Aside from the Colleges permanent staff, lecturers were invited from the various ministries to deal with particular subjects. A large number of lecturers were former students and current participants. Out of the fifty-seven lecturers during the first year, thirty were students.

Indications of the relative success of the program could be seen in various statements made by students of the school. A civilian official expressed his opinion in a yearbook as follows:

> Before coming to study at the National Defense College, most civilian officials do not know too much about the activities of the military. After studying here, we have come to understand and appreciate the importance of the military [in national administration].[28]

Other excerpts are just as revealing. For example,

> What has impressed me most while being a student at the National Defense College is the solidarity among the students. Although there are 77 students, a number that generally would lead to differences in opinions, I find that students in this class think and judge as one.
>
> On the personal level, I have come to meet and associate with other students; I have come to learn the job responsibilities of others; I have come to participate in solving national problems; and I have gone for study tours with others in a very fraternal atmosphere. I have received sincere friendship from fellow students without being friends of theirs since childhood. Our friendship did not have to rely upon studying each other's characters nor on previous ties. Forming a close relationship in adulthood is difficult, for we must understand each other thoroughly. I have met my fellow students and have understood them well, and I have come to understand the needs of the nation. We have also revealed our concerns regarding our respective duties; we have consoled each other and have joined to seek solutions to our problems. Therefore, we have become close friends in a short period of time. The friendship I have received could not be obtained from any other source.[29]

This feeling was also shared by most of the military officials attending the college. Some expressed their sentiments in the following manner:

> After we have completed our studies in this college, we will be able to carry out our duties more competently because we realize that the solution of problems in our work in the future—not only involving matters of defense but also general national problems—will not depend upon our own specialty but must be based upon knowledge gained from our studies at this institution, together with cooperation and coordination of work between us and our official friends in all fields. [30]

Another high-ranking officer from the army expressed his delight at finding new friends and realizing that the military was not solely responsible for security and development. He said that:

---

[28] Witthayalai Pongkan Ratcha-anachak, *Nangsu Prachampi Runthi 8, Ph.S. 2509* [National Defense College Yearbook, 1966], no pagination.

[29] Ibid. Italics added.

[30] Ibid.

... now I realize that all parts of the national bureaucracy are equally important and are interrelated to complement each other's responsibilities.[31]

To foster friendship and a sense of camaraderie, social affairs were organized, golf tournaments were held for students, past and present, and inspection tours were conducted. These tours initially had some intrinsic meaning, as the classes were assigned to visit remote areas within the country. While this type of tour still continues, elaborate trips to Europe and Asia at the end of the academic session have increased and appear to be no more than a reward for participation at the college. Attempts were also made to promote closer relations between the participants: the typical reserve that might otherwise have stifled personal relationships was broken down by the use of familiar names in yearbooks, the introductions of participants' wives, and parties held to establish a sense of esprit de corps. As an outward demonstration of group solidarity and mark of distinction, graduates of the college were entitled to wear a pin or ring as identification.

The participants seemed to gain a heightened sense of their own competence and influence from the opportunity to criticize national conditions and propose solutions to national problems, to have their opinions sought by the regime, and to come into close personal contacts with more important members of the government. Civilian bureaucrats particularly felt a sense of pride at being able to mingle with powerful military personalities on intimate terms. In turn, military officers who did not fully share in the political spoils could find solace in their participation in this exclusive institution of higher learning which added to their status and prestige.

Every effort was made to confer the highest status on the college and its students, not least by the granting of honorary degrees on highly influential Thai leaders. For example, among those who did not attend classes but where included in the roster of graduates because of their "special qualifications" were: the King, the Queen, the Princess Mother, Marshal Phibun, Marshal Sarit, Phote Sarasin, Thanat Khoman, Prince Wan, General Net Khemayothin, Thawee Raengkham, Sukich Nimmanhaemin, Phraya Siwisanwacha, General Sut Sutthisanronnakon, General Jira Wichitsongkhram, and Luang Wichit Wathakan (posthumously). But the "regular students" also were powerful and influential men in many cases. Reading the name list of the first graduating class is like reading from a *Who's Who in Thailand*. The class included such prominent individuals as Marshal Thanom Kittikhachon, Marshal Praphat, Marshal Chalermkiat, Air Marshals Bunchoo and Thawee, Police General Prasert, General Surachit Charusareni, General Chitti Nawisathien, General Kris Punnakan, Dr. Puey Ungphakon, Sanya Thammasak, Sunthon Hongladarom, and Dr. Serm Winichaikun.[32]

An examination of the educational background of the officials who attended the college in the following years is represented in Table 9, below. Data were gathered from what was available from published sources of the college and are scattered at best. What they show, however, is that the officials came overwhelmingly from a handful of prestigious schools and institutions of higher learning. In addition, in many cases, civilian and military officials had attended the same secondary schools,

---

[31] Ibid.

[32] Witthayalai Pongkan Ratcha-anachak, *Thamniep Naksuksa Witthayalai Pongkan Ratcha-anachak Runthi 1-13* [List of 1st to 13th graduating class of the National Defense College], Bangkok, January 1, 1971.

so that their common experience at the National Defense College was a renewal and fostered the solidifying of old ties in a new purposive context.[33]

Table 9
Educational Background of Participants at the National Defense College

	Graduating Classes					
	1956-68	1957-60	1960-65	1962-63	1963-71	1964 72
Total graduates	68	60	65	63	71	72
Elite High Schools						
Suankulab	18	17	20	NA	NA	11
Thepsirin	13	10	12	NA	NA	16
Assumption	6	4	6	NA	NA	6
Wat Bencha	6	0	2	NA	NA	8
Pathum	4	5	4	NA	NA	7
Ban Somdet	3	3	3	NA	NA	5
Percentage of class identified	*74*	*65*	*72*	*----*	*----*	*74*
Higher Education						
Military Academy	27	26	29	21	23	NA
Chulalongkon Univ.	5	9	7	9	13	NA
Thammasat Univ.	1	3	9	12	7	NA
Law School (Min. of Justice)	9	6	10	1	4	NA
Percentage of class identified	*62*	*73*	*83*	*68*	*66*	*----*
Foreign Experience						
United States	8	8	24	26	31	NA
England	13	8	12	8	15	NA
France	6	3	4	8	0	NA
Germany	3	1	2	0	1	NA
Percentage of class identified	*44*	*33*	*65*	*56*	*66*	*----*

NA: Data not available
Up until 1962, there was only one class every two years.

That the aim of the National Defense College was to link military and civilian elites, largely on military terms, however, is suggested by Table 10, below, which shows the composition by profession of those who have attended the school from 1956 to 1963, the years which roughly cover the Sarit regime By the end of 1963, 327 officials had passed through the institution. By 1953, only twenty-five of the total had

---

[33] The importance of the National Defense College in providing solidarity for the bureaucratic elite increased with time. While the older generation of high officials tended to come from a small number of schools, this has been less true with later generations. The recent expansion of educational institutions has been remarkable, and as more National Defense College students are chosen from among younger bureaucrats with diversified backgrounds, the role of the college as a prime socializing institution has become more apparent. This trend became most evident in the years after Sarit's death.

died or had retired, leaving 302 still on active duty. Of these, sixty-five held extremely powerful and sensitive positions in the administration.[34]

Table 10
Participants at the National Defense College by Profession

	Graduating Classes				
Profession	1956	1958	1960	1962	1963
Civilian	26 (38%)	23 (38%)	28 (43%)	30 (48%)	25 (35%)
Army	25	25	21	22	26
Navy	7	4	6	4	9
Air Force	4	6	7	4	5
Police	6	2	3	3	6
% Armed Forces	(62%)	(62%)	(57%)	(52%)	(65%)
Total	**68**	**60**	**65**	**63**	**71**

To support the generalization made earlier that the role of the college was to enhance the sense of efficacy of officials, particularly civilians, as well as socialize this elite into taking the development/national security linkage seriously, I have made a rough content analysis of the research papers submitted for graduation in Table 11.[35] The most striking pattern that emerges from the table concerns the two categories of civilian administrative issues and military administrative issues. The majority of the students wrote on administrative problems within their own areas of expertise, based on experience, making observations and recommendations which they felt would be beneficial to national security. The participants were encouraged to demonstrate their logic to each other, as well as to concretize in their own minds the importance of their respective responsibilities in a national framework. By verbalizing their ideas and by expounding on their own experience to their fellows, they were supposed to highlight the importance of bureaucratic cooperation and, at the same time, increase their own sense of efficacy in national policy-making.

Papers dealing with civilian administrative problems showed a steady rise as a percentage of total as compared to those dealing with military-related themes. This suggests that the heavy contingent of military officers came to recognize the importance of statecraft and national administrative concerns above their earlier narrowly defined military interests and also perhaps saw more clearly the decisive roles the military was actually playing in national politics and administration.

---

[34] This number does not include Directors-General of departments in the various ministries.

[35] The categories are made exclusive of each other. An attempt was made to determine whether each author was concerned with general development, national security problems, or administrative concerns, and his own job responsibilities. For example, "Medicine and National Security" papers dealt mainly with medicine and the problems of administration. The relationship to national security was only very vaguely indicated. In most cases, national security was seen in generalized terms, that is, it was assumed that all parts of the bureaucracy should function at their peak to support national security.

Table 11
Research Papers Presented to the National Defense College, 1958-1970 (percentage of total)

Classification	1958	1960	1962	1963	1964	1965	1966	1967	1968	1969	1970
National development	6.5	10.8	8.0	12.6	15.5	6.8	6.7	12.0	5.4	8.8	0.0
International issues	2.2	14.4	8.0	12.5	5.7	9.5	3.9	6.0	5.4	1.8	7.0
Cold War issues	4.3	3.6	1.4	5.5	5.7	1.4	7.9	3.0	3.6	8.8	1.6
Social and internal issues	34.6	18.0	11.2	9.6	11.3	2.7	10.6	9.0	10.6	10.5	7.0
Civil administrative issues	28.3	28.8	33.4	30.6	29.6	41.8	39.4	40.0	37.6	47.3	54.0
Military administrative issues	21.7	25.2	33.4	23.6	25.2	32.4	23.6	24.0	32.2	17.5	27.0
Miscellaneous topics	2.3	0.0	4.6	5.6	7.0	5.4	7.9	6.0	5.2	5.3	3.4

Table 12
Civilian versus Military/Police Authors of Research Papers Presented to the National Defense College, 1958-1970 (percentage of total)

Classification	1958	1960	1962	1963	1964	1965	1966	1967	1968	1969	1970
Civilian authors	34.6	46.4	47.6	47.6	36.6	37.8	43.1	41.0	39.9	39.6	39.9
Military/Police authors	65.4	53.6	52.4	52.4	63.4	62.2	56.9	59.0	60.1	60.4	60.1

The table also reveals that, on the whole, the participants were not much interested in general development problems, international issues, or ideological conflict with the communist world. An understanding of, or concern for, internal unrest and regional dissent was also not much in evidence. For while the curriculum emphasized all the above-mentioned fields, the final papers presented did not reflect this broad orientation.[36]

HARNESSING THE MILITARY

If Sarit tried to gain support and cooperation from the civilian bureaucracy, he never forgot that the military had brought him to power and was the key pillar of his regime.

Since 1932, the military had played the major role in Thai politics,[37] though some attempts had been made to curb the army, most notably the campaigns led by Pridi and his Seri Thai supporters after the Second World War.

Following its return to power in 1947, the army zealously guarded its political preeminence and proceeded to eliminate all sources of opposition. Even when Khuang was appointed prime minister by the 1947 Coup Group, the military held tight rein over his performance. During a heated debate in parliament over the question of the proper role of the military in politics, it became clear that the military would not tolerate any attempts to eliminate its participation in national decision-making. When Khuang proposed to parliament that it should consider prohibiting the military from engaging in politics, he was vehemently denounced by Lt. Gen. Luang Chatnakrop, a member of the 1947 Coup Group and Minister of Defense. Luang Chat angrily, if confusingly, informed parliament that

> Politics is like a disease. To prohibit the military from participating in politics must be done by a gradual process ... for the disease has been chronic. Nevertheless, the military must understand and be engaged in politics.[38]

It is possible to detect in the years after 1947 a certain development in the military's thinking about its role in politics. Military ideology moved slowly from emphasizing concerns for corporate stability and internal improvement to stressing national political leadership and socio-economic control.[39] To document this trend, to which Sarit certainly contributed, I have made a content and quantitative analysis of the army's service journal, *Yutthakot.*

---

[36] The papers dealing with internal unrest and problems of communism revealed no innovative conceptions. Rather, most of them simply repeated accepted facts—some of which are nevertheless questionable. There was a uniformity of content and structure to these papers that leads one to suspect that either the sources used were always the same or that the authors were merely reproducing what they had heard in class.

[37] See Jin Vibhatakarasa, "The Military in Thai Politics" (PhD dissertation, University of Oregon, 1966). See also Somsak Rakwijit, "The Military in Southeast Asian Politics" (PhD dissertation, Vanderbilt University, 1966).

[38] Phayom Chulanon, "Ratthasapha kap Kanthahan [Parliament and the Mititary]," *Yutthakot* LII (April 1948), p. 128.

[39] The preceding section dealing with the National Defense College showed how that institution assisted this development.

Writing in *Yutthakot* in 1949, Captain Premchai Witta expressed some odd but interesting ideas.[40] He noted that when he was attending the military academy, he was led to believe that soldiers should not be involved with politics because political ideas and ideology could create rifts within the military and would weaken discipline. Yet, he reasoned, by its very name, politics (*kanmuang,* affairs of the city) should be the concern of all city inhabitants, as opposed to farmers and those living in the countryside. Soldiers were stationed in cities and thus should consider themselves *phonlamuang,* or city dwellers. In order to become good *phonlamuang,* soldiers had to be involved in *kanmuang:*

> ... knowing the duties of a city-dweller involves the study and participation in *kanmuang.* The fact that military officers are interested in *kanmuang* means that they are endeavoring to become good city dwellers who are well-versed in *kanmuang* ... [Soldiers] are good *phonlamuang* whose duties are to protect national independence.[41]

Moreover, since military officers had the duty of leading and educating the common soldiers to understand their roles in society, the good military officer must be well-versed in politics. Finally, Premchai said that:

> Because of this strong love for the nation, some military officers have come to realize that on certain occasions they should have the duty of protecting the nation's future. In this instance, the officer is transformed into a *ratthaburut* [statesman] and not a *nakkanmuang* [politician] ... Politicians think of coming elections, but the statesman is concerned with the future of the nation.[42]

The distinction between statesman and politician was and is taken quite seriously by Thai military leaders. They have continued to feel that they have the right to lead the nation and to determine the course of its future. Twenty-one years after Premchai wrote his article, similar sentiments were expressed by Col. Charung Prakob-wannakit while a student at the National Defense College. Col. Charung wrote:

> Barring any prejudices, we can see that soldiers are citizens [*prachakon*] with clean hearts [*chit chai sa-ad*], brave, and worthy of honor ... soldiers have pure hearts almost comparable to monks ... Therefore, it is no surprise that only the best soldiers could become kings in ancient times. As a corollary, it should not be a source of wonder today that the prime minister is forever a soldier.[43]

Yet the two examples, in spite of their similarities, show a changing justification for the military's role in politics. Premchai presented an idealistic picture of the good soldier aware of his contemporary environment. Col. Charung, on the other hand,

---

[40] Captain Premchai Witta, "Sanyalak khong Nakkanmuang [The Sign of a Politician]," *Yutthakot* LVII (June 1949), pp. 87–90.

[41] Ibid., p. 88. This interpretation is very unorthodox, *kanmuang* is usually translated as "affairs of the state, city." *Phonlamuang* is usually translated as "citizen."

[42] Ibid., p. 90.

[43] Colonel Charung Prakobwannakit, "Prachakon kap Khwammankhong khong Chat [Citizens and National Security]," Research Paper, National Defense College, 1970, pp. 71, 75.

evoked tradition and history to justify military leadership in politics. In both cases, of course, the soldier is idolized and bidden to lead and direct the nation's destiny because of his purity of mind and upright moral character. Soldiers could be statesmen according to this interpretation, but never politicians.

In recent years, however, an additional type of justification for political involvement has become very noticeable, based on the role of the military in guaranteeing national integrity and domestic security. The military has come to view itself self-consciously as an internal force for the suppression of internal unrest and strife. A representative example of this perspective is the following:

> A country that possesses a strong military having a leading role in politics could expect other nations to seek its friendship ... In countries where there is the need for internal security ... it is imperative that the military should be relied upon as an institution to suppress unstable forces. In order to achieve that goal, it is necessary to strengthen the military by including it in politics ... In a political situation where the military is involved, as is present today, we have witnessed that it has brought immense political stability to the nation.[44]

In a 1970 article entitled "For Self or Nation," a military officer using a pseudonym declared that the imposition of martial law over the long period since 1958 demonstrated the critical state of national affairs:

> Up to now [1970], the Ministry of Interior has determined that thirty-six provinces have been infiltrated by communists, which constitutes half of the country. This indicates that the national situation is not very normal ... Also, the Ministry of Defense has declared that military officials in thirty-three provinces may make decisions according to powers stipulated under martial law, showing that the national situation is not stable.[45]

By a rather circular process of reasoning, the political acts of the military authorities are interpreted as proofs of internal unrest (rather than the unrest itself), and thus cited to justify further political interventions. One last aspect of the Thai military's changing view of its role is the theme of responsibility for development and progress. An examination of *Yutthakot,* following procedures developed by Maury D. Feld, shows this clearly.[46]

Feld's article proposes to "explore the implications of technological change for the self-image of the military professional" from an analysis of American army and navy journals.[47] Viewing the military as an organization interested and engaged in technical development and innovation, he concluded that the American military was changing from a primitive self-conception to a competitive or managerial

---

[44] Major General Chawaeng Youngcharoen, "Nayobai Kanthahan khong Thai [Thai Military Policy]," Research Paper, National Defense College, 1964, pp. 40, 41.

[45] 666 (pseud.), "Phuaton ru Phuachat [For Self or For Nation]," *Yutthakot* LXXVII (April 1970), pp. 105-112, esp. p. 107.

[46] Maury D. Feld, "The Military Self-image in a Technological Environment," in *The New Military,* ed. Morris Janowitz (New York, NY: John Wiley & Sons, Inc., 1967), pp. 159-188.

[47] Ibid., p. 159.

orientation.[48] Feld assumed that it was technological change alone that had affected the American military's self-image. In the Thai case, however, it is clear that long participation in politics and interaction with other groups in the socio-economic and administrative sectors, rather than technology, actually produced a new self-image. This means that the modern Thai military as a competitive political organization has had to accept the application of some non-military standards to the management of military affairs. In sum, the military has partially internalized civilian standards and procedures for use in running the country.

My hypothesis is that, following Sarit's consolidation of power and the elimination of all major political opposition after 1958, the military, especially the army, enjoyed far wider participation in and control of national administration than ever before, and this made them recognize the complexity and importance of their political role. This transformation should be reflected in *Yutthakot*, where one would expect the articles to show a wider interest in social, economic, and political affairs at the expense of purely military subjects.[49] In general, this would mean that the Thai military's perception of its own role changed from primitive notions (concern for military operations) to competitive ones (where the military recognized that it must internalize civilian and political values in order to improve its ability to rule).

As Feld points out, there is a major difference between the military service journals and those of other professions. Other professional journals serve as an avenue through which recognition is given to industrious and innovative members of the profession. But the military establishment is a more comprehensive institution, and professional soldiers must operate within a structure that defines official behavior as well as providing norms concerning how they are to perform.[50] In this respect, military service journals provide information that the institution feels its officers should know. Thus service journals can be assumed to represent the determined and accepted policies of the corporate entity. This is all the more noticeable in the case of the *Yutthakot* since most of its contributors were on its permanent staff and major authors appeared in the journal at regular intervals, leading one to suspect that they were the spokesmen of the army. In addition, there seems to have been a conscious program to educate officers to understand their new role as political leaders, as indicated by a series of articles written by civilian experts on social, political, and economic problems and their possible solutions.[51]

To trace this changing military perception of its role, it may be useful to compare *Yutthakot* contributions in two major categories: the first can be labeled "broad professional," covering topics of interest to all officers; the second can be labeled "narrow professional," dealing with subjects of particular interest to specialized groups of officers. The assumption here is that "narrow professional" articles reflect the army's concern for primitive values, while "broad professional" articles represent the competitive outlook. In addition, articles in the "broad professional" category can

---

[48] Ibid., p. 188.

[49] The collection used here is from the National Library in Bangkok. Volume 64 was missing. Many single issues also could not be found. During the war years, 1943–1954, publication was suspended. In 1948, volumes 54-56 were lumped together as one to compensate for those three years.

[50] Feld, "The Military Self-image," p. 175.

[51] Shortly after Sarit's takeover, for example, a series of articles dealing with public administration, banking and finance, and economic development were written by Bunchana Atthakon.

be broken up into groups covering: general and historical themes; primarily military-related topics; and political/social/economic subjects. This last category is most significant, for it acts as an indicator of how the army leadership has directed the interest of its officers towards a comprehensive role in administration.

We can see that, following the coup of 1947, which marked the return of the military to political leadership, there were more "broad professional" than "narrow professional" articles in the journal. This can be explained by the fact that after the military was partially discredited by the Seri Thai and civilian political leaders, they had to launch a program to boost the organization's morale and solidarity. Articles appealing to all members of the organization would achieve that goal better than those of interest to only a few. However, after 1950 and especially 1953, there was a sharp rise in the number of "narrow professional" topics addressed in the journal, perhaps because of the Korean war and the shift of the army's structure to approximate that of the American model. After 1957, following the Sarit coup, more articles of the "broad professional" type appeared. A majority of these articles dealt with the social/political/economic themes that were emphasized by the Sarit regime. After the death of Sarit in 1963, there was a gradual decline in specialized military subjects, representing a de-emphasis on the primitive outlook of the army; this trend supports the observation by some scholars that Thanom and Praphat paid little attention to basic military needs and were too busy playing politics.

The significant rise of "broad professional" articles published in *Yutthakot* during Sarit's tenure becomes clearly apparent when we examine Table 14.

After Sarit staged his *pattiwat,* there appeared a gradual increase in contributions dealing with socio-political and economic themes, as compared to general military-related articles and those classified as general-historical. When Sarit became prime minister in 1958, he was able to eliminate all opposition. The army was in firm control of national leadership. It was Sarit's goal that military officers be made aware of their new responsibilities under his regime. Even after Sarit's death, the Thanom regime adhered to his guidelines. The figures reinforce the generalization, made in the above discussion of the National Defense College, that the Sarit government pushed for a greater convergence between military and civilian elites. Under the Sarit system, military officers were supposed to understand the social, economic and political issues that had earlier been mainly the field of the civilian bureaucrats and politicians. Table 15, below, throws further light on the same trend.

Following the Sarit coup of 1957, the ratio of army to civilian authors represented in *Yutthakot* began to narrow. Because Sarit expected the military to become more knowledgeable of social, political, and economic matters, outside help was needed to write the appropriate articles. The years between 1957 and 1965 can be seen as formative in developing military familiarity in dealing with such subjects. After 1965, it is clear that military officers took over the task of dealing with a wide variety of such topics. In essence, a new generation of army officers appeared who were as comfortable dealing with civilian-related questions as with military ones.[52]

---

[52] A word about the large contingent of pseudonymous authors is in order. It is my suspicion that these were mainly military officers. Where the names can be identified, they are usually those of military men.

Table 13
Classification of Articles in *Yutthakot*, 1947–1969
(percentage of total)

Classification	1947	1948	1949	1950	1951	1952	1953	1954...
Broad Professional	58.8	65.3	43.3	38.5	38.8	47.7	25.0	23.7
Narrow Professional	9.8	9.3	12.1	28.2	24.5	16.0	60.7	16.2
Others	31.4	25.4	44.6	33.3	36.7	36.3	14.3	60.1

	...1955	1956	1957	1958	1959	1960	1961	1962...
Broad Professional	14.7	NA	27.4	28.7	21.9	39.0	43.9	22.0
Narrow Professional	25.6	NA	20.5	19.1	11.9	10.0	12.1	18.0
Others	59.7	NA	52.1	52.2	66.2	51.0	44.0	60.0

	...1963	1964	1965	1966	1967	1968	1969
Broad Professional	34.9	52.5	24.0	37.0	41.1	41.4	41.6
Narrow Professional	26.5	15.4	12.0	12.0	9.0	9.9	8.1
Others	38.6	32.1	64.0	51.0	50.9	48.7	50.3

NA – Data not available
Articles classified under "others" include short stories and articles designed for entertainment purposes.

Table 14
Breakdown of Broad Professional Articles in *Yutthakot*, 1947–1969
(percentage of total)

Classification	1947	1948	1949	1950	1951	1952	1953	1954
Historical	25.8	28.0	29.0	27.0	21.1	42.9	50.0	42.1
Military	48.4	52.0	29.0	23.0	15.8	33.3	42.9	21.5
Socio-political & economic	25.8	20.0	52.0	50.0	63.1	23.8	7.1	36.4

	...1955	1956	1957	1958	1959	1960	1961	1962
Historical	41.6	NA	19.0	23.2	22.2	25.5	25.5	11.5
Military	0.0	NA	57.1	38.4	33.3	29.8	38.8	27.0
Socio-political & economic	58.4	NA	23.9	38.4	44.5	44.7	36.7	61.5

	...1963	1964	1965	1966	1967	1968	1969
Historical	14.0	25.9	3.8	16.6	32.6	35.9	36.0
Military	28.0	25.9	3.8	26.2	18.4	12.5	20.3
Socio-political & economic	68.0	48.2	92.4	57.2	49.0	51.6	43.7

NA – Data not available

Table 15
Classification of Authors in *Yutthakot*, 1947–1969
(percentage of total)

Classification	1947	1948	1949	1950	1951	1952	1953	1954...
Military	50.0	39.8	44.3	38.4	40.0	41.8	67.9	31.5
Civilian	26.0	21.5	35.2	21.8	40.0	43.7	27.2	36.1
Pseudonym	24.0	38.7	20.5	39.8	20.0	14.5	4.9	32.4

Classification	...1955	1956	1957	1958	1959	1960	1961	1962...
Military	37.6	NA	67.9	72.3	76.2	73.2	62.3	52.7
Civilian	34.8	NA	20.5	21.3	23.8	26.8	23.7	28.3
Pseudonym	27.6	NA	11.6	6.4	00.0	00.0	14.0	19.0

Classification	...1963	1964	1965	1966	1967	1968	1969
Military	43.9	50.0	38.0	53.5	72.6	95.9	82.5
Civilian	32.6	29.8	36.2	26.1	17.1	4.1	9.3
Pseudonym	23.5	20.2	25.8	20.4	10.3	00.0	8.2

NA—Data not available

In summary, our examination of the army service journal confirms our earlier conclusion that under Sarit the military as a group rapidly acquired expertise in dealing with society, politics, and economic problems. Military officers had to be well-versed in military science, but, more importantly, they had to recognize their role as administrators and potential leaders. The developing pattern in the Thai military officers corps was one of an increasingly competitive outlook and acceptance and mastery of skills hitherto considered within the domain of civilian expertise. It should be added that much of Sarit's legitimacy within the army came from his role in expanding its functions, skills, prestige, and control.

While the above accounts in a broad sense for Sarit's popularity with the military arm of the bureaucracy, it does not show how his personal control was maintained. One likely explanation of Sarit's success in this narrower sense is that he was shrewd enough to build around him a clique of loyal subordinate officers who were promoted to positions of power as their patron rose to the top. Thanom, Praphat, and Kris can be considered members of his "immediate" family of close supporters and subordinates. It was only after the death of Sarit that the army's leadership became divided again and competition among Sarit's heirs for sole control of the army intensified—a crisis which was only finally resolved in October 1973, when General Kris, the army's commander-in-chief, refused to cooperate with Thanom and Praphat in suppressing student demonstrations.

Following the coup of 1947, the most powerful and critical army command was the First Division stationed in Bangkok. Soldiers from this division were responsible for staging the 1947 coup and suppressing the Pridi and Manhattan Rebellions, and they were used by the Phibun government in keeping the peace within the capital area following the dirty elections of 1957. Suffice it to say, the real strength of the government was directly related to support from the First Division. Assured control of the First Division meant the control of political power.

In 1947, Sarit was Commander of the 1st Regiment of the First Division and provided the Coup Group with the soldiers used to carry out the coup. Under him was Lt. Col. Praphat as Commander of the 1st Battalion. Thanom at that time was teaching at the Military Academy; he was responsible for leading the cadets to participate in the coup. In 1948, Sarit was promoted to Major General and Commander of the First Division, while Thanom became Commander of the 11th Regiment under Sarit's leadership. This began the long and close association between Sarit, Thanom, and Praphat. In 1950, Sarit became Commander of the First Army and Thanom was promoted to Deputy Commander of the First Division. In the following year, when Sarit became Deputy Minister of Defense, Praphat was given control of Sarit's former command, the 1st Regiment. Basically, the First Division had two regiments, the 1st and 11th, and these were now under Thanom and Praphat. In 1952, Sarit became Deputy Army Commander-in-Chief, and in 1954 he replaced Marshal Phin. That same year, Thanom assumed command of the First Division and the First Army, succeeding Sarit. When Sarit became Minister of Defense in 1957, Thanom was his deputy, while Praphat was given the position of Commander of the First Division and Deputy Minister of Interior. At this juncture, General Kris's rise to prominence became apparent, for he became Praphat's deputy in the First Division.

After Sarit staged his coup d'état against Phibun in 1957, and following the short interlude of the Phote caretaker government, Thanom became Prime Minister and

Minister of Defense, while Praphat took over the Interior Ministry. When Sarit regained his health, staged his *pattiwat*, and assumed political leadership as Prime Minister, Thanom remained as Defense Minister and Praphat retained his former political position.

Thus we can see that Sarit's ability to control the army, and particularly the strategic First Division, came from entrusting the command of that division to his old associates. A long pattern of parallel promotion assured Sarit of the two commanders' gratitude and support.

Another factor that contributed to the solidarity of Sarit's immediate "family" of allies was marriage. In 1958, the king performed the marriage ceremony between Thanom's son, Lt. Narong Kittikhachon, and Praphat's daughter, Suphaphon Charusathien. This dynastic link also helps to account for the relative solidarity in the leadership of the Revolutionary Council after the death of Sarit in 1963.

Furthermore, after 1947 the army enjoyed great prosperity. In his acceptance speech as the new army Commander-in-Chief on June 25, 1954, Sarit promised that he would see to it that the army would reach its pinnacle of development.[53] As we have seen, Sarit was able to do this with the help of the United States. Two years prior to his assumption of the army leadership, Sarit had been instrumental in helping to reorganize the Thai army along American lines. In 1954, he went to Washington to negotiate for more military aid and was quite successful. It should be noted, however, that, under Sarit, the national budget of the armed forces did not increase drastically by comparison with the funds allotted to education and the Interior Ministry.[54]

Finally, unlike Phibun (who led the government in the middle and late 1940s) and Phin (the early 1950s), both leaders who slowly lost touch with the army's rank and file because of their involvement in politics and business ventures, Sarit tried his best to preserve strong personal ties with the army. He maintained a house in the First Division Headquarters and made it a point to attend all army functions, even when he was sick. His biographer in the Cremation Volume noted Sarit's love for the army by writing that:

> Throughout his life, he was proud and deeply involved with the army. He often said that "I have lived in the army since my youth, and if I had to leave the army

---

[53] Cremation Volume of Sarit Thanarat [Cabinet edition], p. 1.

[54] Budget allocations during the Sarit regime were, by percentage of total:

	1958	1959	1960	1961	1962	1963
Education	4.6	18.4	17.3	15.4	14.9	15.6
Defense	10.2	19.6	17.8	16.6	16.9	15.6
Interior	7.0	16.3	15.1	15.0	13.9	14.3

Source: Computed from *Ratchakitcha, 1958-1963*.
After Sarit's trip to negotiate for defense aid from the United States in 1954, American financial and material aid to the Thai armed forces increased considerably:

1955	1956	1957	1958	1959	1960	1961
90.8	178.7	107.7	113.1	283.6	166.6	116.3

(In million baht.) *Source:* Bunchana Atthakon, "Khwamchuailua chak Tangprathet kap Phatthanakan thang Setthakit khong Prathet Thai [Foreign Aid and Thai National Economic Development]," Research Paper, National Defense College, 1962, p. 139. These aid figures are not complete, for they do not include all other military assistance.

it would break my heart. Therefore, I vow that if I should die, let it happen while I am in the army." He kept that vow, for even if he was promoted to high offices, he never left the army. He did not merely hold on to positions in the army [while engaged in other work], but personally took care of important administrative work. He tried his best to attend all important functions of the army. Often he remarked to his close associates that no matter where he was, nothing could compare with the army. Especially during annual meetings to consider promotions of army officers, he would never be absent, but would attend their opening or closing ceremonies, and he never failed to deliver lengthy speeches. [55]

Thus we find that Sarit, realizing that his ultimate control of Thai politics depended upon the support of the army, tried his best to maintain his hold over the top officers who commanded strategic troops, such as Thanom, Praphat, and Kris, to maintain close contact with the rank and file, and oversee the promotions of all officers. And it should not be forgotten that Sarit represented in many ways the ideal model of the modern Thai army officer—a person who achieved the highest military rank of Field Marshal at the early age of forty-seven and became prime minister at the age of fifty. Within the army officer corps, Sarit was very much a man to be respected and emulated.

THE ROLE OF THE MONARCHY

As a political institution, the modern Thai monarchy has not received its fair share of academic scrutiny. Most scholars have been contented to accept that the Thai monarchy is vital to the stability and well-being of Thai society, representing national unity, a link with the past, a source of legitimacy, and the union of the best values of Thai culture and tradition.

David Wilson did try to deal with kingship, but largely in historical and cosmological terms, failing to point out clearly the roles and functions of the institution within the modern political system. Only in one long paragraph that discusses how Rama IX reacted to certain political situations and the potential significance of those reactions did Wilson move close to contemporary realities:

> The fact that the throne is now occupied by an adult who can manipulate some of the great prestige of the institution would certainly indicate that the political problem of the throne must be faced. Whether the political influence of the king will gradually increase or will suddenly be cut off, as it was in 1935, depends largely upon the discretion of the monarch. [56]

Wilson's observation is valid up to a point. But he did not see the role of the *regime* in actively and consciously directing the activities of the monarchy.

In the constitutional period, the political role of the monarchy was not very clear or developed, at least until the mid-1970s. Following the abdication of Rama VII in 1935, Thailand did not have an adult resident reigning monarch until 1950. In the interim, Rama VIII had returned to Bangkok, but his untimely death in 1946 left the throne vacant until 1950, when King Rama IX came to take up residence in Bangkok.

---

[55] Cremation Volume of Sarit Thanarat [Cabinet edition], p. 53.

[56] Wilson, *Politics in Thailand,* pp. 114, 115.

As a young monarch, Rama IX was not able to exercise any influence on the cabinet or on general political activities. The government leadership under Phibun blocked any attempt by the king to exert some influence on national affairs. It has already been pointed out that when Phibun reinstated the 1932 Constitution in 1951, the king tried to intervene, but his efforts were futile.[57] Wilson has also pointed out that Phibun was disturbed to discover that the king was quite popular with the public when he went on a tour to the Northeast. The prime minister was so alarmed that he refused to finance further trips for the king.[58] Furthermore, to demonstrate his annoyance at Phibun, the king failed to show up at major functions celebrating the Twenty-Fifth Centennial Buddhist Celebrations in 1957.[59] From the above, we can readily see that while the king could withhold active support for a government, he and his advisors felt that he was in no position to take any political initiatives.

The political elite ushered into power by the coup of 1957 accorded the throne much more power and prestige than their predecessors had. The fact that Sarit, Thanom, and Praphat came from a different generation than Phibun, and that they were educated and trained entirely in Thailand, made it easier for them to make accommodations with the throne. These leaders were not identified as anti-royalists and had not participated in the overthrow of the monarchy. They were not directly influenced by Western liberalism, and their political experience was very parochial. The king still had an aura of sacredness and purity for this elite, and its relationship with the throne reflected this perspective.[60]

The Sarit Coup Group also had little historical basis for legitimacy compared with the leaders of the 1932 Revolution, whose claim to power rested on constitutionalism and their role in overthrowing absolute monarchy. The Sarit coup of 1957 initially based its legitimacy solely on the fact that it had responded to public demands that the corrupt Phibun regime be replaced. Sensing the instability of its own foundation, the Sarit clique turned to the throne for support and legitimacy. It has been shown earlier how Sarit proclaimed to the press and public that his position was legal because the king had given his approval and had presented Sarit with a document, which was immediately displayed.[61] Thus in 1957, the monarchy had the function of legitimizing a new political leadership.

As a result, the development of the monarchy as a political institution saw rapid progress after 1957. The Sarit regime made conscious efforts to give the king more exposure domestically and internationally. As the prestige of the king increased, the government's popularity grew. Under Sarit's leadership, elaborate tours of the country and foreign countries were arranged for representatives of the monarchy, traditional ceremonies were revived, the national day was changed to coincide with the king's birthday, and the royal family was encouraged to participate in military affairs.

---

[57] Ibid., p. 114. Also see Phairote Chaiyanam, *Khamathibai kotmai Ratthathammanun Priapthiap* [Lecture Notes on Comparative Constitutions], vol. II, Thammasat University, pp. 151-154.

[58] Wilson, *Politics in Thailand,* p. 114.

[59] See Chapter II.

[60] Thai Noi and Rungrot, *Nayok Ratthamontri khon thi 11,* pp. 222-229. The authors describe the graduation ceremonies of Thanom's class in 1920. The graduates were much impressed and moved by the presence of the king.

[61] See Chapter III.

Under the Sarit political system, the monarchy had two main functions. First and foremost, the throne played the vital function of legitimizer, not only of the seizure of power, but of a wide range of regime policies. It increased the regime's prestige abroad and helped cement regime/elite solidarity through royal sponsorship of ceremonial and social affairs. The second function was to contribute to the paternalistic programs of the regime. The throne in this instance acted as an institution for receiving private contributions for charity work. At the king's discretion, and with the government's acquiescence, these funds were channeled to public programs, enhancing the popularity of both the king and the government in the process.

TRIPS ABROAD

From, the start, the Sarit government gave firm support to the throne, hoping to strengthen its own position domestically and internationally by that means. The king represented the "nation," and the Sarit regime emphasized the fact that it was acting in the name of both. Unlike Phibun, Sarit was not socially sophisticated in the Western sense. He had been described by the foreign press as a brusque military officer. His English was poor, and he was not as gracious in public as Phibun could be. Because of this, Sarit realized that he would be a poor representative of his government and the country abroad. To play down the "vulgarity" of his regime, Sarit turned to the king for help. The king had been brought up in Europe since childhood and spoke many languages. He also had a very attractive queen who was well-adjusted to the ways of the West. To enhance the prestige of the country and the government, Sarit therefore arranged elaborate visits for the royal couple. These official state visits were carried out by the king in the name of the Thai people, but the government realized that the king's exposure to the foreign public would minimize foreign criticism of the regime itself for being dictatorial. Furthermore, with attention diverted to the activities of the throne, the public would be less likely to be critical of the actions of the government.

It is clear from the queen's own account that her trips were carefully planned by the government. Reminiscing about the royal travels, she revealed that from the time she and the king returned to Thailand in 1952, up until 1959, the pair had never ventured out of the country. This was because the king had made a firm decision to remain as close to his subjects as possible. Indeed, the king had never even thought of vacationing anywhere except within the country, according to the queen's memoir.[62] She continued:

> In 1959, I accompanied the king abroad for the first time in making a state visit to the Republic of Vietnam for three to four days. Later, the king traveled to Indonesia and Burma.
>
> During that time, I heard that the government was arranging state visits with the American government and governments of European countries. The total was fifteen nations.[63]

---

[62] Sirikit, Queen of Thailand, "Khwamsongcham nai Kantamsadet Tangprathet thang Ratchakan [Recollection of State Visits]," in *Anuson Phraratchathan Pluengsop Phraya Rattanaphakdi* [Cremation Volume of Phraya Rattanaphakdi], June 19, 1972, p. 1

[63] Ibid., p. 2.

The trial exposure of the king to foreign countries was conducted in late 1959 and early 1960. Within those four months, the king toured three neighboring countries—the Republic of Vietnam, Indonesia, and Burma. He was well received, and both the international and Thai press gave him very comprehensive coverage. The king's performance elicited a very favorable domestic reaction. The public and the newspapers expressed pride in the monarchy and were happy that the government had given support to the throne.

With these initial successes, Sarit planned an elaborate goodwill tour for the royal couple that would include visits to the major powers of the West. Between mid-June 1960 and mid-January 1961, the king and queen visited fourteen countries: the United States, England, West Germany, Portugal, Spain, Switzerland, Denmark, Norway, Sweden, Italy, Belgium, France, Luxembourg, and the Netherlands.[64] By the time of Sarit's death in 1963, the royal couple had visited Malaya, Pakistan, Australia, New Zealand, Japan, and the Philippines. Thus, within a span of five years, the king had made state visits to twenty-three countries.[65]

The most important trip that the king made was the one covering fourteen countries over a six-month period. Accounts of those trips by the queen and those who accompanied the royal couple indicate the hectic and tight schedule that had to be kept. It is clear that the trips were not pleasurable experiences. The reasons behind the royal tours were explained by Sarit when he wished the king good fortune and a safe trip in the following words:

> ... your majesties' absence from Thailand for many months is cause for concern for the government and the people. But ... royal visits abroad have been a tradition that past kings performed, and it will bring closer and friendlier relations with other countries.[66]

In reply the king said:

> We would like to thank the people for understanding and supporting our trip ... The fact that the people support our trip is most important, for without the acquiescence of the people, we would not have been able to go. This trip is for the interest of the nation. We shall carry out our duties as leader and bring with us the goodwill of the Thai people to demonstrate to foreigners that we are friends, would like to be friends, and are willing to cooperate with them.[67]

The exposure of the king to people around the world was a good advertisement for the government. The king and queen left a positive impression of Thailand, its

---

[64] P. Watcharaphon, *Sadet Yuan 14 Prathet* [Royal Visits of 14 Nations] (Bangkok: Kasem Bannakit Press, 1961). Chalerm Wutthikosit, *Sadet Yuan Saharat Amerika* [Royal Visit to the United States] (Bangkok: Phrae Phitthaya Press, 1960). W. Na Pramuanmak (pseud.), *Sadet Phraratchadamoen Pakisathan Sahaphantharat Malaya* [Royal Trips to Pakistan and Malaya] (Bangkok: Phrachan Press, 1963). Mom Chao Wiphawadi Rangsit, *Sadet Phraratchadamnoen Pakisathan, Ph.S. 2505* [Royal Visit to Pakistan, 1962] (Bangkok: Ruamsan Press, 1972).

[65] After Sarit's death, the king only visited four more countries—England in 1966, Iran in 1967, and the United States and Canada in 1967.

[66] Watcharaphon, *Sadet Yuan 14 Prathet,* p. 6

[67] Ibid., p. 8.

government, and the Thai people. Through them, the foreign public became more aware of Thailand and more ready to believe that the Thais were civilized and sophisticated. Thus the king accomplished what Sarit could never have done, and Thailand was not so much identified by its "vulgar" government, but by the graciousness of its monarch and queen.[68]

Upon the return of the king and queen from the United States and Europe, the government prepared one of the largest celebrations ever held in Bangkok. Posters and welcoming signs were erected throughout the capital, and festivities were arranged in many centers. Movies, shows, puppet plays, music, and fireworks were exhibited at four main areas in Bangkok, and the public was given the chance to share in welcoming and celebrating the return of the king to the country. This elaborate plan was carried out to help generate public enthusiasm for the throne, as well as to indicate to the king himself that the government was willing to support the activities of the monarchy as long as the monarchy reciprocated by reinforcing the government's authority.

DOMESTIC LEGITIMIZING FUNCTIONS

In 1957, the monarchy provided initial legitimacy and sanction for a new elite that had seized political power, but which still lacked a firm basis for future control of the government. We have seen how, when Sarit staged his coup against Phibun and Phao, his position was supported by the throne.[69] In a letter addressed to Sarit, the king expressed his confidence in the Marshal and urged him to carry out the duties of government. This document was given wide publicity and became Sarit's legal sanction. The throne's official acceptance of the government was seen as adequate proof of its legitimacy in the eyes of the bureaucracy and general public.

The government was also aware that, through addresses to the nation, the king was in a position to influence public opinion. His voice was usually taken as that of a statesman; he was perceived as a genuine protector of the interests of the nation. It was hard for the Thai public to envision the monarch as someone who might not be concerned for the future of the country whose past had been shaped and protected

---

[68] It is also possible to view this tour as an attempt by the Eisenhower administration to help boost the stability of the Sarit regime. The tour in the United States was the most lavish of all, and press coverage was extensive. Thailand was emerging as an important ally of the United States in Asia, and perhaps the Eisenhower administration wished to introduce the country to the American public. Thus the king's visit was a way to play down the repressive character of the Thai government and present Thailand through a more favorable image—an attractive royal pair.

Another way to bolster the regime's respectability was by attempting to link the Thai monarchy to "international monarchy." Ten of the twenty-three states visited were monarchies. Thus the king's trips to the various countries served the purpose of creating identifications with European and Asian royalty who in turn reciprocated the visits by coming to Bangkok. Among the list of royalty who visited Thailand after the king's trips in 1960 were King Leopold (1963), King Chaosisawangwatthana of Laos (1963), Queen Juliana (1963), Princess Margrethe of Denmark (1963), the King and Queen of Belgium (1964), and the King and Queen of Malaysia (1964). Other royal personages continued to come to Thailand; the British royal family visited Bangkok in 1972.

[69] The king signed into law a decree granting amnesty to the coup leaders of October 20, 1958. See *Ratchakitcha* vol. 76, section 41, 1959, p. 1. It has been widely rumored that the king refused to do the same after the Thanom coup of 1971, indicating somewhat his displeasure.

by his own ancestors. This faith, coupled with the traditional beliefs surrounding kingship—*phokhun, thewarat, chakraphat, chao phaendin, thotsaphiratchatham*—rendered the king's advice powerfully authoritative with the public.[70] Because the king was believed to represent the national interest better than any particular political or military leader, it was prudent for the Sarit regime to cultivate the throne's trust and active support. The king's boycott of the Twenty-Fifth Centennial Buddhist Celebrations had significantly helped discredit Phibun and Phao in the eyes of the public. Indeed Sarit had used their embarrassment to help justify his coup. Thus by persuading the monarch to make speeches and pronouncements on behalf of the government, Sarit gained public credibility for his programs and policies.

While in his past addresses to the nation on New Year's Day, the king had refrained from mentioning the government or showing any outward support for government policies, his address in 1961 was marked by praise for the regime:

> Regarding the domestic scene, I am glad that you live in peace and happiness. Also, the government is trying to promote national development in a most competent way. Today, with the cooperation of responsible public officials and experts in various fields, the government has drawn up a plan to revitalize the economy and improve the education of the people. This plan will be implemented this year. I believe that it will be useful for the nation. However, it is most important that programs be carried out under the plan with unified help from all sides. Only then would the nation profit. I hope that you will cooperate with the government on these matters in the future.[71]

In addition, the king warned the public of political instability in Laos, although he did not mention that country by name. He urged the people to be aware that:

> ... currently, international relation are in flux, and there is tension in all areas of the world. Even in our neighboring countries, events have taken place that cause great concern, and these events will invariably affect our national security. Because of this, I ask you to remain peaceful for the sake of the nation.[72]

In these two passages we see the king first wielding his authority in favor of the Sarit plan for *phatthana*, and then, by urging the people to remain peaceful and calm, indirectly asking the public to support the government's policy on Laos and Cambodia.

The following year the king again commended the government for trying its best to promote national security and economic development and asked the public to cooperate with these regime goals. He also warned the people not to pay heed to the divisive propaganda of the communists whose infiltration was threatening the

---

[70] *Thewarat*, deva raja; *chakraphat*, wheelrolling emperor; *chao phaendin*, lord of the land.

[71] Phumiphon Adunyadet, King of Thailand, "Phraratchadamrat Phraratchathan kae Prachachon Chao Thai nai Okat Wan Khun Pi Mai, Ph.S. 2504 [Royal New Year Address to the Thai People, 1961]," in *Phraratchadamrat lae Phrabaromarachowat khong Phrabat Somdet Phrachaoyuhua Phumiphon Adunyadet lae Somdet Phranangchao Sirikit Phrabaromarachini* [Speeches and Advice of His Majesty King Phumiphon Adunyadet and Her Majesty Queen Sirikit] (Bangkok: Bandansat Press, 1966), p. 110.

[72] Ibid., p. 111.

country.[73] On August 12, 1962, the king addressed a meeting of commune and village leaders from the Northeast to warn them against adverse propaganda and subversion. He urged them to think about national unity and integration and told them that:

> Being Thai does not necessarily depend on the religion one follows nor the customs and language used. There may be variations, but we are all Thai. We follow the same flag and share common aspirations.[74]

It has become customary since this time for the king to remind the people during each new year of the importance of national security and the threats from within and without.

Increasingly then, the king echoed the government's stress on the great danger of communist subversion—and this naturally, if implicitly, underscored the importance of the military and police in national administration. Through his speeches on this theme, the king in effect helped to legitimize the role of the military in Thai politics by strongly urging the public to support the government's internal security policies.

In return for this support, Sarit did much to strengthen and secure the monarchy. The position of the king was made more central under the Interim Constitution,[75] and Sarit staged public spectacles demonstrating military allegiance to the throne. The royal conferring of *Chaichalermphon* flags on regiments—an occasion at which the troops swore allegiance to throne and flag—became a major military ceremony under Sarit. It has been pointed out by Sarit's biographers that even in 1963, when the prime minister was very sick, he forced himself to attend the annual rite despite protests from his doctors. Even on his deathbed, Sarit was honored by the visit of the king and queen. To show his loyalty to the throne, Sarit took the king's hand and placed it on his head. This picture was widely circulated to show the close relationship Sarit had with the monarchy, for it was not customary for a subject to touch the king's person.[76]

On the occasion of the king's birthday on December 5, 1952, and only a year after Sarit became prime minister, the Army's 21st Regiment was transferred to palace duties and the queen became its honorary commanding colonel.[77] Sarit also asked the king to accept the honorary positions of Commandant of the Army Academy, Commander of the 1st Infantry Regiment, the 11th Infantry Regiment, the 1st Calvary Regiment, the 1st Artillery Regiment, and the 1st Engineers Regiment, all of which constituted part of the royal guards.[78] In his address to the king on the occasion, Sarit briefly outlined the role that the king was to play in the future. Because of its importance, the main part of the speech is reproduced below:

---

[73] Ibid., pp. 130, 131.

[74] Ibid., p. 144. "Phraratchadamrat Phraratchathan nai Kanobrom Kamnan Phuyaiban nai Khet Chaidaen Phaktawanok Chiengnua [Royal Address to the Conference of Commune and Village Heads from the Northeast]," August 12, 1962.

[75] The king's position was invoked throughout the document.

[76] After his death, the king sponsored Sarit's cremation rites and declared national mourning.

[77] This regiment went to Korea and Vietnam.

[78] Kongthap Bok [Army], *Yingduai Phrabarami Anuson* (Bangkok: n.p., 1959), p. 22.

It is clear to all both within the country and abroad that your majesty has followed the guidelines of *thotsaphiratchatham* in national affairs and has been the most exalted leader of the nation. Your majesty is very farsighted and is genuinely concerned with the development of the country. One year has passed under the *pattiwat* system, and your majesty has shown that you are a king of great ability and interested in the work of the government, although these involve new methods and plans brought about by the *pattiwat*. You have advised and cautioned me and others to carry out our duties faithfully for the development of the nation and the happiness of the people. All your ideas have been useful and have provided constant encouragement for this government.

I would like to ask for your royal indulgence to state to you from the bottom of my heart that your subjects have realized your great kindness and will revere you within our hearts. All this is because you have a personality worthy of worship. Your visits to the countryside have swayed the hearts of your people towards unity within the nation. Regardless of their race or creed, your subjects are happy with your interest, which has reduced divisive thoughts and unified the country. No other person could have done this. Your activities are comparable to those of King Phrachulachomklao, whose statue is before us. Referring to the hearts of the people, one could guarantee that your majesty is a king who will go down in our history as one who is truly loved and respected by the people.

The love and enthusiasm for you does not merely exist within the country. Foreigners also praise your illustrious personality. Diplomats and foreign dignitaries who have had the opportunity to meet you have spread your fame. It has become internationally well-known that Thailand is lucky to have a king worthy of worship. Therefore, I firmly believe that your state visits this coming year will be beneficial to Thailand and the country's foreign relations. [79]

The sentiments expressed here were put into effect in various interesting ways. For example, when Sarit visited the southern provinces in April 1960, he was concerned enough by what he saw to stress anew the need for better national integration.[80] Aside from telling the public after his return to Bangkok that it was not too late to remedy the situation and that ethnic Thais should settle in the South, he arranged for a seventy-member delegation of southern Thai Muslims to have an audience with the king in 1961.[81] These audiences continued, and from that time on the king regularly attended Muslim Maulid ceremonies marking the birth date of the Prophet.

The government was also instrumental in reviving traditional festivals and ceremonies connected with the Thai monarchy. Many of these had been neglected

---

[79] Sarit Thanarat, "Khamkrabthawai Bangkhomthun khong Phubanchakan Thahan Bok nai Kansuansanam nuang nai Phraratchaphithi Chalerm Phrachonmaphansa [Speech of the Commander-in-Chief of the Army during the Parade to Celebrate the King's Birthday]," December 7, 1959, in ibid., pp. 22–24.

[80] Sarit Thanarat, "Khamprasai nai Kanpaitruad Ratchakan Phak Tai," May 2, 1960, in *Pramuan Sunthoraphot* I, pp. 169–172.

[81] Samnak Ratchalekhathikan [Royal Secretariat], File "Phraratchakit Pracham Wan [Daily Royal Activities]," 1961. This is a semi-official file kept on the daily activities of the king and queen. It covers royal audiences, ceremonies that the king and queen (and other royal representatives) attended, and other general activities.

after the 1932 Revolution. While the regime's main concern was to enhance the monarchy and to strengthen the government's legitimacy, Sarit believed that the revival of some of these traditional ceremonies would promote national unity through the public demonstration of aspects of Thailand's cultural heritage that could be shared by all.[82]

A good example of this cultural revivalism was the Raek Nakhwan, or First Plowing, ceremony, which probably dates from the time of Sukhothai.[83] Simply stated, the ceremony is a brahmanical rite to insure a good harvest, as well as to predict rainfall and the right types of crop to plant. For this ceremony, a substitute king, Phraya Raek Na, is appointed; his election is usually determined by his official position in the bureaucracy. Before the plowing, the Phraya Raek Na blindly chooses a *phanung*,[84] and its length determines the prediction for rain. After the plowing, the Phraya Raek Na sows seeds made potent by *mon* (mantras) chanted by Brahmanical priests and Buddhist monks. After this, seven types of food are presented before an ox to see which he will choose. The one he fancies is predicted to be the most likely to grow in great abundance during the next year.[85]

Prior to the reign of Rama IV, the plowing ceremony, then known as Phraratchaphithi Chot Phranangkhan, was a purely Brahmanical ceremony. Rama IV added a Buddhist component and was the instigator of the elaborate public spectacle involving a Phraratchaphithi Phutmongkhon complete with four queens to accompany the substitute king.[86] These two ceremonies were discontinued in 1936 and were not practiced again until 1947, during Phibun's cultural revitalization program. Phibun only reinstated the Phraratchaphithi Phutmongkhon in which the king merely went to the temple to pray for good crops. The colorful plowing ceremony was not performed again until 1950, when Sarit was prime minister. Under Sarit's leadership, the two ceremonies were brought back to their former splendor with much fanfare, and the king and queen attended the ceremonies. People from all over the country came for this ceremony and at the end of the rite,

---

[82] The crucial difference between Sarit's and Phibun's cultural programs lay in the role and importance of the throne. Phibun minimized the centrality of the throne, while Sarit did exactly the opposite.

[83] The best source for explaining this ceremony is Chulalongkorn, King of Thailand, *Ruang Phraratchaphithi Sipsong Duan* [Treatise on the Royal Ceremonies of the Twelve Months] (Bangkok: National Archives, 1920). The king died before finishing the volume, and there were no ceremonies recorded for the eleventh month. A good English source is H. Quaritch Wales, *Siamese State Ceremonies* (Hertford: Steven Austin and Sons, 1931), chapter XXI. Other contemporary sources are: Siphanom Singthong, *Phraratchaphithi khong Kasat Thai* [Royal Ceremonies of Thai Kings] (Bangkok: Odeon Store Press, 1962); Ukharin Wiriyaburana, comp., *Praphaeni Thai Chabab Phramaharatchakhru* [Thai Customs, Phramaharatchakhru edition] (Bangkok: Prachak Witthaya Press, 1969). The compiler is engaged in conducting Brahmanical ceremonies, and his work is a compilation of the ceremonies that he studied from the Chief Brahman. Also see Phatthayakon (pseud.), *Mongkhon Phithi Sipsong Duan Pracham Chat Thai* [Auspicious Ceremonies of the Thai Nation during the Twelve Months] (Bangkok: Kasem Bannakit Press, 1964); Thawiwong Thawansak, "Phraratchaphithi Prachampi nai Ratchakan Patchuban [Annual Ceremonies of the Present Reign]," in *Phraratchathan Pluengsop Phon Tho Phraya Siharatritthikrai* [Cremation Volume of Lt. General Phraya Siharatritthikrai], (Bangkok: n.p., 1969).

[84] A sarong-like garment.

[85] The seven types of food are paddy, maize, peas, sesame, liquor, water, and grass.

[86] Siphanom, *Phraratchaphithi khong Kasat Thai*, p. 348.

they descended on the newly ploughed field to scrounge for the "blessed" seeds. These seeds were believed to bring luck and prosperity and they were mixed with seeds to be planted later or kept in money sacks to bring good fortune.

A majority of Thais are Buddhists, and the king is in theory the protector, patron, and most devout member of the Buddhist community. Besides being a future Buddha, the king must rule according to Buddhist teachings. Seeing government support for Buddhist religious affairs as conducive to reinforcing the Thai social fabric and national unity, the Sarit regime encouraged the king to set a good public example of religious piety. The royal *kathin* ceremony[87] had been played down in the constitutional period: the royal *kathin* procession down the river in gilded barges was discontinued in the 1930s. This ceremony was now revitalized under Sarit's leadership and the barges were repaired and refurbished.

The *kathin* ceremony is purely Buddhist in contrast to many other ceremonies connected with Thai kingship. Wales has made a good functional analysis of the *kathin* ceremony and concludes that it was important to Thai society in three ways:

1. The king, by the lavishness of his gifts and his personal profession of faith at the altar, impresses upon the people in a truly regal way his belief in the national religion, and thus reinforces the love and respect which the people have for their monarch;
2. The example of the king inspires the people with a desire to emulate his generosity, and by means of the *Kathinas* undertaken by nobles and private persons, which take place on a smaller scale all over the country, every monastery is provided for and the growth of the Buddhist religion is stimulated;
3. The Royal Kathina processions by land and by water are almost the only occasions, other than the Coronation, during which the people can see their monarch pass by amidst the pomp and circumstance characteristic of Old Siam.[88]

In an additional effort to promote national unity and integration through religion, the king was also induced to present robes to monks at monasteries outside as well as within the capital; to perform the ritual of raising the *chofa* of newly constructed temples;[89] and to attend *Wisakhabucha* ceremonies (commemorating the birth, enlightenment, and death of the Buddha) in different parts of the country.

One other interesting role that the monarchy increasingly performed under the Sarit regime was that of legitimizer of newly emerging elites in Thai society. After Sarit's *pattiwat*, the business sector experienced rapid growth. Prominent military and civilian bureaucrats became more and more involved in business enterprises, both directly and indirectly. In the process, marriage relationships developed between elite bureaucratic and newly wealthy business families. To provide a kind of "spiritual" sanction for this elite convergence, the monarchy was extensively employed. In the early period of his reign, the present king performed marriages for members of the royalty and a few members of the political elite. While this has continued, we find that, more and more often, the king has been performing

---

[87] Presenting monks with new robes.

[88] Wales, *Siamese State Ceremonies*, pp. 200, 201.

[89] This is swan-like protrusion at the top of the roof of the temple.

marriages between sons and daughters of these groups and those of the emerging business elite. Since Thai society is very status conscious, the performance of marriages by the king is seen *ipso facto* as conferring elite status. Thus the king in effect performs the function of helping to consolidate a complex of alliances between political, royal, bureaucratic, and business families.[90]

POLITICAL DONATIONS AND REGIME PROGRAM SUPPORT

An important function of the throne which has been overlooked by scholars of modern Thai politics has been its ability to attract donations for charity and building projects, which helped to demonstrate the genuine paternalism of the regime as well as of the throne. Unlike other political systems, where political donations are commonly made to political parties, this practice is not prevalent in Thailand. Perhaps because of the ephemeral nature of Thai political parties and their narrow social base, they do not attract financial support from the public. This is true in the case of government parties. We have seen how Phao had to supply the Seri Manangkhasila Party with funds obtained from the control and sale of opium. Later, when Sarit organized the Sahaphum and Chatsangkhom Parties, he had to finance them through his "own" funds from the Lottery Bureau.

But especially after 1963, donations offered to the king for charity and social welfare work increased substantially. Through this extra-budgetary channel, buildings, hospitals, and new schools were erected without draining government funds; this practice continues even to the present. Because of the increasing popularity and prestige of the throne, private citizens and organizations made sizeable contributions to charity and to educational foundations established by the monarchy. In many cases, donations were clearly marked for use in anti-communist programs, indicating the effectiveness of the government in identifying the throne with anti-communism and using the throne to convince the public that "security" was a national priority. Through donations to the throne, the regime was able to tap private financial resources for use in various projects that would have strained the budget if they had been underwritten with government funds. Thus the regime's investment in the king paid off in the form of financial contributions that flowed indirectly into government hands.

Donations for charity and to monasteries are popular Thai forms of alms-giving and merit-making. Some observers of Thai society have commented that private financial resources have not been put to good public and civic use because charitable contributions—in the form of land and money—are so heavily invested in building pagoda and temples, since these activities bring the donor the greatest merit. However, because the throne came to command such great prestige, donating to the king became a kind of status symbol, for in addition to making religious merit, such

---

[90] In general, looking at the family names, the majority of those honored are still from royalty, the military, and civilian bureaucracy. File, "Phraratchakit Pracham Wan," 1953-1971. From 1953 to 1957, the king married twenty-eight couples, all of whom had had either royal or political backgrounds. Between 1958 and 1963, fifty-two couples were married by the king. While the majority were from elite families, some business families were also involved. Between 1964 and 1971, 192 couples were married by the king. While the names of some identified them as members of wealthy business families, it is hard to make firm generalizations because of the incomplete nature of the data.

donations often secure medals and decorations from the throne.[91] Hence we find that the throne took on the function of channeling money intended for merit-making and redirected it from primarily religious projects into other social activities. A systematic recording of donations began to be kept in the file "Phraratchakit Pracham Wan" in 1963. Not all donations were recorded, for some were put immediately to use.[92]

From Table 16 below, a few things seem to be clear. The donations made by the public to the throne have mainly been for social work. While donations were made for religious purposes, they did not constitute the bulk of the money contributed. The largest amount of money donated went to the Red Cross, which is chaired by the queen. The Thai Red Cross performs many social welfare functions, mainly in health and medicine. The second largest category was for education. Most of the money was given to the Ananda Mahidol and Nowaruk Foundations, the rest being split between donations for school buildings and supplies for needy students.[93]

We also find periodical donations made in the event of natural calamities. In such cases, rice and medicine were donated in addition to money. In most cases, the king would transfer these funds to the government and instruct it to use them to help the victims. Funds received for this purpose and for general social welfare were used by the government to extend its paternalistic reach beyond the span allowed by its actual budgetary capabilities.

Interestingly enough, after 1955 a new category appeared. This consisted of donations made for anti-communist programs and for insuring the welfare of the border police and soldiers in their struggle with the insurgents.[94]

In the nine years for which data are available, we can see that the public donated over 120 million baht to the throne for various purposes. (It should also be kept in mind that there were sizeable material donations as well, but these were not recorded in the available sources.)

What is particularly interesting is that donations to the king were made by a wide spectrum of people and organizations. Private citizens and private organizations constituted the bulk of the donors. Businesses, both domestic and foreign, also made substantial contributions. The frequency of contributions from student groups increased steadily through this period, especially in organizing charity affairs and participating in the annual Red Cross Bazaar. Government agencies and the armed forces also provided periodic contributions of moderate

---

[91] Media coverage also encourages this activity.

[92] Mr. Manop Sirinthu, Assistant Secretary to the Privy Council, believes that the king acted as middleman, receiving donations and directing them to appropriate authorities. Other favors that the king performs involve choosing the names for infants and giving people new surnames. These names themselves are marks of status. Although compared to the national budget, the total amount of the donations received by the king is relatively small, it nevertheless provides him with a means to act on his own and create a psychological impact on the public.

[93] The Ananthamahidon and Nowaruk Foundations were established to support education. The latter was usually applied to Chiengmai University.

[94] Another aspect of this development was the throne's personal patronage of the strategic mountain tribes. The king made frequent visits to the north to distribute clothing, food, and medicine. He organized rain-making teams that were used to help the farmers, as well as to conduct activities related to counterinsurgency. Farmers took up collections to purchase more planes for the king's rain-making efforts. The army was jealous of the throne's success in this venture and wanted to organize its own rival team. Interview with a confidential source.

Table 16
Donations Received by the King, 1963–1971
(in thousand baht; US$1 = 20 baht)

Year	Religion	Social Welfare	Education	Red Cross	Hospital Medicine	Anti-communism	Disaster Victims	Royal Discretion	Others	Total
1963	–	151	886	360	–	–	415	1,956	230	3,998
1964	304	–	1,195	1,198	1,100	–	–	150	748	4,695
1965	906	1,559	1,594	1,223	1,628	–	–	590	320	7,820
1966	100	631	1,217	2,757	560	200	31	650	79	6,225
1967	1,610	15	10,741	3,109	2,210	3	340	341	713	19,088
1968	1,081	1,382	2,730	8,477	2,086	2,006	–	1,606	220	19,588
1969	100	519	1,391	5,001	1,565	1,368	1,530	3,633	1,463	16,570
1970	1,200	247	1,575	6,472	6,242	566	1,526	4,359	955	23,322
1971	–	494	4,102	3,355	1,040	904	461	6,292	3,127	19,775
Total	*5,301*	*4,998*	*25,437*	*31,952*	*16,431*	*5,047*	*4,303*	*19,757*	*7,855*	*121,081*

Source: *Samnak Ratchalekhathikan*, file "Phraratchakit Pracham Wan," 1963–1971

sums. Even *samlo* drivers got into the act and demonstrated their support for the throne from time to time.[95] In general, the composition of the donor groups suggests that the king was able to move closer to his subjects and that the monarchy developed a new, more "human," image as a result of these activities.

Clearly, this popularization of the throne, encouraged by Sarit, substantially altered the kinds of activities in which the king became engaged. The parameters of this change are suggested by Table 17, below, which analyzes the daily activities of the king from 1954 to 1971. The table categorizes the monarch's activities according to the type of functions he attended.[96]

During the Phibun period, we can see that the king was effectively restricted to the role of titular head of state. He attended government affairs, received foreign dignitaries, performed traditional and state ceremonies, conducted private ceremonies connected with the kingship, and rarely gave audiences to private citizens. The only time he went to visit his subjects was the trip to the Northeast in 1955. His popularity during that tour was so unnerving to Phibun that no funds were made available for future tours.

With the advent of the Sarit regime in 1958, the king began to give audiences to the private sector, and more foreign dignitaries were presented to him. It was the policy of the government to increase the prestige and popularity of the king by making him more accessible to these groups. While the king still did not go out much to visit his subjects, he was sent abroad to represent the country and to promote goodwill with other nations. Domestic tours were handled by Sarit himself. Particularly after 1961, the king granted audiences to private citizens and groups on a scale hitherto unimaginable. Together with the fact that the king spent more time attending to the affairs of the private sector, this clearly indicates that the throne was developing links with the rising (private) Thai middle-class. Undoubtedly, the government initially encouraged this development, but as the position of the throne became stronger with time and the king expanded his contacts with the public, it became harder for the regime to exercise firm control and direction over the monarchy. Towards the end of the Sarit regime, and more so after his death, the king increased his interaction with the students. While originally he had done little more than hand out graduation certificates annually, now he began to visit the campuses, to attend student affairs, and generally make himself more accessible to the student body. In 1966, the king began to visit the people, and as the years passed, his visits increased in frequency. The king's newly powerful position in national politics was evidenced by the number of scheduled audiences with the prime minister and other cabinet members. After the death of Sarit, the Thanom government turned increasingly to the king for support and advice. The large number of audiences in

---

[95] Pedicabs were banned from the capital area by Sarit in 1959, but motorized trishaws still existed.

[96] The category "recreation and entertainment" was left out because it was difficult to determine whether an affair attended was for charity or for pleasure. Under this category one might include summer holiday trips to Hua Hin and Chiengmai. It is also customary for the king to attend horse races to raise funds and to be present at annual balls attended by students who have studied abroad. However, recently the kings has been represented by some other high royalty or official. Activities of the throne increased in the early 1970s, when the king and queen had to separate to attend different functions. The Royal Secretary revealed in a conversation that the king was truly interested in national affairs and regularly summoned the prime minister and members of the cabinet to keep him abreast of issues. Many of these meetings were not officially recorded.

1964 and 1965 indicate that the Thanom government particularly needed the support of the throne to be able to weather the Sarit corruption scandal (See below, Conclusion). At the same time, the throne also moved closer to the military, as indicated by the number of military-sponsored events the king attended after 1963.[97]

In conclusion, it is clear that the monarchy came to exercise increasingly important functions in the politics of Thailand following the Sarit coup of 1957. The institution more and more often played the role of legitimizer of political power, supporter/legitimizer of broad regime policies, promoter and sanctioner of intra-elite solidarity, and "broker" for transferring funds from the private sector to the state treasury, in addition to becoming the symbolic focus for national unity. These dramatic changes were the result of the policies of Sarit, whose political thinking, with its emphasis on recreating a stable, traditionalist, three-tiered society, and search for legitimacy for a "second generation" politico-military elite pushed in the same direction: toward the closest possible identification between regime and throne. But in so doing, Sarit made it possible, without perhaps intending this result, for the monarchy to grow strong enough to play an independent role after his death. The relative political weakness of Sarit's successors brought the throne even more clearly to the center of the political stage.

---

[97] Close identification between the monarchy and the military is reflected in the fact that the king and queen frequently wear military uniforms to visit their subjects as well as when attending various government functions. Also, the Crown Prince was sent to Australia to study at a military academy, thus making Thailand's future king a military person.

Table 17

Activities of the Thai Monarchy, 1954-1971 (frequencies of occurrence)

Year	Gov't Functions	Military Functions	Private Sector Functions	Cabinet Audiences	Bureaucr'l Audience	Citizen Group Audience	Foreign Dignit'ry Audience	Royal Audience Ceremony	Tradit'l Ceremony	Private Ceremony	Meetings With Students	Meetings With Subjects	Visits Abroad
1954	18	10	17	3	14	2	24	12	27	11	0	1	0
1955	10	18	15	7	12	0	40	7	25	21	0	7	0
1956	8	5	17	1	1	1	31	2	18	22	0	0	0
1957	22	7	15	6	7	1	25	6	34	12	0	0	0
1958	8	6	28	1	11	7	61	10	36	17	0	6	0
1959	5	9	39	11	10	9	59	4	28	23	0	0	1
1960	5	3	26	5	5	5	52	5	30	17	0	0	2
1961	22	9	35	1	10	45	66	10	24	26	3	0	14
1962	16	5	46	9	12	67	102	10	33	22	1	0	3
1963	20	17	43	7	21	91	99	13	31	29	3	3	3
1964	26	18	71	20	23	79	22	4	26	22	8	5	0
1965	16	11	73	18	18	18	92	12	41	28	14	0	0
1966	16	18	71	13	16	116	98	11	58	27	9	5	0
1967	19	21	75	13	17	115	117	9	43	26	10	17	3
1968	38	23	84	9	32	154	87	11	38	19	16	20	0
1969	21	22	117	13	35	139	98	13	52	13	16	23	0
1970	16	26	102	10	26	190	116	9	41	12	7	25	0
1971	22	20	121	8	26	191	85	8	54	20	10	31	0

Source: *Samnak Ratchalekhathikan, file "Phraratchakit Pracham Wan," 1954-1971*

Sarit originated the idea of the Royal Guards Oath of Loyalty to the King and instituted the ceremony as public pageantry, January 3, 1962.

The Supreme Military Commander inspecting troops from the three military forces pledging their allegiance to the national victory flag, Equestrian Monument Plaza, November 8, 1963. Sarit was very sick by this time.

A week before Sarit's death, the King visited him, and against court tradition, Sarit asked for permission to hold the king's hand and placed it on his forehead as a sign of his ultimate devotion to the crown.

CONCLUSION

Sarit's career ended on a sour note. Shortly after his death, it became evident that he had misappropriated a large amount of government funds for personal entertainment and investment in business ventures. While it had been an open secret that the prime minister had an insatiable appetite for sex, the public was not aware of the extent of his wealth nor the sources of his riches. This unsavory side of Sarit was a shock to the public, which had just witnessed elaborate ceremonies and eulogies commending the "greatness" of the man. After the initial shock, however, the public settled back and enjoyed the drama of the fight over the division of Sarit's wealth between Thanphuying Wichitra, his last wife, and his children from previous marriages. On balance, Sarit came out quite well, while the "villain" in the affair was identified as his "greedy" wife. Corruption was not novel to Thai politics, but apparently a leader who could get things done was. Thus, in spite of the scandalous revelations, many people still believed that Sarit was better than past leaders. According to their logic, although it was true Sarit had *kin* (literally "eaten", i.e., taken money), the country nevertheless prospered. In contrast, many others had *kin* but were unable to achieve any visible results for their administration.

THE SCANDAL

One month after the death of Sarit, his heirs began to quarrel over the division of the prime minister's large fortune.[1] On February 14, 1964, Sarit's seven children sued Wichitra for trying to deprive them of their rightful shares.[2] Because of its dramatic appeal, the public became very interested in the case, and the news media picked it up as the ultimate scandal of modern Thai times. Public interest in the trial forced the Thanom government to intervene and investigate the background of Sarit's affluence.

The reading of Sarit's will took place at Thanom's house in the presence of lawyers and prominent military officers close to Sarit. The will itself was dated February 19, 1959, shortly after Sarit became prime minister. The main points in the document stated that all of Sarit's wealth would be left solely to his wife, Wichitra, with the condition that she give her stepsons, Settha and Somchai, one million baht

---

[1] Khon Khao boe "O" (pseud.), *Buanglang Khadi Moradok 2,874 lan* [Inside Story of the 2,874 million baht Inheritance] (Bangkok: Chaichana Press, 1964). Wat (pseud.), *Suk Ching Moradok* [Battle over the Inheritance] (Bangkok: Mit Charoen Press, 1964). Khon Khao (pseud.), *Buanglang Phinaikam Chomphon Sarit Thanarat* [Inside Story of Marshal Sarit Thanarat's Will] (Bangkok: Prachak Witthaya Press, 1964). All these books written by newsmen give thorough accounts of the court battle over Sarit's inheritance.

[2] The principle plaintiffs were Lt. Colonel Settha and Lt. Somchai Thanarat, Sarit's eldest sons by his first wife. The other five children were represented by their mothers. The defendants were Wichitra , her mother (Sarit's cousin), Sanguan Chantarasakha (Sarit's half-brother), and Sanguan's wife (Wichitra 's sister).

each and a house appropriate to their positions. This provision, however, would be carried out only if Sarit's total cash assets were in excess of ten million baht. In addition his farm was to be divided equally between his two eldest sons.

The plaintiffs contended that Sarit had written another will which was destroyed by Wichitra following an illegal raid of Sarit's personal hide-away at the First Division camp.[3] They accused Wichitra of trying to hoard all of Sarit's wealth, which they claimed amounted to 2,874,009,794 baht (approximately 140 million dollars), plus many intangibles that could not be accounted for. Wichitra, on the other hand, countered by saying that there was only twelve million baht that she knew of.

While waiting for the outcome in the courts, Sarit's children petitioned Thanom to use his special authority under Article 17 of the Constitution to investigate the whole matter. After a brief deliberation, the government felt that if it did not act swiftly, it would be jeopardizing its position vis-à-vis the public, Thus, on June 16, 1964, Thanom announced that he was invoking Article 17 to confiscate Sarit's wealth and establish an investigating committee to determine the extent of Sarit's corruption.

Through the work of this committee, it was found that Sarit had used government funds to maintain his mistresses and invest in business.[4] The three major items of interest to the government were approximately 394 million baht belonging to the Secret Investigation Fund of the Prime Minister's Office, 240 million baht from the Lottery Bureau, and about 100 million baht that should have gone to the army from its percentage cut from the sale of lottery tickets.[5]

During the investigation, the Director-General of the Commerce Department revealed that Sarit and Wichitra held an interest in forty-five companies. One of their largest holdings was in the Bangkok Gunny Sack Company, amounting to over twenty million baht. Later, a member of the board of directors of the company testified that these shares had been transferred to two of Sarit's brothers. This meant that Sarit had made considerable profits from the rice industry, which was forced by law to buy gunny sacks from the company. Aside from stocks and large bank accounts, Sarit had possession of a tremendous amount of land: the Director of the Land Department said that Sarit owned over twenty thousand rai of land in the countryside, and innumerable plots in and around Bangkok. In cash reserves at various banks, Sarit had some four hundred and ten million baht, which was confiscated to determine whether any of it belonged to the government.[6]

The fight over Sarit's wealth was finally resolved by the court in a decision rendered on October 22, 1964. The court proposed a compromise, whereby Wichitra and Lt. Colonel Settha would become co-executors of the will and any settlements

---

[3] Sarit maintained a house-cum-harem there, which was off-limits to Wichitra . He usually spent his time there among his mistresses. Sarit also had other mistresses located around Bangkok in houses he had ordered built for them. In general, the titles to the land were not given to these mistresses until they proved themselves trustworthy. In most cases, the titles were registered in the name of one of his close military aides. See Phichit Santiraksa, *Rang Sawat lang Phon 1* [Love Nest Behind the First Division] (Bangkok: Phatthana Press, 1964). Dom Daenthai, *Chomphon khong Khun Nunu* [The Girls' Marshal] (Bangkok: Kiatisak Press, 1964). The authors compiled a list of eighty-one women in Sarit's life.

[4] See *Samut Pokkhao* [White Notebook], published sometime in late 1964.

[5] Wat, *Suk Ching Moradok*, p. 581.

[6] Thanom Kittikhachon, Press interview, *Sayam Nikon*, July 17, 1964.

would be made privately, conditional upon the final outcome of the government investigation.

SARIT'S POLITICAL LEGACY

Despite his corruption, Sarit had left his mark firmly on Thai politics. People still debate whether he intended to return the money to the government, whether his position as *pattiwat* leader compelled him to centralize his position through the control of the government's finances on a personal basis, or whether he was an out-and-out swindler. Many Thais see Wichitra as the greedy villain who tried to claim all of Sarit's riches, even those that belonged to the government. Some still believe that, because of the delicate nature of secret service investigations and the highly centralized nature of the prime ministership, Sarit had to transfer government funds to his own bank accounts to facilitate his particular style of leadership. But the interesting thing is that, while the public in general did condemn him for using government funds for his own personal enjoyment, he was widely admired for having the effrontery to acquire mistresses on such a grand scale. Practically no one was immune to his overtures—beauty queens, movie stars, night club hostesses, university and secondary school students, the young and not so young. His elaborate network of procurers was the envy of many.

It seems that it was precisely his paradoxical image and interesting personality that made Sarit good material for folklore. On the one hand, he was seen as the completely dedicated leader, a firm and decisive person who made great personal sacrifices for the people.[7] As the powerful *pattiwat* leader, he had been able to institute *phatthana* programs and made that concept part of Thai daily life. As a paternal leader, he had frequently visited the public to find out their needs. He was remembered as a doer and not a talker, whose firmness reduced the frequency of arson, got roads repaired, cleaned up the cities, improved communications, and advanced the economy.

On the other hand, Sarit was also seen a *nakleng*, a person who was not afraid to take risks, a person who "lived dangerously," kind to his friends but cruel to his enemies, a compassionate person, a gambler, a heavy drinker, and a lady-killer. In short, he was the kind of person who represented one central model of Thai masculinity. (The word *nakleng* itself has ambiguous connotations, but in male circles it is desirable to have friends who are *nakleng* at heart, for they will be loyal and trustworthy in times of need.)[8]

---

[7] The taking of life, especially human life, is unacceptable according to Buddhist teachings. Sarit, however, accepted all the consequences for ordering the execution of arsonists, the *phi bun*, and communist suspects. The public noted his intense involvement in the fight against arson; even when he was sick, he would immediately go to supervise fire-fighting whenever it occurred, many times against the orders of his doctors.

[8] Phaithun Khruekaew postulates that there are nine basic Thai values—wealth, power, seniority, *chit chai nakleng*, status, charity, gratitude, wisdom, and propriety in etiquette. Phaithun Khruekaew, *Laksana Sangkhom Thai* [Thai Social Characteristics] (Bangkok: Liang Sieng Chungcharoen Press, 1970), pp. 84–103. He distinguishes three components in the *nakleng* value—sportsmanship, manliness, and benevolence. See especially pp. 96-98. Interestingly enough, Sarit himself made an effort to make the idea of *nakleng* less ambiguous by popularizing the term *anthaphan*, or hooligan. In everyday language, hooligans were commonly referred to as *nakleng*, but through Sarit's example, uncontrolled, renegade *nakleng*

We may recall Sarit's orders for the public execution of arsonists and suspected communists. In those orders, Sarit accepted sole responsibility for , although to kill is highly sinful according to Buddhist ethics. Sarit was thought *nakleng* enough to take on the burden of these sins for his country.[9] The heroes of Thai folklore are often just such persons, who combine daring, courage, compassion, cruelty, and gentlemanly debauchery. Thais seem to enjoy a gentleman crook. Most popular movies and novels revolve around a leading man with such characteristics. In addition, in the not-so-distant past, kings and aristocrats maintained large retinues of concubines and wives.[10] The practice was taken as a sign of magical virility and mystical power. While one would not go so far as to suggest that Sarit attempted to imitate the life-style of the former monarchs, it is possible to say that his activities were not too severely criticized because of such recent promiscuous precedents.

Thus, while in another society, and perhaps in other situations, a scandal of such magnitude would have ruined a man's reputation, Sarit's image has weathered criticism well. It is still possible to find people making remarks such as "We need a person like Sarit to make the streets safe again," or "If only Sarit were alive, he could solve this problem." Sarit's forceful and unwavering character also profited from a sharp contrast with the character of Thanom, his successor. While people accepted Thanom as a well-meaning person, they doubted whether he could provide decisive leadership as Sarit had done.[11] It is curious in this regard that Sarit was successful in projecting an aura of *phokhun*-ship, while Thanom failed to do so.

In sum, Sarit's success depended partly upon his ability to project the *phokhun* image as a basis for legitimacy: it was an image of a strong, benevolent and decisive leader-statesman, whose responsibility was to the nation and not to groups of voters. This reputation enabled him to portray parliamentary democracy in Thailand as an obstacle to national development and the root cause of dangerous divisive tendencies. His *pattiwat* was supposed to create a political system basically Thai in form, where the leader was the father to the nation and could determine what was good and what was bad for the national family. Thus, Sarit's approach to government constituted both a break with the past and an attempt to create new links with it.

Phokhun-ship was not enough to insure long-term political control, and Sarit proved adept in generating support from other power groups in Thai society to sustain his regime. The most important of these were the bureaucracy and the throne. Through his concept of *phatthana*, he was able to provide new roles for these groups and enlist their help for his paternalistic programs. Yet one must understand

---

are more and more often described as *anthaphan*, leaving *nakleng* with decidedly better connotations than hitherto.

[9] In contrast, when Thanom ordered the executions of bank robbers and other petty criminals following his 1971 coup, the rumor was that he immediately tried to make merit and wash his hands of responsibility by inviting monks to his house for a feast.

[10] It is still a popular practice of wealthy Thai males to have a wife and, additionally, "minor wives," or mistresses.

[11] It is my suspicion that the public's continuing trust in Sarit can be traced to the fact that he was seen as having possessed the attributes of a *nakleng*, while Thanom was not. This points to a possible connection between the concept of *nakleng* and that of *phokhun* which needs further study. Since the "father" in this case ruled over so large a family as a nation, it was perhaps necessary and acceptable that the modern *phokhun* be a severe and stern person who could be compassionate or cruel as the occasion demanded.

that these programs, administered from the top down, were inaugurated to consolidate his political authority much more than to achieve national development and modernization. *Phatthana* was always oriented to the political end of legitimacy.

After the death of Sarit, Thanom was entrusted with the responsibility of carrying on his system of government. Thanom claimed at the start that his government would not depart from the guidelines laid down by the dead marshal. Government would be based on a strong executive, and development would be the government's major task. Cooperation with the throne and the bureaucracy would continue, and close relationships with the United States would be maintained.

To reinforce the ideas of Sarit and try to overcome the scandals that followed his death, Thanom presented new slogans. While Sarit had emphasized good roads, running water, and bright lights, Thanom tried to convince the public that his government was an honest one; the official slogan became "Do good, do good, do good." The government went to great lengths to point out to the public that they should not judge Sarit by his personal activities, but should remember his public deeds and principles. A revival and elaboration (with subtle changes) of Sarit's basic political philosophy was propagandized in the series of radio lectures entitled *"prachathipatai baeb Thai"* (Thai Democracy) over army radio "20." What Sarit had conveyed by personal charisma the government now attempted to project by disseminating what can almost be called the doctrines of Sarit-ism.[12]

The rapid socio-economic changes that occurred as the result of Sarit's development plans, the government's close relationship with the United States, and business generated by the Indochina war, urban expansion, and social differentiation were phenomenal in the period of the 1960s.[13] Not only did business prosper (mainly in the service sector), but more and more people flocked to the major cities looking for jobs and opportunities. With rapid urbanization came severe problems of unemployment, housing shortages, educational bottlenecks, transportation needs, a rising crime rate, and so forth, all complications that gradually led to a new mood of public disenchantment.

The problems caused by rapid urbanization, in addition to widespread rural unrest resulting from inequitable implementation of the rural development plan, plus a growing number of "floating intellectuals" produced by the unbalanced and erratic expansion of the educational system,[14] forced the Thanom government to look

---

[12] These lectures were delivered in 1965 when the Thanom government felt that it had to reassure the public of the government's intention to provide the nation with a proper constitution. It attempted to use constitutionalism ("democracy") as a legitimizing principle while making it clear that the new constitution would reflect the special characteristics of Thai society and its traditional political heritage.

[13] For a study of social differentiation and political awareness, see Joyce Nakahara and Ronald A. Witton, *Development and Conflict in Thailand*, Cornell University Thailand Project, interim Report Series, No. 14, June 1971.

[14] The figures below indicate clearly what was happening in the educational sector:

Comparison of Budget Allocations for Education, Defense, and Interior (% of Total)

	1953	1954	1955	1956	1957	1958	1959
Education	14.2	14.7	12.7	5.8	2.6	4.6	18.4
Defense	24.8	29.1	30.0	17.2	15.0	10.2	19.6
Interior	20.5	19.5	19.5	12.9	10.4	7.0	16.3

for sources of legitimacy that Sarit had not found necessary. To divert the attention of the public from social and political problems, the government announced that the Constituent Assembly had finally produced a satisfactory constitution for the country after deliberating for ten years. In 1968, this constitution was promulgated and signed by the king with great pomp and ceremony. It was well received by the public, and elections were planned for the following year. The Thanom constitution acknowledged the special characteristics of the Thai political system as envisioned by Sarit. Executive supremacy over a weak legislature was assured by providing that parliament was to be bicameral, with the Senate composed of appointed members subject to cabinet nomination.[15]

In the elections of February 10, 1969, the government party, the United Thai People's Party, in fact obtained a majority of seats in the lower house. Thus Thanom was again appointed prime minister although he was not chosen through popular vote by the electorate. While the 1969 parliament was weak and basically controlled by the government, some of its members did attempt to perform the duties of a legislative branch. At times, MPs severely criticized government policies, and there were attempts to block government budget bills. As a result, as had happened in the 1950s, the government grew increasingly unhappy with parliament.

Without having given any indication that such a plan was in the works, Thanom staged a coup d'état on November 17, 1971, and imposed martial law. It was uncanny to witness Thanom's replay of the Sarit coups of 1957 and 1958 all at once. Parliament was dissolved, political parties banned, and a Sarit-type Revolutionary Council formed. Finally, Thanom proclaimed that his coup too was *pattiwat*, though he failed to present any new rationale for this and merely restated the old Sarit

	1960	1961	1962	1963	1964	1965	1966
Education	17.3	15.4	14.9	15.6	15.4	15.3	14.3
Defense	17.8	16.6	16.9	15.6	15.4	15.5	15.0
Interior	15.1	15.0	13.9	14.3	15.5	16.9	17.1
	1967	1968	1969	1970	1971	1972	1973
Education	13.2	5.8	5.5	5.9	6.2	6.0	6.7
Defense	13.6	15.3	15.7	17.0	17.9	18.2	18.2
Interior	15.6	20.7	21.3	20.7	21.5	22.1	23.5

(*Computed from*: Bureau of the Budget, *Thailand's Budget in Brief*; and *Ratchakitchanubeksa*)

We can see that, during the Phibun regime, allocations for education were very small compared to those for defense and interior. However, beginning in 1959, Sarit saw to it that the budget for education was increased to the levels of the other two ministries. After his death in 1963, the budget for education continued to hold its own in comparison with the other two until 1968, when it drastically declined. One can thus see from these figures that there was an "education boom" between 1959 and 1968. The major increases were made at the local level; new local schools were organized for primary and secondary education. See Ministry of Education, *Educational Developments in Thailand, 1949-1963* (Bangkok: Ministry of Education, n.d.). On the university level, Chiengmai and Khonkaen Universities were established in 1964 (plans had been drawn up during Sarit's administration). In 1962, Sarit limited enrollment at Thammasat University by reducing admissions to 1,700 a year, as compared to 8,000 to 10,000 previously. However, the demands for higher education resulted in the opening of Ramkhamhaeng University in Bangkok in 1970; this new university had an open admissions policy.

[15] *Constitution of the Kingdom of Thailand*, 1968. Article 78, paragraph 2 stipulated that the Senate should be 75 percent the size of the lower house.

formula.[16] And, like Sarit, Thanom obtained a letter from the king and publicized it in the newspapers and television. He ceremoniously appeared on national television to show the people that the king's message was genuine. During this appearance, the king was symbolically present in the form of a large picture to which Thanom bowed at intervals as though he were addressing the king personally. The message for the public was clear—the Revolutionary Council had been sanctioned by the monarchy.

Although the coup was initially justified by citing "security" concerns, it was clear that many other factors were at work. The government had experienced a close call with regard to its unpopular budget in the lower house; it felt very uncertain of the position of Thailand within the changing international system following the United States-China rapprochement and the announcement of the Nixon doctrine; it faced the problem of political succession since Thanom, Praphat, and other old Sarit hands were reaching retirement age; and it was frustrated by its inability to cope with rapid and unexpected political and social change. Of these, the last two were the most immediately decisive.

Because of the effective elimination of all rivals to its leadership, the old Sarit clique in the army had to create a plan for succession and choose candidates out of its own ranks. The most obvious candidate was Thanom's young son, Lt. Colonel Narong, who was also Praphat's son-in-law. He was an ambitious army officer who openly hinted to the press that he was the one responsible for persuading his father to stage the coup. Thus the coup became a means for Narong to stake out a claim to the succession ahead of many more senior officers. (This created serious tensions within the army, a factor that weakened Thanom's position and ultimately led to his forced exile.)

Yet Thanom perceived that threats posed by new social forces to the basic political ideology of Sarit were potentially more dangerous than problems concerning succession. The sharpened political and social consciousness of a larger number of students, the growing middle class, and a more informed public began to threaten the foundations of regime supremacy: paternalism and an all-powerful political leadership. The advancement of education and the development of the mass media had made Thais much more aware than hitherto of deteriorating social conditions and political inequalities. More and more, people demanded a share in politics, and the growing popularity and power of parliament, which flourished despite tight government controls, proved alarming to the Thanom leadership. The Sarit hierarchical structure of *rat/ratthaban, kharatchakan, prachachon* seemed endangered, as the boundaries between the three tiers were visibly weakening.

It was a sign of the changes that had taken place after Sarit's death, and largely as a result of his policies, that when Thanom tried to impress the public with his *pattiwat* by ordering the execution of a few petty thieves, his actions were seen as overly harsh, and he himself was tagged not as a *nakleng,* but just a bully.[17]

---

[16] Many MPs realized that the coup was really intended to suppress the opposition and so immediately went into hiding.

[17] The rise of petty thievery was an inevitable byproduct of rapid, disorganized urbanization. But instead of trying to treat the malady, Thanom only paid attention to the symptoms. In contrast, Sarit's programs for clearing out *anthaphan* and opium users from the cities were backed up with plans to help rehabilitate them. Job training was given to former *anthaphan,* and health centers were provided for opium addicts while opium consumption and sale were outlawed.

Immediately following the coup, Thanom summoned all top bureaucrats to a "clarification" session. The response from the leadership of the *kharatchakan* was good. They readily accepted the explanations of the Revolutionary Council. However, the knowledgeable sectors of the *prachachon*, which included former MPs, students, teachers, and those who had been closely following events since 1969, were frankly skeptical of Thanom's explanation that the country faced grave internal and external dangers and that the throne was in jeopardy. Consequently, three ex-MPs filed a civil suit against the Revolutionary Council for violating the constitution. The court referred the case to the Revolutionary Council, which promptly sent the three to jail on charges of treason.

The Thanom government's repression of the parliamentarians did not generate an immediate public outcry. University students who had been very active in supervising the 1969 elections on a voluntary basis and who, judging from their publications, had been showing signs of political militancy were caught by surprise. But while the majority of the students felt a sense of despair, a few began planning future actions to regain rights of free expression, a new constitution, and national elections.

In June 1973, in reaction to unconventional tactics employed by the government in its efforts to manipulate and effectively corrupt university admissions, a number of articles appeared in student publications that indirectly attacked the government. These students were summarily expelled. This incident touched off a sizeable (20,000 participants) student demonstration that demanded and got a promise from the government that the students would be reinstated. The demonstrators also demanded a new constitution. The outcome of this incident encouraged a group of students, professors, politicians, and other prominent figures to work more vigorously for a restoration of constitutionalism. This group of citizens formed the *"klum riakrong ratthathammanun"* or "The Call for a Constitution Group." The Group was not formed secretly, but it made public the names of its member and the goals for which it was working. In early October 1973, twenty members of this group began distributing leaflets in downtown Bangkok, and thirteen were arrested by the police. They were immediately declared martyrs for democracy, and student leaders called for a mass demonstration against the government. Unlike the demonstration in June, the university students were now joined by secondary and technical school students, as well as students from the provinces. The occasion drew from 200,000 to 500,000 participants, including participants ranging from junior bureaucrats down to common vendors. The demonstrators demanded that the government release the thirteen detainees and agree to promulgate a constitution within a year. Again the government grudgingly and partially capitulated. In the meantime, some demonstrators went to see the king, who agreed to look into the whole matter on their behalf. While the students were dispersing, clashes with the police occurred.

In response, angry demonstrators attacked police stations, police outposts, and government offices. The situation reached a critical point when the government ordered in troops equipped with combat gear and backed by tanks and helicopters to suppress the protestors. This took place on October 14. But the government's attempt to suppress the demonstrators failed because it lost the backing of the key First Division, which had been historically vital in the seizure and maintenance of political power since 1947. The commander of the First Division, Lt. General Prasert Thammasiri, had been generally accepted, before Thanom's coup, as the person most likely to follow in the footsteps of Sarit and Thanom, both of whom had risen to authority from that position. For Prasert, one suspects, the student demonstration was an opportunity to eliminate his young rival, Colonel Narong. In any case, brutality by the police and soldiers resulted in a large number of civilian casualties, which angered and consolidated public opinion in demanding that Thanom, Praphat, and Narong be arrested and brought to trial for murder. At this point, the king intervened with the backing of General Kris Siwara, the army chief. Thanom and Praphat were forced to resign and go into exile. The king subsequently appointed Professor Sanya Thammasak, rector of Thammasat University and a member of the Privy Council, as prime minister. So the Sarit system came to a (temporary?) end. Sarit's political order, based upon clear divisions between *rat/ratthaban*, *kharatchakan*, and *prachachon* seemed to have disintegrated, with the top two tiers divided and the third unwilling to remain passive and accept government paternalism.

One final question may be asked: were Sarit and his system anachronisms? Is it possible that some future leader with the personal style of Sarit will capture the allegiance of the Thai public? My answer is that it is possible.[18] While we have seen that in the recent past there has been an increase in the politically aware public, and Thai society has become much more differentiated, there still exists a large section of the *prachachon* who are conservative and politically unmobilized and therefore likely to welcome the advent of a strong, decisive, and paternalistic national leader. Just prior to the Thanom coup, it was not uncommon to hear even well-educated people talking nostalgically about the early sixties, when there had been a real feeling of impending change for the better under the leadership of Sarit.

POST-SCRIPT: THAI POLITICS AFTER OCTOBER 14, 1973

The period of political stability under the Sarit, Thanom-Praphat leadership spanned a period of fifteen years. In that time, the regimes were not threatened from within the elite ranks, as had happened prior to 1958. Sarit's despotic repression of opposition and other heterodox elements had guaranteed the regime's internal stability. Under this facade of political calm, authoritarian rule was seen as capable of generating national progress under the *phatthana* programs.

Initially, up until the late 1960s, paternalistic despotism seemed to have worked—there was stability both politically and economically—in part thanks to the Indochina policy of the United States. Thailand's external security was assured by

---

[18] During a 1971 conference on "Thai Society: Present and Future" held at Chulalongkorn University, Thai scholars from various universities examined the problems faced by Thai society. In the course of the discussions involving the panel on "Political Problems," one of the panelists expressed a common sentiment about Sarit: "When Field Marshal Sarit Thanarat became prime minister, he ruled as a dictator. Nevertheless, he accomplished many good things. Even *achan mom* [Kukrit Pramote] himself has said that he missed Sarit. Why then do a large number of people still think of this person? This is because the people have never before witnessed a true leader, and when a strong leader appeared, they believed that he would release the country from its chronic problems and bring in wealth. However, when he died, there were initial condemnations, but later people began to miss him because they realized that he had done a lot of good, which is more than could be said for the present regime. Many people really believe this. Therefore, we can see that people are willing to accept a person with a good and firm political ideology." See Chulalongkorn University, Alumni Association, *Patchuban lae Anakhot khong Sangkhom Thai* [Thai Society: Present and Future] (Bangkok: Akson Sampban Press, 1971), p. 51.

the military presence of the United States. In this regard also, *phatthana* was successful owing to the funds invested by the United States in its attempt to stabilize Thailand, the location of which was critical for the prosecution of the American Vietnam offensive.

As *phokhun*, Sarit had unquestionably far more power than his predecessors to act swiftly and decisively on matters pertaining to policies that he considered essential to implement *phatthana*. As a result of his strong-arm tactics, which involved political repression and an outward demonstration of anti-communism, Sarit's Thailand was viewed by the United States as a stable staging area for its war efforts. This perception by Washington led to the great influx of funds for "development and security" programs. Guided by its own *phatthana* policies, the Sarit government was also readily open to accepting advice from US-trained technocrats, who acted as advisers from the United States. Furthermore, having ensured political stability, Sarit sought out foreign capital to implement economic development, which he saw as a long-term guarantor for his regime. Through providing economic prosperity, he had hoped to consolidate his rule. To attract foreign investment, his government banned strikes and dissolved unions. Tax breaks for foreign firms were implemented, and those companies were permitted to buy land. Thus the political and economic bases for the boom of the 1960s were laid out under Sarit's leadership.

Following the death of Sarit in 1963, Thanom and Praphat carried on with the basic policies of their benefactor. Their administration was authoritarian, but lacked the "ferocity" of the Sarit era, which had "normalized" Thai politics and implemented the strong orthodoxy that was the basis for their rule. The Johnson administration's escalation of the Vietnam War brought new "prosperity" to Thailand. The construction of bases and other installations, together with the steady flow of American servicemen on a grand scale, led to the war-related expansion of the service industries as well as low-level manufacturing industries. Also, because of Thailand's relative stability, tourism became a multi-million dollar business.

The rapid growth of the Thai economy created, in turn, changes in the Thai social structure—a prismatic diffusion of the *prachachon*—which was to compromise Sarit's three-tiered static hierarchy. Because of the profusion of infrastructure construction intended to satisfy development and security objectives, land speculation became big business in Bangkok, as well as in the surrounding areas. Sarit's decree eliminating restrictions on the size of land-holdings (previously set at 50 rai) helped bring about this new basis for wealth for the traditional Sino-Thai businessmen and high-ranking bureaucrats who had access to information about development plans. Activities of this sort established a foundation for a new business elite composed of businessmen and civilian military officials whose newly acquired riches came from land speculation, investment in the services business, and other war-related enterprises.

Ultimately, the economic boom filtered down to the lower stratum of society as well. The tourist trade and the inflow of foreign firms gave rise to the rapid development of the middle class, members of which were now able to send their offspring to universities both in Thailand and, more importantly, to universities abroad. Also, the prosperity of the cities attracted rural migration, as rural laborers rushed in to fill up the lower ranks of the service-oriented job market. In sum, the authoritarian political regime was secure as long as it was seen as producing progress and prosperity for the nation led by a burgeoning middle class that was, by nature, conservative in outlook.

However, while economically the Vietnam conflagration was beneficial to Thailand, on the intellectual level it gave rise to political dissension and resentment of the military regime's political authoritarianism and its collaboration with the Untied States. As the Vietnam conflict began to stagnate, domestic opposition to the war in the United States and elsewhere, on social and moral grounds, found ready audiences in Thai universities and intellectual circles. The radicalization of the student population in the late 1960s and early 1970s resurrected the challenging intellectual ideas that had been repressed during the Sarit period, and these ideas were then supplemented with leftist critiques generated by the international anti-war movement. Despite its authoritarian nature, the military regime was not able to repress this development immediately, as Sarit had done before them. The power of the government to stifle the debate was hampered by a development that had taken place during the Sarit period, when economic and educational expansion had increased the numbers of emergent potential dissidents.

The other complexity was a social and economic one. The new middle class soon became disenchanted with the military rulers, as the basis for their newly acquired prosperity (i.e., American commitment in Vietnam and Thailand) became uncertain. The United States' decision to begin withdrawing troops from Vietnam incited fears of communist reprisals and expansion into Thailand. Many began to blame the military for bringing the country to such a crisis. A number of worrisome conditions led to widespread disillusionment: these included escalating international oil prices, domestic inflation in double figures, fear of communist reprisals, open corruption of military leaders, and the prospect that an authoritarian political dynasty would rule Thailand for years to come (through the promotion of Thanom's political and natural heir, Colonel Narong). Hence, when the October 14 demonstrations took place, the urban middle class supported the actions of the students.

When the American position in Indochina suddenly collapsed in the spring of 1975, the exhilaration of October 14 successes was largely forgotten by this middle class. Insecure with their newly acquired status and lacking any real historical political experience of democratic rule, the majority of urbanites began to identify student violence, demonstrations, labor strikes, peasant demands, and inter-party conflict as the underlying characteristics of liberal political behavior. Just as they had grown disillusioned with the military regime, they now came to dread open democracy.

Therefore, the middle class soon became the target for intensified rightist propaganda generated by the former elite groups. The ensuing political polarization of Thai society was in essence one of generational, as well as ideological, conflicts. The radicalized students in the universities increasingly demonstrated socialist sentiments bent on social, political, and economic reforms that threatened to compromise middle-class gains. Furthermore, Marxist ideas were openly discussed, and the most influential ideas of Chit Phumisak were circulated—those that critically reevaluated the historical position of the Thai monarchy. These ideas shocked the sensibilities of their middle-class parents and the public at large. The student's scorn for authority and their dismissal of orthodox Thai propriety and cultural norms (actively promoted during Sarit's time) further exacerbated the ideological and generational tension. Their forays into the rural areas to provide political education for the peasant farmers (as well as for their own practical experiences) were interpreted as subversive and disruptive.

Rightest groups and newspaper articles began to surface in response to the student activism. Most visible of these groups were the Nawaphon, the Krathing Daeng (Red Gaur), the Village Scout movement, and the Chomrom Witthayu Seri (Independent Radio Club). The Nawaphon group was loosely organized. It recruited members from among middle-class conservatives, businessmen, bureaucrats, and academicians with the main purpose of defending the monarchy against attack and defamation. The Krathing Daeng were rightist storm-troopers recruited from ex-mercenaries, hooligans, and other hard cases by elements from within the Internal Security Operations Command. They were responsible for various atrocities; the deadly counterattack against student demonstrators at Thammasat on October 6, 1976 ranked foremost. The Village Scout movement was organized in 1971 by the Border Police in support of rural security and anti-communism. It quickly acquired an urban component and in general was led by business leaders, civil servants, and other prominent social personalities. This group enjoyed the direct patronage of the royal family, which had become alarmed by the country's shift to the left as well as by the increasingly powerful communist regimes situated around Thailand's borders. This group provided the "popular" grist for rightist activity whenever its members were summoned en masse for political rallies by controlling authorities as well as other right-wing groups, such as the Chomrom Witthayu Seri. This latter organization was composed of radio stations that followed the Armored Division Radio controlled by a colonel with family ties to the queen. It was responsible for fueling anti-student/leftist/communist hatred and was instrumental in polarizing Thai society.

Guided by such organizations, the blood-letting at Thammasat University was carefully orchestrated. That same day, the military declared a coup d'état and helped set up a civilian cabinet and an appointed legislature. The coup leaders subsequently formed themselves into the National Policy Council to oversee important policy decisions.

The interregnum of the Thanin civilian authoritarian government was a disaster in many ways. This short-lived regime carried out political repression, intellectual intimidation, and widespread despotism. It was, in essence, a rule characterized by despotic nepotism, and for that reason it alienated the bureaucracy (and the military which had originally supported it). Thanin and his cabinet failed miserably as national leaders. Unlike the former military leaders, who fashioned themselves somewhat on the Sarit prototype, these conservative civilian leaders were perceived as decisively petty, arrogantly weak (Thanin likened his government to the meat of an oyster, with the military as the shell; the army immediately rejected the metaphor, which it considered an offensive misrepresentation), and blindly reactionary. This type of civilian leadership was in stark contrast to the "golden days" of Sarit's military authoritarianism, and major segments of the frustrated public openly longed for a return to military dictatorship.

The Thanin interlude appears to have been a calculated move. Firstly, it shifted the responsibility for the October 6 affair to civilian reactionary groups and sentiments; by this means, the military was able to pose as a force capable of "rescuing" society from social malaise and further decay. Secondly, the interval gave military leaders some breathing space to regroup and partially settle internal service conflicts. And thirdly, it paved the way for the "natural" return of military domination of the Thai political life. On the whole, the public welcomed the Kriangsak coup of 1977.

The legacy of Sarit's authoritarian rule, revised with some adjustments, reappeared. Decisive military leadership returned. However, because of new ideological and social developments, despotic paternalism of the Sarit type was diluted and liberalized. Nevertheless, Thai politics is still authoritarian in nature, as indicated by the fact that the position of the prime minister continues and would continue to be central in the decision-making process. Political participation would be allowed to satisfy middle-class demands for more rational politics, yet this accommodation of liberalized politics is to be guaranteed by strong and decisive leadership, intended to shield the state against the "excesses" of the 1973–1976 democracy. All this has become necessary since the nature of political succession has shifted from one determined by internal elite *coups de main* to one where the solvency of any political regime depends on support from emergent social clientels. The lesson learned from October 6 clearly indicates the significant changes in the nature of Thai politics, especially the stronger role and function of the manipulation of the masses.

Thus, the roots of present-day political dynamics could be attributed to Sarit's "despotic paternalism," which assumes that the Thai sociopolitical structure should be fundamentally atavistic, static, and neatly compartmentalized. While initially *pattiwat* was necessary for *phatthana*, in the long run *phatthana* would undermine and weaken *pattiwat*. So long as socioeconomic progress continues without parallel political development (for various reasons), the probability of a return to "despotic paternalism will remain high. As a prototype for military political leadership, the Sarit example appears to have more adherents than the Phibun type of authoritarianism. Needless to say, Thai politics even today is just one step removed from "despotic paternalism," and the possibility of a political relapse demands that we seriously contemplate its past meaning and form, especially the likelihood and implications of a future, adaptive resurrection of paternal rule, *mutatis mutandis.*

Sarit and Wichitra, no recorded date.

Wichitra and family waiting at Wat Thepsirin for the arrival of Sarit's remains,
December 9, 1963.

Sarit's first wife, Chawee, at his funeral with their sons, Army Major Settha and Lieutenant Somchai.

Nuanchan, one of Sarit's partners, and their children; Praima, another one of Sarit's partners, and her two children. These two families were not mentioned in Sarit's will.

Miss Thailand pageant winners of 1961. All five were said to have been Sarit's mistresses.

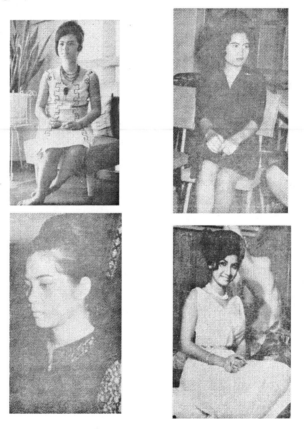

Some of the more than eighty beauty queens and starlets who were supposed
to be Sarit's mistresses.

APPENDIX I

PLANNED ROAD CONSTRUCTION, 1961-1970

The map shows planned road construction between 1961 to 1970. As we can see, road construction contemplated under the National Economic Development Plan, 1961-1966, was quite sparse and scattered. The new road construction program approved by the Sarit cabinet in July 1962 showed extensive new planning, which attempted to provide a highway network to all the various regions. Its most striking feature was the road plan for the Isan region, which contained the only "loop" (between Korat to Ubon and swinging north to Roi Et, Mahasarakham, before joining the Friendship Highway leading to Khonkaen, Ubon, and Nongkhai). This strategic loop was meant to link up the network of American bases at Khorat, Ubon, Khonkaen, Udon, and Nongkhai. United States financial aid for road construction was initially heavily concentrated on the Friendship Highway, part of which was completed in the mid-fifties. United States funds for this highway linking Bangkok to Nongkhai near Vientiane in Laos was aimed first at improving the Bangkok to Saraburi route (1959-1964), and then the Khorat to Nongkhai stretch (1957-1965). It is interesting to note that the major planning for these highways occurred in 1962, after the Rusk-Khoman agreements of March 6, 1962, which were interpreted as a commitment by the United States to defend Thailand against possible "aggression" from Laos. We should recall Sarit's ordering of the mobilization of troops from Phitsanulok and Khorat to the Laotian border in February 1962, during the Pathet Lao offensive, and the subsequent SEATO nations' show of force in April. By this time, the Sarit government was very concerned with the situation in Laos, and we can fairly conclude that of these revised plans for the national highway system in July 1962 were a quick response to these developments.

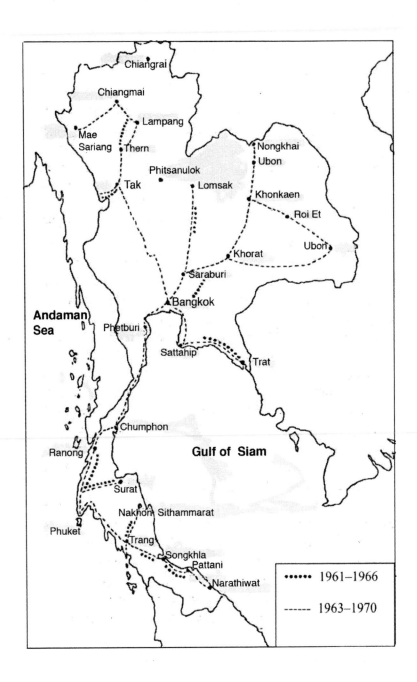

RE-EXAMINING THE DOMINANT NATIONAL NARRATIVE AND AN INTERPRETATION OF THE SARIT MONUMENT IN KHONKAEN

At the Conference on Thai Studies held in Amsterdam in 1999, Professor Charnvit Kasetsiri read a paper titled "Is 'Thai' Studies still Possible?"[1] His paper gave a provocative review of recent developments in the conceptualization of Thai history. He calls into question the real definition of "Thai" and asks who could lay claim to its representation. He, like many other scholars, has been struggling to find the place for the "Other" in Thai society. The issue of how to deal with the Other in the retelling of the dominant Thai national narrative is also manifested in the narrative of memories and the role that national monuments play in reminding or educating the public about that particular narrative. Events can be commemorated in various ways that may lead to different interpretations of their significance. Monuments, in particular, are susceptible to political manipulation, both by what is visually highlighted and what is recorded epigraphically. This fascination with monuments is not the monopoly of academics,[2] for the significance of monuments is also debated publicly. Recently, articles that discussed the politics of monuments also appeared in the Bangkok papers, calling into question not just the monuments themselves but who should be included in "Thai" history.[3]

This postscript examines the recent challenge to the dominant Thai-centric national narrative by scholars attempting to make room for non-Thai and non-elites. The second part of this postscript will examine how the Sarit Thanarat monument in Khonkaen can be interpreted as a way for the people of Isan to be included in this history. The term "Isan" refers to provinces in the northeast of Thailand inhabited by a large number of Lao speakers. Many of these Isan people were forcefully resettled in present-day Thailand from Laos after the suppression of a rebellion against Bangkok by the Laotian prince, Chao Anuwong, in 1827. Thai speakers from the Chaophraya river basin generally look down on their Lao-speaking cousins from Isan. But during the Sarit regime, the backward and neglected Isan region was targeted for rapid economic development, partly because Sarit had relatives there, and partly because the American counterinsurgency strategy was to make sure that

---

[1] Charnvit Kasetsiri, "Is 'Thai' Studies Still Possible?" Keynote address at The Seventh International Conference on Thai Studies, Amsterdam, July 4-8, 1999.

[2] Thongchai Winichakul, "Thai Democracy in Public Memory: Monuments of Democracy and Their Narratives," Keynote address at The Seventh International Conference on Thai Studies, Amsterdam, July 4-8, 1999.

[3] *The Nation*, August 14, 1999.

the poor in rural areas did not fall under communist influence. Sarit made Khonkaen an economic and educational hub for the northeast.

The significance of the Sarit monument will also be examined in the context of the controversy over another monument in Isan, namely, the Thao Suranari monument erected in Khorat. Thao Suranari was believed by many Thais to have been a pivotal leader who helped her husband suppress the Chao Anuwong rebellion. The monument dedicated to her heroism is well-known and revered, while Sarit's monument, on the other hand, is obscure in the minds of most Thais. In spite of this difference, I argue that both cases address the same issue, that is, how the local people of Isan attempt to make a space for themselves in the narrative of a Thai-centric history. The erection of the Sarit monument is a way for the people of Khonkaen to claim Sarit as a favorite son of Isan who became the prime minister of Thailand.

The venerated Thao Suranari Monument erected in 1934 following the failed royalist attempt to overthrow the People's Party.

In his most famous political novel, *Lae Pai Khangna*, written while he was in jail in 1957, Kulab Saipradit showed that he was clearly aware of the injustice of the politics of memory in Thai historiography.[4] Kulab penned a marvelous incident illustrating his concerns by pitching the scholarly Nithat against the bullying aristocratic M. R. Rujirek, thus illustrating the potential tension between writing a people's history and writing a history based on the Royal Chronicles. Speaking through the voice of Nithat, Kulab questions the validity of a "Thai identity" that ignores the role of the local Chinese and other common folks from the provinces. In response to a boast from Mom Ratchawong Rujirek that people should feel grateful to his ancestors who saved the Thai nation from its enemies, Nithat reminds his fellow students that many others also fought bravely besides those who were named in the Chronicles. Nithat goes on to praise King Taksin and his Chinese soldiers, along with the heroes of other wars who were "Thai" peasants from the provinces. These unsung "Thai" heroes and heroines were the Sino-Thai and Isan peasants who were ignored in the national narrative and whose brave acts were not part of the Thai national memory. We should note here that Kulab purposely chose two outsiders as his main characters to represent the "future" of the Thai people. Chantha Nondindaeng is from Isan, a country bumpkin who yearns to fit into the Bangkok-dominated Thai state. The other character is the kind, smart, loyal, Christian and international Seng, the son of a Chinese watch repairman who later becomes a newspaper reporter. It is clear that Kulab—and, I am sure, other enlightened Thai of that period—saw the need to reconfigure a national narrative that is more inclusive of important contributors to the Thai state, and to redefine "Thai identity" in a way that is more magnanimous.[5]

The fascination with the problem of how to interpret the past has always troubled scholars of Southeast Asia. David Steinberg's book, *In Search of Southeast Asia*, opens with this wonderful passage:

> On the small island of Mactan in the Philippines there is a monument erected by the Spanish in the nineteenth century to glorify God, Spain, and Ferdinand Magellan. In 1941, during the American era, a historical marker inscribed "Ferdinand Magellan's Death" was erected nearby. It stated: "On this spot Ferdinand Magellan died on April 27, 1521, wounded in an encounter with the soldiers of Lapulapu, Chief of Mactan Island. One of Magellan's ships, the Victoria, under the command of Juan Sebastian Elcano, sailed from Cebu on May 1, 1521, and anchored at San Lucar de Barrameda on September 6, 1522, thus completing the first circumnavigation of the earth." Exactly a decade later, the by then independent Republic of the Philippines erected a second marker, entitled "Lapulapu." It read: "Here, on 27 April 1521, Lapulapu and his men repulsed the Spanish invaders, killing their leader, Ferdinand Magellan. Thus Lapulapu became the first Filipino to have repelled European aggression."[6]

---

[4] Kulab Saipradit, *Lae Pai Khangna* (Bangkok: Chapit Co., BE 2516).

[5] The reinterpretation of the master narrative and the democratization of Thai "history" has some of its roots in Ithaca, New York, where Professor Charnvit studied.

[6] David Steinberg, ed., *In Search of Southeast Asia* (Honolulu, HI: University of Hawaii Press, 1970).

This passage illustrates that "history" serves the purposes of the state and those who control it. Memory and the selective recording of events and actors in the historical narrative ultimately shape the present and future of the state and its people. Therefore, the decision to (re)interpret history by constructing particular national monuments has far-reaching implications.

THAI HISTORY, AND WHAT OR WHO IS THAI?

The official state narrative of Thailand's—or Greater Siam/Ayutthaya's—history focuses on race and the glorification of militaristic leaders whose love for "freedom"—a (re)interpretation of the word "Tai"—forced them to lead a somewhat passive peasantry southwards to an empty golden land (*Suwannaphum*). The idea of this southbound exodus is not unique to the Thai narrative. Writing about Vietnam, Keith Taylor had something very important to say about such myths:

> The category of "nam tien," "the march to the south," has been established in modern Vietnamese historiography to cover an imagined event extending across many generations and hundreds of kilometers and commonly essentialized as something inherent in a presumed Vietnamese character, a process that has operated throughout Vietnamese history. I do not believe that such an event ever took place and I will speak no further of it.[7]

The finality of Taylor's statement is enviable. Even though some Thai historians have questioned the genetic imperative of this southward march by the Thai tribes who sought to escape the oppressive Chinese, no Thai scholar has yet addressed the question as defiantly as Professor Taylor. In the Thai case, attempts to re-evaluate the official paradigm have taken two forms. The first form of history writing follows the example of Kulab Saipradit in *Lae Pai Khangna*. These relatively more recent works involve a writing of "Thai" history that highlights the contributions of Thais with other-than-Thai racial backgrounds. These studies have implicitly questioned the narrow definition of "Thai-ness" based on race, exclusive of culture. The second form of re-examining "Thai" identity, albeit by breaking down the boundaries of the nation-state, focuses on a form of irredentism that by definition racializes the term "Thai/Tai," making Tai history inaccessible to the non-Thai. Professor Charnvit also addressed the existence of these two schools in his keynote address at the 1999 Amsterdam Thai Studies Conference.

Studies of the first type have been labeled the "*Jek*" school of history. *Jek*, of course, is a derogatory label for the Sino-Thai.[8] In 1986, Professor Niddhi Eawsiwong

---

[7] Keith W. Taylor, "Surface Orientations in Vietnam," *Journal of Asian Studies* 57,4 (November, 1998): 981.

[8] See *The Nation*, editorial and Opinion, August 14, 1999. A scholarly study of the epistemology of and evolution of this label has yet to be written. Niddhi cites Phraya Anumanrachadhon, who explains that "Jek" is related to the word "Trok" in the Yakhai language, to "Toyok" in Burmese, and the work "Khae" in Chinese. He reasoned that the original meaning of these words must have been "Khaek" or "strangers" (this category also refers to Siam's early visitors, who were Indians, Arabs, and Malayan Muslims). Furthermore, he thinks that, in fact, "Khaek" and "Jek" could be one and the same. Although I am not a linguist, common sense compels me to think that the word "Jek," which is a somewhat derogatory term, may have

of Chiangmai University published his landmark study of King Taksin of Thonburi. The study began with an examination of the Chinese roots of this "Thai" hero and the role played by his Chinese allies.[9] Niddhi—whose name, incidentally, sounds very close to Nithat, the protagonist of *Lae Pai Khangna*—is perhaps the first serious scholar to admit that his fascination with and admiration of King Taksin came about because both he and Taksin were *Jek*. Although Taksin's reign and life have been the subject of more scholarly books than those of any other Thai monarch, no previous study dealt squarely with the importance of his Chinese-ness.[10]

Niddhi defines *Jek* as the ethnic Chinese in Siam. *Jek* is not exactly the same as *Jin* (native Chinese). *Jek* culture is an admixture of Thai and Chinese and is in itself a distinct category. Curiously, Niddhi attempts to explain the term *Jek* inside the framework of conventional Thai historiography. And although Niddhi's study does not reject the basic premise that underlines Greater Siam/Ayutthaya history, his meticulous narrative portrays Taksin as an outsider and not purely as an aristocratic Thai. Taksin's "Thai-ness" derives from his mother, an alleged noblewoman forced to marry a rich Chinese man from Swatow. Niddhi suggests, however, that Taksin's mother may have been, in fact, *Jek* herself, thus making Taksin a full-blooded Chinese. But to make Taksin more legitimate in the chronology of succession that records the line of Thai kings, Thai historiography has traditionally identified Taksin as an aristocratic Thai raised within the compounds of the king. His half-Chineseness has been downplayed. Yet Niddhi insists that, even though he had an aristocratic Thai upbringing, Taksin exploited his *Jek* connections during the struggle to re-establish Ayutthaya and to consolidate power as the new Thai King. Taksin's campaigns along the Eastern seaboard relied heavily on his contacts with the *Jek* in Siam and the Chinese from abroad. As king, Taksin even used his father's Taechiu Chinese surname, *Sae Tae* or *Tia*, or the Mandarin *Cheng*, in conducting diplomatic relations with China. In Vietnam, he was known under the family name, *Trinh*. Also, according to Niddhi, Taksin made little effort to hide his *Jek* heritage.

---

come from the Thai making fun of the Chinese by using the word for number "one" in Taechiu as a representation of all Chinese. Another plausible explanation is that the word is derived from "Ah Jek," a reference to "Number One Brother." I have also learned from my *Peranakan* friends that elderly Chinese are sometimes given the honorific "Inchik" in Malaya. Regardless of the roots of this term, it is clear that many "Thai" of clearly questionable ancestry have been practicing racial amnesia by denying their own Chinese-ness. In fact, the *Jek* background of the Thai monarchy and most of its old aristocracy, while widely known, is not often publicly acknowledged. The exception to this rule, perhaps, was the late iconoclast, Mom Ratchawong Kukrit Pramote, who practiced Chinese ceremonies during Chinese New Year festivities. Niddhi's study of King Taksin brought this issue into the open, where it was subjected to public debate and scrutiny.

[9] Niddhi Eawsiwong, *Kanmuang Thai Samai Phrachao Krung Thonburi* (Bangkok: Silapa Watthanatham Press, 1986).

[10] In the introduction of his book, Niddhi thanked both Benedict Anderson and David Wyatt for giving him ideas about writing such a controversial history. Niddhi took Anderson's famous "Plural Societies" course in the early 1980s and wrote a paper about people in Thailand who wore their hair in a "*pia*" or Chinese (Manchu) queue. I am quite certain that David Wyatt's influence had something to do with his study proving that the leadership of the Ayutthaya and early Bangkok aristocracy was highly cosmopolitan and that Taksin relied on his Chinese connections to help him win the struggle against the Burmese after the fall of Ayutthaya in 1767. See David K. Wyatt, "Family Politics in Nineteenth-Century Thailand," *Journal of Southeast Asian History* 9,2 (September 1968): 208-228.

Niddhi's book caused quite a stir. Since he is one of modern Thailand's most respected historians, his meticulous research and narrative were hard to ignore. The new interpretation compelled orthodox Thai history to make a space for the ethnic Chinese, and, by implication, also compelled it to make room for other excluded groups. Niddhi declares his Sino-Thai roots in the preface of his book. He writes: "a society that is dynamic is one where there is room for a multiplicity of cultures, ways of life, values, and tastes. *Jek* is one aspect of cultural wealth in Thai society."[11] And below his name, the date of the message is inscribed as "Chinese Moon Festival," but with the Thai Buddhist calendar year, 2529.

Another blow to the orthodoxy of the Greater Siam/Ayutthaya history was Sujit Wongthet's book, written with the tongue-in-cheek—or cheeky—title, *Jek Pon Lao* (Chinese Mixed with Laotian); it appeared the year after Niddhi's book. The fact that Sujit is the owner and editor of the *Silapa Watthanatham Journal*, which published Niddhi's book, may give the impression that a conspiracy to create a new school of Thai history was in the making.[12]

Sujit's slim volume, written soon after his return from a trip to Laos, had quite an impact on the academy, greater than one might expect from a non-academic work. But more importantly, it struck a chord with the reading public. Even though Sujit wrote about Laotian history and Thai-Lao relations, the biggest impact of the book was the visual immediacy of its assertive, in-your-face title, "*Jek Pon Lao*," which literally labeled the Thai as "ethnic Chinese mixed with Lao." On one level, Sujit makes the case (also a personal one) that the "Thai" are in fact a mixture of two or several races and cultures, and that "Thainess" is a cultural, and not a racialized, concept. In fact, it was the state that created the category "*Chuechat Thai*," or "Thai race." This designation is quite ambiguous and legally unenforceable. In many cases, people cannot differentiate "*Chuechat Thai*" from "*Sanchat Thai*," meaning "Thai nationality." It is very easy for *Jek* or *Khaek* (Indian, Arab, Muslim), after several generations in Thailand, to declare themselves "*Chuechat Thai*" and to ignore or conveniently set aside the race of their forefathers.[13]

Thai readers, many of whom were of mixed ancestry, loved Sujit's book. The psychological release that the book provoked permitted many to declare openly that they are Thai and *Jek* at the same time. It also allowed others to declare themselves "*Thai Pon Khaek*," "*Mon Pon Jek*," "*Khamen Pon Thai*," and other interesting permutations. Suddenly, the idea that Siam was a racially pure Thai state became something of an indefensible concept. It seems clear that Sujit's book created more

---

[11] Niddhi Eawsiwong, *Kanmuang Thai Samai Phrachao Krung Thonburi*, preface.

[12] Sujit spent a year in Ithaca in the early 1970s when his wife, Pranee, was studying in the Anthropology department. Sujit left shortly before Niddhi arrived in Ithaca to write his dissertation. Sujit Wongthet, *Jek Pon Lao* [Chinese Mixed with Laotian] (Bangkok: Silapawatthanatham, 1987).

[13] The irreverent Sujit was also poking fun at the proud graduates of the Thai Military Academy, who were the protectors and defenders of the orthodox version of Thai history. Sujit humorously declared himself "Jau Pau Lau," the acronym for "Jek Pon Lao," in contra-distinction to "Jau Pau Rau," the acronym that stood for the Royal Military Academy. Charnvit suggests that the naughty Sujit, in effect, "turns racially derogatory terms into something culturally positive, but at the same time has fun teasing Military Cadet graduates who have been very much up and about in Thai politics." Charnvit, "Is 'Thai Studies' Possible?"

space for the *Jek* and others in "Thai" history, even more than Niddhi's book had done.

Sujit had cleverly laid the groundwork for his assault on the Greater Siam/Ayutthaya narrative when, two years later, he published *Khon Thai mai dai ma chak nai* (The Thai Did Not Come from Somewhere Else).[14] That book, a semi-serious travelogue, chronicled his visit to Sipsongpanna and Nanchao, in China, to search for the Thai. The book was filled with pictures of happy Tai people still living in parts of China. Sujit's research asserted that the story of the southern exodus of the Thai people was actually the brainchild of an Englishman who invented the tale in 1885.[15] And later, according to Sujit, it was Prince Damrong who legitimized this story in a lecture at Chulalongkorn University in 1924. The idea that the Thai loved freedom so much that they left their homeland to escape Chinese domination was later canonized in 1939 by nationalistic songs composed by Luang Wichit Wathakan and aired on national radio.

Sujit's assertions that the Tai were spread over a large area that included large portions of present-day Southeast Asia and that they had not been driven south by the Chinese struck two blows at the interpretation of Thai-ness. First, Thai-ness has been defined as different from the *Other*. That *Other* has, for some time, been conveniently defined as the Chinese. Thai nationalism was founded on the narrative relating how the Thai were pressured by the Chinese and forced to leave their ancestral homeland in the foothills of the Autai mountain range; this heroic exodus and struggle against the powerful Chinese helped define the collective personality of the Thai people. Thai nationalism continued to target the Chinese during the 1930s to the mid-1960s. The closing of Chinese language schools and the elimination of Chinese surnames for those who joined the bureaucracy during the Phibun ultra-nationalist period were carried out by the Thai state in the name of nationalism.

Sujit's contention that the Thai were never driven out by the Chinese, and that the Tai people had, in fact, lived all over southern China, took the wind out of the sails of nationalistic historiography. Furthermore, Sujit argued that the "Thai" in Thailand are not comprised exclusively of the Tai race, but are a new people formed out of a mixture of various ethnic groups and races. The new Thai race no doubt includes the local Chinese, the Mon, the Khmer, the Khaek, the Lao, and many others. Sujit also boldly asserted that *Jek* culture is a legitimate part of Thai culture and that the ethnic Chinese played and continue to play an important role in Siam's development.[16]

---

[14] Sujit Wongthet, *Khon Thai mai dai ma chak nai* (Bangkok: Silapawatthanatham, 1984).

[15] Ibid., p. 163.

[16] Already we are witnessing the "coming out" of many leading Thai political and business leaders. This new openness and the broadening of "Thai identity" has allowed politicians to acknowledge publicly their *Jek* ethnicity. Recent examples are Chamlong Srimuang, Banharn Silapa-acha, and Prime Minister Chuan Leekpai. It appears that the ethnic Chinese in Thailand have been accepted as full and equal members of the nation more easily than ethnic Chinese in some other Southeast Asian countries; in Malaysia and Indonesia, for example, ethnic Chinese still find themselves categorized as a different kind of citizen. This is because, in Thailand, unlike the other two countries, there is no category for "native" that is the equivalent to Malaysia's *bumiputera* or Indonesia's *pribumi* and thus no barrier to prevent the *Jek*, and others, from becoming entirely "Thai" and participating fully in the political and economic system.

Sujit was not alone in writing about the Thai in their ancestral land. Many scholars have pursued research on the Tai/Dai.[17] As Charnvit pointed out in his 1999 keynote address, fascination with the Tai/Dai is the basis for another so-called school of Thai history.[18] There are many serious researchers and scholars who continue to study the Tai/Dai as a major race comparable to the Chinese. The Tai are alleged to have been scattered all the way from China to Vietnam, to Siam, to Burma, and all the way to India. Ironically, scholars tend to avoid studying the Tai in Thailand because the culture of "Thai" in their homeland is seen as the most corrupt version of Tai culture.[19]

Studies of the Tai living outside of Thailand found the essence of Tai culture to be a peasant-based society, and therefore inherently anti-state. However, the efficacy and popularity of this school of history is quite limited, as Charnvit argues. Many of these esoteric, yet trendy precolonial/postcolonial transnational studies are heavily subsidized academic exercises. (Paradoxically, some of these studies were supported by the Thai royalty, perhaps to legitimize their role as the leaders of the universal Tai race, an ambition apparently unfazed by the fact that they themselves are "Thai Pon Jek.") According to Charnvit, the "Studies of Cultures of the Tai people" Conference in 1993 drew 700 participants; 1,500 reports documenting the proceedings were printed and later distributed free of charge. Professor Shalardchai Ramitanond's project on "Cross Countries Comparative Studies on Societies and Cultures of the Tai Speaking Peoples in Northern Thailand, the Shan in Burma, and Assam in India" resulted in a voluminous publication; 500 of those were printed. Again, paradoxically, these research findings, while appearing rather dull and innocent, further undermined the validity of the Greater Siam/Ayutthaya historical tradition. The Tai school findings assert that the Tai people, intrinsically, are not as passive nor as ignorant as they have been represented by the royalist/nationalist historians, and that the southern exodus actually never occurred. Also, as corollary, these scholars argue that the Thai should stop blaming the Chinese for historical slights.[20]

---

[17] One can visit the famous Cornell Echol's collection and check out voluminous studies of these people, who must seem to modern Thai urbanites as oddities. See Sisuphon Chuangsakun, Atthittaya Charuchinda, *Bannanukrom Kansuksa Kieokap Chonchat Thai* [Bibliography of Studies about the Tai People] (Bangkok: Khrongkan Ruapruam Khomun Kansuksa Kieokap Chonchat Thai, 1995).

[18] Charnvit identifies three projects that have been carried out by Professor Shalardchai Ramitanond (Chiangmai University), Professor Chatthip Natsupha (Chulalongkorn University), and Professor Sumit Pitipat (Thammasat University). I remember my own exposure to my ancestral cousins on May 12, 1978, when I visited the Chinese National Institute of Minorities in Peking. There, I met two Tai students, a man in a Mao jacket, and a woman dressed in a costume no different from that worn by northern Thai women today. As I towered over them, I attempted to seek some common ground for our "Tai-ness." I did not experience the out-of-body giddiness that I had expected would seize me if I were to look at myself from another dimension. In the end, we found a meeting ground in some basic words, such as I=*khai*, you=*mung*, speak=*wao*, good=*dii*, like=*yiam*, eat=*kin*, and shit=*khii*. The realization that "you are what you speak" convinced me that the category "race" is overblown in its importance and is much misused. Race is insufficient bonding material. Language and culture are much stronger.

[19] See *The Nation*, August 14, 1999.

[20] Charnvit argues that the *Jek* school of history seems to have had a greater impact on the Thai than the Tai school, if publication figures are any indication. Of recent books that are fun, or *sanuk*, to read and have attracted a substantial audience, Chitra Konanthakiat's *Tung Nang Kia* (Descendents of the Chinese) stands out; this book has gone through sixteen printings and

In defense of the Chinese, Professor Zhu Liangwen's book, *The Dai: Or the Tai and their Architecture and Customs in South China*, made a point of linking the archeological findings in Ban Chiang to the existence of the Tai, showing that the Tai had lived in Southeast Asia many thousands of years ago. Though he subscribed to the theory that the Tai had migrated south, the fact that many are still living happily in Southern China suggests that the Chinese had no hand in driving this minority out of the region. Professor Zhu also claimed, with nationalistic zeal, that the Tai language belonged to the Zhuang-Dong branch of the Sino-Tibetan language, perhaps implying that there would be no reason for the Chinese to drive away its own people.[21]

ISAN AND LOCAL NARRATIVES OF MEMORY

Once again, Kulab Saipradit, writing in *Lae Pai Khangna*, was very perceptive when he lamented the fact that the people of Isan, a significant Thai ethnic group, have had to struggle for a place in the dominant national narrative. Northeasterners have been looked down by the Central Thai as poor, uneducated, and bumbling provincials. But more importantly, they have been viewed by Bangkok as politically untrustworthy. Isan's problematic struggle for regional identity and inclusion into the Thai state have created tensions in the past, and these tensions seem to lie just beneath the surface of the apparently placid nation, as evidenced by a recent incident in Khorat.

In 1995, a book based on a Thammasat masters thesis by Saipin Kaewngarmprasert, titled "Kanmuang nai Ausawari Thao Suranari" (The Politics of the Thao Suranari Monument), was published.[22] The study is a typical postmodernist, deconstructionist look at historical inconsistencies and "the political premises that have shaped the successive versions of the dominant narrative," in this case, the significance of the Thao Suranari, or *Ying Mo/Ya Mo* (Lady Mo, or Grandmother Mo), statue in Khorat.[23] The monument was first erected in 1934 and restored in 1967. Simply put, Saipin's conclusion was that this minor historical actress was singled out for glory by leaders of the new Thai state under the leadership of Marshal Phibun Songkhram for political reasons, and that political exigencies shaped narratives associated with the monument. Saipin's study proved to be controversial and prompted mass protests in early 1996. The public outcry clearly demonstrated the

---

sold over 100,000 copies. With typical self-effacing modesty, Charnvit explains in his address that the books he publishes as an academic author only number between one to three thousand and take years to sell out.

[21] Zhu Liangwen, *The Dai: Or the Tai and their Architecture and Customs in South China* (Bangkok: D. D. Books, 1992), p. 2.

[22] Saipin Kaewngarmprasert, "Kanmuang nai Anusawari Thao Suranari" (MA thesis, Thammasat University, 1996. Bangkok: Silapawatthanatham, 1996). Charnvit was Saipin's thesis adviser, and Sujit is the publisher of Silapawatthanatham. Perhaps their detractors associated this book with the continuing revisionist effort to weaken the prevailing Greater Siam/Ayutthaya school of history.

[23] For a discussion of the monument, see Charles Keyes, "National Heroine or Local Spirit?: The Struggle over Memory in the Case of Thao Suranari of Nakhon Ratchasima" in *Cultural Crisis and Social Memory: Modernity and Identity in Thailand and Laos*, ed. Shegeharu Tanabe and Charles E. Keyes (Honolulu: University of Hawaii Press, 2002), chapter 4.

sensitivity of the politics of memory and the importance of the symbolism of monuments.

The book caused quite a stir in Khorat, even though Charles Keyes suspects that few people there have actually read it. Nevertheless, incendiary fliers were distributed to the public urging them to demonstrate against the desecration of the memory of Isan's major heroine. Organizers of the protest accused Saipin of questioning not only Thao Suranari's heroic actions, but her very existence. Both accusations were unfair to the author.

It is recorded that Thao Suranari, the historical figure, was the wife of the deputy governor of Khorat at the time of the Chao Anuwong rebellion in 1827. She was said to have joined—and some say she led—the fight against Chao Anuwong's soldiers at Thung Samrit. According to Thai historians, the decisive defeat at Thung Samrit led to the eventual withdrawal of Chao Anuwong. Although the Chao Anuwong rebellion was documented by Chaophraya Thipakorawong in his *Royal Chronicle of the Third Reign*, Mayoury and Pheuiphanh Ngaosyvathn in their book, *Paths to Conflagration*,[24] assert that, in fact, it was Prince Damrong, the first modern Thai historian, who credited Ying Mo for her heroic deeds; Charles Keyes makes a similar assertion. Prince Damrong praised Ying Mo as a "clever" person in his 1926 publication, *Jotmaihet ruang prap khabot wiangchan*. The Phibun propagandists of the late 1930s and early 1940s accomplished even greater leaps of imagination and invention when they set out to identify and canonize Thai heroes and heroines—Ying Mo included. Phibun's nationalist ideologue, Luang Wichit Wathakan, was instrumental in popularizing the deeds of these "nationalists" through plays and songs that were broadcast over the radio. Amazingly, Luang Wichit's songs are still aired today.

The inscription that was placed at the Thao Suranari monument in 1967, when the new statue was erected, states:

> In 1826, Cao Anuwong of Vientiane rebelled against Bangkok. He brought his army and seized Nakhon Ratchasima. Then he [ordered] that the population of Nakhon Ratchasima be moved [to Vientiane]. [When] they reached Thung Samrit, Lady Mo, with the backing of the [captive] women and men [of Khorat], fought in hand-to-hand combat with the Vientiane troops and annihilated them. Cao Anuwong withdrew his forces. Subsequently, a Thai army was mobilized, suppressed [the rebellion], and captured Cao Anuwong.[25]

For this heroic act, Rama III bestowed upon Ying Mo the title Thao Suranari, and her husband was given the title and rank of Chaophraya Mahitsarathibodi.

The excellent study of the event by Mayoury and Pheuiphanh Ngaosyvathn in *Paths to Conflagration* argues that, as with all historical incidents, conflicting accounts

---

[24] Mayoury and Pheuiphanh Ngaosyvathn, *Paths to Conflagration: Fifty Years of Diplomacy and Warfare in Laos, Thailand, and Vietnam, 1778–1828* (Ithaca, NY: Cornell Southeast Asia Program, 1998). It should be noted here that parts of this book were previously published in Sujit's *Silapa Watthanatham Journal*, which some could interpret as another attempt by this author to promulgate a more balanced and broad view of Thai history, one that would include regional (now foreign) perspectives. Ironically, the transnational interest in the Tai may lead to important (re)writing of Thai history.

[25] Translated by Charles Keyes, "National Heroine or Local Spirit?," p. 7.

can be unearthed. One conclusion seems clear to them, and that is, the so-called battle at Thung Samrit was not the turning point in the war, as suggested by the Thai chroniclers. And although the details of the conflict will not be covered here, it is sufficient to state that, in the Lao view, the involvement of Ying Mo was inconsequential and most probably non-existent. Mayoury and Pheuiphanh concluded that it was her husband who used trickery to massacre the small contingent of Lao police escorts. They write,

> Then, Plat [Phraya Plat, i.e., deputy governor of Khorat] returned to Anou's camp to convince him that the evacuees were exhausted and unable to walk further. He argued that they needed their knives and axes returned, as well as nine to ten flintlocks to hunt for food. With arresting generosity, Anou gave his approval. Made confident by Anou's clemency and the kindness shown by their forty Lao police guards, Phraya Plat's men massacred their Lao escort.[26]

Thai writers have generally viewed this event as a rebellion by a vassal state and would not acknowledge the Lao as a different people attempting to regain their national independence. Lao writers, on the other hand, see the struggle in racial terms. This issue is difficult to resolve because before nation-states came into being, allegiance to kings determined the boundaries of political units, and empires did not depend upon racial homogeneity as a basis for their existence. Therefore, in its historical context, this rebellion would not have involved race as a factor in the logic of the rebels or their opponents. It is by using modern lenses that scholars can now distinguish the Isan people as Lao living in Siam, thus problematizing Isan identity. Furthermore, the birth of the modern Thai state in 1932 also necessitated the redefinition of the state as the home of the Thai people. Thailand would be the home of the Thai, and, at least on the surface, non-Thai would henceforth become Thai. Thus, the modern Thai state officially declared in Ratthaniyom (State Preference) No. 3, "appellation of the Thai people," that:

> As the Government is of the opinion that the names by which the Thais in some parts of the country have been called do not correspond to the name of the race and the preference of the people, so-called, and also that the appellation of the Thai people by dividing them into many groups, such as the Northern Thais, the Northeastern Thais, the Southern Thais, Islamic Thais, is not appropriate, for Thailand is one and indivisible ... It thereby, notifies that the State Preference is ... [the] use of the word "Thai" for all of the Thais without any of the above-mentioned divisions.[27]

But the distinction between *chuechat* and *sanchat* would continue to plague national ethnic identities, and the existence of regional identities are still issues to many—witness the use of terms such as *khon Thai, khon Isan, khon Nueu,* and *khon Tai.*

Saipin's book was interpreted in Khorat as an attempt to make Chao Anuwong (or Chao Anou) a Laotian hero and to reinterpret the struggle as a nationalistic one.

---

[26] Mayoury and Pheuiphanh Ngaosyvathn, *Paths to Conflagration,* p. 190.

[27] In Thak Chaloemtiarana, ed., *Thai Politics* (Bangkok: Social Science Association of Thailand, 1978), p. 24.

Paradoxically, if one were to agree with the Phibun nationalists, Ying Mo can be a nationalist *only if she were herself Thai and fighting a foreign force,* but not if the incident was part of an internal rebellion. But in pre-nation-state Siam, Ying Mo could have been a Lao who was loyal to Siam. The dilemma today is how to assert and maintain regional identity as Isan/Lao, yet remain part of modern Siam and maintain a place in the dominant national narrative.

Saipin's research discovered that the original monument built in 1934 was the first of its kind erected after the revolution of 1932. She concluded that it was constructed to "demonstrate" Khorat's *allegiance* to the Thai state, and therefore, conceptually it was not an integral part of the Thai nation-state whose history is dictated by Bangkok. The statue was constructed soon after the Boworadet rebellion, during which Prince Boworadet brought provincial troops to Bangkok to try to wrestle power away from the People's Party in 1933. This interpretation of the statue's original meaning fits in well with the Greater Siam/Ayutthaya historical tradition, since it proposes that the monument was meant to demonstrate that the people of Khorat were still loyal to Bangkok, and that Isan was still a part, albeit a lesser one, of Greater Siam. Following this line of reasoning, my guess is that the restoration of the statue in 1967 was intended to remind people in Isan once again that loyalty to Bangkok is critical, especially when an internal communist insurgency is threatening national integrity, as it allegedly was in the late 1960s and early 1970s.

THE SARIT MOUMENT IN KHONKAEN

Another monument that plays upon the themes of national memory and national integration is the statue of Field Marshal Sarit Thanarat in Khonkaen city. This monument stands in a prominent and quiet area in the old part of Khonkaen. The life-size statue of the former prime minister faces the main street. The monument itself is framed by well-kept gardens backed by a series of plaster bas relief panels highlighting Sarit's life. Unlike Ya Mo's monument, which has turned into a major shrine, replete with soothsayers and Ya Mo cultists, the Sarit monument does not seem to attract worshipers ... or lottery and garland vendors. In fact, when I visited the monument, graffiti desecrated the plaque extolling his virtues. Nevertheless, Sarit's monument is probably the only one in Thailand erected to commemorate the deeds of a prime minister, making this monument somewhat unique as a regional and even a national icon.

But before proceeding to analyze the visual elements of the monument, we should briefly review Sarit's life and deeds.[28] After serving briefly in WWII, Colonel Sarit Thanarat became the Army's rising star through his involvement in the 1947 coup and his role in suppressing the 1949 Pridi coup attempt. By 1956, and at the age of forty-eight, Sarit became the youngest non-royal Field Marshal in Thai military history. The following year, he staged a coup d'état against his former boss, Marshal Phibun. Thanom Kittikhachon was then installed as prime minister. A few years later, after returning from treatment at Walter Reed hospital in 1958, Sarit staged a *coup de main* against his deputy, Thanom. Sarit took over as prime minister until he succumbed to cirrhosis of the liver, caused by too much drinking and partying, in 1963. He was fifty-five years old. Ten years after his death, in 1973, his regime fell

---

[28] For a more thorough discussion of Sarit's life, please refer to earlier chapters of this book.

following student demonstrations that forced out his lieutenants, Marshal Thanom Kittikhachon and Marshal Praphat Charusathien.

Sarit popularized the idea of *phatthana,* or "development," as the panacea for Thailand's political, social, and economic troubles. His regime was led by the *khana pattiwat,* or the "Revolutionary Council," named to distinguish it from the leadership of the previous regime, which had purportedly stirred up chaos in Thailand through its flirtation with Western-style democracy. Later military coup leaders would try to emulate Sarit's success by using the pretentious term *pattiwat,* and not the more appropriate *ratthaprahan,* or "coup d'état," to describe their actions. Sarit also convinced technocrats to join him in implementing his concept of national development. Under pressure from the World Bank, Sarit's government drafted Thailand's first National Development Plan, which laid the foundation for attracting foreign investment, promoting industrialization, and encouraging rural development.[29] Sarit believed that strong leadership and close ties with the United States were necessary for development, and that political and human rights should be suspended to achieve political stability and economic prosperity.

Even though he was the harsh, dictatorial father figure exercising "tough love"—unlike his predecessor, Phibun—Sarit made room for the monarchy to play an important, and gentler, role as the symbol of the Thai nation. Sarit promoted the monarchy as a symbol of national unity and pride, and he took every opportunity to demonstrate his loyalty to the throne and to show the public that the king's opinion mattered. He was able to do this because he had not been part of the group that overthrew the absolute monarchy. Sarit's political legitimacy was thus buttressed by royal patronage. He also based his legitimacy on dubious Thai ideas about democracy without representation. Under his scheme, Thailand could be considered democratic, even if there were no elected MPs, just so long as those leaders who were selected worked for the common good. His regime further popularized a state political ideology based on the triology "*chat, satsana, phramahakasat*"—Nation, Religion, and King.[30]

It was clear that the Sarit regime privileged the bureaucracy and big business. Sarit laid the foundation for Thailand's future industrialization by promising that the government would not compete with investors by creating new state enterprises, and also by promising tax breaks to foreign investors. Under the new economic system, however, farmers and peasants did not fully reap the benefits of *phatthana*; instead the senior bureaucrats and rich businessmen enjoyed a profitable symbiotic relationship that conveniently married, figuratively and literally, politics, power, and wealth. One can trace the rise of many new ethnic Chinese business tycoons and bureaucrats to the Sarit regime. The middle-class academics—teachers, white-collar workers, and middle- to low-ranking government officials—would not enjoy the profits of "*Yuk Phattana*" (era of development) until the 1980s.

On the negative side, Sarit's regime institutionalized the political role of the military, and, in turn, marginalized democratic political processes. Censorship of all types was enforced: movies were closely reviewed, newspapers were warned to be friendly. No Elvis or Beatle haircuts were allowed in Thailand, and even the "twist,"

---

[29] See Robert J. Muscat, *The Fifth Tiger* (Tokyo: The UN University Press, 1994), Chapter 4.

[30] The incantation was designed by King Vajiravudh, an Anglophile who borrowed the phrase "God, Country, and King/Queen."

a popular new Western dance, was banned.[31] Sarit was notorious for enforcing his conservative view of Thai culture. He engaged in blatant social engineering by rounding up "hooligans," "teddy boys," prostitutes, and drug addicts and sending them off to reform prisons. He even personally lectured them on the occasion of their release—a final "spanking" from father, as it were. Sarit's rule was despotic. He used his authority under Article 17 of the Interim Constitution to summarily execute arsonists, most of whom were Chinese, and alleged communists and political dissenters from Isan. It is surprising that the people of Isan did not focus on his repression of regional dissent and identity but instead embraced him as one of their own ... and a benefactor to boot.

Sarit's orthodox rule was absolute. Everybody in Thailand was afraid of him. He appeared unexpectedly everywhere and was very unpredictable—qualities that are important for a dictator. His attention to small details made people feel that they could not hide from him. At times, he would make surprise inspection visits to marketplaces to check for price gouging. He would check public toilets for cleanliness and arrest people for littering the streets. On one highly publicized occasion, Sarit stopped and arrested a motorist in Bangkok who threw Lamyai peel out of his car window.

His personal life, however, was not immaculate. It was public knowledge that he was a heavy drinker and a womanizer, but this reputation only added to his powerful image as *"nakleng,"* or tough guy. No beautiful woman was safe from his lust. When he died, it was discovered that he had amassed a fortune of over two billion baht, most of it gained through corruption. Nevertheless, Sarit remains an potent icon for the military, for arch-conservatives, some royalists, and even big business. But even though his dictatorial and self-indulgent lifestyle may have some appeal to conservative elements in Thai society, his corrupt personal life scandalized the monarchy. And thus, Sarit's place in Thai history is not as prominent as it might have been.

Although the Sarit regime promoted economic development, it stunted the political growth of Thai civil society. James Ockey, who has studied Thai politics of the late 1950s, has argued that there is evidence that Thai civil society was already in its formative years by the end of the 1950s, and that it was suppressed by the Sarit regime.[32] Ockey's close study of the Hyde Park movement led him to that conclusion.

The Thai "Hyde Park" movement mimicked the English practice of permitting political speeches to be delivered at Hyde Park in London. Prime Minister Phibun encouraged this practice after his return from a tour of Europe and America in 1955. For the following two years, citizens, politicians, and others were allowed to speak freely about politics at the speaker's corner at Sanam Luang, Thailand's "Hyde Park." Several of these speeches, in fact, led to protest marches to the Government

---

[31] Sarit's police would round up young men who wore tight pants as *anthaphan* (hoodlums) if their trousers were so snug that a Coca Cola bottle could not be passed up the legs. And even though the twist was banned for its sensual and sexually suggestive movements, it did not seem to bother the king and queen. In the early 1960s, the royal couple visited the Philippines. At a social gathering for Thai students held at the Ambassador's resident, the king played jazz with Senator Raul Manglapus's band. The students were encouraged to dance to the music, and the queen's ladies in waiting encouraged those present—myself included—to dance the twist. The ambassador at that time was Mom Chao Rangsiyakorn Aphakorn.

[32] James Ockey, "Civil Society and Street Politics: Lessons From the Fifties" (paper presented to the Thai Studies Conference, Amsterdam, July 4-8, 1999).

House. In his paper, Ockey accuses Sarit of "side-tracking the political impulses of civil society" by refocusing its attention on economic competition and national development. It is therefore ironic that, twenty years after his death, Sarit was honored by the budding representatives of the Isan civil society—leaders from the business, political, administrative, and educational communities—as a hero of its cause.

The Sarit Thanarat statue was erected in Khonkaen in 1983. Because there is no special convention concerning celebrations marking the twentieth anniversary of a person's death, other explanations are in order. The text on the plaque at the base of the statue provides a partial explanation. It reads:

> Thailand's 11th Prime Minister
> Served from February 9, 1959 to December 8, 1963
> [Field Marshal Sarit] was a person who administered the country with bravery, resolution, and firmness that help build stability for the nation. Furthermore, he was the person who initiated the National Economic and Educational Development Plan that permitted every region in the nation to become modernized [*charoen*] equally. In the Northeast, Khonkaen province quickly developed and modernized.
> Therefore, the people and government officials of Khonkaen joined together to build this monument to commemorate his good deeds.

The Sarit Thanarat Monument, a shrine without worshippers.

Plaster casts of scenes depicting the highlights of Sarit's life and his
connection to the Northeast.

Additional information found on the base behind the statue records the
astrological date of the laying of the auspicious cornerstone. The plaque also reveals
that General Athit Kamlang-ek, the then Army Commander-in-Chief, presided at the
ceremony. A garden and bas relief plaster impressions of scenes commemorating
important milestones in Sarit's life provide a backdrop for the statue. More
information is provided by a larger plaque on the back wall.

This plaque outlines briefly Sarit's life, beginning with his birth in Pak Khlong
Talad, in Bangkok's Phahurat district. It records the names of his parents, his
graduation from the Military Academy, his wedding to his niece Wichitra, the
daughter of his first cousin, his career in the military service (he held high ranks in
all the services except the police force), his political career, and his premiership, up
until his death in 1963. The narrative singles out Sarit's concern for the well-being of
the people, especially those in Isan. Sarit is credited with writing a development plan
for the Northeast, with Khonkaen at its center. More importantly, accordingly to the
plaque, it was because of Sarit's good deeds on behalf of the Isan that local
government officials, businessmen, and the people of Khonkaen joined together to
erect his statue as part of the "Bicentennial Celebration of the Founding of the
Rattanakosin Dynasty." We also learn that Khunying Wichitra, Sarit's widow,
attended the ceremony.

The life-sized statue shows Sarit resplendent in the King's Guard dress uniform.
The statue was cast in Bangkok at Wat Phromsuwansammakhi on May 23, 1983. And
similar to what happened with Ya Mo's ashes, Sarit's ashes were interred in the base

of his statue, a ritual that would make the statue more *saksit* and magical.[33] The unveiling of the statue itself was presided over by the crown prince on behalf of the king on May 31, 1984. A fence was eventually built around the statue in 1990, and the Khonkaen ZONTA raised funds for a garden and a pavilion. The series of white plaster panels was constructed in 1993; the artists who created the bas relief scenes came from local Khonkaen University.

The monument clearly gives Sarit credit for the development of Isan and, perhaps more importantly, its inclusion into the Thai state. As pointed out earlier, since the beginning of the Bangkok period, Isan, or the *Lao Lan Sang* region, has figured as a political challenge to the Bangkok government. The region is always suspected of harboring separatist aspirations. Until the Sarit regime, Isan was a neglected region. But because of other mitigating circumstances, and not primarily because Sarit was a northeasterner, Isan became central to the regime's conception of a prosperous modern Thai nation-state.

Compared to other regions, Isan was seen as the most backward and politically the most problematic. During the early democratic period immediately following World War II, Isan representatives in parliament were the only ones who voted as a regional bloc. These politicians were the first to look at issues that came before parliament with a regional perspective. The Bangkok leaders were aware that the Northeast had a different ethnic and linguistic tradition that was perhaps more closely linked to—and therefore vulnerable to political influences from—Laos, Cambodia, and Vietnam. Conversely, to the people of Isan, Bangkok was seen more as foe than friend.[34]

Perhaps because it was perceived as a potential breeding ground for resistance against the Thai state, American concerns about communist advances in Indochina prompted a massive influx of aid to Isan. The famous Friendship Highway was completed in 1957, linking Bangkok to Nongkhai, just across from Vientiane. The highway was the first major all-season hard surface road linking the Northeast to Bangkok. The new infrastructure made it easier to integrate the region into the Thai state, and it led to a minor agricultural boom in maize and kenaf production, goods that were then exported, mostly to Japan. Thus, under the Sarit regime, Isan was brought closer into the Thai state for reasons having to do with the Cold War. The regime needed better control of this volatile region. Thanks to the advice of the World Bank and the foreign policy dictates of the United States, Isan was finally accorded space in the Greater Siam/Ayutthaya national history.

The conflation of the "regional" and the "national" narratives was facilitated by the joining of the two in Sarit's public identity. In the regional narrative, Sarit is seen as a native son of northeast Thailand who became a great national leader and an advocate for Isan, and especially Khonkaen. In fact, at the time of the bicentennial,

---

[33] However, during a recent visit, I did not find any Sarit cultists hanging out near his statue waiting for some sign or signs that could be used to select lottery tickets. This is surprising because people have probably forgotten that Sarit funded his early political machine from money skimmed from the Lottery Bureau. He, if anybody, would know what the winning numbers were.

[34] In the 1950s, US aid agencies (USOM) conducted several studies on political leadership, sanitation, and soil and water conditions in Isan. One study, in particular, surprised researchers. In response to the question "List the top foreign powers that you have heard of," peasants in Isan put "Bangkok" at the top of their list. Eugene Black, *Alternative in Southeast Asia* (New York, NY: Frederick A. Praeger, 1969), p. 39.

rumors circulated that Khonkaen was to be renamed *"Sarit Thani,"* or Sarit city. The people of Khonkaen who represented modern Isan yearned to be included in the national narrative. By embracing Sarit as their native son, and by honoring him as part of the celebration of Bangkok's bicentennial celebrations, they were able to lay claim to a legitimate place in the Greater Siam/Ayutthaya narrative.

It is interesting to note which public figures appeared to honor Sarit's memory. Thailand's crown prince was present at the ceremony; the Thai king and queen were not.[35] There are two possible explanations for the presence of General Athit at this event. The first one was suggested to me by Professor Likhit Dhiravegin. Likhit is certain that Athit was one of the junior officers who commanded troops sent out to Makkhawan bridge to stop the Hyde Park demonstrators from marching to the Government House on March 2, 1957 to protest the February elections. This incident ultimately made Sarit the darling of the press and champion of the people, not because he supported the troops, but because he controlled them. Sarit heard that his troops were ready to open fire on the demonstrators and arrived in time to stop them. It was he who let the peaceful demonstrators pass through the lines. He then went ahead by car to the Government House to convince Phibun and other government leaders to come out to hear the grievances of the demonstrators. When the crowd arrived, they were surprised to find Phibun and other cabinet members there, ready to listen to them. However, to the chagrin of Prime Minister Phibun, the crowd called for "Commander Sarit" to speak to them. The protesters were angry about the February elections, which had been marred by widespread cheating. Sarit cleverly disarmed the mob by telling them that he, too, agreed that the elections were dirty—the dirtiest in Thai history, in fact—and that corruption was rampant. To the delight of the crowd, he admitted that "everyone cheated ... "

To maintain order, the young Field Marshal Sarit was subsequently appointed by Phibun as Peacekeeper of the Capital City, with authority to command all military and police forces to make sure that the mob would not get out of hand. Calm returned to Bangkok after two weeks, and Sarit's job was done. Before he left, he uttered the famous words that were echoed by the media—*"phob kan mai mua chat tongkan"* [We shall meet again when the nation calls]. Sarit became the first modern Thai politician to master the use of the media to benefit his career. Six months later, Sarit "heard the nation's call" and staged a coup d'état against his former superior, Phibun.

General Athit's presence at the opening ceremonies could therefore be interpreted as a show of respect to his former commanding officer. As commander-in-chief, Athit had the duty of representing the Army in honoring one of its most distinguished icons. Another explanation for Athit's presence, however, relates to his political ambitions and his attempt to strengthen his hand against Prime Minister Prem Tinsulanon. In 1983, Athit had hoped to unseat Prem and assume the premiership. Unfortunately, Prem had the king's backing and was adept in forming coalitions with the various political parties in parliament. Prem was also able to extract himself from the controlling influence of the military's "Young Turks," who had helped install him as prime minister. A group of colonels in the Thai army, the

---

[35] Although the presence of the crown prince at the ceremony links Sarit to the monarchy, I suspect that, following Sarit's death, when the embarrassing details of his sexual exploits and corruption became public, his reputation came to be so tarnished that years later the Thai king and queen were unwilling to make an appearance at an event commemorating his life.

Young Turks were fed up with parliamentary politics, and on April 1, 1981 they staged a coup and asked Prem to lead a Sarit-style government. To his credit, General Prem would not agree and escaped with the royal family to Khorat, thus taking the wind out of the sails of the young coup plotters.

It is therefore conceivable that Athit attended the commemorative ceremony because he wanted to establish a link to Sarit and keep his memory alive in order to pave the way for another Sarit-style coup. Athit's bid for power ultimately failed. Nevertheless, the efficacious Sarit model had other admirers in the Thai Army. Many years later, in 1991, General Athit's successors, Generals Sunthorn Khongsomphong (of the same class as Athit) and Suchinda Khraprayoon (Class 5) staged a coup of their own against General Chartchai Choonhavan.

The 1991 coup was reminiscent of Sarit's 1958 coup; in fact, the coup group's proclamations and announcements were copied almost verbatim from Sarit's pronouncements of thirty-three years earlier. The coup leaders saw no reason to change a model that had worked so superbly in the past. But time had changed Thailand, and the praetorian state no longer existed. The stubborn Suchinda government met with bitter opposition from city dwellers. That government ended abruptly in 1992, when the king responded to public outcry against the illegal seizure of power. In this instance, the world witnessed an unusual scene, broadcast by CNN, showing the king scolding General Suchinda and the other protagonist, General Chamlong Srimuang. The incident raised the king's stock while tarnishing the army's image. The 1992 Bloody May clashes between the public and the military, which were also shown on CNN, came to be known as the "mobile phone" (connoting middle-class) revolt against absolute rule. The mobile phone symbolized the burgeoning "new rich" and civil society in Thailand, the very same group that Ockey identified as having lost out under the Sarit's "development" regime.

ANALYSIS OF THE SARIT MONUMENT

The Sarit monument's bas relief series is a rendition of important scenes from his life. Perhaps the poor quality of the art work can be explained by the materials: it was executed in plaster and not in stone. One can think of the scenes in these panels as "modern pictographs," rich with meaning and symbolism that recount a regional narrative contextualized by the nation and its goal of modernization. The visual multi-vocal narratives on the wall emphasize local values, Isan's claim on Sarit, and legacies that are important to Khonkaen as the major political, cultural, and economic center of Isan, a city committed to modernization and development.

Visually, the series is read from left to right. There are eleven distinct scenes, but there is no clear demarcation between scenes, a style reminiscent of traditional religious mural paintings. The scenes flow from one to the next, separated in each instance by blank space. There are no epigraphical guides posted under each scene, but the implications seem to be quite clear. Because the pictures are not accompanied by explanations or the figures identified with names, one can assume that the local people viewing them would be expected to immediately identify and interpret the scenes and the characters without difficulty.

In deference to religion, and perhaps to make Sarit's harsh rule palatable to the public, the series of panels is bracketed on each end with religious symbols. On the left, where viewers begin their circuit of the bas reliefs, the observer sees a large Lao Buddhist pagoda, reminiscent of the famous Phrathat Phanom—clearly the best visual representation of Lao/Isan and also a comment on Sarit's piety, suggesting that he led a devout Thai Buddhist life. The last panel of the series shows Sarit and his wife, Wichitra, making merit by giving food to monks. It is quite startling to find that, in death, Sarit's image was given a more mellow and religious overtone, one that was never emphasized in his lifetime.

Panel 1

The second pictograph represents Isan's claim on Sarit as a native son. The picture shows acting Lieutenant Sarit standing next to his first cousin (and mother-in-law), Prathiap Chonlasap, alongside children who are only identified by name. His mother is seated in the middle. The scene is taken from a picture in Sarit's cremation volume and captioned "Sarit and mother with relatives." (See original photo at end of chapter.) Clearly, the picture claims Sarit as Isan's native son surrounded by his loving Lao/Isan relatives.

Panel 2

Sarit's mother, Chanthip Thipayawong, was a native of the Mukdahan district in Nakhon Phanom Province, near the border of present-day Laos. There is no doubt that she came from a prominent Lao family. In fact, General Phoumi Nosavan of Laos, who briefly became prime minister in the early 1960s, was Sarit's cousin. Chanthip met Lieutenant Thongdee Thanarat, Sarit's father, in Nongkhai, and they were married there. Lieutenant Thongdee was an expert in Khmer, Thai, and French and was sent to the border area as an interpreter in the Thai expeditionary force dispatched to repel marauding "Haw" brigands. After Siam ceded its provinces east of the Mekong to the French in 1893, the family moved to Udon, where the Thai Northeast Army command center had been relocated. In 1899, Thongdee and his family returned to Bangkok. Sarit was born in 1908 in Bangkok, the third child, following his sister, Thin, and brother, Sawat. Three years later, for unexplained reasons (one of which may well have been passionate homesickness), Sarit's mother decided to return to Nakhon Phanom without her husband's knowledge or permission. She took her two sons with her. Tragically, Sarit's elder brother died on the way of jungle fever.

The heartbreak over the death of her eldest son was the reason cited officially to explain why Chanthip refused to return to Bangkok. Family stories suggest that Sarit yearned for the return of his father, who did not show up for another two years. Sarit would remain in Mukdahan for two more years, at the request of his mother, before returning to live with his father in Bangkok, at age seven or eight, for schooling. It is rather puzzling that Sarit's mother did not return to Bangkok to be with her young son and fulfill her obligations to her husband. Fortuitously, her refusal to return to Bangkok and insistence on remaining in Isan helped, in the end, to sanctify, to reconfirm and ultimately strengthen, Isan's claim that Sarit was one of its true sons. It is not evident whether his mother ever remarried.

The third panel of the series shows Sarit walking with his officers in front of the Parliament building. The juxtaposition of the Parliament building and Sarit and his fellow officers, who later staged a coup against Phibun, is quite disturbing. In reality, it was Sarit and his cohorts in that picture who were instrumental in closing Parliament and who were responsible for stunting the growth of participatory democracy in Thailand. The implied message is that the Sarit-style democracy, in which civil liberties were curtailed and elections banned, was necessary for Thailand's economic development. This portrayal of a "democratic" Sarit ignores the fact that he had ordered the execution of Isan dissidents who were accused of communism, as well as the execution of a man accused of leading a separatist millenarian movement.[36] The panel is based on a picture taken at the Makkhawan Bridge, where Sarit appeared to stop his troops from shooting at the election protestors, an action that won him public adoration.

The next scene, panel 4, shows Sarit conducting a cabinet meeting in Government House. Sarit is wearing a Western-style suit and is shown with reading glasses. This visual image suggests modernity, studiousness, and hard work.

Moving on from the lofty conference rooms of Government House, panels 5 and 6 shows the prime minister dressed in military fatigues, smoking a pipe, and talking to civilian officials in the field. These officials are his eyes and ears, as he so often said. The entourage stands amid a group of peasants, including a marked assembly of women and children, seated respectfully on the ground. Here, Sarit is acting out his role as father of the nation visiting his children. In panel 6, he is shown touching a poor country girl's shoulder. (In the actual photo, below, the girl actually has her back to the viewer). The military uniform suggests ruggedness, firmness, and decisiveness, and the pipe represents his cosmopolitan and modern outlook. On his trips to visit citizens in the country, Sarit preferred to camp out.

---

[36] In January 1959, Sarit's police arrested forty-seven people in Srisaket—all associates of Thep Chotinuchi—for planning a communist uprising. Then, in 1961, Sarit arrested Khrong Chandawong and Thongphan Suttimat in Sakon Nakhon. Hundreds were arrested as communists during the Sarit regime. Khrong was an MP from Isan, who was accused of urging his Lao constituents in Isan to ally with Laos and secede from Bangkok. Khrong and Thongphan were executed by Sarit. Sarit also executed Sila Wongsin, a farmer who declared himself *phi bun* and established a small kingdom in a village in Nakhon Ratchasima. He had about two hundred villagers as "subjects." The police killed eleven and arrested eighty-eight of these subjects. See Chapter IV.

Panel 3

Panel 3 is based upon a picture of Sarit walking across the Makkhawan Bridge to greet the masses protesting the dirty elections of April 1957. This panel suggests that Sarit was protecting democracy, as depicted by the image of parliament building at his back.

Panel 4

Picture of Sarit convening a meeting of the National Economic Development Board, Government House, August 4, 1959.

Panel 5

Panel 6

Actual picture of Sarit giving a young girl some clothing during his visits to the countryside.

Panel 7 portrays Sarit again in a Western suit, conferring the university charter to Khonkaen University. This panel is the only one with writing showing the name of the university at the top of the picture. The suits represent modernity, Westernization, and new ideas. A similar scene is depicted on panel 8. This is most likely a picture of Sarit talking to local business leaders, who are wearing suits. The background of the picture appears to be filled with some sort of factory building spouting an impressive array of steel pipes.

Panels 9 and 10 show Sarit again in military fatigues, talking to engineers wearing hard hats. Sarit sports an army cap, thus distinguishing himself as a military leader who listens to technocrats. The group is discussing the construction of a dam, most likely the Ubonrat Dam, and the prospects of more energy production for factories in Isan. Scene 10 is framed by a steel electrical tower. These scenes recall one of Sarit's famous slogans: "*Nam lai, fai sawang, thang di, mi ngan tham, bandan suk*" (Water flows, the lights are bright, the roads are good, there is work for the people. Such is happiness).

Panel 7

Panel 8

Panel 9

Panel 10

Panel 11 shows Sarit standing over his lovely cousin, and considerably younger wife, Wichitra. Wichitra also had Isan roots on her mother's side. This picture is a (mis)representation of the ideal and loving couple. It was widely known that Sarit had many affairs and numerous minor wives and mistresses—traditional signs of a man of means and prowess. He was anything but a good husband and family man.

Panel 11

This final scene again shows Sarit and Wichtra together, this time offering food to a monk. Although it is very possible that Sarit and his wife regularly performed this ritual, devout religious observance was never a part of his public persona. Sarit was known for his willingness personally to shoulder all the consequences of his actions, especially his decisions to execute those accused of undermining the state and his regime. His declaration, "*khaphachao rabphitchob tae phudiew*," meaning, "I, alone, am responsible," would have been a more appropriate epitaph and ending to the series of panels, rather than "*tak baat*" (giving food to the monks).[37]

Curiously, none of these depictions attempted to represent the harsh nature of his regime. And even more surprising, the series left out an important pillar of the Sarit legacy, that is, the prime minister's close relationship with the monarchy. One of the most famous pictures of Sarit shows him, on his dying bed, holding the king's

---

[37] A commemorative plaque depicting a monk would have been more appropriate for Sarit's successor, Thanom Kittikhachon. Following one of his rare orders to execute a prisoner, newspapers published pictures of Thanom offering food to monks. The public saw this action as Thanom's way of accruing more merit to balance the taking of a person's life. Strangely, however, even in Buddhist Thailand, the gesture was perceived—contextualized by Sarit's example—as a sign of a weak leader. To many Thais, Sarit was "*Than huana khana pattiwat*," meaning "His excellency the Head of the Revolutionary Council." Thanom, on the other hand, earned the title "*Je Nom*." *Je* is Chinese for "elder sister."

hand to his forehead, a gesture that is at once bold and touching. The king's body is sacred, and it is not customary for his subjects to touch any part of his body, let alone to hold his hand. Perhaps the local artists chose to omit this image so that their regional narrative would suggest the callous treatment Isan had suffered under the rule of the Bangkok dynasty. On the other hand, the artists may have omitted the scene out of respect for the wishes of the palace, which did not want the monarchy linked too closely to Sarit. Through this omission, the chance to link Isan to Thai kingship, and therefore to the dominant national narrative, was missed. In the final analysis, a close reading of the monument shows that Isan is connected to the nation through Sarit, the native son and prime minister who brought Khonkaen into the national narrative celebrating the modernization of Thailand.

CONCLUSION

The struggle over the dominant national narrative of the Thai state, while still in flux, has, at the very least, made room for the ethnic Chinese and other ethnic groups. Creating a historical space for the *Jek* in Thai political memory will allow Thailand to continue to tap into this source of energy and leadership. The Sarit monument suggests that people from Isan are central to the history of the Thai state, to its security and economic development. Isan's place in Thai history is also assured because of its claim to a favorite son. No longer will people have to repress their ethnic identities, pick sides, or consciously practice racial and cultural amnesia in their quest to become more Thai. The reinterpretation of history will also allow regional identities to reinvent themselves and to find a place in the dominant national narrative. The Bangkok government's paranoia that a multi-racial, multi-ethnic population would threaten national integrity no longer holds.

More recently, it is common to see television shows that feature Thais from different ethnic backgrounds speaking in different accents. And, refreshingly, advertisements, and even news programs, show people who now freely speak local dialects, and not the official Central Thai. Also, the globalization of the entertainment business has led to the acceptance of new personalities—young Amerasian entertainers and actors—as genuine "Thai," even though they do not speak perfect Central Thai and do not look very Asian. In the most famous case, the Thai have embraced Tiger Woods as one of their own.[38] More importantly, at the other end of the socio-economic spectrum, Bangkok Thais are beginning to accept their compatriots who speak with accents that used to be considered "up-country" as legitimate and full-fledged Thais. The situation seems ripe for a serious reexamination of "Thai identities" in the modern period, which ought to include studies of the Thai diaspora that are not tied to the anachronistic concept of the nation's "Tai/Dai" ancestry.

---

[38] This recognition and adoration of the successful golfer is indeed a welcome sign. Not that long ago, the Thai regarded Africans and African-Americans with distrust and anxiety. It is still common to hear blacks referred to as *Ai mued*, meaning "the darkies." Even as late as the 1940s, state propaganda aimed at bringing Thailand into the ranks of the civilized world would urge people not to act like the Africans. Thais were advised to emulate the modern Englishman, not the primitive black people, who were said to eat with their bare hands, sleep on the ground, and wear barks and skins. See the dialogues between Nai Munchuchart and Nai Khong Rakthai in Thak Chaloemtiarana, ed., *Thai Politics*, pp. 271-272.

The second panel of the Sarit Monument was based upon this picture taken in 1929 of Sarit and his mother and relatives from the northeast.

INDEX

replaces Constitution of 1949, 44, 51, 52

Constitution of 1946 (Pridi), 19: bans army officers from politics, 27; replaced, 32

Constitution of 1949 (Khuang): replaced, 44, 51; restricts powers of government and military officials, 42, 50

Constitution of 1952, amends that of 1932, 69

Constitution of 1959 (Interim): espouses traditional Thai concept of state, 95, 97, 98, 99, 108; grants Sarit power to order executions, 127–28; provides for Constituent Assembly, 186; strengthens and secures the monarchy, 210; stipulates reorganization of the Office of the Prime Minister, 183. *See also* Article 17 of the Interim Constitution of Thailand (M 17)

Constitution of 1968 (Thanom), 228

constitutionalism: advent of, 115; decline of, 44; Western concept of, 2, 99. *See also* constitutional democracy

constitutional democracy, 92, 93, 94, 99, 181. *See also* Thai democracy; Western-style democracy

coup d'état of 1932, 20: and the bureaucracy, 115, 181–82; conflict between merit and blood, 6; and the installation of constitutional rule, 93, 99, 115, 181; and the monarchy, 2, 7, 115

coup d'état of 1947, 8, 29–32: and the decline of constitu-tionalism, 44; events leading to, 20–25; return of the military to political leadership, 198. *See also* Coup Group (1947)

coup d'état of 1948 (October 1st Rebellion), 35–36

coup d'état of 1951. *See* Radio Coup ("Silent Coup")

coup d'état of 1957, 9, 80

coup d'état of 1958, 81, 92–93: factors leading to, 94–96, 107, 121; ideology of, 147; and police supervision, 85; and censorship of press, 83. *See also* Revolutionary Council

coup d'état of 1971, 228–29

coup d'état of 1976, 137, 234

coup d'état of 1991, 259

Coup Group (1947), 32, 35: chief planners of, 28–29; control over cabinet and parliament, 52–54; drafts new constitution, 31; eliminates Luang Kat, 36–37; forces Khuang to resign,

34; forms Legislative Committee (Sapha Nittibanyat), 56–57; handling of the Manhattan Rebellion, 41; power struggle within, 33–34; relationship to Thai political system, 43; suppression of the Palace Rebellion, 38–39; senate acts against, 50; six reasons for coup, 29. *See also* coup d'état of 1947

Coup Group (1958). *See* Military Group

Cremation Volume (Sarit), 94–95, 114–15, 203

Crime Suppression Bureau, 59, 84, 127

Criminal Investigation Division, 59

Crosby, Sir Josian, 54–55

D

Declaration of the Neutrality of Laos (1962), 165

Defender of the Capital, 82, 84, 86

Defense of the Realm Council, 185

Democrats (conservative royalists), 19, 20, 47, 85: boycott elections of 1952, 54, 56; call for vote of confidence, 46; capture majority in parliament, 34; contest Phibun's leadership, 72; criticize Thamrong's government, 25; in general debate, 77; pledge aid to Isan, 75; question King Ananda's death, 24, representation on Phibun's cabinet, 45

Department of Administrative Inspection, divided (1960), 185

despotism, 133: benevolent, 3, 92, 94, 97, 104–5, 133; despotic paternalism, 231, 234. *See also* Thai paternalism

det khat (decisiveness), 123, 27

devaraja, 113, 114: cult of, 1–2, 115

Director General of the Police Department, 186

Direk Chaiyanam, 18, 38

E

economic aid. *See* United States; World Bank

Economic Assistance Program, 169

Economic and Technical Cooperation Agreement (1950), 68, 156

economic development, 10, 253: historic lack of, 130; immediate public assistance as, 97, 119–21, 133; impact of foreign policy on,

SOUTHEAST ASIA PROGRAM PUBLICATIONS
Cornell University

Studies on Southeast Asia

Number 42   *Thailand: The Politics of Despotic Paternalism* (revised edition), Thak Chaloemtiarana. 2007. 284 pp. ISBN 0-8772-7742-7 (pb).

Number 41   *Two Views of Seventeenth-Century Vietnam: Christoforo Borri on Cochinchina and Samuel Baron on Tonkin*, ed. Olga Dror and K. W. Taylor. 2006. 290 pp. ISBN 0-8772-7741-9 (pb).

Number 40   *Laskar Jihad: Islam, Militancy, and the Quest for Identity in Post-New Order Indonesia*, Noorhaidi Hasan. 2006. 266 pp. ISBN 0-877277-40-0 (pb).

Number 39   *The Indonesian Supreme Court: A Study of Institutional Collapse*, Sebastiaan Pompe. 2005. 494 pp. ISBN 0-877277-38-9 (pb).

Number 38   *Spirited Politics: Religion and Public Life in Contemporary Southeast Asia*, ed. Andrew C. Willford and Kenneth M. George. 2005. 210 pp. ISBN 0-87727-737-0.

Number 37   *Sumatran Sultanate and Colonial State: Jambi and the Rise of Dutch Imperialism, 1830-1907*, Elsbeth Locher-Scholten, trans. Beverley Jackson. 2004. 332 pp. ISBN 0-87727-736-2.

Number 36   *Southeast Asia over Three Generations: Essays Presented to Benedict R. O'G. Anderson*, ed. James T. Siegel and Audrey R. Kahin. 2003. 398 pp. ISBN 0-87727-735-4.

Number 35   *Nationalism and Revolution in Indonesia*, George McTurnan Kahin, intro. Benedict R. O'G. Anderson (reprinted from 1952 edition, Cornell University Press, with permission). 2003. 530 pp. ISBN 0-87727-734-6.

Number 34   *Golddiggers, Farmers, and Traders in the "Chinese Districts" of West Kalimantan, Indonesia*, Mary Somers Heidhues. 2003. 316 pp. ISBN 0-87727-733-8.

Number 33   *Opusculum de Sectis apud Sinenses et Tunkinenses (A Small Treatise on the Sects among the Chinese and Tonkinese): A Study of Religion in China and North Vietnam in the Eighteenth Century*, Father Adriano de St. Thecla, trans. Olga Dror, with Mariya Berezovska. 2002. 363 pp. ISBN 0-87727-732-X.

Number 32   *Fear and Sanctuary: Burmese Refugees in Thailand*, Hazel J. Lang. 2002. 204 pp. ISBN 0-87727-731-1.

Number 31   *Modern Dreams: An Inquiry into Power, Cultural Production, and the Cityscape in Contemporary Urban Penang, Malaysia*, Beng-Lan Goh. 2002. 225 pp. ISBN 0-87727-730-3.

Number 30   *Violence and the State in Suharto's Indonesia*, ed. Benedict R. O'G. Anderson. 2001. Second printing, 2002. 247 pp. ISBN 0-87727-729-X.

Number 29   *Studies in Southeast Asian Art: Essays in Honor of Stanley J. O'Connor*, ed. Nora A. Taylor. 2000. 243 pp. Illustrations. ISBN 0-87727-728-1.

Number 28   *The Hadrami Awakening: Community and Identity in the Netherlands East Indies, 1900-1942*, Natalie Mobini-Kesheh. 1999. 174 pp. ISBN 0-87727-727-3.

Number 27   *Tales from Djakarta: Caricatures of Circumstances and their Human Beings*, Pramoedya Ananta Toer. 1999. 145 pp. ISBN 0-87727-726-5.

Number 6	*Trends in Khmer Art,* Jean Boisselier, ed. Natasha Eilenberg, trans. Natasha Eilenberg, Melvin Elliott. 1989. 124 pp., 24 plates. ISBN 0-87727-705-2.
Number 5	*Southeast Asian Ephemeris: Solar and Planetary Positions, A.D. 638–2000,* J. C. Eade. 1989. 175 pp. ISBN 0-87727-704-4.
Number 3	*Thai Radical Discourse: The Real Face of Thai Feudalism Today,* Craig J. Reynolds. 1987. 2nd printing 1994. 186 pp. ISBN 0-87727-702-8.
Number 1	*The Symbolism of the Stupa,* Adrian Snodgrass. 1985. Revised with index, 1988. 3rd printing 1998. 469 pp. ISBN 0-87727-700-1.

SEAP Series

Number 23	*Possessed by the Spirits: Mediumship in Contemporary Vietnamese Communities.* 2006. 186 pp. ISBN 0-877271-41-0 (pb).
Number 22	*The Industry of Marrying Europeans,* Vũ Trọng Phụng, trans. Thúy Tranviet. 2006. 66 pp. ISBN 0-877271-40-2 (pb).
Number 21	*Securing a Place: Small-Scale Artisans in Modern Indonesia,* Elizabeth Morrell. 2005. 220 pp. ISBN 0-877271-39-9.
Number 20	*Southern Vietnam under the Reign of Minh Mạng (1820-1841): Central Policies and Local Response,* Choi Byung Wook. 2004. 226pp. ISBN 0-0-877271-40-2.
Number 19	*Gender, Household, State: Đổi Mới in Việt Nam,* ed. Jayne Werner and Danièle Bélanger. 2002. 151 pp. ISBN 0-87727-137-2.
Number 18	*Culture and Power in Traditional Siamese Government,* Neil A. Englehart. 2001. 130 pp. ISBN 0-87727-135-6.
Number 17	*Gangsters, Democracy, and the State,* ed. Carl A. Trocki. 1998. Second printing, 2002. 94 pp. ISBN 0-87727-134-8.
Number 16	*Cutting across the Lands: An Annotated Bibliography on Natural Resource Management and Community Development in Indonesia, the Philippines, and Malaysia,* ed. Eveline Ferretti. 1997. 329 pp. ISBN 0-87727-133-X.
Number 15	*The Revolution Falters: The Left in Philippine Politics after 1986,* ed. Patricio N. Abinales. 1996. Second printing, 2002. 182 pp. ISBN 0-87727-132-1.
Number 14	*Being Kammu: My Village, My Life,* Damrong Tayanin. 1994. 138 pp., 22 tables, illus., maps. ISBN 0-87727-130-5.
Number 13	*The American War in Vietnam,* ed. Jayne Werner, David Hunt. 1993. 132 pp. ISBN 0-87727-131-3.
Number 12	*The Voice of Young Burma,* Aye Kyaw. 1993. 92 pp. ISBN 0-87727-129-1.
Number 11	*The Political Legacy of Aung San,* ed. Josef Silverstein. Revised edition 1993. 169 pp. ISBN 0-87727-128-3.
Number 10	*Studies on Vietnamese Language and Literature: A Preliminary Bibliography,* Nguyen Dinh Tham. 1992. 227 pp. ISBN 0-87727-127-5.
Number 8	*From PKI to the Comintern, 1924–1941: The Apprenticeship of the Malayan Communist Party,* Cheah Boon Kheng. 1992. 147 pp. ISBN 0-87727-125-9.
Number 7	*Intellectual Property and US Relations with Indonesia, Malaysia, Singapore, and Thailand,* Elisabeth Uphoff. 1991. 67 pp. ISBN 0-87727-124-0.

Number 6   *The Rise and Fall of the Communist Party of Burma (CPB)*, Bertil Lintner. 1990. 124 pp. 26 illus., 14 maps. ISBN 0-87727-123-2.

Number 5   *Japanese Relations with Vietnam: 1951–1987,* Masaya Shiraishi. 1990. 174 pp. ISBN 0-87727-122-4.

Number 3   *Postwar Vietnam: Dilemmas in Socialist Development,* ed. Christine White, David Marr. 1988. 2nd printing 1993. 260 pp. ISBN 0-87727-120-8.

Number 2   *The Dobama Movement in Burma (1930–1938),* Khin Yi. 1988. 160 pp. ISBN 0-87727-118-6.

Cornell Modern Indonesia Project Publications

Number 75   *A Tour of Duty: Changing Patterns of Military Politics in Indonesia in the 1990s.* Douglas Kammen and Siddharth Chandra. 1999. 99 pp. ISBN 0-87763-049-6.

Number 74   *The Roots of Acehnese Rebellion 1989–1992,* Tim Kell. 1995. 103 pp. ISBN 0-87763-040-2.

Number 73   *"White Book" on the 1992 General Election in Indonesia,* trans. Dwight King. 1994. 72 pp. ISBN 0-87763-039-9.

Number 72   *Popular Indonesian Literature of the Qur'an,* Howard M. Federspiel. 1994. 170 pp. ISBN 0-87763-038-0.

Number 71   *A Javanese Memoir of Sumatra, 1945–1946: Love and Hatred in the Liberation War,* Takao Fusayama. 1993. 150 pp. ISBN 0-87763-037-2.

Number 70   *East Kalimantan: The Decline of a Commercial Aristocracy,* Burhan Magenda. 1991. 120 pp. ISBN 0-87763-036-4.

Number 69   *The Road to Madiun: The Indonesian Communist Uprising of 1948,* Elizabeth Ann Swift. 1989. 120 pp. ISBN 0-87763-035-6.

Number 68   *Intellectuals and Nationalism in Indonesia: A Study of the Following Recruited by Sutan Sjahrir in Occupation Jakarta,* J. D. Legge. 1988. 159 pp. ISBN 0-87763-034-8.

Number 67   *Indonesia Free: A Biography of Mohammad Hatta,* Mavis Rose. 1987. 252 pp. ISBN 0-87763-033-X.

Number 66   *Prisoners at Kota Cane,* Leon Salim, trans. Audrey Kahin. 1986. 112 pp. ISBN 0-87763-032-1.

Number 65   *The Kenpeitai in Java and Sumatra,* trans. Barbara G. Shimer, Guy Hobbs, intro. Theodore Friend. 1986. 80 pp. ISBN 0-87763-031-3.

Number 64   *Suharto and His Generals: Indonesia's Military Politics, 1975–1983,* David Jenkins. 1984. 4th printing 1997. 300 pp. ISBN 0-87763-030-5.

Number 62   *Interpreting Indonesian Politics: Thirteen Contributions to the Debate, 1964–1981,* ed. Benedict Anderson, Audrey Kahin, intro. Daniel S. Lev. 1982. 3rd printing 1991. 172 pp. ISBN 0-87763-028-3.

Number 60   *The Minangkabau Response to Dutch Colonial Rule in the Nineteenth Century,* Elizabeth E. Graves. 1981. 157 pp. ISBN 0-87763-000-3.

Number 59   *Breaking the Chains of Oppression of the Indonesian People: Defense Statement at His Trial on Charges of Insulting the Head of State, Bandung, June 7–10, 1979,* Heri Akhmadi. 1981. 201 pp. ISBN 0-87763-001-1.

Number 57   *Permesta: Half a Rebellion,* Barbara S. Harvey. 1977. 174 pp.
             ISBN 0-87763-003-8.

Number 55   *Report from Banaran: The Story of the Experiences of a Soldier during the
             War of Independence,* Maj. Gen. T. B. Simatupang. 1972. 186 pp.
             ISBN 0-87763-005-4.

Number 52   *A Preliminary Analysis of the October 1 1965, Coup in Indonesia (Prepared
             in January 1966),* Benedict R. Anderson, Ruth T. McVey, assist.
             Frederick P. Bunnell. 1971. 3rd printing 1990. 174 pp.
             ISBN 0-87763-008-9.

Number 51   *The Putera Reports: Problems in Indonesian-Japanese War-Time
             Cooperation,* Mohammad Hatta, trans., intro. William H. Frederick.
             1971. 114 pp.
             ISBN 0-87763-009-7.

Number 50   *Schools and Politics: The Kaum Muda Movement in West Sumatra (1927–
             1933),* Taufik Abdullah. 1971. 257 pp. ISBN 0-87763-010-0.

Number 49   *The Foundation of the Partai Muslimin Indonesia,* K. E. Ward. 1970. 75 pp.
             ISBN 0-87763-011-9.

Number 48   *Nationalism, Islam and Marxism,* Soekarno, intro. Ruth T. McVey. 1970.
             2nd printing 1984. 62 pp. ISBN 0-87763-012-7.

Number 43   *State and Statecraft in Old Java: A Study of the Later Mataram Period, 16th
             to 19th Century,* Soemarsaid Moertono. Revised edition 1981. 180 pp.
             ISBN 0-87763-017-8.

Number 39   Preliminary Checklist of Indonesian Imprints (1945-1949), John M.
             Echols. 186 pp. ISBN 0-87763-025-9.

Number 37   *Mythology and the Tolerance of the Javanese,* Benedict R. O'G. Anderson.
             2nd edition, 1996. Reprinted 2004. 104 pp., 65 illus. ISBN 0-87763-041-0.

Number 25   *The Communist Uprisings of 1926–1927 in Indonesia: Key Documents,* ed.,
             intro. Harry J. Benda, Ruth T. McVey. 1960. 2nd printing 1969. 177 pp.
             ISBN 0-87763-024-0.

Number 7   *The Soviet View of the Indonesian Revolution,* Ruth T. McVey. 1957. 3rd
             printing 1969. 90 pp. ISBN 0-87763-018-6.

Number 6   *The Indonesian Elections of 1955,* Herbert Feith. 1957. 2nd printing 1971.
             91 pp. ISBN 0-87763-020-8.

Translation Series

Volume 4   *Approaching Suharto's Indonesia from the Margins,* ed. Takashi Shiraishi.
             1994. 153 pp. ISBN 0-87727-403-7.

Volume 3   *The Japanese in Colonial Southeast Asia,* ed. Saya Shiraishi, Takashi
             Shiraishi. 1993. 172 pp. ISBN 0-87727-402-9.

Volume 2   *Indochina in the 1940s and 1950s,* ed. Takashi Shiraishi, Motoo Furuta.
             1992. 196 pp. ISBN 0-87727-401-0.

Volume 1   *Reading Southeast Asia,* ed. Takashi Shiraishi. 1990. 188 pp.
             ISBN 0-87727-400-2.

Language Texts

INDONESIAN

Beginning Indonesian through Self-Instruction, John U. Wolff, Dédé Oetomo, Daniel Fietkiewicz. 3rd revised edition 1992. Vol. 1. 115 pp. ISBN 0-87727-529-7. Vol. 2. 434 pp. ISBN 0-87727-530-0. Vol. 3. 473 pp. ISBN 0-87727-531-9.

Indonesian Readings, John U. Wolff. 1978. 4th printing 1992. 480 pp. ISBN 0-87727-517-3

Indonesian Conversations, John U. Wolff. 1978. 3rd printing 1991. 297 pp. ISBN 0-87727-516-5

Formal Indonesian, John U. Wolff. 2nd revised edition 1986. 446 pp. ISBN 0-87727-515-7

TAGALOG

Pilipino through Self-Instruction, John U. Wolff, Maria Theresa C. Centeno, Der-Hwa V. Rau. 1991. Vol. 1. 342 pp. ISBN 0-87727—525-4. Vol. 2., revised 2005, 378 pp. ISBN 0-87727-526-2. Vol 3., revised 2005, 431 pp. ISBN 0-87727-527-0. Vol. 4. 306 pp. ISBN 0-87727-528-9.

THAI

A. U. A. Language Center Thai Course, J. Marvin Brown. Originally published by the American University Alumni Association Language Center, 1974. Reissued by Cornell Southeast Asia Program, 1991, 1992. Book 1. 267 pp. ISBN 0-87727-506-8. Book 2. 288 pp. ISBN 0-87727-507-6. Book 3. 247 pp. ISBN 0-87727-508-4.

A. U. A. Language Center Thai Course, Reading and Writing Text (mostly reading), 1979. Reissued 1997. 164 pp. ISBN 0-87727-511-4.

A. U. A. Language Center Thai Course, Reading and Writing Workbook (mostly writing), 1979. Reissued 1997. 99 pp. ISBN 0-87727-512-2.

KHMER

Cambodian System of Writing and Beginning Reader, Franklin E. Huffman. Originally published by Yale University Press, 1970. Reissued by Cornell Southeast Asia Program, 4th printing 2002. 365 pp. ISBN 0-300-01314-0.

Modern Spoken Cambodian, Franklin E. Huffman, assist. Charan Promchan, Chhom-Rak Thong Lambert. Originally published by Yale University Press, 1970. Reissued by Cornell Southeast Asia Program, 3rd printing 1991. 451 pp. ISBN 0-300-01316-7.

Intermediate Cambodian Reader, ed. Franklin E. Huffman, assist. Im Proum. Originally published by Yale University Press, 1972. Reissued by Cornell Southeast Asia Program, 1988. 499 pp. ISBN 0-300-01552-6.

Cambodian Literary Reader and Glossary, Franklin E. Huffman, Im Proum. Originally published by Yale University Press, 1977. Reissued by Cornell Southeast Asia Program, 1988. 494 pp. ISBN 0-300-02069-4.

HMONG

White Hmong-English Dictionary, Ernest E. Heimbach. 1969. 8th printing, 2002. 523 pp. ISBN 0-87727-075-9.

VIETNAMESE

Intermediate Spoken Vietnamese, Franklin E. Huffman, Tran Trong Hai. 1980. 3rd printing 1994. ISBN 0-87727-500-9.

* * *

Southeast Asian Studies: Reorientations. Craig J. Reynolds and Ruth McVey. Frank H. Golay Lectures 2 & 3. 70 pp. ISBN 0-87727-301-4.

Javanese Literature in Surakarta Manuscripts, Nancy K. Florida. Vol. 1, *Introduction and Manuscripts of the Karaton Surakarta.* 1993. 410 pp. Frontispiece, illustrations. Hard cover, ISBN 0-87727-602-1, Paperback, ISBN 0-87727-603-X. Vol. 2, *Manuscripts of the Mangkunagaran Palace.* 2000. 576 pp. Frontispiece, illustrations. Paperback, ISBN 0-87727-604-8.

Sbek Thom: Khmer Shadow Theater. Pech Tum Kravel, trans. Sos Kem, ed. Thavro Phim, Sos Kem, Martin Hatch. 1996. 363 pp., 153 photographs. ISBN 0-87727-620-X.

In the Mirror: Literature and Politics in Siam in the American Era, ed. Benedict R. O'G. Anderson, trans. Benedict R. O'G. Anderson, Ruchira Mendiones. 1985. 2nd printing 1991. 303 pp. Paperback. ISBN 974-210-380-1.

To order, please contact:

Cornell University
Southeast Asia Program Publications
95 Brown Road
Box 1004
Ithaca NY 14850

Online: http://www.einaudi.cornell.edu/southeastasia/publications/
Tel: 1-877-865-2432 (Toll free – U.S.)
Fax: (607) 255-7534

E-mail: SEAP-Pubs@cornell.edu
Orders must be prepaid by check or credit card (VISA, MasterCard, Discover).